CW01478594

 **Evening Standard**

Where to Get the Look

BARBARA CHANDLER

SIMON & SCHUSTER
A VIACOM COMPANY

This book is dedicated to my husband Ben Tewson

Research assistants: Anna Blackburn, Louise Palmer, Antonia Faust

First published in Great Britain by Simon & Schuster UK Ltd, 1999
A Viacom Company

1 3 5 7 9 10 8 6 4 2

Simon & Schuster UK Ltd
Africa House
64–78 Kingsway
London WC2B 6AH

Text design: Rachel Hardman Carter
Typeset by: Stylize Digital Artwork
Printed and bound in Italy

A CIP catalogue record for this book is available from the British Library

ISBN 0 671 03336 0

Also published in this series:
The London Pub & Bar Guide
Children's London
Where to Live in London

**Always telephone to check addresses and opening hours
before setting out.**

CONTENTS

continued overleaf

continued overleaf

FOREWORD BY SIR TERENCE CONRAN

Shops play a vital role in shaping the taste of the nation: the clothes we wear, the food we eat, and the things with which we furnish and fill our homes are all, by and large, bought from shops, supplemented with the odd home-grown vegetable, car-boot treasure, or found object.

Of course, magazines and newspapers and television and adverts all also play a part in providing sources of visual stimulation from around the world.

But unless a consumer is especially entrepreneurial or determined, it is likely that his or her tastes will largely be shaped by whatever selection of products are being offered by retailers. You can, after all, only buy what you are offered, so it is up to retailers to be sniffing the ether and scouring the world in search of innovative and beautiful new products that fulfil emerging tastes and aspirations.

When retailers get it right, I believe shopping can be an exciting and fun experience, and London has a good many retailers determined to prove that that's true.

INTRODUCTION

'Mid pleasures and palaces though we may roam.
Be it ever so humble, there's no place like home...'
J H Payne (1791–1852)

When you're shopping for your home, retail therapy is a myth. Nobody goes out on a spree, returning with glossy designer carrier bags and a feeling of well-being. Yes, buying for the home is ultimately a source of pleasure, because in an age where the exterior environment is increasingly polluted, vandalised, and strewn with litter, that old adage is truer than ever: 'There's no place like home'.

But the way to the perfect room or house is as fraught with difficulties as Christian's path in Pilgrim's Progress. How do I know? Firstly, because I've had several homes in London myself, and laboriously furnished them on a limited budget. Even then they were far from perfect.

Secondly, because I have been writing about shopping for the home in London for over 30 years. In that time, I have visited innumerable shops, by foot, tube, bus, car, taxi, mini-cab, and even helicopter (admittedly the company itself organised the trip to their rather grand out-of-town showroom).

I'm lucky to have many of London's more imaginative and enterprising shopkeepers, old and new, as personal friends. I have dealt with countless enquiries from readers, mostly stylish and fully clued-up when shopping for clothes, but completely stymied when it comes to the home. When friends/relatives/ colleagues ring me up unexpectedly, sometimes it's because they care about me, but often cursory enquiries into health/wealth etc rapidly lead to a 'By the way, I was just wondering where I could get so-and-so...'

It's not surprising shopping for the home is difficult. We shop for a tie or a top perhaps every month or so, but only buy one to three sofas in a lifetime. We spend years acquiring fashion expertise – what to wear with what and where to get it – but are suddenly faced with the reality of home furnishing virtually overnight. And nobody wakes up in the morning just knowing instinctively what to do and where to go. It's knowledge hard won, and often eagerly swapped with friends.

Regard this book as part of the info-swapping exercise. It can take some of the aggro out of the whole business. It should be regarded as my personal compilation.

There have been a lot of improvements in London home shopping in the last couple of years. The biggest is the advent of Sunday shopping – providing a chance to catch up on perhaps your only free day. In particular I'd recommend a stroll down the King's

Road, but now Oxford Street and Tottenham Court Road are catching on, and numerous more adventurous individual retailers see Sunday shopping as a big consumer service – which indeed it is. Thank you to them and their long-suffering staff.

Then there's electronic shopping – I've bitten the bullet and included web sites in this guide so you can browse and in some cases order even in the wee small hours.

Catalogues too have proliferated. Some enable you to order over the phone or by post, others are intended more as a reference point and for inspiration. Again a big investment for the shops concerned, but invaluable for homemakers with a busy life. I've divided London's home shops according to their type (eg DEPARTMENT STORES, DIY SUPERSTORES), or according to the goods they sell (eg FURNITURE) subdivided to be as helpful as possible (eg FURNITURE: UPHOLSTERY). Inevitably classifications overlap, so there are cross-references. At the back you will find an alphabetical list of shops in this book. (But always *check* before making a special journey.)

KEY

	Out of Town
	Money Saver
	By Phone, By Post

UNDER ONE ROOF

FURNISHING SPECIALISTS

Life for many Londoners is in permanent overdrive. Surrounded on every side by beautiful pictures in the multiplying media that deal with home design, we have little time to implement the ideas and aspirations generated. Fortunately, London's shopkeepers appreciate the needs of the capital's stressed-out homemakers, and an increasing number of stores offer as much as possible under one roof – a wide range of furnishing goods (from a soap dish to a sofa), plus perhaps services for interior design or making curtains.

ALSO LOOK AT FURNITURE: GENERAL, page 149, as many large modern furniture stores have bedroom and/or kitchen departments, and may offer a complete interior design service. Some shops listed under INTERIOR DESIGN, page 16, offer a complete home furnishing service – some even do building work. Some of the shops listed in ACCESSORIES: SHOPS WITH FURNITURE, page 22, are making efforts to provide a whole-house service.

THE CONRAN SHOP
ADDRESS Michelin House, 81 Fulham Road, SW3 6RD
TEL 0171 589 7401   **FAX** 0171 823 7015
A splendid store in a modern airy space in the exuberantly-restored Michelin building. It's energised by an unequivocal commitment to modern design for the home, and charged up by its team of enterprising young buyers. Good ranges of furniture by many leading young designers, supplemented by modern classics and pieces from abroad. Also good for fabrics, china and glass (some handmade or hand-decorated), cutlery, bedlinens, carpets and rugs – many from The Conran Collection (see ACCESSORIES, page 22). Plus a food shop with utensils for every cuisine. Books and lots of imaginative children's furnishing. Interesting plants and dried flowers, and garden accessories.
TUBE *South Kensington* • **OPEN** *Mon Tues Fri 10am–6pm. Wed Thurs 10am–7pm. Sat 10am–6.30pm. Sun 12 noon–6pm* • **SERVICES** *Gift wrapping. Wedding lists. Furniture catalogues* • **ALSO AT** *55 Marlborough High Street, W1M 3AE (0171 723 2223). Conran at Bluebird, 350 King's Road, SW3 5UU (0171 559 1140) sells a changing selection of best-sellers. Conran Collection, 12 Conduit Street, W1R (0171 399 0710)*

HABITAT

ADDRESS 196 Tottenham Court Road, W1P 9LD
TEL 0171 631 3880   **FAX** 0171 255 6012 (head office)
TEL 0645 334433 (information line); 0845 601 0740 (for local branches and wedding list service)

Habitat tirelessly pushes out the boat for home design, with a new pilot, design director Tom Dixon, acclaimed master of sculptural shapes. The original sixties image of earthenware and pine has been ousted by modes for the new millennium – concrete, stone, and metals galore, tied in with streamlined wood, plus innovative ceramics and fabrics. Enthusiastic and focused buying teams fill the stores with good-looking stylish merchandise which is remarkably avant-garde for a national chain. Stores are pleasantly laid out. Particularly good for large pieces of furniture, and tableware. Also for lighting and accessories – and good for gifts at Christmas. A constantly updated colour palette is reflected in its own paint range.

OPEN *Mon–Wed 10am–6pm. Thurs 10am–8pm. Fri Sat 10am–6.30pm. Sun 12 noon–6pm* • **WEBSITE** *www.habitat-international.com* • **SERVICES** *Extensive, inspirational catalogue, £2. Cafe. Deliveries. Wedding lists. China registration service – advance notification when a pattern is being discontinued, so you can stock up. Home assembly. Blinds made to order* • **ALSO AT** *206 King's Road, SW3 (0171 351 1211). 195 Finchley Road, NW3 (0171 328 3444). 19 King's Mall, Hammersmith, W6 (0181 741 7111). 1 Drury Crescent, Pearly Way, Croydon (0181 681 3818);* ☞ *here you can find discontinued lines at reduced prices.*

HEAL'S

ADDRESS 196 Tottenham Court Road, W1P 9LD
TEL 0171 636 1666   **FAX** 0171 637 5582

It's always been there – a large beautiful store championing good design since the turn of the century. Heal's lost its way a bit in the eighties, but bounced back under new independent management to become a modern mecca for bright design, much of it exclusive. Good as always for modern furniture, and for fabrics, with plenty in stock and off the roll. Famous for handmade beds. Plus innovative lighting, linens, china, and very good for gifts at Christmas. Humpherson's kitchen and bathroom studio on second floor. Newer store on the King's Road has its own buzz, an essential part of the busy Sunday shopping scene in a street that refuses to go out of fashion.

OPEN *Mon–Wed 10am–6pm. Thurs 10am–8pm. Fri 10am–6.30pm. Sat 9.30am–6.30pm* • **SERVICES** *Cafe, restaurant. Interior design. Wedding lists. Curtain and blind making* • **ALSO AT** *234 King's Road, SW3 5UA (0171 349 8411); open Sun 12 noon–6pm*

IKEA

ADDRESS Brent Park, 2 Drury Way, North Circular Road, NW10 0TH
TEL 0181 208 5600

24-hour automatic answering to check whether an item is in stock. Personal customer advisers during store hours. Ten years ago, IKEA arrived in London from Sweden – a megastore of modern design entering a lion's den of traditional furnishings. It has been a mega-success and proved once and for all that if you make good design affordable and accessible, it becomes appealing to the mass-market in a big way. It can be cheaper to buy a shelving system from IKEA than to make it yourself from purchased timber. They employ top international designers in their Swedish studios – some of the rug patterns and ceramic shapes are stunning. Sections for

bedrooms, kitchens (particularly popular), all kinds of furniture and upholstery, fabrics by the metre plus ready-made curtains and curtain poles, china, glass, kitchenware, accessories, plants, floorings, rugs, children's equipment, and the home office. But it pays to know the ropes. Never attempt to shop at a peak period – the till queues are horrendous. Don't attempt to do one big shop, try and spread your visits. Study the free catalogues well in advance, but remember they are for guidance only, not mail order. You can load smaller items straight into vast unwieldy trollies off the shelves, but self-assembly furniture has to be tracked down, part by part, from racks of warehouse shelving. It takes time and a steady nerve.
TUBE *Neasden* • **OPEN** *Mon–Fri 10am–8pm. Sat 10am–6pm. Sun 11am–5pm. Bank holidays 10am–6pm* • **SERVICES** *Supervised playroom for children, and free video cinema for older children. Personal shopping advisers by appointment. Kitchen planning help (0181 459 3497). Recommended kitchen installers. Home delivery service* • **ALSO AT** *Croydon and West Thurrock*

LAURA ASHLEY

TEL 0990 622116 for number of nearest store
ADDRESS 7–9 Harriet Street, SW1X 2JS
TEL 0171 235 9797
It's worth knowing that this is a dedicated store for home furnishings – and the Laura Ashley look still has a lot to offer. Still difficult to beat for affordable florals, but watch out for more recent exotic touches – velvets and chenilles. Plus furniture. Brilliant interior decorating advice (includes home visit) costs £50, refundable against an order.
TUBE *Knightsbridge* • **OPEN** *Mon–Fri 10am–6pm. Sat 9.30am–6pm*

PURVES & PURVES

ADDRESS 80–81 and 83 Tottenham Court Road, W1P 9HD
TEL 0171 580 8223   **FAX** 0171 580 8244
In the teeth of the recession, Andrew Purves opened a small modern furnishing shop opposite Heal's. His aim: a centre of excellence, taking its products from home and abroad. Soon people hungry for modern design were beating a path to his door. The next bold step: acquiring a large adjacent corner site (7,000 sq ft) and filling it with furniture and lighting drawn from the best contemporary companies – B & B Italia, Riva, Naver Mobler, Kartell, Hitch Mylius. The original store now houses accessories and gifts, with fab kitchen section downstairs. Andrew and wife Pauline tirelessly update stock, combing trade fairs abroad and at home. Success rewards their flair – yet Andrew remains ever the same modest entrepreneur, finding time to turn over precious selling space to inspirational exhibitions. This is where I spend my slender budget.
TUBE *Goodge Street* • **OPEN** *Mon–Sat 9.30am–6.00pm. Late night Thurs 7.30pm* • **WEBSITE** *www.purves.co.uk* • **SERVICES** *Free mail order catalogue (0870 603 0205). Stimulating exhibitions. Interior design. Full soft furnishings service. Wedding lists*

DEPARTMENT STORES

'No minute gone comes ever back again,
Take heed and see ye nothing do in vain.'
Inscription over the arch in Liberty's famous mock-Tudor building in Regent Street

As little as ten years ago, pessimistic retail pundits prophesied the international demise of the department store, condemned in New York, Paris, London and Rome, as a 'retail dinosaur' that couldn't survive the threat of self-service supermarkets and out-of-town shopping complexes. Around this time, London had some ominous casualties – notably Whiteleys – now an upmarket shopping centre in Bayswater, W2 – and Bourne and Hollingsworth – now The Plaza shopping centre in Oxford Street, W1. But other stores have held their own, spending vast sums of money on refurbishment and merchandise, to provide an all-in-one shopping experience. The major stores date back many decades, so you get architecture thrown in for free – the magnificent Victorian tiled food halls at Harrods, the sumptuous Art Deco entrance of Selfridges, and the charming turn-of-the-century Arts and Crafts Movement façade and interiors of Liberty, where even the lifts are lined with dark-stained oak linenfold panelling, reminiscent of a stately home. You also get handy places to eat and drink, toilets, baby-changing rooms and various other services.

BARKERS (HOUSE OF FRASER)
ADDRESS 63 Kensington High Street, W8 5SE
TEL 0171 937 5432; 0171 963 2236 (enquiries for all House of Fraser Stores, including merchandise availability)
Re-vamped flagship store for House of Fraser homewares, which are on the second floor. Stylish furniture, lighting, rugs, carpets, kitchenware, china and glass, well laid out and displayed . Plus a Designers Guild concession.
TUBE *High Street Kensington* • **OPEN** *Mon–Wed Friday, 10am–7pm. Thurs 10am–8pm. Sat 9.30am–7pm. Sun 12 noon–6pm* • **ALSO AT** *D H Evans, 318 Oxford Street, W1A 1DE (0171 629 8800). Army & Navy, 101 Victoria Street, SW1E 6QX (0171 834 1234). Dickins & Jones, 224/244 Regent Street, W1A 1DB (0171 734 7070); good tableware/ accessories department on the fourth floor*

DEBENHAMS
ADDRESS 334–348 Oxford Street, W1A 1EF
TEL 0171 580 3000
Home department is on the second floor – reliable for bedlinens, china, glass, cookware and home accessories – including designer ranges from Jasper Conran, Cath Kidston and Kelly Hoppen. In summer, the 'outdoor living' section is particularly jolly. Custom-made and ready-made curtains by Montgomery Tomlinson, and Mostyns. Also concessions for Christy towels, Dorma bed linens, Coloroll fabrics and papers, Sheridan bed linens, and Sanderson.
TUBE *Bond Street* • **OPEN** *Mon Tues 9.30am–7pm. Wed 10am–8pm. Thurs–Fri 9.30am–8pm. Sat 9am–7pm. Sun 12 noon–6pm* • **SERVICES**

Basement cafe, second floor restaurant. Baby-changing. Deliveries from £7.50. Mail order Direct Bed and Bath catalogue and Christmas Direct catalogue: 0870 600 3333

HARRODS

ADDRESS 87–135 Brompton Road, SW1X 7XL
TEL 0171 730 1234

Harrods is a top tourist attraction, with 35,000 customers a day and over 40 per cent of purchases going abroad. This and its sheer size – 300 departments on seven floors over 20 acres – considerably dilutes its appeal as a home shopping destination for Londoners. The second floor cookshop is particularly popular, with all main brands as well as exclusives like Alessi and Fissler. The major electricals department has top of the ranges – Viking and Thermadore (used by Gary Rhodes) plus Amana and Sub Zero. In the china and crystal rooms, find exclusive brands like Richard Ginori and William Yeoward, as well as Harrods own successful contemporary china in plain pastel shades of lilac, pink and Tiffany blue. Sound & Vision on the third floor has individual areas for all the major brands – Sony, Linn, Akai, Philips, and Bang & Olufsen. A recent arrival is ABC Rugs from New York – anything from a rag rug to an antique Persian. Plus fitted carpets with large selection of Wools of New Zealand.

TUBE *Knightsbridge* • **OPEN** *Mon Tues Sat 10am–6pm. Wed–Fri 10am–7pm* • **SERVICES** *Numerous cafes, bars, restaurants. Deliveries. Interior design*

HARVEY NICHOLS

ADDRESS 109–125 Knightsbridge, SW1X 7RJ
TEL 0171 584 0011

At this, London's most glamorous department store, the big home attraction is the fourth floor jam packed with concessions – mini shops for all kinds of big names in the furnishing world. So a leisurely browse brings you bang up to date with trends and merchandise. You'll find Belinda Coote (tapestries); Besselink Jones & Milne (lighting); Bridgewater (modern china); Catherine Memmi (luxurious French bed linens); Designers Guild (fab fabrics, linens etc); Jerry's Home Stores (kitchen style); Kenneth Turner (flowers); La Maison de la Fausse Fourrure (fake fur throws, cushions); Mulberry at Home (luxury fabrics, furniture, accessories; Nina Campbell (pretty gifts/accessories); Nick Monro (modern metalwork); Ralph Lauren Home (see page 37); Smythson (posh stationery); The Candle Collection; The Monogrammed Linen Shop.

TUBE *Knightsbridge* • **OPEN** *Mon–Sat 10am–7pm. Late night Wed–8pm. Sun 12 noon–6pm* • **SERVICES**. *Cafe, restaurants, bars. Deliveries. 5th Floor food hall*

JOHN LEWIS

ADDRESS Oxford Street, W1A 1EX
TEL 0171 629 7711

Part of a nationwide group where all staff are partners, sharing equally in profits. This flagship store has been a bedrock for generations of furnishers, who rely on their slogan 'never knowingly undersold' for keenest prices. Once the merchandise was reliable and worthy rather than smart, but now there's a strong emphasis on design, particularly in the furnishing departments, which are more extensive than any other department store. Own brand is Jonelle – goods are exclusive and particularly good value for money. Very good for kitchen appliances (basement). Kitchenware is also strong, with all those mundane items (brooms, plate racks, washing up bowls) often given that little extra design twist. Lighting is good, as is china and glass. On the second floor is the showpiece fabric department – huge selections off the roll, plus designer fabrics to order. Adjacent is excellent department for cushions – instant brighteners for any room – plus blinds and handy curtain hardware – like portière rods that swing back for door curtains, and clip-on curtain hooks. Also, carpets and flooring, and linens. Also good for tv and hi-fi, with extended warranties. No 'sales' as such, but 'events' with splendid special purchases and seconds in January and June. **TUBE** *Oxford Circus* • **OPEN** *Mon Tues Wed Fri 9.30am–6pm.Thurs 10am–8pm. Sat 9am–6pm* • **SERVICES** *Own credit card with better interest rates than most – won't accept other credit cards though will accept debit cards. Coffee shop and busy counter-style restaurant. Extensive service for all soft-furnishing making (own workshops). Carpet and floor laying. Kitchen planning* • **ALSO AT** *John Lewis Brent Cross, NW4 3FL (0181 202 6535); Mon–Fri 10am–8pm; Sat 9am–6pm. And at Kingston (0181 547 3000); and at High Wycombe (01494 462666; splendid furnishing and leisure store)*

LIBERTY

ADDRESS 214 Regent Street, W1R 6AH
TEL 0171 734 1234
Liberty takes furnishings very seriously, and has marvellous merchandise. Pay a reverential pilgrimage to the Arts & Crafts department on the fourth floor which sells original furniture and accessories from the movement in which the store was so prominent. Then fast forward to the modern furniture and lighting at the very cutting edge of design. A well-kept secret is The Hole in the Wall, for handmade designer accessories – door knobs, curtain poles, mirrors, lamps in metal, wood and glass. British Crafts on the ground floor is equally stimulating, with spirited ceramics and groovy glass. Third floor has beds and bed linens, oriental carpets, tapestries and furnishing fabrics. China, glass and funky accessories for kitchens and bathrooms are in the basement.
TUBE *Oxford Circus* • **OPEN** *Mon–Wed Fri Sat 10am–6.30pm. Thurs 10am–7.30pm. Sun 12 noon–6pm* • **SERVICES** *Restaurant, coffee shop and cafe. Curtain-making and sewing school. Wedding list*

PETER JONES

ADDRESS Sloane Square, SW1W 8EL
TEL 0171 629 3434
Branch of John Lewis Partnership (see above), with similar range of goods and services, but particularly strong on interior design.
TUBE *Sloane Square* • **OPEN** *Mon Tues Thurs–Sat 9.30am–6pm. Wed 9.30am–7pm*

SELFRIDGES

ADDRESS 400 Oxford Street, W1A 1AB
TEL 0171 629 1234
Thanks to recent (and very costly) revamps and facelifts, this deliciously art deco edifice, built by American retail magnate Gordon Selfridge and completed in 1928, is relaxed and inspirational. Furniture, floorings, lighting, and linens on the fourth floor are stimulating and eclectic –

exotic silk cushions, exclusive Cappellini furniture, crisp modern rugs by Christopher Farr, antique pieces from China and India. Lower ground floor: great garden furniture department, good selections of appliances, and tableware. An Oriental Cooking department caters for current culinary trends. Best of all are the individual displays devoted to British artist-craftsmen – you can buy a beautiful handmade vase or a turned wafer-thin wood bowl by a top maker without trekking to a specialist gallery.
TUBE *Bond Street* • **OPEN** *Mon–Wed 10am–7pm. Thurs Fri 10am–8pm. Sat 9.30am–7pm. Sun 12 noon–6pm* • **WEBSITE** *www.selfridges.co.uk*
• **SERVICES** *Thirteen restaurants and bars. Curtain-making and carpet-laying. Personal home shopping consultant (0171 318 3323). Interior design service (0171 318 3480). Florist (0171 318 3894). Trained store guides (called ambassadors) speak French, German, and Italian, with other translators drawn from Selfridges' multinational employees. One ambassador sourced, bought and exported everything for a complete house overseas*

INTERIOR DESIGN

'It's beige! My colour!'
Elsie De Wolfe (1865-1950). Celebrated designer and leader of fashion, on first sighting the Acropolis

Interior design is not a prerogative of the elite – it simply means having your home the way you want it: comfortable, attractive, efficient, stylish. In a sense, therefore, the whole of this book is about interior design, but this chapter highlights some of the specialist design services now available to help you implement the look you covet. The good news is that interior design is now more affordable and accessible – and less intimidating – than ever before.

There are many reasons why you may want to consult an interior designer.

FUNCTION/PLANNING A professional makes rooms work better – particularly relevant for kitchens and bathrooms, of course.
CO-ORDINATION A designer's training and experience helps to pull a room together even when the main ideas are your own.
COLOUR, PERSPECTIVE, PROPORTION The designer dovetails all these elements into a unified whole.
VISUALISING A designer can help you imagine what a room will look like when it is finished – this is tricky for the inexperienced.
ACCESS AND SOURCING A designer puts you in touch with services and merchandise that you would not otherwise have known about.
SUPERVISION A designer takes charge, saving time and trouble.
MONEY-SAVING A designer can prevent costly mistakes. Many will deduct their initial charges if you implement their scheme by buying merchandise through their shop.

USEFUL CONTACTS

THE INTERIOR DECORATORS' AND DESIGNERS' ASSOCIATION (IDDA)
ADDRESS 1–4 Chelsea Harbour Design Centre, Lots Road, SW10 0XE
TEL 0171 349 0800   **FAX** 0171 349 0500
The IDDA (founded in 1966) has around 300 designer/decorator members
working throughout the UK and abroad. Their free leaflet, *Why you should
use an interior designer*, is a guide to professional working practices, and
explains fees and charging. You can also consult the database at their
offices to find a designer particularly suited to your needs.
TUBE *Sloane Square + bus, Fulham Broadway*

DULUX COLOUR ADVICE LINE
TEL 0891 515 222
Talk over your colour problems with a trained adviser – calls charged at
49p a minute.

RIBA CLIENTS' ADVISORY SERVICE
TEL 0171 307 3700
A good architect will analyse your problems and produce imaginative,
original and up-to-date solutions. He or she will submit draft proposals,
followed by detailed designs and deal with planning permissions. He will
suggest materials and find the workforce, negotiate fees and supervise the
work. An architect's fee for conversion work is around 16^1/$_2$ per cent
of the total cost – however the expertise of a good architect will usually
save you at least their fee. Phone the RIBA Clients' Advisory Service for
architects' names and a leaflet called, *Why Use an Architect?*

The shops listed below are perhaps one of the most valuable and
often least utilised resource for London's homemakers. Virtually all
of them are run by practising interior designers, and stock a huge
variety of the latest fabric and pattern books – and the staff (often
the owner him or herself) know what's in them. They've done the
searching and editing for you. What's more, the staff are usually
prepared to offer you free design advice on the spot, helping you
to implement your ideas and pointing out any flaws. If you want
more detailed advice, then these shops offer a full interior design
service, and are perhaps the least intimidating way of using an
interior designer. They will come to your home, talk through your
needs and ideas, assess your property, measure up, and then
come up with sample boards and sketches. How they charge for
this service varies from shop to shop. In many instances, there is an
initial charge which is refundable from any merchandise/making-up
services you purchase through the shop, thus giving you in effect
free interior design advice. Alternatively, the design fees are
charged separately, either by the hour or day, or by the job.
Check on charges at the beginning of your negotiations.

BATTERSEA DESIGN COMPANY
ADDRESS Chivalry House, 167 Battersea Rise, SW11 1HP
TEL 0171 228 3957/0171 228 1115   **FAX** 0171 738 2909
Giles Paul and Fiona Common have run their design practice for nearly
15 years. They have a showroom with a comprehensive range of fabric
and paper samples, plus carpets and various floor finishes. Also examples

of Hatt fitted kitchens and alternative worktops, and Neff appliances/Franke sinks. If you buy through them, their design service is free. They can arrange literally everything for you – getting estimates for the making-up of curtains, decorating, construction of wardrobes, alcove cupboards etc, planning and installation of kitchens and bathrooms. 'We will organise and oversee any work to the home to the point of loft conversions and small extensions – but we stop short at building a new house!' They promise to devote as much time and detail to helping a client choose, have made up and hang a blind as to a house full of curtains and decoration work – a pleasant and sympathetic approach.

RAIL Clapham Junction • **OPEN** Mon–Fri 9.30am–6pm. Sat 9.30am–1pm

BELLHOUSE AND COMPANY

ADDRESS 33 Kensington Park Road, W11 2FU
TEL 0171 221 0187   **FAX** 0171 792 0467
Showroom packed with pattern books – 'we'll sell you a metre of fabric and a couple of rolls of paper, or we'll do up your entire house.' Own workshops for all soft furnishings, including curtains, blinds, and pelmets, adding braids and tassels. Beautifully quilted bedcovers, bedhangings, and valances, plus own range of traditional upholstery, mostly buttoned. Full range of carpets, including wools and sisals, with special colours and borders to order. They can arrange special finishes and stencilling by experienced artists – 'no commission is too insignificant.'

TUBE Notting Hill Gate/Ladbroke Grove • **OPEN** Mon–Fri 9.30am–1pm; 2pm–5.30pm. Open Sat by appointment • **SERVICES** All interior design services

CHEONG INTERIORS

ADDRESS 84–86 Stoke Newington Church Street, N16 0AP
TEL 0171 923 7894   **FAX** 0171 923 7895
Sarah Cheong offers a full interior design service, with comprehensive selections of pattern books from all leading makes.

RAIL Stoke Newington • **BUS** 73 • **OPEN** Mon–Sat 10am–5.30pm
• **SERVICES** Full interior design, flooring and soft-furnishing service

COLOUR COUNSELLORS

ADDRESS 3 Dovedale Studios, 465 Battersea Park Road, SW11 4LR
TEL 0171 978 5023   **FAX** 0171 924 3008
Headquarters for a network of consultants who can bring their expertise and samples to your home and then arrange to implement anything from a pair of curtains to a room to a whole house, producing schemes and sample boards and drawings. This organisation has been successfully trading for 29 years under the guidance of its innovative and hard-working founder Virginia Stourton – 'With the huge number of fabrics, papers and paints now on the market, a Colour Counsellor will take the agony out of making a choice'.

COLOUR COUNSELLORS covering the London area include:

Penelope Maitland, N4	Susan and Steven Nicoll, Bromley, Kent
TEL 0181 800 0688	**TEL** 0181 460 9945
	FAX 0181 466 7465
Penny Wicks, Chorley Wood, Herts	Juliet Robinson, West Hampstead, NW6
TEL/FAX 01923 283174	**TEL** 0181 208 2914

Susan Wauchope, SW4
TEL 0171 720 8253
FAX 0171 498 9927

Pauline Worley, Ruislip, Middx
TEL/FAX 01895 638661

FABRIKA
ADDRESS 6 Church Road, Teddington, Middx, TW11 8PB
TEL 0181 943 2685   **FAX** 0181 943 1631
This shop is a well-known local landmark – they've been going for 17 years. Full interior design service, with their own soft furnishing workshop on the premises, where they make hand-sewn curtains, bedcovers and so on. Also quality wallpapers, fabrics, and blinds.
RAIL *Teddington* • **OPEN** *Tues–Fri 10am–4.30pm. Sat 10am–2pm*
• **SERVICES** *All interior design and soft furnishing services*

INTERIOR OPTIONS
ADDRESS 25 Horsell Road, N5 1XL
TEL 0171 609 8023   **FAX** 0171 609 9669
Friendly design team with a wide range of samples at their busy workshop – 'A complete service, down-to-earth advice, everything is one-off.' High-quality hand-finished soft furnishings: all styles of curtains, blinds, and upholstery, plus special paint effects. They'll bring samples and ideas to you, if you are too busy to come and see them, and they can work within traditional or modern idioms. 'We'll take away the headaches, supervise all the work, and keep within your budget.'
RAIL *Drayton Park* • **TUBE** *Holloway Road* • **OPEN** *Mon–Fri 9am–6pm by appointment* • **SERVICES** *All interior design services. Free estimates. Free parking*

INTERIORS AND FURNISHING
ADDRESS 224–226 York Road, SW11 3SD
TEL 0171 924 2400   **FAX** 0171 924 3420
Formerly known as Pullingers, this shop opened here in 1987. Room settings show off a full range of fabrics and wallpapers, plus carpets, upholstery and beds.
RAIL *Clapham Junction* • **OPEN** *Mon–Sat 10am–6pm* • **SERVICES** *All interior design and soft furnishings. Re-upholstery and furniture restoration*

INTERPRETATIONS
ADDRESS 308 Worple Road, Raynes Park, SW20 8QU
TEL 0181 879 0103   **FAX** 0181 879 7645
Friendly, personal service from a large bright showroom with three interconnecting rooms full of samples: fabrics, wallcoverings and carpets. Sofas and sofabeds, occasional furniture and mirrors. All curtain making, quilting, cushions, loose covers, upholstery and carpet fitting. Fabrics from around £12 a metre, and wallpapers from £15 a roll.
RAIL *Raynes Park* • **OPEN** *Mon–Sat 9.30am–5pm. Early closing Wed 3pm*
• **SERVICES** *All interior design services*

KENSINGTON DESIGN

ADDRESS 12 Stratford Road, W8 6QD
TEL 0171 938 4388   **FAX** 0171 376 2320
Friendly shop with a relaxed, pleasant atmosphere – they'll loan out their
books of fabric and wallpaper samples, and boast 'the best selection of
fabrics in the neighbourhood'. Import their own kilims direct from Turkey.
Good for decorative accessories – the interior designer owners are always
adding something fresh and interesting at prices from £5.
TUBE Earls Court/Kensington High Street • **OPEN** Mon–Sat 10am–6pm
• **SERVICES** All interior design services

LA MAISON CREATIVE

ADDRESS 43 England's Lane, NW3 4YD
TEL 0171 586 4747   **FAX** 0171 483 0191
Adrian and Michelle Green (established for 12 years) offer a full interior
design service, including all building works. 'We'll do absolutely everything,
down to the last picture,' promises Adrian. They employ all their own
bricklayers, carpenters and plumbers. Own soft-furnishings workshop and
own upholstery can be custom-designed. 'We do smaller jobs, too,' they
stress, adding that their motto is: 'From a cushion to a castle.'
TUBE Belsize Park • **OPEN** Mon–Fri 9am–6pm • **SERVICES** Complete interior
design and soft furnishings, including re-upholstery and loose covers, and
all decorative effects

LIPP INTERIOR DESIGN

ADDRESS 118a Holland Park Avenue, W11 4UA
TEL 0171 243 2432   **FAX** 0171 792 8872
Modern classic is the style at this adventurous interior design showcase, run
by interior designer Tara Ford, and ex-Pentagram industrial designer Heike
Brandt. Anything from general advice to complete project management,
with access to other specialists as needed. Furniture from B & B Italia,
Max Alto, Arrben and Porro, with suede cube seating by Ochre, offset by
contemporary glassware. Access to the work of more than 50 international
companies and designers, including Julian Brown, Antonio Citterio, Joe
Columbo, Philippe Starck and Terence Woodgate. Not forgetting classic
pieces by Le Corbusier, Charles Eames, Arne Jacobsen, Erik Magnussen,
Vernon Panton, Enzo Mark and more.
TUBE Holland Park • **OPEN** Mon–Fri 10am–7pm. Sat 11am–7pm. Sun
11am–5pm • **SERVICES** Complete interior design and making-up services

MR JONES

ADDRESS 175–179 Muswell Hill Broadway, Muswell Hill, N10 3RS
TEL 0181 444 6066   **FAX** 0181 883 6958
Despite the masculine moniker, it's the friendly and experienced Susan
Jones who runs this designer fabric and wallpaper shop (established in
1986). The staff will happily help you sift through an extensive range of
fabrics and wallpapers from Designers Guild, Osborne & Little, Mulberry
et al, plus the Zoffany paint range. Prices can vary from £19 a metre for
a Designers Guild plain cotton to £98 a metre for a Mulberry chenille.
The interior design service can be tailored to your budget. Home visits
for a small fee which is refundable against purchase.
TUBE Highgate + 134 bus • **OPEN** Tues–Sat 10am–5pm • **SERVICES** All
interior design and soft-furnishing services

PENNYBEE INTERIORS
ADDRESS 53–54 High Street, Wimbledon Village, SW19 5AX
TEL 0181 947 7224/5 **FAX** 0181 947 1988
A family business, with an 'all under one roof' slogan – 4,500 sq ft, two
floors. Everything from fitted kitchens, bathrooms and bedrooms to carpets,
curtains, all interior decoration, and even building work. German modern
and English solid wood kitchens; made-to-order bathroom and living-room
furniture; exclusive hand-forged wall-lights and candelabra. Extensive
range of wallpaper and fabric samples.
TUBE/RAIL *Wimbledon* • **OPEN** *Mon–Fri 9am–5.30pm. Sat 9am–5pm*
• **SERVICES** *Interior design and building, including planning applications.
Kitchens and bathrooms. Soft furnishings*

ST JOHN'S WOOD INTERIORS
ADDRESS 27 St John's Wood High Street, NW8 7NH
TEL 0171 586 5807 **FAX** 0171 586 5058
Longest-established family-run interior design business in North West London
– a husband-and-wife partnership. 'We've survived on recommendations
and by good value and service'. Relaxed and comfortable atmosphere –
browse through their large library of wallcoverings, fabrics and trimming
samples, covering a wide range of tastes and prices. Children's department
has toys, gifts, children's pine, and custom-made furniture. Get ideas and
inspiration from their large portfolio of previous jobs.
TUBE *St John's Wood* • **OPEN** *Mon–Sat 9am–6pm* • **SERVICES** *Full interior
design service, with free advice and estimates – 'no design fees'. All soft
furnishings, decorating, carpet laying and wood flooring, kitchens/
bathrooms, and building work*

SCHEMES
ADDRESS 56 Princedale Road, W11 4NL
TEL 0171 727 3775/1148 **FAX** 0171 792 0294
Fabrics are the main emphasis here – showroom is packed full of samples,
with own range of printed linen unions.
TUBE *Holland Park* • **OPEN** *Mon–Fri 9.30am–6pm* • **SERVICES** *All interior
design/soft-furnishing services*

TESSUTI CASA
ADDRESS Units 3 and 5, 36–40 York Way, N1 9AB
TEL 0171 837 6888 **FAX** 0171 833 9686
Tessuti means fabrics in Italian. 'We're like a mini Chelsea Harbour,' says
interior designer owner Patricia Berry. 'We've got all the latest books.
Come and see us and we'll put you a room together.' Curtains, blinds,
carpets, flooring, furniture.
TUBE *King's Cross* • **OPEN** *By appointment* • **SERVICES** *All interior design
and soft-furnishing services including special paint effects and re-upholstery*

TOP LAYER
ADDRESS 5 Egerton Terrace, SW3 2BX
TEL 0171 581 1102 **FAX** 0171 589 9043
Small friendly shop, established for around 20 years. Current owners Alain
Judd and Barrie Coppin claim 'one of the largest selections of fabric and
wallpaper books in London'. Own designers and architects, and own

workroom for fine hand-sewn curtains, blinds, tented ceilings and all other soft furnishings. Plus their own team for track fitting and curtain installation.
TUBE *Knightsbridge* • **OPEN** *Mon–Fri 9.30am–5.30pm, or by appointment*
• **SERVICES** *All interior design and soft-furnishing services*

WATERCOLOUR INTERIOR DESIGN
ADDRESS 6 Springbridge Road, W5 2AA
TEL 0181 579 3688/3228   **FAX** 0181 579 1237
Helpful shop with full interior design and soft-furnishings service for every aspect of home decoration – 'we'll do anything required'.
TUBE/RAIL *Ealing Broadway* • **OPEN** *Mon–Sat 9.30am–5.30pm*
• **SERVICES** *All interior design services*

ACCESSORIES

Change the look of a room with accessories – cushions, lamps, flowers, pictures and general bits and pieces. But if minimalism is your mission, leave them out. Most people find that accessories rapidly clone into clutter, and a good-tempered pruning from time to time may help preserve the basic bones of your original look.

SHOPS WITH FURNITURE

AFTER NOAH
ADDRESS 121 Upper Street, N1 1QP
TEL/FAX 0171 359 4281
Furniture restorer Matthew Crawford and his wife Zoe, who makes mosaics, pack out two floors with an idiosyncratic mix of merchandise. Their own popular metal beds include an unusual deco model; they also restore antique wrought-iron bedsteads. Chunky Shaker/Mission-style turn-of-the-century furniture in faded distressed paint finishes is imported from America (rocking chairs from £275). Plus masses of other old pieces – chairs, china, lamps, glass, metal and so on, culled from provincial shops and auctions. Lively modern accessories such as witty shower curtains. Downstairs is jewellery, plus cases of tiny vintage gifts which include cigarette cases, wallets, cufflinks, and boxes.

TUBE *Angel* • **OPEN** *Mon–Sat 10am–6pm. Sun 12 noon–5pm* • **SERVICES**
Beds/mosaic made to order • **WEBSITE** *www.afternoah.demon.co.uk*
• **ALSO AT** *261 King's Road, SW3 (0171 351 2610)*

ECCENTRICS

ADDRESS 3–5 Fortis Green Road, Muswell Hill, N10 3HP
TEL 0181 883 8030   **FAX** 0181 883 5030
Flying the flag for modern design in suburban North London is former
Liberty interior designer Nicola Steer, who has a degree in textiles. She has
filled a showroom by the cinema at Muswell Hill with colourful furnishings.
'I want to promote the current wealth of British designer-makers.' Furniture,
lighting, glassware, ceramics and accessories. Also hand-crafted jewellery
and textiles. Windows look particularly brilliant at night with glowing
displays. The look is funky, bright and accessible.
TUBE *Highgate + 43 or 134 bus* • **OPEN** *Mon–Sat 10am–6pm* • **SERVICES**
Full interior design service. Curtain making. Mosaic fireplaces to order.
Special furniture and mirrors. Mail order catalogue: phone 0181 458 9697
• **ALSO AT** *21 Market Place, NW11 6JY (0181 458 9697)*

ELEPHANT

ADDRESS 230 Tottenham Court Road, W1P 9AE
TEL 0171 637 7930   **FAX** 0171 637 7940
Wide variety of colourful furnishings from this growing group of stores.
Three floors of upholstered furniture, plus ethnic pieces from India, China,
and Indonesia, and iron furniture. Indian carved door cupboard, £1500,
Chinese antique wedding cabinets, £550. Comfortable and colourful, with
ethnic overtones.
TUBE *Goodge Street/Tottenham Court Road* • **OPEN** *Mon–Fri 10am–6.30pm.*
Sat 10am–6pm. Sun 11am–5pm • **ALSO AT** *94 Tottenham Court Road, W1*
(0171 813 2092). 169–171 Queensway, W2 (0171 467 0630). 18-24
Westbourne Grove, W2 (0171 243 0203). 11 Howland Street, W1 (0171
813 2092)

THE GENERAL TRADING COMPANY

ADDRESS 144 Sloane Street, Sloane Square, SW1X 9BL
TEL 0171 730 0411   **FAX** 0171 823 4624
The word is eclectic. GTC built its name on fine china, silver and glass
enlivened with the finest antiques. You'll still find all of these but spiced up
with leather, modern linens and exotic oriental artifacts. Wander through
the warren of room-like departments and if your purse is reasonably well-
lined, you're almost certain to solve a present problem or indulge in a gift
for your home – from a huge raffia curtain tie-back to a lacquered bowl,
from a horn beaker to a china planter or a shower curtain printed with
goldfish. One of only eight companies to hold four royal warrants, run by
the same family since 1920. This is the heart of Sloane Ranger territory,
but everyone gets personal service and staff are genuinely unpatronising.
A move is scheduled to Pavilion Road in autumn 2000.
TUBE *Sloane Square* • **OPEN** *Mon–Sat 9.30am–6pm. Late night Wed 7pm*
• **WEBSITE** *www.general-trading.co.uk* • **SERVICES** *Wedding lists. Cafe.*
Mail-order catalogue, £2

GRAHAM & GREEN

ADDRESS No 4 (home furnishings), No 7 (gifts & kitchenware), and
No 10 (fashion) Elgin Crescent, W11 2JA
TEL 0171 727 4594 **FAX** 0171 243 3695
Antonia Graham is the motivating force behind a much-loved group of
shops for unusual furnishings and fashion. She goes on regular buying trips
searching for the best in contemporary design, sometimes as near as Paris,
other times as far away as India. Stock is a rich mix of ethnic textiles,
including kilims, and ahead-of-the-trend merchandise.
TUBE *Notting Hill Gate* • **OPEN** *Mon–Fri 10am–6pm. Sat 9.30am–6pm.
Sun 11am–5pm* • **SERVICES** *Interior design* • **ALSO AT** *164 Regents Park
Road, NW1 8XN (0171 586 2960)*

GRAND ILLUSIONS (MAISON)

ADDRESS 2–4 Crown Road, St Margarets, Twickenham, Middx, TW1 3EE
TEL 0181 744 1046 **FAX** 0181 744 2017
Based loosely on modern French country style, the shop is crammed with
seductive home accessories at very reasonable prices – a set of 18 Bistro
glasses for £12.99. Plus pottery, wirework, lamps, baskets, pictures,
frames. Satisfyingly solid range of over 50 pieces of furniture made from
re-claimed timber, some in natural or waxed finishes, others painted in two
layers of different coloured paint, with the top rubbed back to show the
underneath – all done using Grand Illusions' own chalky paints. Owners
Nick Ronald and David Roberts, who've starred on TV's Home Front, have
crammed all their original decorating ideas into two successful books –
Grand Illusions, and now *New Decorating*. Own range of beautiful paint
colours, plus fabric paints. And they've just launched their own range of
fabrics and wallpaper.
RAIL *St Margarets (every half hour from Waterloo)* • **OPEN** *Mon–Sat
10am–6pm* • **SERVICES** *Mail-order catalogue, £2.50, refundable against
order. Courses in painting walls, floors, furniture and fabrics* • **ALSO AT**
*Clocktower Place, The Square, Richmond, TW9 1DZ; Sunday 12 noon–5pm
(0181 332 0420)*

THE HOLDING COMPANY

ADDRESS 241–245 King's Road, SW3 5EL
TEL 0171 352 1600 **FAX** 0171 610 9166 (head office); 0171 352
7495 (shop)
Say goodbye to domestic disorder. Well, give it a try, anyway. 'Who says
storage can't be fun?' is the slogan for a large bright space that's gobbled
up three shops, plus their basement area. It sells every way possible to
keep your household goods under control – hangers, boxes, racks,
baskets, bags, hooks, and stylish furniture in materials as diverse as
canvas, zinc, chrome, rattan, teak and bamboo. Plus the fearsome 'drawer
organiser', a nifty concertina-shaped bit of white plastic that spells death to
muddled socks. This retail mini-empire has grown from Canadian Dawna
Walter's 1995 mission vision to bring Londoners 'design-led storage
solutions.' For possession obsessionals, the place is a dream. Those of us
whose socks, even when tidy, remain obstinately single can at least enjoy
the bright hues and witty shapes, and vow to try harder. As Dawna says:
'If the right systems are in place, it's incredible how much time, energy
and anxiety are saved.' Yes, indeed. Now surely I haven't lost that
catalogue again...

TUBE *Sloane Square + bus/Fulham Broadway* • **OPEN** *Mon–Sat 10am–7pm.
Sun 12 noon–6pm* • **WEBSITE** *www.theholdingcompany.co.uk* • **SERVICES**
Mail-order catalogue: phone 0171 610 9160

THE HOME PLACE

ADDRESS The Hyde, Edgware Road, Hendon, NW9 7TH
TEL 0181 200 5588   **FAX** 0181 205 8657
American-style furnishings and housewares superstore, with 28,000 sq ft
of glass, cookware, ceramics, linens, rugs and flooring, soft furnishings,
bathroom and bedroom accessories, lighting and some furniture.
TUBE *Hendon Central* • **OPEN** *Mon–Fri 10am–8pm. Sat 9am–6pm.
Sun 11am–5pm* • **SERVICES** *Cafe. Plentiful parking. Occasional
kitchen/product demos*

JERRY'S HOME STORE

ADDRESS 163–167 Fulham Road, SW3 6SN
TEL 0171 581 0909   **FAX** 0171 584 3749
Eat your dinner in a diner – all the way from the US of A – furnished with
tables and chairs that are sturdy, shiny, practical and fun. Jerry's also has
Fiesta ware, the chunky pottery made from original Art Deco moulds. Plus
steel office and hospital pre-war American furniture, with shabby paint
stripped off, and polished to a cool gleam – desks, chests of drawers,
bathroom cabinets. Also Mission solid cherrywood furniture from Vermont,
including a desk and filing cabinet. Plus sophisticated New York armchairs
and sofas in weathered brown or soft black leather. Masses of practical
good-looking table- and kitchenware – pans for serious cooking, and shakers
for serious cocktails. Heavy-duty juicers and mixers, authentic pizza-makers.
Brilliant cookery books. Clever gifts and no holds barred at Christmas.
TUBE *South Kensington* • **OPEN** *Mon–Fri 10am–6pm. Sat 10am–6.30pm.
Sun 12 noon–5.30pm* • **SERVICES** *Mail-order on 0171 581 0909* • **ALSO
AT** *57–61 Heath Street, NW3 (0171 794 8622). 4th Floor, Harvey
Nichols, SW1 (0171 245 6251). Kingston (0181 549 5393)*

MILLENNIUM

ADDRESS 1b Barnes High Street, Barnes, SW13 9LB
TEL 0181 876 1112   **FAX** 0181 876 2105
Tallboys, chests, tables, dressers can be made to any measurements within
three to four weeks – finishes from a light limewash to deep rich colours.
Dressers from around £650. Metal and glass furniture can also be made to
measure – metal shelving from £30. Plus accessories which include mirrors,
hooks, lamps, and mosaic tables.
RAIL *Barnes Bridge/Barnes* • **OPEN** *Mon–Sat 10am–6pm. Sun 11.30am–
4.30pm* • **SERVICES** *Custom-made furniture including mosaic to order*

MUJI

ADDRESS 26 Great Marlborough Street, W1V 1HL
TEL 0171 494 1197
This was the first store for a retail 'no brand' concept from Japan which
hooked Londoners on to unadorned basics in simple materials and natural
colours. Minimal look, and happily, minimal prices, based on 'kanketsu'
(Japanese for simplicity). Newer branches (see below) are much larger.
Simple furniture in fibreboard, ply, and card – storage boxes, shelving,
tables. Plus thick towels and no-nonsense bedlinens, basic white/oatmeal

ceramics, stainless steel kitchenware, and clear plastic accessories. Card storage boxes from £2.95; shelving in steel and wood veneer, from £125. Steel clothes rail, £9.50, and canvas baskets, £15. Well worth careful exploration.

TUBE *Oxford Street* • **OPEN** *Mon–Wed 10.30am–6.30pm. Thurs 10am–7pm. Fri Sat 10am–6.30pm. Sun 12 noon–6pm* • **ALSO AT** *187 Oxford Street, W1 (0171 437 7503). 39 Shelton Street, WC2 (0171 379 1331). 157 Kensington High Street, W8 (0171 376 2484). 77 King's Road, SW3 (0171 352 7148). 135 Long Acre, WC2 (0171 379 0820). Whiteleys Shopping Centre, W2 (0171 792 8283)*

MCCORD ✉

TEL 0870 908 7020   **FAX** 0645 533 533/0870 908 7050
Free mail-order catalogue for good value pleasant furnishings, many exclusive. From large items of furniture to small accessories. Invaluable.
WEBSITE *www.mccord.uk.com*

OCEAN ✉

TEL 0870 8484840   **FAX** 0870 848 4849
Frequently up-dated catalogue of designer furniture and accessories for style slaves. Brilliant selections of well-illustrated products, sourced tirelessly from home and abroad.
SERVICES *48-hour delivery. Gift wrapping. 24-hour 7-day orderline*
• **ALSO AT** *Ocean Warehouse Shop, 9 Hardwicks Way, SW18 4AW (0171 670 1222).* ☞ Warehouse shop for discontinued lines, seconds and returned orders, with up to 80 per cent savings on continually changing merchandise.
RAIL *Wandsworth Town* • **OPEN** *Mon–Sat 10am–6pm*

OLIVER BONAS

ADDRESS 801 Fulham Road, Fulham, SW6 5HE
TEL 0171 736 8435   **FAX** 0171 731 6913
Growing chain of shops for attractive furniture and accessories. Side tables, dining tables, and other furniture in oak, metal and glass. Coffee tables, from £150 to £400; dining room chairs, £100 to £250. Plus glassware, including vases from the Polish factory Krosno, from around £10 to £90. Ironwork lamps £25 to £80. Plus mirrors, many small accessories, and gifts.
TUBE *Parson's Green* • **OPEN** *(all branches) Mon–Fri 10am–6.30pm. Sat 10am–6pm. Sun noon–5pm* • **SERVICES** *Wedding lists* • **ALSO AT** *137 Northcote Road, Battersea, SW11 6PX (0171 223 5223). 113 Shepherds Bush Road, Brook Green, W6 7LP (0171 371 2662). 416 Richmond Road, Richmond Bridge, TW1 2EB (0181 892 0808). 23 The Pavement, Clapham Common, SW5 0JA (0171 720 8272). 24 Turnham Green Terrace, Chiswick, W4 1QP (0181 994 9894)*

THE PIER

ADDRESS 200 Tottenham Court Road, W1
TEL 0171 637 7001   **FAX** 0171 637 3332
High style, low price for an affordable mix of mainly imported handicrafts, thanks to the tireless energy of founder director Alison Richards, who now

has 14 shops around the country. Cane furniture is particularly good. Chow chair in white plus colours is £29; sofas including seat cushion from £185 – good for that budget first flat. Plus cane wardrobes, trunks, bedheads and sets of storage drawers. Also colourful tableware, with new themes each season – candles, linens and china. Stylish rugs, cushions, screens, and masses more smaller accessories.

TUBE *Goodge Street* • **OPEN** *Mon Wed Fri 10am–6.30pm. Tues 10.30am–6.30pm. Thurs 10am–7.30pm. Sat 9.30am–6.30pm. Sun 11am–5pm*
• **SERVICES** *Mail-order: call Pier Direct for a catalogue, 0171 814 5004*
• **ALSO AT** *91–95 King's Road, SW3 (0171 351 7100). Upper Level, Centre Court Shopping Centre, Wimbledon, SW19 (0181 879 1046). Kingston (0181 974 8262). Bromley (0181 466 8090)*

RUTH ARAM SHOP

ADDRESS 65 Heath Street, NW3 6UG
TEL 0171 431 4008   **FAX** 0171 431 6755
Vivacious always-ahead outpost for groovy home design amidst the sedate fashion boutiques of Hampstead. Ruth Aram is a determined young woman whose sound design education is pepped up by personal panache. Her stock puts the message over; from small witty gifts and funky accessories such as door handles through impressive lighting selections (all wired up in radiant display) to furniture which includes cutting-edge upholstery and bold blow-up chairs. All underpinned with serious design classics. Shop here and the West End may be irrelevant.

TUBE *Hampstead* • **OPEN** *Mon–Sat 10am–6pm. Sun 11.30am–5.30pm (winter); 12 noon–6pm (summer)* • **SERVICES** *Mail-order. Will post/ship stock anywhere*

TOBIAS AND THE ANGEL

ADDRESS 68 White Hart Lane, SW13 0PZ
TEL/FAX 0181 878 8902
Angel very much exists but Tobias remains biblical. She's built up a devoted clientele for rustic and country antiques, and has her own range of solid wood furniture, painted and with a rubbed-back finish. Simple Swedish-style country chairs, £200; plain pine tables, £85 per sq foot. Plus all kinds of hand made delights, mostly from old fabrics – lamps with old baluster stands and removable washable shades, and exquisite Christmas decorations. Plus of course, an angel for your tree. Prices on the steep side – but swollen by hours of labour.

RAIL *Barnes Bridge* • **OPEN** *Mon–Sat 10am–6pm*

VIVI LIGHTING AND INTERIOR

ADDRESS 201 Lower Richmond Road, SW15 1HJ
TEL 0181 780 1199   **FAX** 0181 780 3311
Vivi Ind sells modern classics from France, Sweden, Norway, Denmark and the UK – accessories and some small pieces of furniture. Her criteria: arresting shapes, innovative materials, and bright colours – home linens, wool blankets, photo frames, suede cushions (ready-made and to order), luscious fake fur throws, and chairs printed with huge flowers and fruits.

RAIL *Mortlake* • **OPEN** *Mon–Fri 10am–5.30pm. Sat 10am–5pm*

SHOPS WITH SMALLER ACCESSORIES

AMERICAN RETRO
ADDRESS 35 Old Compton Street, W1V 5PL
TEL 0171 734 3477 **FAX** 0171 734 6885
Buyer Sue Tahran tirelessly circles the globe (Japan, America, Continental
Europe – you name it, she's been there) to bring London the most
fashionable *objets* for home and wardrobe. Drop-dead style over two
floors. Inflatable cushions, Philippe Starck toothbrushes, Cowsticks to give
your fridge a cow-hide pattern, flat-pack fruitbowls, bear-shaped candles –
if it's wild and wacky, you'll find it here. Just the job for cheering up a bleak
corner, and brilliant for presents. So when next in town, go there.
TUBE *Leicester Square/Piccadilly/Tottenham Court Road* • **OPEN** *Mon Tues
Wed Fri Sat 10.15am–7pm. Thurs 10am–8pm*

BARCLAY AND BODIE
ADDRESS 7 Blenheim Terrace, NW8 OEH
TEL 0171 372 5705 **FAX** 0171 328 4266
Idiosyncratic is the only word. In 1988, Ruth Barclay and her niece Sherrie
Bodie set up shop so successfully they soon gobbled up next door. 'We
scrutinise every item personally – we shop for ourselves – practicality and
originality are our watchwords.' Trays, wastebins, cushions, embroidered
towels, candlesticks, boxes, screens, antique furniture, kitchen accessories:
exclusive and covetable. My favourites: the shower curtains with black-and-
white classical figures (£25) and the risqué ironing board cover with a
naked man (£17.50). Plus the handy armchair leather organiser to keep
all those elusive electronic controls in order (£49).
TUBE *St John's Wood* • **OPEN** *Mon–Sat 9.30am–5.30pm* • **SERVICES**
Free gift wrapping. Mail order catalogue

BRATS
See DECORATING: PAINT SPECIALISTS, page 96
The very latest in funky home accessories and gifts – just this side of
kitsch. Bright bead curtains, day-glo plastics, blow-up furniture, and
much, much more.

CHAIRWORKS
ADDRESS Unit 77, Chelsea Business Centre,
326–342 Queenstown Road, SW8 4NE
TEL 0171 498 7611 **FAX** 0171 498 7613
Battersea's little-known best basket store fills two huge warehouses under
railway arches by the Dog's Home. They're stashed floor to ceiling with
wicker every which way you turn. Choose from styles that go to all the chic
shops – ring for free catalogue and price list. Director Nick Smyth has
bullied and cajoled suppliers in the Far East to make thick Western-style
willow baskets, many based on traditional European shapes. This means
lower prices. Colours vary from smooth peeled white (which can be
stained) to rougher rustic wood with bark.
RAIL *Battersea Park* • **OPEN** *Mon–Fri 9am–5.30pm*

CLASSIC ROBES AND INTERIORS
ADDRESS Old Spitalfields Market, 57-59 Brushfield Street, E1 6AA
TEL 0171 375 1844   **FAX** 0171 375 1886
A sweet-scented hideaway whose main line is luxurious printed towelling
robes with exotic towels to match. Also good for designer accessories –
from glass knobs to knobbly mugs.
TUBE Liverpool Street • **OPEN** Sun–Fri 11.30am–6pm

CXV
ADDRESS 376 King's Road, SW3 5UZ
TEL/FAX 0171 351 5975
Marine themes proliferate in this tiny shop with pointy Gothic windows –
shells are heaped high into an iridescent cone to decorate a lampbase and
glinting fish frolic around a gilded mirror frame. These and other natural
motifs contrast with more formal glass and china gifts, plus sophisticated
decorator accessories, such as a huge selection of framed classical prints.
A spiral stairway leads to larger pieces – clocks, mirrors, screens, sconces,
and cupboards.
OPEN Mon–Thurs Sat 10am–6.30pm. Fri 10am–6pm. Sun 12 noon–4pm
• **TUBE** Sloane Square + 11, 19, 22 bus

EMMA BERNHARDT
ADDRESS 301 Portobello Road, W10
TEL 0181 960 2929   **FAX** 0171 935 4080
Mexico run riot – everything's colourful and some is unashamedly kitsch.
Loads of woven baskets, plus tin trays, juice squeezers, street decorations,
fabric off the roll, feather dusters – whatever caught Emma's fancy on the
latest trip.
TUBE Ladbroke Grove • **OPEN** Tues 12 noon–5.30pm. Wed Thurs
10.30am–5.30pm. Fri Sat 10.30am–6pm

FIELDHOUSE
ADDRESS 89–91 Wandsworth Bridge Road, Fulham, SW6 2LF
TEL 0171 736 7547   **FAX** 0171 731 0150
Rosie Bartlett runs this charming shop with best friend Bunty Ross. For
12 years, they kept on growing – now they're 'opening up the back'.
Carefully chosen decorative accessories and gifts – always a bit different –
huge range from all over the world. Mirrors, candlesticks, sconces, boxes –
something for everyone and every room. Presents and accessories with a
romantic flavour.
TUBE Parsons Green • **OPEN** Mon–Sat 10am–8pm. Sun 11am–5pm

GALERIE SINGLETON
ADDRESS 40 Theobalds Road, WC1X 8NW
TEL 0171 831 6928   **FAX** 0171 831 8307
Here's an unlikely outpost for modern handmade design, on such a bleak
metropolitan highway. The colourful characterful window is hypnotic –
you're inside before you know it, to find handmade pottery, papier mâché,
boxes, candelabra and ceramics, often with a quirky twist. Originality is
guaranteed. Shop for a present, but many things are just too good to give
away. Clocks are a speciality. 'Prices are as affordable as possible'.
TUBE Holborn • **OPEN** Mon–Fri 10.30am–6.30pm. Sat 11am–5pm

GEORGE PEDERSEN
ADDRESS 152 Upper Street, N1 1RA
TEL 0171 359 5655   **FAX** 0171 359 2056
This interesting shop, owned by George Booker (formerly of Gore Booker)
has an intriguing mix of wrought-iron furniture and small pieces in ceramic
and glass. Mirrors, picture frames – 'you name it, we sell it – from a door
knob to an old chest of drawers'.
TUBE *Angel or Highbury & Islington* • **OPEN** *Mon–Sat 10am–6pm.
Sun 1pm–5pm* • **SERVICES** *Mirrors and furniture made to order*

GREEN & PLEASANT
ADDRESS 129 Church Road, Barnes, SW13 9HR
TEL 0181 741 1539   **FAX** 0181 741 0816
They describe themselves as a lifestyle shop – with fashions as well as
furnishings. Merchandise is very pretty, with unusual lamps, candles,
ceramics, toys, mobiles. Early summer or Christmas are the best times to
visit. Some furniture and lamps from Morocco.
RAIL *Barnes Bridge* • **OPEN** *Mon–Sat 9am–6pm* • **SERVICES** *Top florists do
flowers for all occasions – very popular*

IN
ADDRESS 13a Lamb Street, Old Spitalfields Market, E1 6EA
TEL 0171 247 3561   **FAX** 0171 426 0401
Tucked alongside the old market is an outpost for modish modern
accessories, from kitchen kitsch to leopardskin lamps and velvet cushions.
TUBE *Liverpool Street* • **OPEN** *Mon–Sun 10am–6pm*

INDISH
ADDRESS 13 Broadway Parade, Crouch End, N8 9DE
TEL 0181 340 1144   **FAX** 0181 340 1188
Indian & English equals Indish. Anglo-Indians Melanie Silgardo and Kash
a Dalal – pleasant, imaginative and resourceful – fill this shopping gem
with vibrant colourful cotton tablemats and napkins, cushions, bed linen,
sheer voile curtains, pyjamas and bathroom accessories – all hand-woven
exclusively for them in South India. Plus a complementary range of bits and
pieces from around the world – Turkish kilims, British lighting, Vietnamese
laquerware and Kenyan sisal baskets, Danish hand-thrown porcelain.
TUBE *Finsbury Park + W3, W7 bus* • **OPEN** *Mon–Sat 10.30am–5.30pm*

INVENTORY
ADDRESS 26–40 Kensington High Street, W8
TEL 0171 937 2626   **FAX** 0171 938 4079
Started life as The Source, then got bought out, and confusingly changed
its name. A vast ex-industrial building crammed with stylish home goods at
unpretentious prices. For example, 16-piece black and white cutlery set,
£30; natural blankets in cream and taupe, £27.50; square linen baskets,
£15; heart nightlight holders, £5. In the basement: storage, lighting, books
and the kids' department. On the ground floor: kitchen, china, glassware,
accessories, and gifts. First floor: bedding, bathroom, and textiles.
TUBE *Kensington High Street* • **OPEN** *Mon–Sat 10am–7pm. Sun 12 noon–6pm*

LA MURRINA

ADDRESS 79 Ebury Street, SW1W 0NZ
TEL 0171 730 7922 **FAX** 0171 730 7920

Fabulously fragile glass chandeliers hang from the ceiling of this large and luscious shop, with exquisite handmade glass from the famous island of Murano in the Bay of Venice. Perfume bottles, glass fruit, fish sculptures, statuettes, paperweights, dishes, bowls, wine glasses, cocktail sets in rich colours enhanced with gold, silver and frosting.

TUBE *Sloane Square/Victoria* • **OPEN** *Mon–Fri 10am–5.30pm. Sat 10am– 4pm* • **SERVICES** *Gift wrapping*

OGGETTI

ADDRESS 133 and 143 Fulham Road, SW3 6RT
TEL 0171 581 8088/0171 584 9808 **FAX** 0171 581 9652

This shop was way ahead in presenting well-designed accessories as mini works of art in gleaming glass showcases. Now the world has caught up. Alessi is (almost) a household word and Porsche is roaring up on the design agenda. Tableware, luggage, bar goods, watches, sunglasses, coffee makers, kettles, silver, ceramics, plastic. 'Leading design mixed with classics – for the kitchen, home and beyond.'

TUBE *South Kensington* • **OPEN** *Mon–Sat 9.30am–6pm. Sun 12 noon–5pm* • **SERVICES** *Gift wrapping*

OUT OF EARTH

ADDRESS 83 Church Road, Barnes, SW13 9HH
TEL/FAX 0181 563 9991

The mission here is to mix the work of new young designers with those already famous. Spread over two floors, against a background of warm ochre-glazed brick, an eclectic mix of ceramics, furniture and glass. Plus fun and often inexpensive presents for your home or a special gift.

RAIL *Barnes* • **OPEN** *Mon–Sat 10am–6pm. Late hours for Christmas – please phone* • **SERVICES** *Wedding lists, mail order, gift wrapping/ posting. Commissions for ceramics, furniture and jewellery*

STEPHEN EINHORN

ADDRESS 210 Upper Street, N1 1RL
TEL 0171 359 4977 **FAX** 0171 354 0953

Maverick designer Stephen Einhorn crowds his little shop with imagination and wit. Peep around the back to see his workshop. From bird feeders to corkscrews, from candleholders to chocolates...you never know quite what you'll find or what it will be made of, so prepare for surprises. For example, Gothic taps, in skull and cross-bone shapes (from £170.65 a pair). Or the Nail range, from a single hook (looks like a nail banged in the wall, but more refined) to the large nail stool. Bottle openers and keyrings; skulls, UFOs, flowers, birdcages, from £9.95.

TUBE *Highbury & Islington* • **OPEN** *Mon–Sat 10am–6pm* • **SERVICES** *Bespoke jewellery*

THE TARTAN CUPBOARD
ADDRESS 2a The Market, Greenwich, SE10 9HZ
TEL 0181 858 0038
Savour the delights of bonnie Scotland at Daphne Hirons' small but much loved boutique. Tourists fall with glee on excellent authentic ties and kilts. But there's also tartan home accessories including fabric by the metre.
RAIL *Greenwich* • **OPEN** *Tues–Sun 11.30am–5pm*

TESSA FANTONI GIFTS AND ACCESSORIES
ADDRESS 77 Abbeville Road, SW4 9JN
TEL 0181 673 1253
Making beautiful books by hand is Tessa Fantoni's special art. Handmade photo albums are covered in a choice of decorative papers with elegant buckram bindings. Add a few family snaps, for a very personal present. Prices from £20.95 to £65. Plus pottery, photo frames, jewellery, handbags.
TUBE *Clapham South* • **OPEN** *Mon–Sat 10am–6pm. Sun 12 noon–5pm. Extended hours at Christmas – please phone for details* • **ALSO AT** *Tessa Fantoni Decorative Objects for the Home, 73 Abbeville Road, SW4 9JN*

VERANDAH
ADDRESS 15b Blenheim Crescent, W11 2EE
TEL 0171 792 9289
Anne Jaye opened Verandah on a Friday the Thirteenth in April 1990. A lucky date all round – she's much loved locally for her quirky affordable home accessories. 'Everything is handmade, but most things are usable as well as decorative.' Moroccan lanterns from £12.50. Also rustic glass, and small wooden items, candle holders, bright baskets, mosaic-framed mirrors, disco balls from £2.15 to £50. Glowing shelves of turquoise and blue pottery. Plus beautiful handmade papers to wrap everything in.
TUBE *Ladbroke Grove/Notting Hill Gate* • **OPEN** *Mon 1–6pm. Tues–Sat 10am–6pm. Extended opening hours at Christmas – phone for details*

VILLAGE INTRIGUE
ADDRESS 10 Crown Road, Twickenham, TW1 3EE
TEL 0181 892 4140   **FAX** 0181 892 3419
Recycled oak furniture from the 1920s for today's interiors. Stunning modern mirrors, burrwood photo frames, handmade paper. Hand-cut stencils. Established for 18 years, they are firm local favourites and were one of the first importers from Northern Thailand, whose craftsmen still make wood sculptures, architectural corbels, and mirror frames exclusively for them. Also garden seats and tables.
RAIL *St Margarets* • **OPEN** *Mon–Sat 10am–6pm* • **SERVICES** *Stencil cutting*

WONG SINGH JONES
ADDRESS 253 Portobello Road, W11 1LR
TEL 0171 792 2001   **FAX** 0181 968 5030
Colourful kitsch reigns supreme at this corner shop crammed with beautiful – and bizarre – imports. Almost anything goes, from Indian film star postcards to clip-on anodised aluminium lights, from fortune cookies to polka-dot plastic tumblers, from cardboard star-lights to henna hand stencils. Magical, mysterious and a must.
TUBE *Ladbroke Grove* • **OPEN** *Mon–Sat 10.30am–6.30pm. Sun 11am–5.30pm*

SHOPS RUN BY DESIGNERS/INTERIOR DECORATORS

Particularly worth visiting are the shops run by London's top decorators, as listed below. Maybe you can't afford their internationally-acclaimed services, but through the bits and pieces in their shops, you can acquire a little of their look.

BILL AMBERG

ADDRESS 10 Chepstow Road, W2 5BD
TEL 0171 727 3560   **FAX** 0171 727 3541
Leather is simple, sensuous, natural and feels good to the touch – and Bill Amberg is London's Mr Leather. Handbags and luggage are his mainstay, but he also does leather floor tiles (not cheap at £250 a square metre) and leather panelling. Leather cushions in coloured leather and suede are around £100. Plus screens, desks, chairs, umbrella stands and storage units.
TUBE *Notting Hill Gate* • **OPEN** *Mon–Sat 10am–6pm. Late night Wed 7pm*
• **SERVICES** *Leather floor installation*

CARDEN CUNIETTI

ADDRESS 83 Westbourne Park Road, W2 5QH
TEL 0171 229 8559   **FAX** 0171 229 8799
A very personal selection from designers Audrey Carden and Eleanora Cunietti who garner globally and then show off their finds on decorative antiques. Cushions made from treasured fragments of antique fabrics, comfortable cutlery from Germany, and designer glass from Sweden, alongside lacquer from Vietnam, handmade American crockery, and scented Oregon candles. Prices from £7.50 for a pretty shell cabinet handle to £2,000 for a Murano glass floor lamp. 'But our backbone is our all-encompassing interior design service – from foundations to a finished home full of luxurious creature comforts.'
TUBE *Westbourne Park/Royal Oak* • **OPEN** *Mon–Sat 10am–5.30pm*
• **SERVICES** *Interior design, including all building work*

CONRAN COLLECTION

ADDRESS 12 Conduit Street, W1R 9TG
TEL 0171 399 0710   **FAX** 0171 399 0711
A large shop over two floors, showing Terence Conran's definitive range of products for the home. Says Sir Terence: 'The Conran Collection is quietly modern, comfortable and beautifully made... it's modern living made simple.' He's worked with a team of four other designers to produce furniture, lighting, bedlinen, glass, crockery, cushions, rugs, and candles that are elegantly understated and not inordinately expensive. It is difficult to leave without making a purchase.
TUBE *Oxford Circus* • **OPEN** *Mon–Fri 10am–6.30pm. Late night Thurs 7.30pm. Sunday 12 noon–6pm* • **WEBSITE** *www.conran.co.uk*
• **SERVICES** *Catalogue, £2.50 + postage*

DAVID CHAMPION

ADDRESS 199 Westbourne Grove, W11 2SB
TEL 0171 727 6016   **FAX** 0171 792 2097

Destination discovery: exotic, eclectic, and individual with treasures trawled from all over the world. Vietnamese ceramics are particularly popular, as are African tribal carvings and masks. These could be mixed with Art Deco, or classic chairs from the fifties. Go to get ideas and stretch your imagination.
TUBE *Notting Hill Gate* • **OPEN** *Mon–Sat 10am–6pm* • **SERVICES** *Tables and upholstery made to order*

DESIGNERS GUILD

ADDRESS 267–277 King's Road, SW3 5EN
TEL 0171 351 5775   **FAX** 0171 243 7710

Here in living glowing technicolour is the 3D rendition of Tricia Guild's inimitable style, known worldwide through her brilliant books on colour. Avant-garde furniture (Cappellini, B & B Italia, Tom Dixon), their own range of sofas and armchairs, plus galvanised-frames for beds and four-posters. Also bright, bright, bright looks for linens, china, cushions and so on. Plus Tricia's own very personal take on crafts, and a pleasant courtyard out the back for garden items. Just a few doors down the road is the corner showroom for fabrics and papers to complete your Go Guild lifestyle (see FABRICS AND SOFT FURNISHINGS: FABRIC MANUFACTURERS WITH SHOWROOM SHOPS, page 68)
TUBE *Sloane Square + 11, 19, 22 bus* • **OPEN** *Mon Tues 9.30am–5.30pm. Wed Thurs Fri Sat 10am–6pm. Sun 12 noon–5pm* • **SERVICES** *Wedding list. Gift wrapping. Capuccino bar*

JOANNA WOOD

ADDRESS 48a Pimlico Road, SW1W 8LP
TEL 0171 730 5064   **FAX** 0171 730 4135

Joanna Wood is one of Britain's best-known decorators, beloved by an international clientele for her very 'English style'. Her Pimlico port-of-call is crammed with accessories and gifts picked up all over the world. China, lamps, candlesticks, mirrors, frames, small pieces of furniture, cushions, pill boxes, bedlinen and objets d'art. Elegant and Wood-be-good.
TUBE *Sloane Square* • **OPEN** *Mon–Fri 10am–6pm. Sat 10am–4pm*

LOUISE BRADLEY

ADDRESS 15 Walton Street, SW3 2HX
TEL 0171 589 1442   **FAX** 0171 589 2009

Decorator gifts and home accessories, including carved stone-effect candles, beaded candle-holders, lampshades, and drink mats, wrought-iron lamps with ecru shades, hugely tall champagne flutes, and an exclusive tortoiseshell glass collection.
TUBE *Knightsbridge/South Kensington* • **OPEN** *Mon–Sat 10am–6pm*
• **SERVICES** *Gift service catalogue – use instead of sending flowers. Full interior design service*

MICHAEL REEVES

ADDRESS 33 Mossop Street, SW3 2NB
TEL 0171 225 2501   **FAX** 0171 225 3060

This small shop reflects the taste of the winner of the Interior Designer of the Year Award, 1988. Artefacts from all around the world and every period

including art deco originals offset contemporary pieces, including his own range of sofas, chairs and occasional tables.
TUBE *Sloane Square* • **OPEN** *Mon–Fri 9.30am–5.30pm. Sat 10am–5pm*

NICHOLAS HASLAM

See FABRICS AND SOFT FURNISHINGS: FABRIC MANUFACTURERS WITH SHOWROOM SHOPS, page 69. Lighting, furniture, cushions, screens, and lots of unusual touches.

NINA CAMPBELL

ADDRESS 9 Walton Street, SW3 2JD
TEL 0171 225 1011   **FAX** 0171 823 8353
Nina is our decorating grande dame. Her colour palette is unique, expressed in her own papers, fabrics and carpets, shown in her own showroom shop and distributed by Osborne & Little – (see FABRICS AND SOFT FURNISHINGS: FABRIC MANUFACTURERS WITH SHOWROOM SHOPS, page 69). This shop has the prettiest accessories in town, including exquisite French porcelain and glass from famous names and small workshops. Plus lamps, cushions (in Nina's fabrics), trays and so on. Perhaps you don't have a mansion, but a visit to Nina's is a good objects lesson: how to choose them, where to place them and how to group them.
TUBE *South Kensington/Knightsbridge* • **OPEN** *Mon–Fri 9.30am–5.30pm. Sat 10am–4pm* • **SERVICES** *Full interior decorating service* • **ALSO AT** *7 Milner Street (0171 589 8589)*

RENWICK & CLARKE

ADDRESS 190 Ebury Street, SW1W 8UP
TEL 0171 730 8913   **FAX** 0171 730 4508
This amazing shop is filled with lavish largesse by interior designer George Renwick and partner Hugh Meyer. Huge contrast of materials, from bronze for urns and vases, to faux croc for wastepaper baskets and accessories. Linens, furniture, lighting, cutlery, glassware and richly-embossed gilded and hand-painted leather panels. Particularly good for table-setting ideas.
TUBE *Sloane Square* • **OPEN** *Mon–Fri 9.30am–6pm. Sat 10am–4pm*

ROSEMARY HAMILTON

ADDRESS 44 Moreton Street, SW1V 2PB
TEL 0171 828 5018   **FAX** 0171 828 1325
Catch up on all the latest designs at this small shop which sells decorative accessories, objets d'art and small pieces of furniture.
TUBE *Pimlico* • **OPEN** *Mon–Fri 9.30am–5.30pm* • **SERVICES** *Full interior design service. China mending service*

STEPHEN RYAN

ADDRESS 7 Clarendon Cross, Holland Park, W11 4AP
TEL 0171 243 0864   **FAX** 0171 243 3151
Exclusive furniture and lamps, plus contemporary art and decorative accessories to re-create the style of this award-winning designer. Sofas in exotic textures – leathers, wool, velvets and lace. Candles, cushions, burnished metals, etched glass and feathers.
TUBE *Holland Park* • **OPEN** *Mon–Sat 10am–6pm* • **SERVICES** *Full interior design service. Library of fabrics and materials for public use*

TINDLE
ADDRESS 162–168 Wandsworth Bridge Road, SW6 2UQ
TEL 0171 384 1485   **FAX** 0171 736 5630
Professional interior decorators go to Tindle for finishing touches – wonderful lamps, rugs, cushions, objets d'art. Frankly, it's not cheap but browsing through huge stocks over three floors could yield an exquisite treasure.
TUBE *Fulham Broadway* • **OPEN** *Mon–Fri 9.30am–5.30pm. Sat 10am–5pm*

FASHION SHOPS WITH HOME COLLECTIONS

DEBENHAMS
See UNDER ONE ROOF: DEPARTMENT STORES page 13. Affordable home range from Jasper Conran, who's done big bold duvet covers and knitted throws. Attractive and unpretentious.

DONNA KARAN
ADDRESS 19 New Bond Street, W1Y 9HF
TEL 0171 495 3100   **FAX** 0171 495 3500
DK is big on lifestyle with big prices for a range that's rich in feely-touchy textures and natural materials like leather and linen. A candle, albeit beautifully packaged, and pungent with essential oils, could cost £100. A changing selection of other accessories show a fashionably oriental influence – lacquerware, huge platters, and big silver bowls.
TUBE *Bond Street/Green Park* • **OPEN** *Mon–Sat 10am–6pm. Late night Thurs 7pm*

GIANNI VERSACE
ADDRESS 34–36 Old Bond Street, W1
TEL 0171 499 1862   **FAX** 0171 499 1719
Richly ornate, and unmistakably Versace, so at least you are buying into obvious exclusivity. Extensive luxury homewares include bed linen, cushions, cutlery, china, towels, bath robes, glassware, vases, lamps, and frames. A set of silk sheets could set you back £1000. Or you could simply buy two cotton pillowcases for £35.
TUBE *Green Park* • **OPEN** *Mon–Sat 10am–6pm*

GUCCI
ADDRESS 18 Sloane Street, SW1X 8NE
TEL 0171 235 6707   **FAX** 0171 838 9541
It's difficult to see how things can be so expensive. Cushions, tableware, vases, lighters, photoframes, cigar cases. Rabbit fur cushion for £225 or a leather one for £250, and for the designer dog, a lead for £95.
TUBE *Knightsbridge* • **OPEN** *Mon–Sat 10am–6pm. Late night Wed 7pm*

HERMES INTERIORS
ADDRESS 179 Sloane Street, SW1
TEL 0171 823 1014   **FAX** 0171 823 1458
This famous fashion house was ahead in the home chic game when they

first produced an ashtray in 1950. Now they've added porcelain, cutlery, glassware, tableware, furniture and accessories – and even H for Hermes bookends.

TUBE *Knightsbridge/Sloane Square* • **OPEN** *Mon–Sat 10am–6pm*

JOSEPH

ADDRESS 74 Sloane Avenue, SW3 3DZ
TEL 0171 591 0808   **FAX** 0171 591 0880

Sleek furniture in fashionably-dark wenge wood, plus leather-covered items. Coffee tables cost around £950. Daybeds from £1295. Magazine racks are £240.

TUBE *Sloane Square and South Kensington* • **OPEN** *Mon–Fri 10am– 6.30pm. Late night Wed 7pm. Sat 10am–6pm. Sun 12pm–5pm*

MARGARET HOWELL

ADDRESS 24 Brook Street, W1Y 1AE
TEL 0171 495 4888   **FAX** 0171 495 2313

Margaret Howell uses lots of lovely natural fibres for Irish linen sheets, cashmere and merino blankets, calico mattress covers. She also has antique household linens, simple glazed bowls and jugs, and hand-thrown pottery in creamy whites.

TUBE *Bond Street* • **OPEN** *Mon-Sat 10am-6pm* • **ALSO AT** *29 Beauchamp Place, SW3 1BR (0171 584 2462)*

NICOLE FARHI HOME

ADDRESS 17 Clifford Street, W1X 1RG
TEL 0171 494 9051   **FAX** 0171 494 9052

Essentially the favourite designer of the smart girl about town, NF enters the furnishing market with a typically of-the-moment collection in lots of natural materials including the inevitable leather but also (more distinctive and cheaper) wood and horn. Her dinner service is pure white, of course, with contrasting matt/gloss finish. Plus pure Irish linen and Egyptian cotton sheets, silk organza throws in steely greys and granite shades, and a selection of art deco and forties pieces, including leather chests.

TUBE *Bond Street/Green Park/Oxford Circus* • **OPEN** *Mon–Sat 10am–6pm. Late night Thurs 7pm*

RALPH LAUREN HOME

ADDRESS 4th Floor, Harvey Nichols, Knightsbridge, SW1X 7RJ
TEL 0171 235 5010   **FAX** 0171 235 9940

Of all the fashion designers, Ralph Lauren is the one that takes the home most seriously and he has built up a large and well-deserved following for his fabrics, linens, furniture, ceramics, glass and accessories. In the true style of a fashion king, he brings out new home collections twice a year, but usually keeps popular merchandise from previous seasons in production. Thus you will find a good choice of various looks – from his particularly chic versions of leopard-skin prints (extended even on to bedlinen and towels) to denim to tartan, tweeds and Aran knits.

TUBE *Knightsbridge* • **OPEN** *Mon–Sat 10am–7pm. Late night Wed 8pm. Sun 12 noon–6pm*

FRAMES AND FRAMING

BOURLET FINE ART FRAMERS
AND PICTURE GALLERY

ADDRESS 32 Connaught Street, W2 2AY
TEL/FAX 0171 724 4837
Fine pictures deserve expert surroundings. This old-established company is famous for its splendid hand-carved frames in fruitwood, veneer, or inlaid with marquetry, plus carving, gilding and painting. Their service takes from two weeks to two months – 'the more you pay, the longer you wait.'
TUBE *Marble Arch/Lancaster Gate* • **OPEN** *Mon–Fri 10am–5.30pm. Sat 10am–4pm* • **WEBSITE** *www.bourlet.co.uk* • **SERVICES** *Specialised picture lighting*

COUTTES FRAMING

ADDRESS 75 Blythe Road, Brook Green, W14 OHP
TEL 0171 603 7475   **FAX** 0171 602 3980
This highly experienced company, established for 15 years, offers high-class bespoke framing, with unique gilded and hand-painted frames and mounts. They also do unusual mantle mirrors.
TUBE *Hammersmith/Olympia* • **OPEN** *Mon–Fri 9am–5pm. Sat by appointment* • **SERVICES** *Framing and restoration*

FIX A FRAME

ADDRESS 280 Old Brompton Road, SW5 9HR
TEL 0171 370 4189   **FAX** 0171 244 7876
Learn all the trade tricks of frame making and mount cutting – and get your picture framed quickly by doing it yourself with expert guidance.
TUBE *Earls Court* • **OPEN** *Tues–Fri 10.30am–7pm. Sat 10am–6.30pm* • **SERVICES** *Bespoke framing also available*

FRAME

ADDRESS 137 Portobello Road, W11 2DY
TEL 0171 792 1272   **FAX** 0171 792 1272
Fine quality mouldings are turned into sophisticated frames to produce an amazing variety of unusual styles, at off-the-peg prices.
TUBE *Notting Hill Gate* • **OPEN** *Mon–Fri 10am–6pm. Sat 8am–5.30pm. Sun 11am–5pm*

FRAME EMPORIUM

ADDRESS 123–129 St Pancras Road, NW1 1UN
TEL 0171 387 6039   **FAX** 0171 388 2691
Here the claim is 'London's cheapest framers – by 30 to 50 per cent', and the service takes five working days. An average poster 20 by 30-in with glass and ½-in wooden moulding would cost around £20.00 plus VAT. They also have a selection of original antique French drinks posters, and a huge selection of decorative mirrors. The business has been established for 24 years.
TUBE *King's Cross* • **OPEN** *Mon–Fri 10am–6pm. Sat 11am–5pm* • **SERVICES** *Frames and mirrors made to order* • **ALSO AT** *589–591 Holloway Road, N1 (0171 263 8973)*

GREEN AND STONE

See DECORATING: SPECIALIST DECORATING SUPPLIERS, page 99

At one of the oldest shops in the King's Road (established 1927) you will find a good range of picture framing services.

FRAME EXPRESS

ADDRESS 82 Charing Cross Road, WC2H OBA
TEL 0171 836 2948

It's quick, as you might expect. They offer over 400 mouldings and a good choice of mounts, in traditional or modern styles, and take two to three working days. There are clear sample displays with prices. You'll also find clip and photo frames, cards, and posters. Prices for ready-made frames range from £10 to £70.

TUBE *Leicester Square* • **OPEN** *Mon–Sat 9.30am–6pm* • **SERVICES** *Express service. Bespoke serve within 3 days* • **ALSO AT** *81 Baker Street, W1M 1AJ (0171 935 7794). 266 Kensington High Street, W8 6ND (0171 602 2277). 111 Old Brompton Road, SW7 (0171 589 7635). 34 Wormwood Street, EC2 (0171 256 6537). 1 Queens Road, Wimbledon, SW19 8NG (0181 947 7838). Unit 15, Putney Exchange, High Street Putney, SW15 1TW (0181 785 6360)*

FRAME FACTORY

ADDRESS 20 Cross Street, Islington, N1 2BQ
TEL 0171 226 6266   **FAX** 0171 226 0078

This firm offers a complete range of framing services, including bespoke and contract framing. Also a big choice of simple clip frames, and, from stock, frames in black lacquer or varnished pine. They also do box and display framing and conservation framing, and can dry mount posters. Plus a range of mirrors.

TUBE *Angel/Highbury and Islington* • **OPEN** *Mon–Sat 9.30am–6pm* • **ALSO AT** *92 Stoke Newington, Church Street, N16 OAP (0171 254 0066). Streatham High Road, SW16 6GH (0181 677 1882). 159 Haverstock Hill, NW3 4QT (0171 483 2050)*

POSTERS AND PRINTS

Art college degree shows are always a good source of inexpensive art work. You can also find excellent folios of posters in all London's big museums and art galleries. Of necessity, the shops below are just the tiniest taste of what London has to offer. A small bi-monthly magazine called *Galleries* lists art dealers by areas and is free from art galleries (or send sae to 54 Uxbridge Road, W12 8LP; 0181 740 7020).

CINE GRAPHIX GALLERY

ADDRESS 4 Copper Row, Shad Thames, Tower Bridge Piazza, SE1 2LH
TEL 0171 234 0566   **FAX** 0171 234 0577

Affable Greg Edwards runs the largest gallery for international film posters in the UK. His specialities are rare originals from 1920 onwards but he does not do current releases. Prices from £10 to £4,500 – on average, people spend £100 to £200.

TUBE *Tower Hill* • **OPEN** *Tues–Sat 11am–7pm*

FLASHBACKS
ADDRESS 6 Silver Place, W1R 3LJ
TEL/FAX 0171 437 8562
Well-established source for movie posters – around 15,000 in stock.
Recent releases cost from £9.75. Fifties posters, around £25.
TUBE *Piccadilly Circus* • **OPEN** *Mon–Sat 10.30am–7pm* • **SERVICES**
Framing, from around £60

GREENWICH PRINTMAKERS
ADDRESS 1a Greenwich Market, SE10 9HZ
TEL 0181 858 1569
Allow plenty of time for a serious browse through this well-established
showcase for a group of around 45 local artists, who display an
impressive and professional selection of affordable art, from £1 cards
to framed pictures from £50. Each artist has their own display drawer
in this organised shop so you can easily find your favourites.
RAIL *Greenwich* • **OPEN** *Tues–Sun 10.30am–5.30pm*

GROVESNOR PRINTS
ADDRESS 28 Shelton Street, WC2H 9HP
TEL 0171 836 1979   **FAX** 0171 379 6695
Print dealer established over 20 years with one of the largest stock of
antique prints in London.
TUBE *Covent Garden* • **OPEN** *Mon–Fri 10am–6pm. Sat 11am–4pm*

HABITAT
See UNDER ONE ROOF: FURNISHING SPECIALISTS, page 11. Attractive
selections of framed and unframed prints.

LONDON TRANSPORT MUSEUM SHOP
ADDRESS The Piazza, Covent Garden, WC2E 7BB
TEL 0171 379 6344
Historic London transport posters, and contemporary posters commissioned
from leading artists.
TUBE *Covent Garden*

RENNIE'S
ADDRESS 13 Rugby Street, WC1N 3QT
TEL 0171 405 0220
This is a treasure trove of pre-war posters (eg Shell, GPO, the old railway
companies, The Empire Marketing Board), mainly printed lithographically
in up to 40 colours, and supervised or even executed by artists such as
Paul Nash and Ben Nicholson. Prices from go from £800 to £1500 for
'without question an authentic artistic artefact'.
TUBE *Holborn/Russell Square* • **OPEN** *Wed–Sat 12 noon–6.30pm*

VINTAGE MAGAZINE STORE
ADDRESS 39–43 Brewer Street, W1R 3FD
TEL 0171 439 8525   **FAX** 0171 439 8527
Movie maniacs can buy their cine posters here – both originals and
reprints, from Europe and the US. The stock includes current releases,
which usually cost around £6.99. But move fast in case your fave film

becomes a cult. The Titanic, for example, was originally £6.99, but rapidly reached double figures and is rising as fast as the flood water in the hold.
TUBE *Piccadilly Circus* • **OPEN** *Mon–Wed 10am–7pm. Thurs 10am–8pm. Fri Sat 10am–10pm. Sun 12 noon–8pm* • **WEBSITE** *www.vinmag.com*
SERVICES *Framing* • **ALSO AT** *55 Charing Cross Road, W1 (0171 494 4064). 247 Camden High Street, NW1 (0171 482 0587)*

RUGS

CHRISTOPHER FARR
ADDRESS 212 Westbourne Grove, W11 2RH
TEL 0171 792 5761 **FAX** 0171 792 5763
Pioneers of the modern designer rug – their thick luxurious carpets are modern art for the floor, with pure wool hand-tufted pile. Designs are commissioned from leading textile artists such as Allegra Hicks, Kate Blee, and Cressida Bell, and fashion designers such as Rifat Ozbek. Expect to pay on average £2,000 for a rug around 2 metres by 3 metres – unless you can catch a half-price bargain in the twice-yearly sales. Allow plenty of time for a considered choice.
TUBE *Notting Hill* • **OPEN** *Mon–Fri 11am–6pm. Sat 11am–5pm*
• **SERVICES** *Commissions*

DAVID BLACK
ADDRESS 96 Portland Road, Holland Park, W11 4LN
TEL 0171 727 2566 **FAX** 0171 229 4599
A respected source for oriental carpets – including knotted carpets and flat weaves. Antique and new vegetable-dyed carpets with lovely soft rich colours at prices from £150 to £40,000. Changing programme of exhibitions.
TUBE *Holland Park* • **OPEN** *Mon–Fri 10am–6pm. Sat 11am–5pm*

DAVID J WILKINS
ADDRESS 27 Princess Road, Regent's Park, NW1 8JR
TEL 0171 722 7608 **FAX** 0171 483 0423
They claim discount prices for a wide range of rugs from Iran, Russia, Turkey, and Afghanistan – 'we specialise in large sizes'.
TUBE *Camden Town* • **OPEN** *By appointment*

GALLERY ZADAH
ADDRESS 35 Bruton Place, W1X 7AB
TEL 0171 493 2622 **FAX** 0171 629 6682
These dealers are a family business run by Alex Zadah (second generation). They have antique carpets for collectors and interior decorators – expect to pay from £1000 upwards.
TUBE *Oxford Circus* • **OPEN** *Mon–Fri 10am–5.30pm, Sat by appointment*

JACK FAIRMAN CARPETS
ADDRESS 218 Westbourne Grove, W11 2RH
TEL 0171 229 2262 **FAX** 0171 229 2263
In a cool gallery atmosphere, admire Iranian nomadic rugs – each is different, but patterns have a surprisingly modern twist which makes them

well-suited to contemporary interiors. Also antique Tibetan and Chinese rugs. Harvey Page is the fourth generation of a respected rug-dealing family – 'what we sell will hold its value'.

TUBE *Notting Hill Gate* • **OPEN** *Mon–Sat 10am–6pm* • **SERVICES** *Rugs woven to any design by Tibetan weavers in Nepal – costs £450 a square metre, and takes three months. Cleaning, restorations, valuations*

KILIM AND NOMADIC RUG GALLERY

ADDRESS 5 Shepherds Walk, Hampstead, NW3 5UE
TEL/FAX 0171 435 8972   **FAX** 0171 435 9739
Del Blacker hunts down kilims, from antique to merely second hand, and has a gallery at the bottom of his house. Prices from £50 to £10,000 for very valuable pieces. Also kilim-covered cushions.

TUBE *Hampstead* • **OPEN** *By appointment* • **SERVICES** *Rug repairs and restoration on premises*

KILIM WAREHOUSE

ADDRESS 28a Pickets Street, SW12 8QB
TEL 0181 675 3122   **FAX** 0181 675 8494
Kilim simply means a flat woven rug. Once they were considered poor relations to oriental carpets with a knotted pile. Since 1982, Jose Lczyc-Wyhowska has helped put the world straight, amassing huge selections. Here you'll find a wide variety of old and antique kilims, and woven tribal artifacts. There are also new designs, commissioned exclusively. In all, it probably amounts to the largest selection in the UK, with stock coming from Turkey, Afghanistan, Yugoslavia, Persia and Romania. Prices start at around £100 and go up to £3,000.

TUBE *Clapham South* • **OPEN** *Mon–Fri 10am–5.30pm. Sat 10am–4pm* • **WEBSITE** *www.kilim-warehouse.co.uk/kilim* • **SERVICES** *Brochure. Cleaning and restoration*

THE LOOM

ADDRESS 4 Greenwich Market Square, SE10 9HZ
TEL/FAX 0181 293 9178
Turkish Tarik Safa regularly tours the villages of his homeland to seek out rugs and kilims, also selling some Afghan and Persian rugs, and Indian cotton throws. Runners are particularly popular, at prices from £20 to £300.

RAIL *Greenwich* • **OPEN** *Mon–Fri 10am–5pm. Sat Sun 9am–6pm* • **SERVICES** *On approval loan service. Rug cleaning and restoration*

OMAR MASOM

ADDRESS 8 Eccleston Street, SW1W 9LT
TEL/FAX 0171 730 8848
Rugs and kilims from Turkey and Central Asia.

TUBE *Victoria* • **OPEN** *Mon–Sat 10am–6pm* • **SERVICES** *Restoration. Special exhibitions*

ORIENTALIST

ADDRESS 74 and 78 Highgate Road, NW5 1PB
TEL 0171 482 0555   **FAX** 0171 267 9603
Ground floor displays, workshops above. Oriental handmade rugs, carpets, textiles, tapestries, cushions, needlepoint and kilims

TUBE *Kentish Town* • **OPEN** *Mon–Sat 10am–6pm, Sun 11am–4pm*
• **SERVICES** *Expert repair of antique rugs and textiles*

ROBERT STEPHENSON

ADDRESS 1 Elystan Street, SW3 3NT
TEL/FAX 0171 225 2343
Large and valuable antique Persian and oriental carpets, at prices
from around £2,950. Old kilims from around £750. Also 17th and
18th-century Flemish tapestries. Helpful, friendly staff.
TUBE *South Kensington* • **OPEN** *Mon–Fri 9.30am–5.30pm. Sat
10.30am–2pm* • **SERVICES** *Cleaning and restoration on premises*

THE RUG COMPANY

ADDRESS 124 Holland Park Avenue, W11 4UE
TEL 0171 792 3245   **FAX** 0171 352 5122
With wood and stone floors so fashionable, Chris Sharp sees his shop
as a logical progression. 'The emphasis is on decorative rugs for interior
design.' His speciality is handmade Indian reproductions of 18th-century
European-designed rugs. Plus Aubusson woven tapestry-style reproductions
made in China to original French 18th-century designs and colours
(9 ft by 6 ft, £1,400). Some very large pieces also available. Also hand-
embroidered needlepoint rugs for the look at half the price – eg 5 ft by
3 ft, £220. Also some modern rugs.
TUBE *Holland Park* • **OPEN** *Mon–Sat 10am–6pm* • **SERVICES** *Rugs on
approval. Catalogue* • **ALSO AT** *103 Lots Road, SW10 0RN (0171 352
0012); open Sundays*

SOVIET CARPET AND ART GALLERIES 🐷

ADDRESS 303–305 Cricklewood Broadway, NW2 6PG
TEL 0181 452 2445   **FAX** 0181 450 2642
Rugs from the East at trade prices – around 50 per cent of big-store prices.
Also a huge selection of Russian art – one of the three largest Russian art
collections in the world, they say, with thousands of watercolours and prints
at prices from £25 to £150, and oil painting from £10 to £400. Reputedly
the work is from top Russian artists, including promising young graduates.
RAIL *Cricklewood* • **OPEN** *Mon–Fri by appointment only. Sun 10.30am–5pm*

CUSHIONS

You can change a look in an instant with a heap of cushions.
Remember, too, they're very easy to make yourself. Save money
by keeping the posh fabrics for the front and using cheap cottons
for the back.

CRESSIDA BELL

ADDRESS 10–22 Lamb Lane, E8 3PL
TEL 0181 985 5863   **FAX** 0181 533 3675
Beautiful Bloomsbury printed velvets by the granddaughter of Vanessa Bell.
From £85. Plus lampshades, throws, scarves. Phone for brochure.
RAIL *London Fields* • **OPEN** *By appointment*

HERAZ

ADDRESS 2 Halpin Arcade, Motcomb Street, SW1X 8JT
TEL 0171 245 9497   **FAX** 0171 235 7416
Treasured remnants of antique textiles – silks, velvets, brocades – make
glorious cushions with a history, finished off with antique trimmings
(fringes and braids). Prices start at around £100. You'll also find a
selection of old tapestries and needlepoint.
TUBE *Knightsbridge* • **OPEN** *Mon–Fri 10am–1pm; 2pm–6pm. Closed for
lunch 1pm–2pm*

INVENTORY

See ACCESSORIES: SHOPS WITH SMALLER ACCESSORIES, page 30.
Particularly good for cushions in unusual textures and patterns.

JOHN LEWIS

See UNDER ONE ROOF: DEPARTMENT STORES, page 14. Very good
displays of colour-grouped cushions at can't-beat-it prices. Also good for
feather cushion pads and bolsters for DIY.

NICE IRMA'S BY POST ✉

ADDRESS Unit 2, Finchley Industrial Centre, 879 High Road, N12 8QA
TEL 0181 343 7610   **FAX** 0181 343 9590
Excellent selections of colourful cushions from India, together with other
accessories, in this excellent mail-order catalogue (sadly the shop in
Goodge Street has closed down).

THE PIER

See ACCESSORIES: SHOPS WITH FURNITURE, page 26. Excellent for
inexpensive original cushions with embroidery or appliqué.

SAVILLE-EDELLS

ADDRESS 123 Sydney Street, SW3 6NR
TEL 0171 351 1221   **FAX** 0171 351 0390
Embroidered hand-finished cushions with a seemingly endless fund of
messages are the stock-in-trade of this pretty little shop, which is also
packed with accessories and gifts for the home.
TUBE *Sloane Square/South Kensington* • **OPEN** *Mon–Sat 10am–6pm.
Sun 12 noon–6pm*

SUSSEX HOUSE

ADDRESS 92 Wandsworth Bridge Road, SW6 2TF
TEL 0171 371 5455   **FAX** 0171 371 7590
Gaynor Churchward has become famous for her constantly evolving
designs based on old textiles. Intricate raised designs of velvet appliqué
have embroidered gold cording. Rich crushed velvet is appliquéed for
bedspreads and throws. The Colonial Collection has embroidered pastel
and ecru hand-woven raw silk cushions and bedcovers, whilst the
Hollywood ensemble is enhanced with silver threads. Divinely decadent
are the embroidered muslin curtains and velvet appliquéed nets to suspend
at a window, or to use for bed hangings. Cushion prices start at around £40.
TUBE *Parsons Green/Fulham Broadway* • **OPEN** *Mon–Fri 10am–6pm.
Sat 10.30am–5pm*

VENETIA STADIUM
ADDRESS 13 Grafton Street, W1
TEL 0171 495 7634   **FAX** 0171 495 7635
Rich and glorious silks hand-dyed in Venice are made into cushions, lamp-
shades and fashion accessories. Small plissé silk cushions are edged with
hand-blown Murano glass beads. Silk tassles are trimmed with beads or brass.
TUBE *Green Park* • **OPEN** *Mon–Fri 10.30am–6pm. Sat 11am–6pm*

TABLEWARE, GLASS AND CERAMICS

*'Curtains in orange nylon and no place mats,
there's not even the veneer of civilisation.'*
Alan Bennett, Talking Heads

London is traditional tableware centre of the world, as any of our
department stores will show you. A walk along Regent Street, W1
will also introduce you to the showrooms of leading brands such as
Waterford Wedgwood and Royal Doulton. They speak for themselves.
Also explore the galleries listed under CRAFTS AND DESIGNER-MAKERS,
page 52. For stylish, money-saving tableware it is difficult to beat
IKEA – see *UNDER ONE ROOF: FURNISHING SPECIALISTS*, page 11. There
are also excellent selections at Habitat – again see *UNDER ONE ROOF:
FURNISHING SPECIALISTS*, page 11 – who will register the pattern you
buy, and let you know if there are any plans to discontinue it.

ARIA
ADDRESS 133 and 295 Upper Street, N1 1QP
TEL 0171 704 1999   **FAX** 0171 704 6333
A browser's delight. Here you'll find elegant tableware and home accessories
well-arranged on shelves and tabletops, in an intriguing mix of styles. Other
goods include baskets, glass, metalware, lighting, trendy plastics and even
some furniture – chairs and tables by Philippe Starck, from £85.
TUBE *Angel/Highbury & Islington* • **OPEN** *Mon–Fri 10am–7pm. Sat 10am–
6.30pm. Sun 12 noon–5pm* • **SERVICES** *Mail-order. Gift-wrapping*

BRIDGEWATER
ADDRESS 739 Fulham Road, SW6 5UL
TEL 0171 371 9033   **FAX** 0171 384 2457
Emma Bridgewater made her name with pretty stencilled patterns on
classic shapes in fine English earthenware. Here's the full selection, from
dinner services to bowls, jugs, and mugs. In the Bridgewater pottery cafe
next door try your own hand at china painting, or simply have a snack.
TUBE *Parsons Green* • **OPEN** *Mon–Fri 10am–5.30pm. Sat 10am–5pm*
• **SERVICES** *Wedding lists*

CERAMICA BLUE
ADDRESS 10 Blenheim Crescent, W11 1NN
TEL/FAX 0171 727 0288
Ten years ago, Lindy Wiffen started importing bright Sicilian hand-painted
ceramics, specialising in the work of Giovanni Simone. Today, stock has

grown to over 30 tableware ranges from Britain, Europe, and even Mexico, America, South Africa. Prices start at under £10 for mugs and demi-tasse cups. Pasta, fruit and salad bowls, platters, vases, casseroles, teapots and complete tableware ranges.

TUBE *Ladbroke Grove/Notting Hill Gate* • **OPEN** *Mon 11am–5pm. Tues–Sat 10am–6.30pm* • *Discontinued ranges and seconds: first Sun of month, 12 noon–4pm* • **WEBSITE** *www.ceramicablue.co.uk*
• **SERVICES** *Wedding lists. Commissions*

CLAUDIA MEYNELL

ADDRESS 33 Winchester Avenue, Queens Park, NW6 7TT
TEL 0171 625 4966   **FAX** 0171 461 0665
Hand-painted bone china – motifs include flowers, fruit, hearts and marine themes, personalised if requested. Also hand-painted tiles, and mosaic work.
RAIL *Brondesbury Park/Queens Park* • **TUBE** *Queen's Park/Kilburn* • **OPEN** *By appointment*

COLLECTOR AND TABLEWHERE

ADDRESS 4 Queen's Parade Close, Friern, Barnet, N11 3FX
TEL 0181 361 6111   **FAX** 0181 361 4143
Thousands of patterns from leading makers of china are registered on a computer database – director Tom Power reckons he has around a million pieces, some dating as far back as 1900. He's always buying discontinued designs from trade and private sources. So don't despair if you break a plate or two: this is where to replace it, and the cost is usually around the same as today's retail price. Most frequent requests are for the popular patterns of the sixties, seventies, and eighties – Rose Elegans, Yorktown, and Old Colony from Royal Doulton; Hathaway Rose and Florentine from Wedgwood; and Greenwheat, Gypsy and Arabesque from Denby.
TUBE *Arnos Grove* • **OPEN** *Mon–Sat 9.30am–5.30pm*

DAVID MELLOR

See KITCHENS: KITCHENWARE, page 124. Excellent choice of David Mellor's own beautiful modern cutlery, plus good craft pottery.

ILLUSTRATED POTTERS

ADDRESS 70 Camden Lock Place, Camden Lock, NW1 8AF
TEL 0171 485 5116
Jo Crouch runs a gallery/workshop for contemporary pottery, with simple shapes and bold colourful brush strokes. Particularly popular are her own vivid floral designs, which people love to collect into sets. Hand-painted dinner plates here cost from around £13.60 to £16.25; mugs cost from £10.45 to £12.55; and jugs from £12.50 to £15.50.
TUBE *Camden Town* • **OPEN** *Tues–Sun 10am–6pm (summer); Wed–Sun 10am–6pm (winter)* • **SERVICES** *Special designs to commission*

INFINITY

ADDRESS 8 Upper Saint Martin's Lane, WC2 9DL
TEL 0171 497 1011
Handmade glass from all over the world – goblets, platters, bowls, vases, candlesticks, in a rainbow of colours.
TUBE *Leicester Square* • **OPEN** *Mon–Fri 11am–7pm. Sat 11.30am–7pm*

MAP
ADDRESS 165a Junction Road, N19 5PZ
TEL 0171 263 8529   **FAX** 0171 263 8523
Glass is hand-decorated on the premises using a variety of techniques –
sand-blasting, engraving, frosting. Also hand-painted bone china. Goblets
from £14.50. Vases, £28.95.
TUBE *Tufnell Park* • **OPEN** *Mon–Sat 10am–6.30pm*

PORTMEIRION
ADDRESS 13 Kensington Church Street, W8 4LF
TEL 0171 938 1891   **FAX** 0171 376 1770
Complete range (lots of different shapes) of Susan Williams-Ellis' deservedly
perennial Botanic Gardens designs, introduced in 1972, and based on
32 flowering plants and butterflies taken from 19th-century hand-coloured
natural history books. Dinner plates, £9.50 each. The patterns romp over
all over crockery, kitchenware, and cookware, plus co-ordinating tiles,
trays and mats. Fabric accessories, and fabric by the metre.
TUBE *Kensington High Street* • **OPEN** *Mon–Sat 10am–6pm*

REJECT POT SHOP 🐷
ADDRESS 56 Chalk Farm Road, NW1 8AN
TEL/FAX 0171 485 2326
The enterprising owners buy seconds weekly from the potteries. Lots of
plain white china, from a 50p mug to a £4 bone china cup-and-saucer.
Also many popular traditional patterns. Other lines include roll-up bamboo
blinds, and black or white venetian blinds.
TUBE *Chalk Farm* • **OPEN** *Tues–Sun 11am–5.30pm* • **SERVICES** *Free delivery
in London on orders over £150*

THOMAS GOODE
ADDRESS 19 South Audley Street, W1Y 6BN
TEL 0171 499 2823   **FAX** 0171 629 4230
Thomas Goode (founded 1827) – 'the most beautiful china shop in the
world' – has been in the same premises since 1845. Magnificent ceramic
elephants guard the entrance – part of a Minton collection from the Paris
Exhibitions of 1878 and 1889. The mechanical front door opens
automatically under your weight – it was very advanced for its time. Inside:
traditional top makes of china, glass and silverware, and the store's own
exclusive designs, in distinctive gift boxes. Visiting is a visual treat. Even if
you don't have a luxury lifestyle, you can always have tea in the restaurant.
Contemporary ranges include in-house designer Peter Ting's cutting-edge
designs acquired by the V & A Museum for their permanent collection.
TUBE *Green Park/Bond Street* • **OPEN** *Mon–Sat 10am–6pm* • **WEBSITE**
www.thomasgoode.com • **SERVICES** *Bespoke china – monograms, coats
of arms and so on. Restaurant. Wedding lists. Mail order. Gift vouchers*

VILLEROY & BOCH 🐷
ADDRESS 267 Merton Road, SW18 5JS
TEL 0181 870 4168
V & B is one of Europe's largest and poshest tableware manufacturers and it's
worth trekking to the end of the District Line to find seconds and discontinued
lines for their china, crystal and cutlery – reductions are substantial.
TUBE *Southfields* • **OPEN** *Mon–Sat 10am–5pm. Sun 10am–5pm*

CANDLES AND CANDLESTICKS

ANGELIC

ADDRESS 194 King's Road, SW3 5ED
TEL/FAX 0171 351 1557

The complete candle emporium, from nightlights to candelabra and chandeliers. Scented candles, including therapeutic aromas such as geranium, rosemary, pine and jasmine. Floating candles look pretty in a shallow bowl with coloured glass nuggets – one customer even included her goldfish, or so the story goes. Chunky plain church candles are in high demand, the perfect partner for black iron holders. For outdoor entertaining: terracotta pots filled with wax and a wick, in all sizes, plus garden flares.

OPEN *Mon–Sat 10am–7pm. Sun 12 noon–6pm* • **TUBE** *Sloane Square* • **ALSO AT** *6 Neal Street, WC2 (0171 240 2114). 177 Regent Street, W1 (0171 437 6015). 42 Carnaby Street, W1 (0171 439 3717). Whiteleys, Bayswater, W2 (0171 221 3414)*

THE CANDLE SHOP

ADDRESS 30 The Market, Covent Garden, WC2E 8RE
TEL 0171 379 4220 **FAX** 0171 240 8065

This shop was way ahead of the candle craze – it's been going for nearly 30 years, and claims the largest selection of candles in London. Certainly the range is diverse, from simple candles in pure beeswax to novelty candles modelled as politicians. Plus ceramic and wrought-iron candlesticks and chandeliers.

TUBE *Covent Garden* • **OPEN** *Mon–Sat 10am–8pm. Sun 10.30am–7.30pm* • **ALSO AT** *50 New King's Road, SW6 4LS (0171 736 0740). Warehouse outlet with wholesale prices. For example, box of 100 10-in dinner party candles, £19.50*

PRICE'S PATENT CANDLE CO

ADDRESS 110 York Road, SW11 3RU
TEL 0171 801 2030 **FAX** 0171 738 0197

This is the factory shop for the biggest flame in the candle business – trading for 170 years – with a huge range (around 2000 lines). From tea lights to garden flares, prices are at least 15 per cent lower than normal. Also decorative candle holders. Plus seconds, ends of lines, special offers and promotions. Worth a good browse – particularly just before the festive season, or if you're giving a big party. Prices from 20p to £100 (for a giant church candle).

RAIL *Clapham Junction* • **OPEN** *Mon–Sat 9.30am–5.30pm. Sun 11am–5pm*

WAX LYRICAL

ADDRESS 61 Hampstead High Street, NW3 1QH
TEL 0171 435 5105

Candles get interior design status, with themed collections – from leopard prints to jewel colours. Good for dinner party inspirations – mats, napkins and rings to complete the look. Particularly pretty at Christmas.

TUBE *Hampstead* • **OPEN** *Mon–Fri 10am–6.30pm. Sat 9.30am–6pm. Sun 11.30am–6pm* • **ALSO AT** *U 226, Old Town Hall Court Centre, Wimbledon SW19 8YA (0181 879 3905). Unit 9, 53 The Broadway Centre, W5 (0181 840 9829). UR2, Mall 5, Brent Cross Shopping Centre, NW4 3FP (0181 202 8524)*

MIRRORS

HOUSE OF MIRRORS
ADDRESS 597 King's Road, SW6 2EL
TEL 0171 736 5885   **FAX** 0171 610 9188
Browse through a stock of around 300 genuine 19th-century mirrors at any one time in a shop that's been going for 30 years. Mirrors can cost anything from £500 to £20,000.
TUBE *Fulham Broadway* • **OPEN** *Mon–Fri 9am–6pm; Sat 10am–6pm*
• **SERVICES** *Carving, gilding and mirror restoration on site*

JUST MIRRORS
ADDRESS 141 Greyhound Road, W6 8NJ
TEL 0171 385 9613   **FAX** 0171 385 9604
These well-established specialists in handmade, reproduction period frames were previously in the Fulham Road. Frames feature gold leaf, bronze, Dutch gold, or various veneers. Other frames are stained or marbled or you can have one made from your own wallpaper or fabric. Prices from £25 to £4,000.
TUBE *Barons Court* • **OPEN** *Mon–Sat 9.30am–5.30pm* • **SERVICES** *Frame restoration. Picture restoration (oils and watercolours). Mirrors made to measure. Special designs to order. Mail-order catalogue*

OVERMANTELS
ADDRESS 66 Battersea Bridge Road, SW11 3AG
TEL 0171 223 8151   **FAX** 0171 924 2283
Every mantelpiece needs a mirror to set it off, and this is where you find it. (But never lean over an unguarded open fire). Well known for well-made reproduction mirrors for chimney breasts, in many traditional Victorian and Regency styles. Triptychs (designs in three sections) are particularly impressive. Also antique mirror frames, from around £950.
RAIL *Clapham Junction* • **OPEN** *Mon–Sat 9.30am–5.30pm*
• **WEBSITE** *www.overmantels.co.uk*

THROUGH THE LOOKING GLASS
ADDRESS 563 King's Road, SW6 2EB
TEL 0171 736 7799
For romantic reflections, gaze into a 19th-century antique mirror. This shop has various styles, shapes and sizes – mainly French or British. Prices from around £400.
TUBE *Fulham Broadway* • **OPEN** *Mon–Sat 10am–5.30pm* • **SERVICES** *Restoration and cleaning* • **ALSO AT** *137 Kensington Church Street, W8 7LP (0171 221 4026)*

PATIO IDEAS

AVANT GARDEN

ADDRESS 77 Ledbury Road, W11 2AG
TEL 0171 229 4408   **FAX** 0171 229 4410

Joan Clifton bridges the inside/outside divide, with stylish ideas for conservatory and garden. Forged iron tables, chairs, candelabra and plant stands, with blown-glass amphora-style vases supported by elegant frames. Rustic hazel wood chairs, with willow plant trainers, trugs and weeding baskets. 'Topiary' frames, made from antiqued wire and fitted with hand-thrown Long Tom pots for climbing plants (which don't need to be anything more complicated than ivy).

TUBE *Notting Hill Gate/Westbourne Park* • **OPEN** *Mon–Sat 10am–6pm*

THE CHELSEA GARDENER

ADDRESS 125 Sydney Street, SW3 6NR
TEL 0171 352 5656   **FAX** 0171 352 3301

Inspirational garden centre with good selection of plants for both inside and outside – ideal port of call for those that crave a little green within the city. Urns, statues, pots, conservatory furnishings. Incredibly realistic fake flowers.

TUBE *Sloane Square* • **OPEN** *Mon–Sat 10am–6pm. Sun 12 noon–6pm*

CLIFTON NURSERIES

ADDRESS 5a Clifton Villas, off Warwick Avenue, W9 2PH
TEL 0171 289 6851   **FAX** 0171 286 4215

There's been a nursery on this site since the last century – it's one of London's most appealing, full of decorative features, such as trellis, pots and attractive benches. Antique statues and ornaments a speciality, plus a wide range of indoor tropical plants. At the back, through a secret overgrown courtyard with fountains, discover Clifton Little Venice, with old gardening tools, and charming wirework – chandeliers for nightlights or plant pots, and wire topiary balls in four sizes. Also replicas of antique statues, heads, urns and plinths. Romance runs riot.

TUBE *Warwick Avenue* • **OPEN** *Mar–Sept: Mon–Sat 8.30am–6pm; Sun 10.30am–4.30pm. Oct–Feb: Mon–Sat 8.30am–5.30pm; Sun 10am–4pm* • **SERVICES** *Landscape gardening/design. Expert advice/leaflets*

THE CONSERVATORY AND WITHIN

ADDRESS 162 Fortis Green Road, Muswell Hill, N10 3DU
TEL 0181 883 7700   **FAX** 0181 442 1303

Furniture in cane or iron, plus kilim rugs, candelabra candles, and mirrors with wrought-iron frames.

TUBE *Highgate/East Finchley + bus or 10 minute walk* • **OPEN** *Mon–Sat 10am–6pm. Sun 11am–4pm*

FULHAM PALACE GARDEN CENTRE
ADDRESS Bishops Avenue, SW6 6EE
TEL 0171 736 9820 **FAX** 0171 736 2640
Enthusiastic team of previously unemployed gardeners provide first-class
plant selections for outdoors or inside, on a previously derelict site. Unusual
and exotic flowers, old-fashioned roses. All profits go to Fairbridge Inner-
city Youth Charity.
TUBE *Putney Bridge* • **OPEN** *Mon–Thurs 9.30am–5.30pm, Fri Sat
9.30am– 6pm. Sun 10am–5pm* • **SERVICES** *Planting tubs and window
boxes*

THE GARDEN CENTRE
ADDRESS Alexandra Palace Road, N22 4BB
TEL 0181 883 7937 **FAX** 0181 444 2555
Extensive garden centre with shop for imaginative house/conservatory
plants, plus pots and tubs and conservatory and garden furniture. Pots
from Malaysia, Greece, North Africa, Poland and Egypt.
TUBE *Finsbury Park* • **RAIL** *Alexandra Palace* • **OPEN** *Mon–Sat
9.30am–6pm. Sun 10.30am–4.30pm*

GARDEN CRAFTS
ADDRESS Sissinghurst Road, Biddenden, Kent, TN27 8EJ
TEL 01580 292070 **FAX** 01580 292131
Garden ornaments and furniture, with arresting outdoor displays of
classical reproductions. Specialists for over 65 years – they used to
be in Fulham. Wooden table £180, aluminium chair £48.
Five minutes from Sissinghurst castle.
OPEN *Mon–Fri 9am–5pm. Sat 10am–5pm*

HANNAH PESCHAR SCULPTURE GARDEN
ADDRESS Black and White Cottage, Standon Lane, Ockley, Surrey, RH5 5QR
TEL 01306 627269 **FAX** 01306 627662
Modern sculptures/ceramics for gardens/exteriors, displayed in
landscaped gardens, where the wilderness is carefully ordered to create
visionary vistas. Essential viewing for garden/fine art lovers. Admission
£7, concessions £5, children 4–16 £4. Sculptures start at £5000 and go
up to £30,000.
OPEN *First weekend in May till last weekend in October, Fri Sat 11am–6pm,
Sun 2pm–5pm. Other times by appointment*

POTS AND PITHOI
ADDRESS The Barns, East Street, Turners Hill, West Sussex, RH10 4QQ
TEL 01342 714793 **FAX** 01342 717090
A stash of around 12,000 terracotta pots, up to 45-in/115-cm tall,
imported from four potteries in Crete where they are made by hand.
93 styles, 230 sizes. Prices from £10 up to £750.
OPEN *Summer, 7 days a week 10am–5pm; winter 10am–4pm*
• **SERVICES** *London deliveries*

CRAFTS AND DESIGNER-MAKERS

- **Galleries, studios and workshops** *page 52*
- **Craft supplies** *page 56*

'We know that the tail must wag the dog, for the horse is drawn by the cart:
But the Devil whoops as he whoops as old: 'It's clever, but is it Art?''
Rudyard Kipling (1865–1936), The Conundrum of the Workshops

If you can't find exactly what you want from displays at the galleries listed below, consider commissioning – especially if it is for a special piece to fit into a particular space or for a particular occasion. Give the artist as many guidelines/references as possible.

GALLERIES, STUDIOS AND WORKSHOPS

CECILIA COLMAN GALLERY
ADDRESS 67 St John's Wood High Street, NW8 7NL
TEL/FAX 0171 722 0686
Popular well-established gallery for one-off ceramics and glass, plus unusual items in carved and turned wood, with good modern jewellery. Potters include Ben Arnup and Dorothy Gill, with wood vessels and sculptural pieces by Malcolm Martin. Glass is by Catherine Hough, Will Shakspeare, Jane Charles, Peter Layton, and Malcolm Sutcliffe. Prices from £20 to £450. Plus a selection of clocks.
TUBE *St John's Wood* • **OPEN** *Mon–Fri 10am–5.30pm. Sat 2pm–5pm*

CHALK FARM GALLERY
ADDRESS 20 Chalk Farm Road, NW1 8AG
TEL/FAX 0171 267 3300
Paintings, prints, and sculpture, offset by smaller pieces of glass, ceramics, and jewellery. The gallery has been going for 17 years; regular programme of special exhibitions.
TUBE *Chalk Farm* • **OPEN** *7 days 10am–6pm* • **WEBSITE** *www.chalk-farm-gallery.co.uk* • **SERVICES** *Commissioning*

CONTEMPORARY APPLIED ARTS
ADDRESS 2 Percy Street, W1P 9FA
TEL 0171 436 2344   **FAX** 0171 436 2446
Smart and lofty exhibition space over two floors for the work of 250

members, Britain's finest makers of ceramics, glass, textiles, jewellery, wood, furniture, metalwork and bookbinding. 1998 was their 50th anniversary – join their Friends Scheme for £20 a year. Shows on the ground floor change every five weeks, selling area is in the basement. Prices from £15 to £5000.

TUBE *Goodge Street/Tottenham Court Road* • **OPEN** *Mon–Sat 10.30am– 5.30pm* • **SERVICES** *Commissioning – they have a register of over 250 artist makers, together with slides, catalogues and so on*

CONTEMPORARY CERAMICS

ADDRESS William Blake House, 7 Marshall Street, W1V 1LP
TEL 0171 437 7605

Textured clay, smooth rich glazes, hand-thrown vessels, vivid brush strokes – this is the best place in Central London for off-the-shelf British modern ceramics . This recently re-vamped corner shop is the retail outlet for The Crafts Potters Association, with a membership of over 300. 'We specialise in British studio pottery, widely acclaimed as the best in the world.' Anything from a simple little milk jug to an elaborate colourful abstract ornament. Splash out and order a complete dinner service, or settle for a set of satisfyingly handmade soup bowls or an arresting fruit dish or salad bowl. The work of nearly 100 potters is always on show, from top-quality table and kitchenware to ceramic sculptures. Brilliant for gifts – for friends, family or just for your home. Prices from a modest £5 to a thumping £2000. Plus books and a selection of potters' materials.

TUBE *Oxford Circus* • **OPEN** *Mon–Sat 10am–5.30pm. Late night Thurs 7pm* • **SERVICES** *Commissioning*

COSMO PLACE STUDIOS

ADDRESS 11 Cosmo Place, WC1N 3AP
TEL 0171 278 3374   **FAX** 0171 430 9156

Just a short walk from the British Museum, a group of freelance artists sell exclusive hand-painted English bone china in a wide range of vibrant and innovative designs. The decoration is applied using on-glaze enamels and then fired in their kiln. Images vary from witty animals to romantic flowers and fruits. Items can be personalised with names and messages to celebrate special occasions – please allow around one week for this service. Prices range from £10 to £100.

TUBE *Russell Square* • **OPEN** *Mon–Sat 10am–6pm* • **SERVICES** *Gift-wrapping. Personalised china. Ceramic commissions*

CRAFTS COUNCIL GALLERY SHOP

ADDRESS 44a Pentonville Road, N1 9BY
TEL 0171 806 2559   **FAX** 0171 837 6891

Exhibitions change every six weeks. Work for sale in the shop is selected from the Crafts Council Index (a register of high-quality British makers); for example, ceramics by Rupert Spira, glass by Galia Amsel, textiles by Rebecca Earley, jewellery by Kate Wilkinson.

TUBE *Angel* • **OPEN** *Tues–Sat 11am–6pm. Sun 2pm–6pm* • **WEBSITE** *www.craftscouncil.org.uk* • **SERVICES** *Mail order, gift vouchers/wrapping. Cafe. Commissioning service includes their Photostore computer – on this they can call up selected images of over 30,000 pieces of craftwork – these can be posted on together with relevant biographies the next day for a fee of £2*

CRAFTS COUNCIL SHOP AT THE V&A

ADDRESS Victoria and Albert Museum, South Kensington, SW7 2RL
TEL 0171 589 5070   **FAX** 0171 581 2128
Within the vaulted galleries of the V&A, catch up with lively contemporary
British design from members of the Crafts Council Index. You'll find
ceramics, glass, textiles, wood and metal, from artists such as Richard
Batterham, Walter Keeler, Wendy Ramshaw and Gerda Flockinger.
Exhibitions change every four to six weeks – and you can get to the shop
without buying a museum entry ticket.
TUBE *South Kensington* • **OPEN** *Mon 12 noon–5.30pm. Tues–Sun
10am–5.30pm* • **SERVICES** *Commissioning service*

FRIVOLI

ADDRESS 7a Devonshire Road, W4 2EU
TEL 0181 742 3255   **FAX** 0181 994 7372
Lively selection of handmade ceramics, glassware, textiles and jewellery.
TUBE *Turnham Green* • **OPEN** *Mon–Sat 10am–6pm* • **SERVICES** *Bespoke
picture framing*

GABRIEL'S WHARF

ADDRESS 56 Upper Ground, SE1 9PP
TEL 0171 401 2255 (general enquiries)
Nicest way to get to Gabriel's Wharf is to walk along the South side of
the Embankment from the Festival Hall. You'll find a charming enclave of
specialist shops around a courtyard, with handmade crafts and fashions,
plus restaurants and snackbars.
TUBE *Waterloo/Blackfriars* • **OPEN** *Tues–Sun 11am–6pm (applies to all
studios below)* • **SERVICES** *Most of the artists will work to commission*

STUDIO ½
TEL 0374 162149
Four designers produce paintings, ceramics, hand-painted waistcoats and
painted glass.

SKYLARK
TEL 0171 928 4005
Watercolours and inkwash figure and plant drawings by artist Angie Brew.

PHLOX
TEL 0171 401 8244
Florist Emilia Chroscicka does unusual plants and flower arrangements.

GANESHA
TEL 0171 928 3444
Indian textiles and crafts bought by partners Purnendu Roy and Jo
Lawbuary from co-ops and small cottage industries.

LAUREN SHANLEY
TEL 0171 928 5782
From her unique store of old materials, piled high on shelves behind her
sewing-machines, Lauren Shanley pieces together incredible cushion
covers, throws, hangings and clothes.

MARK BONOMINI
TEL 0171 928 4904
Furniture maker using wood and metal.

ELF
TEL 0171 620 2682
Handmade and hand-painted wooden trays, mirrors, frames, mobiles, letter-racks and more.

VIVIENNE LEGG
TEL 0171 401 2240
Fine hand-thrown and hand-painted porcelain – vases, mugs, teapots with delicate floral designs.

T2
TEL 0171 928 1122
Re-cycled materials and bold bright colours for hand-crafted mirrors, boxes, bowls, letter-racks, mobiles, tablelamps and so on

GALERIE BESSON
ADDRESS 15 Royal Arcade, 28 Old Bond Street, W1X 3HB
TEL 0171 491 1706   **FAX** 0171 495 3203
Fine world-class ceramics. Regular artists include Coper, Rie, Leach, Cardew, Henderson, Fritsch, Lee, Casanovas, and de Waal. Also potters from Denmark, Russia, Spain and Japan. Prices from £100 to £5000.
TUBE *Green Park* • **OPEN** *Mon–Fri 10am–5.30pm* • **WEBSITE** *www.galeriebesson.co.uk*

JON OLD
ADDRESS 9 Stratford Road, W8 6RF
TEL 0171 565 8808   **FAX** 0171 564 8877
With energy and enthusiasm, Jon Old has collected a diverse range of handmade objects to fill his quirky gallery – from salad bowls to sculpture, from pottery to candleholders, vases and lamps. He represents around 60 contemporary artist craftsmen, and has become the first port of call for many looking for an unusual present.
TUBE *Kensington High Street* • **OPEN** *Mon–Sat 10am–6pm* • **WEBSITE** *www.jonold.co.uk* • **SERVICES** *Active commissioning service*

LONDON GLASS BLOWING WORKSHOPS
ADDRESS 7 The Leathermarket, Weston Street, SE1 3ER
TEL 0171 403 2800   **FAX** 0171 403 7778
See the magic of mouth-blown glass at master glass-blower Peter Layton's workshop. Shimmering iridescent colours for vases, perfume bottles (from £30 to £70), and wine goblets (from £25). Glass pebbles from £2 to £20 – pile them in bowls or scatter along shelves. There's always a shelf stacked with 'seconds', or phone for details of special sale weekends.
TUBE *London Bridge* • **OPEN** *Mon–Fri 10am–5pm. Weekends by appointment* • **SERVICES** *Blown glass light fittings, screens, sculptures, fountains and other large pieces of glass.*

NEW DESIGNERS IN BUSINESS
ADDRESS 9 Burgess Hill, NW2 2BY
TEL 0171 431 6329 **FAX** 0171 435 5487
An organisation representing young designers who can send an illustrated guide to 80 modern makers for £6.50.

OXO TOWER WHARF
ADDRESS Bargehouse Street, South Bank, SE1 9PH
TEL 0171 401 2255
Studio complex on the first and second floors includes lighting, rug, ceramic and furniture designers – plus artists and jewellery makers. Ring for small free illustrated index.
TUBE/RAIL Waterloo/Blackfriars • **OPEN** Tues–Sun 11am–6pm • **SERVICES** Commissioning. Bars and restaurants

PLATEAUX GALLERY
ADDRESS 1 Brewery Square, Tower Bridge Piazza, Butlers Wharf (off Shad Thames or Gainsford Street), SE1 2LF
TEL 0171 357 6880 **FAX** 0171 357 8265
Large (1,700 sq ft) and elegant gallery in a pleasant and tranquil square, just three minutes walk from the Design Museum. Leo Duval presents avant-garde art and craft from leading designer makers, including furniture, glass, ceramics, wood, and sculpture. The gallery holds regular exhibitions.
TUBE Tower Bridge • **OPEN** Tues–Fri 11am–6pm. Sat Sun 12 noon–6pm
• **SERVICES** Commissioning service

THE ROOM
ADDRESS 158 Walton Street, SW3 2JL
TEL/FAX 0171 225 3225
See silver, pewter, glass, ceramics and furniture, from £25 to £5,000, in a relaxed tranquil atmosphere. The shop's name sums up its atmosphere and philosophy. 'We're not a formal gallery,' stresses owner Philip Evans. 'We're presenting an eclectic mix as it might appear at home.' Particularly beautiful are Anthony Stern's wineglasses, Keith Tyssen's simple pewter bowls, and charming oyster-shell silver and gilt salt and pepper sets by Patricia Hamilton.
TUBE South Kensington • **OPEN** Mon–Sat 10.30am–5.30pm • **SERVICES** Gift wrapping. Wedding list. Free deliveries within London area

CRAFT SUPPLIES

BEADS (NECKLACE MAKER)
ADDRESS 259 Portobello Road, W11 1LR
TEL/FAX 0171 792 3436
Explore an incredible variety of beads (rare, antique, ethnic and precious) and buy what you need to make a curtain, or trim a blind or lampshade or a host of other creative projects. Even better, go to a workshop and learn expert techniques.
TUBE Ladbroke Grove • **OPEN** Mon–Fri 11am–5.30pm. Sat 10am–6pm
• **SERVICES** Re-stringing and repairs. Workshops

CANDLE MAKERS' SUPPLIES

ADDRESS 28 Blythe Road, W14 0HA
TEL 0171 602 4031 **FAX** 0171 602 2796
All materials for candlemaking, including convenient kits, plus materials for
silk-painting, batik, mould-making and resin-casting – from the people who
started the hippy candle-making boom and have been in business ever since.
TUBE *Olympia* • **OPEN** *Mon–Fri 10.30am–6pm. Sat 10.30am–5pm*
• **SERVICES** *Mail order. Candle-making courses*

THE CANE STORE

ADDRESS 207 Blackstock Road, N5 2LL
TEL/FAX 0171 354 4210
This is where you can find all materials for cane and basketwork, including
re-caning. Benefit from their large selection of books backed up by expert
advice. For creative home ideas, find attractive panels of woven cane,
split bamboo, reed screening, and grass/straw. For example, bamboo
rods from 1 cm to 17 cm diameter, cost from 45p to £31 – wonderful for
curtain rods, and easily split to use as furniture edgings. Split bamboo
screening is £63.45 a roll (1.8 by 4.5 metres). Woven cane (46 cm wide)
costs £11.67 a metre.
TUBE *Arsenal/Finsbury Park* • **OPEN** *Mon–Thurs 10am–7pm. Fri 10am–1pm.
Sat 10am–6pm* • **SERVICES** *Cane and rush repairs. Mail order for materials*

CREATIVITY NEEDLECRAFTS

ADDRESS 45 New Oxford Street, WC1A 1BH
TEL 0171 240 2945 **FAX** 0171 240 6030
These large needlecraft specialists prove handicrafts are not dead in
central London. They have everything you need to pursue a project –
yarns, needles, patterns and kits for tapestry, knitting and machine-knitting,
embroidery, rug-making, and crochet. Plus good selections of haberdashery
and a wide choice of books.
TUBE *Tottenham Court Road/Holborn* • **OPEN** *Mon–Sat 9.30am–6pm.
Late night Thurs 7pm*

EHRMAN

ADDRESS 14–16 Lancer Square, Kensington Church Street, W8 4EH
TEL 0171 937 8123 **FAX** 0171 937 8552
There are a lot of people out there still stitching by hand – and this shop is
packed high with tapestry kits to keep them happy, mainly for cushions, but
also rugs, chair seats, slippers, and smaller items like needlecases. Their
own stable of designers is led by the inimitable Kaffe Fasset – but contains
many other artists, so choice is wide-ranging. Average cost is around £40,
but look out for sale bargains.
TUBE *High Street Kensington* • **OPEN** *Mon–Fri 9.30am–5.30pm. Sat
10.30am–4.30pm* • **SERVICES** *Mail order catalogue: £2 refundable
with order*

HANDWEAVERS' STUDIO AND GALLERY

ADDRESS 29 Haroldstone Road, E17 7AN
TEL 0181 521 2281
A specialist outlet for weaving, spinning and dyeing run by and for
dedicated craftspeople. They stock yarns, fibres, fleece, looms, spinning
wheels, and books.

TUBE *Blackhorse Road* • **OPEN** *Tues–Sat 10am–5pm* • **SERVICES** *Second-hand notice board. Mail order. Commissioning advice. Weekend courses*

POTTERYCRAFTS
ADDRESS 8–10 Ingate Place, SW8 3NS
TEL 0171 720 0050   **FAX** 0171 627 8290
Part of a big national craft supplies group, based in Stoke-on-Trent. They sell all basic materials for potters, ceramic artists and sculptors, including clays, paints, brushes, pigments, glazes and so on. Also blank pottery to paint at home.
RAIL *Queenstown Road* • **OPEN** *Mon–Sat 9am–5pm* • **WEBSITE** *www.potterycrafts.co.uk* • **SERVICES** *Catalogue. Mail order. Classes* • **ALSO AT** *Unit 2, Norbury Trading Estate, Craignish Avenue, Norbury, SW16 4RW (0181 679 7606)*

TAPISSERIE
ADDRESS 54 Walton Street, SW3 1RB
TEL 0171 581 2715   **FAX** 0171 589 8609
Exclusive hand-painted tapestry canvasses, plus all wools and some kits. Top-quality accessories include needle threaders, and gold- or platinum-plated needles.
TUBE *Knightsbridge* • **OPEN** *Mon–Fri 10am–5.30pm. Sat 10am–4pm* • **SERVICES** *Blocking and stretching tapestries, making into cushions if required*

LOOKS FROM ABROAD

'We just sold coloured silks from the East – nothing else. The sort of thing that William Morris, Alma Tadema and Burne-Jones and Rossetti used to come in and rave about.'
William Judd, long-serving Liberty employee, speaking of the early days

The world is your oyster. No need to leave London to buy Chinese wedding cabinets, colourful Mexican pottery, Jali tables with fretwork grilles, cool Swedish Gustavian dining-chairs, Indian silks, Burmese bamboo, Sri Lankan planter's chairs. Ethnic is elegant, say the style pundits. Families find with relief that furniture from India, Indonesia and South America is surprisingly affordable, functional and robust. It's all part of the modern mix-it movement that combines old and new, East and West, naturals and synthetics, brights and pastels, into metropolitan eclectic.

ALTERNATIVE EAST
ADDRESS 48 Upper Street, Islington, N1 0PN
TEL 0171 226 9504   **FAX** 0171 354 4103
'We don't deal with large importers, and we believe in fair trading.' A popular policy on which this shop has thrived for eight years. Focal

point is a large glass display case gleaming with semi-precious stones and high-quality silver – jewellery from Central America, Brazil, India, Nepal, Thailand, and North America Indians. Also Indian furniture (thakat tables and grinding-wheel tables, £95 to £120), plus furniture in reclaimed teak from Thailand. Glass tables, wine racks, polished iron mirrors. Giant iron screens from India – over 6 ft tall and six panels wide – cost around £350. Lanterns and shades from Morocco in brass and iron, £20 to £90 for a giant centre piece. Amusing tables with elephant heads and legs (£55 to £120) from Thailand, which also supplies rocking horses, and buddha masks. Plus trinket boxes, nickel and iron candlesticks, and lots of accessories/gifts from £9 to £65.

TUBE *Angel* • **OPEN** *Mon–Sat 10am–6.30pm. Sun 12pm–4pm*

ALTFIELD

ADDRESS 2–22, Chelsea Harbour Design Centre, Lots Road, SW10 0XE
TEL 0171 351 5893 **FAX** 0171 376 5667
Those distinctive oriental blue-and-white china vases, lamps, bowls and so on are made in their own factory in the time-honoured traditional way – hand-painted, dipped in glaze, and coal-fired in a sealed container for around 72 hours. Prices from around £20 to £150. Plus beautifully-restored authentic old furniture, including 18th-century pieces, and Chinese reproductions made from old rosewood. Chinese silks, Japanese screens and original Chinese paintings.

TUBE *Sloane Square + 11, 22 bus/Earls Court + C3 bus* • **OPEN** *Mon–Fri 9am–5pm* • **SERVICES** *Brochures. Deliveries in UK and Europe*

ANTEAKS

ADDRESS 57 Queenstown Road, SW8 3RG
TEL/FAX 0171 720 4259
Specialists in furniture made from tropical hardwood teak. Genuine antiques (about 180 years old) come from remote areas of Central and Eastern Java. Reproductions are made from old wood – the teak is at least 20 and often 50 years old or more, and comes from floors, walls and ceilings of demolished houses.

RAIL *Queens Town Road* • **OPEN** *Mon–Sat 10am–5.30pm. Sun 12 noon–5.30pm or by appointment*

THE BLUE DOOR

ADDRESS 74 Church Road, SW13 0DQ
TEL 0181 748 9785 **FAX** 0181 563 1043
Gustavian-style furniture made and hand-painted to order, plus cotton fabrics, mirrors, glass and pottery to complete the look.

TUBE *Hammersmith + 209 bus* • **RAIL** *Barnes Bridge* • **OPEN** *Mon–Sat 10am–5pm*

CANE & ABLE

ADDRESS 73–74 Camden Lock Place, Camden Lock, NW1 8AF
TEL 0171 485 2350 **FAX** 0171 284 4973
Old country-style furniture in weathered dark woods, culled from all over India by Manhar Savla, spilling out from the shop interior on to the pavement outside. Occasional tables are just a few inches high: Indians are used to sitting on the floor. Some are made from old windows, with

bevelled glass tops over the original ornate iron grilles. Plus chests and cupboards, small boxes and gift ideas.
TUBE *Camden* • **OPEN** *Sat Sun 10am–5pm. Or by appointment*

CASA CATALAN
ADDRESS 15 Chalk Farm Road, NW1 8AG
TEL 0171 485 3975
Famous for well-priced terracotta pots – a huge selection of all sizes from Spain, Portugal and Thailand. Plus throws, rugs, tablecloths and general giftware, jewellery and some furniture – a busy, bright selection.
TUBE *Camden Town* • **OPEN** *7 days 10am–6pm* • **ALSO AT** *16–18 Heath Street, NW3 (0171 431 6002)*

CHINA MAINLAND
ADDRESS 172 Kensington High Street, W8 7RG
TEL 0171 376 0304   **FAX** 0171 376 0309
Container-loads of furniture direct from their Chinese workshops. Lacquered pieces have 20 coats in black, ivory or red, hand-painted and highly-polished – exotic but gaudy. Plainer styles are in solid rosewood from managed Chinese plantations worked with age-old craft techniques.
TUBE *Kensington High Street* • **OPEN** *Mon–Fri 9am–6pm. Late night Thurs 7pm. Sun 11am–6pm*

CIEL DECOR
ADDRESS 187 New Kings Road, SW6
TEL 0171 731 0444   **FAX** 0171 731 0788
Can't go to Provence? Well, let its sun-soaked furnishings come to you via this vibrant boutique which gently spreads over two floors. It even smells right, what with lavender-bags, and special fragrant room sprays. Numerous accessories and speciality foods, but fabrics steal the show – those typical small-scale Provençal block-prints. The paisley and other motifs go back to the port of Marseilles' early Indian imports, now interpreted in vibrant saturated dyes of mustard, terracotta, cobalt, emerald and indigo. From around £29.95 to £45 a metre (150 cm wide); plus some wipe-clean plasticised versions.
OPEN *Mon–Fri 10am–5.30pm* • **TUBE** *Parsons Green* • **SERVICES** *Interior design, and full soft furnishings service, including curtain-making*

THE COLONIAL HOUSE ✉
TEL/FAX 0181 993 7679
Colonial 17th-century-style planter's chairs and tables in hardwood, imported directly from Sri Lanka at very reasonable prices, plus attractive range of accessories.
SERVICES *Catalogue. Or please phone for appointment to view*

DAVID WAINWRIGHT
ADDRESS 63 Portobello Road, W11 3DB
TEL 0171 727 0707   **FAX** 0181 960 8484
Around ten years ago, David Wainwright trailed the 'silk route' from the tip of India to China. He visited remote tribes in the deserts of India to small Tibetan communities and hauled back large antiques, statues, bits of wood and stone from old houses, and colonial furniture plus smaller artifacts and

ornaments. The result: ethnic for every budget – from £1 to £1000s. Furniture here is often a re-cycling exercise – Indian doors turn into tables as do 18th-century Chinese shop signs. Wainwright supplied the fash-pack's East-meets-West minimalist Hempel Hotel in Bayswater. Nevertheless atmosphere is friendly and he promises a 'non-elitist approach.' However, celebrity punters include pop stars, actors and models – Madonna, Kylie Minogue, Bjork, All Saints, Stella McCartney, Hugh Grant, Helen Mirren et al.

TUBE *Notting Hill Gate/Ladbroke Grove* • **OPEN** *Mon–Sat 9am–6pm. Sun 11am–6pm* • **SERVICES** *Interior design. Deliveries* • **ALSO AT** *251 Portobello Road, W11 (0171 792 1988) and 28 Rosslyn Hill, Hampstead NW3 1NH (0171 431 5900)*

THE EGYPTIAN HOUSE ✉

ADDRESS Unit A2, Hatcham Mews Business Centre, Hatcham Park Road, SE14 5QA
TEL 0171 732 4321   **FAX** 0171 732 6543

The exotic Wigmore Street emporium has closed down, but the same range of Egyptian goods is in a mail-order catalogue – hand-painted papyrus pictures, embroidered table cloths and napkins, crocheted and embroidered bed covers, traditional bright turquoise pottery, decorated glass perfume bottles and mother-of-pearl inlaid boxes. Also brass pots and urns, small wool kilims, and brass lanterns.

SERVICES *Catalogue*

GANESHA

ADDRESS 6 Park Walk, SW10 0AD
TEL 0171 352 8972

For 21 years, London's shopping cognoscenti have sought out this fascinating little shop – you never know quite what you'll find, amongst the curios, carvings, candles and jewellery, from India and South East Asia, to the larger pieces of furniture/sculpture down the very steep stairs.

TUBE *South Kensington* • **OPEN** *Mon–Sun 12 noon–6pm*

THE INDIA SHOP ✉

TEL 01672 515585   **FAX** 01380 728118

Anne Wyles adores the vibrancy of India handicrafts – despite her large family (11 children) she goes personally to source the imports that fill her brilliant catalogue, packed with hand-blocked fabrics, rugs, small pieces of furniture, brassware and so on. Essential viewing.

INDIGO

ADDRESS 275 New King's Road, SW6 4RD
TEL 0171 384 3101   **FAX** 0171 384 3102

European antiques are getting scarce. Their place is taken by the type of old Indian pieces you'll find here, sourced mainly from Rajasthan, and restored in their own country workshops. 'We've developed a lot of knowledge and a first class reputation for quality.' Older pieces, usually teak or rosewood, date from the 19th century. They include chunky cupboards (from £250 to £1000, depending on size and age), handsome chests (from £150 to £500), spice boxes (from £20 to £60), and large, useful occasional tables (from £130 to £900). From China: sideboards from Beijing and Taijing, and altar tables for around £820 to £840.

19th-century Chinese wardrobes cost around £1850; leather Chinese
trunks are £320 to £420. Also brassware, textiles, pillars, carved beams,
and smaller home accessories, including brass inlaid jewellery and writing
boxes. Plus contemporary ironwork.

TUBE *Parsons Green* • **OPEN** *Mon–Sat 10am–6pm*

JACQUELINE EDGE

ADDRESS 1 Courtnell Street, W2 5BU
TEL 0171 229 1172   **FAX** 0171 727 4651

Jacqueline Edge has brought beautiful furniture and accessories from
Burma in appealing natural materials – bamboo, rush, clay and teak. Her
best finds are the enticing frostproof pots and urns, each one hand-thrown
from natural clays, and roughly-glazed in green, yellow, cream or blue.
In their homeland, they are used to store water, but planted up, they add
impact to any London balcony or garden. Stand them on the large clay
columns or metal stands, which are also sold here. Bamboo makes an
attractive slatted chair, and teak is turned into a handsome bench, a
lounge steamer chair, and a folding table. Orchid 'boxes' deliberately
expose the roots of these exotic flowers – apparently that's what they like.
For barbecue addicts, the clay Balticue is one of the most attractive versions
on the market. Made from tough Irrawaddy terracotta, it heats rapidly to
an even high temperature. Grill on its top, or pop on a lid for roasting.
Then lounge around in all-silk pyjama suits from Vietnam.

TUBE *Notting Hill Gate* • **OPEN** *Mon–Fri 10am-6pm. Sat 11am–4pm*

JAIPUR DESIGNS

ADDRESS 13 Goodge Street, W1P 1FE
TEL 0171 636 5560

A brilliant touch of affordable India against drab grey pavements. Furniture
(cupboards and tables) from old shesham wood (rosewood). Beautiful
textiles – cushions made from patchworks of old embroideries and saris.
Printed and embroidered duvet covers. Embroidered antique torans
(decorative arches). Just off Tottenham Court Road, and always worth
a detour – friendliest of service.

TUBE *Goodge Street* • **OPEN** *Mon–Sat 10am–6.30pm*

JAVA COTTON CO

ADDRESS 3 Blenheim Crescent, W11 2EE
TEL 0171 229 3212   **FAX** 0181 964 0758

Genuine hand-printed batiks from Indonesia. Fabrics are £17.50
a metre, 1 metre wide. Also made into bedspreads, quilts, cushions,
and children's clothes.

TUBE *Ladbroke Grove/Notting Hill Gate* • **OPEN** *Mon–Sat 10am–6pm*

JOSS GRAHAM

ADDRESS 10 Eccleston Street, SW1W 9LT
TEL/FAX 0171 730 4370

Heaps of hangings, embroideries, shawls, cushions, rugs, and throws
from India, Central Asia and the Middle East, from textiles old and new.
Also ceramics, Vietnamese lacquerware, glass and other accessories.

TUBE *Victoria* • **OPEN** *Mon–Sat 10am–6pm* • **SERVICES** *Textile mounting
and restoration. Special exhibitions.*

KARA KARA

ADDRESS 2a Pond Place, SW3 6QJ
TEL 0171 591 0891 **FAX** 0171 591 0890

An eclectic and elegant mix of Japanese handmade textiles and tableware, plus 'organic' furniture from Indonesia in solid teak, with chairs and tables fashioned roughly from fallen logs – prices from around £300.

TUBE *South Kensington* • **OPEN** *Mon–Sat 10am–6pm*

KOTIZAEN

ADDRESS Unit 75, West Yard, Camden Lock, NW1
TEL 0171 284 0310 **FAX** 0171 284 4973

Hitesh Savlas searches India for old textiles, and sells them mainly to private collectors. Spreads and throws from India, including nomadic pieces, and textiles from Zaire such as raffia cloth. Plus rugs and cushions and lots of small gifts, at very affordable prices.

TUBE *Camden* • **OPEN** *Fri 11am–5pm. Sat Sun 10am–6pm. Or by appointment*

LOMBOK

ADDRESS 4 Heathmans Road, SW6 4TJ
TEL 0171 736 5171 **FAX** 0171 371 5931

Alex Cresswell-Turner was working in Jakarta when he fell in love with Indonesian woods and furniture. Last autumn, he and partner Sara Morison converted an old classic car garage into a atmospheric warehouse for furniture made from reclaimed teak. Wooden objects such as work benches and old doors are reworked into simple classic designs, offset by lamps and smaller accessories. Coffee tables from around £300; dining tables from £600; chairs from £80.

TUBE *Parsons Green* • **OPEN** *Mon–Fri 10am–7pm. Sat 10am–6pm. Sun 11am–4pm*

MEXIQUE

ADDRESS 67 Sheen Lane, SW14 8AD
TEL 0181 392 2345

A boon of a boutique fighting off British grey days with sun-saturated Mexican crafts – pottery, glass, tiles, amazing carved hangings, jewellery, furniture and much more.

RAIL *Mortlake* • **OPEN** *10am–6pm Mon–Fri. Early closing Wed 1pm. Sat 10am–5pm*

MINH MANG

ADDRESS 182 Battersea Park Road, SW11 4ND
TEL 0171 498 3233 **FAX** 0171 498 3353

Anne Harris and Lilly Warwich (who is half-Vietnamese) have a love affair with Cambodian and Vietnamese silks, which are tie-dyed into a myriad of intricate patterns, according to the weaver's district and family. Silks and linens from £10 to £32 a metre, from a large selection of bolts, which also include raw linens. Plus cushions (from £40), throws (made to order in any fabric), frames and albums, lacquer bowls, and seductive fashion accessories, such as embroidered tee-shirts and silk pyjies.

TUBE *Sloane Square + 319 or 137 bus, Vauxhall + 344 bus* • **RAIL** *Battersea Park Road, Vauxhall + 344 bus* • **OPEN** *Mon–Fri 10am–5.30pm. Sat 10am–5pm*

NASSERI FABRICS
ADDRESS 38 Atlantic Road, SW9
TEL 0171 274 5627   **FAX** 0171 978 9526
Designs on fine pure cotton are authentically African, but (for reasons of quality) production is mainly European. Shades are bold and vibrant, in distinctive colour combinations – geometrics or simple patterns with butterflies, elephants, peacocks and so on. The long narrow bazaar-like shop has lengths of cloth hanging from the ceiling, piled on shelves and stacked high on counters. Mostly sold in lengths of six yards, cost is anything from a bargain £5 (find lots of these on their market stall opposite) to £50.
TUBE *Brixton*

NEAL STREET EAST
ADDRESS 5 Neal Street, WC2H 9PU
TEL 0171 240 0135   **FAX** 0171 836 4769
Christina Smith trail-blazed Oriental imports as long ago as 1972, with countless buying trips to China and India. She's created a spacious enticing emporium full of unexpected departments on different levels. Textiles include throws, cushion covers, wallhangings and Kalimkari block-printed bed-spreads. Ceramics come from Japan, China and Morocco. Paper lighting from Nepal, Japan and China. Basketware from China and the Philippines. Cookshop with Japanese, Chinese and Indian ironware, ceramics, woks, kebab sticks, trays, laquerware, herbs and spices. Shoji screens, tatami mats, futons. Big Buddhas and masks, decorative birdcages, and dog baskets. Amazing artificial flowers, and a basement full of party toys and stocking fillers. Lacquer chests from £70. Bamboo matchstick blinds from £5.50. Bamboo tables from £79, shelves from £33.80. Plus inexpensive Chinese butterfly kites (two for £10), temple rubbings, chopsticks, tableware, large decorative fans and parasols, and lots of books.
TUBE *Covent Garden* • **OPEN** *Mon–Wed 11am–7pm. Thurs–Sat 10am–7pm*

NEW RAINBOW TEXTILES
ADDRESS 98 The Broadway, Southall, Middx, UB1 1QF
TEL 0181 574 1494   **FAX** 0181 574 0410
In little India, behind an unpretentious façade, Mr Ahluwalia and sons Kamal and Shashi have amassed probably the finest selection anywhere of Indian fabrics all under one roof. Some buyers come straight from Heathrow airport. Exclusive designs are sold off the roll, rather than as sari lengths (which can restrict projects). The ground floor is packed with polyester – a stunning rainbow of colours, but disappointingly synthetic. Those in the know – including London's leading designers – head straight for the silk basement to find metallic gauze, organzas, shot silks, traditional silk and cotton weaves, and mirror work.
RAIL *Southall* • **BUS** *207 from Ealing Broadway* • **OPEN** *Mon–Sat 9.30am–5.30pm. Wed 9.30am–3pm. Sun noon–6pm*

NINE SCHOOLS
ADDRESS Ifield Galleries; 121 Ifield Road, SW10 9AX
TEL 0171 835 2202   **FAX** 0171 565 0305
Named after the nine 'schools' of traditional Chinese thought. Here you'll find hand-carved and hand-painted Ch'ing Dynasty furniture and ornaments collected from rural towns and villages in Northern and Central

provinces of China. Red and black lacquer wedding chests (£950), leather trunks (£350), plus demi-lune (half-circle) tables, rice pots, water carriers and other unusual pieces. Bed linen collection printed with Chinese calligraphy.

TUBE *Earls Court or Fulham Broadway* • **OPEN** *Mon–Sat 10am–6pm*
• **WEBSITE** *www.thenineschools.com*

NORDIC STYLE
ADDRESS 109 Lots Road, SW10 0RN
TEL 0171 351 1755   **FAX** 0171 351 4966
During the 18th century, the Swedes perfected their own version of elegance, known as Gustavian style, after King Gustaf III (1771–1792). Come here to recreate its airy look, with pale painted furniture and elegant shapes, combined with simple fabrics, pewter tableware, and wood floors. They'll even install you a traditional tiled Swedish stove – but it will cost around £6,000 complete.

TUBE *Fulham Broadway/Sloane Square* • **OPEN** *Mon–Sat 9.30am–5.30pm* • **SERVICES** *Mail order. Catalogue from 0171 351 1755*

THE ORANGE TREE
ADDRESS 123 High Street, Wanstead, E11 2RL
TEL/FAX 0181 530 4621
Chinese, Moroccan, Japanese and Indian pieces, plus soft furnishings and gifts. Chinese chests for around £165, plus Japanese stair cupboards, stepped up the side for plants or ornaments.

TUBE *Wanstead* • **OPEN** *Mon–Sat 9.30am–5.30pm. Sun 10am–3pm*
• **SERVICES** *Curtain making/fitting*

THE PUKKA PALACE ✉
TEL 0345 666660
Neat little catalogue gives postal access to Raj-style furniture, textiles, ironwork and glass – backed up by a huge Shropshire warehouse (01588 672999) of Indian furniture, much of it antique.

QUETZAL TRADING
ADDRESS 1 The Market, SE10 9HZ
TEL 0181 305 0429   **FAX** 0181 692 1858
Simon Pollock travels the world to pack this colourful capsule with vibrant Latin American crafts (jewellery, mobiles, windchimes, wallhangings) and goods from Indonesia, which include inlaid shell work for mirrors, frames, chests and pyramid sets of drawers, plus primitive carved work from Bali. Hand-loomed men's shirts and batik clothing

RAIL *Greenwich* • **OPEN** *Wed–Fri 12 noon–5pm. Sat Sun 11am–5.30pm*

SOO SAN
ADDRESS 239a Fulham Road, SW3 6HY
TEL 0171 352 8980   **FAX** 0171 352 9880
Chinese furniture and accessories include original old Ch'ing (1644–1911) furniture from Northern China. Leather trunks, from around £350; large wedding cabinets, around £2,000. Plus tables, chairs, rice buckets (£150), and original Ming china.

TUBE *South Kensington* • **OPEN** *Mon–Sat 10am–6pm*

TUMI

ADDRESS 23 Chalk Farm Road, Camden Town, NW1
TEL 0171 485 4152.

Tumi source gifts, fashions and furnishings from ten Latin American countries. The result is a brilliant selection of handicrafts. Well known for their delightful balsa-wood carvings – for example, brightly-painted parrots and toucans. Also jointed wooden toys, and little wooden chairs plus dishes and bowls fashioned from sun-dried gourds. Plus furniture, intricate mirrors, textiles and other home accessories.

TUBE *Camden Town* • **OPEN** *Mon–Sat 10am–6pm*

FABRICS AND SOFT FURNISHINGS

- **Fabric manufacturers with showroom shops** *page 66*
- **Fabric shops** *page 71*
- **Soft furnishing shops and services** *page 77*
- **Ready-made and second-hand curtains** *page 82*
- **Curtain trimmings, tracks and poles** *page 83*
- **Blinds and awnings** *page 85*
- **Antique textiles** *page 86*

> *'I have tried for instance to make woollen substances as woollen as possible, cotton as cotton as possible, and so on; I have only used the dyes which are natural and simple.'*
> William Morris (1834–1896)

FABRIC MANUFACTURERS WITH SHOWROOM SHOPS

Most manufacturers sell their fabrics through department stores, soft furnishers, interior design shops and so on. But an increasing number also have London showrooms which welcome the public, and sell 'direct'. These showrooms are really good news – visiting them is an interior decorating treat. Service is well-informed, with high standards of display – lots of ideas for different looks. You can view long lengths on large racks, and get a good idea of pattern repeats and drape. This is in many cases essential, because fabrics can look completely different bunched up over a large area, than they do in a smallish flat sample. You can usually take away small cuttings on the spot.

ANDREW MARTIN

ADDRESS 200 Walton Street, SW3 2JL
TEL 0171 584 4290   **FAX** 0171 589 4957
There isn't an Andrew (he left long ago). The Martin is Martin Waller,
one of the most charismatic and enterprising personalities in the furnishing
trade. His fabrics (from around £29 a metre) sell worldwide yet he still
spends weeks in China and India researching his best-selling designs...
calligraphy prints, Chinese lettering, Indian elephants, African themes.
Fabulous Kravet fabrics from America. And so much more: mock suedes,
real leather, weaves, chenille, voile, velour, silk. Plus oriental furniture –
(old leather trunks and tables) and a new sofa collection. Get a firm fix on
furnishing fashion in an unintimidating atmosphere.
TUBE *South Kensington* • **OPEN** *Mon–Fri 9am–5.30pm. Sat 10am–5pm*
• **SERVICES** *Mail-order catalogue for household linens*

ANNA FRENCH

ADDRESS 343 King's Road, SW3 5ES
TEL 0171 351 1126   **FAX** 0171 351 0421
So easy to live with – that's Anna's special gift: a soft up-to-date look that's
not aggressively modern. She's continually updating her collections of
printed fabrics, weaves and voiles, with papers and borders to co-ordinate.
Reasonable prices for decorator merchandise – prints start at around £18 a
metre. Also designs for children. Hanging at the back of this airy showroom
are magnificent collections of lace panels, made on rescued Victorian looms
to original period designs. Friendly atmosphere, essential viewing.
TUBE *Sloane Square + 11, 19 or 22 bus* • **OPEN** *Mon–Fri 9.30am–5.30pm.
Sat 10.30am–5.30pm* • **SERVICES** *Curtains and soft-furnishings made to order*

BEAUMONT & FLETCHER

ADDRESS 261 Fulham Road, SW3 6HY
TEL 0171 352 5594   **FAX** 0171 352 3546
Inspirations for richly-coloured linen union prints and weaves come from
diverse and romantic design sources – Aubusson tapestries, petit-point
needlework, French toiles, 18th-century English calico prints, even Raphael's
decorations for the Vatican. Roses, fruits, leaves and scrolls in glorious
abundance, shown off in a recently-decorated showroom, with traditionally-
made furniture, wall-lights and mirrors. Expect to pay around £65 a metre,
though linen union stripes and plains are from £28.40 a metre.
TUBE *South Kensington* • **OPEN** *Mon–Fri 9.30am–5.30pm. Sat 11am–5pm*
• **SERVICES** *Interior design. Curtain-making*

CELIA BIRTWELL

ADDRESS 71 Westbourne Park Road, W2 5QH
TEL 0171 221 0877   **FAX** 0171 229 7673
Exotic exclusive fantasy designs in voile, silks, and large painterly patterns.
TUBE *Royal Oak/Westbourne Park* • **OPEN** *10am–5pm Mon–Fri* • **SERVICES**
Free samples. Large basket full of bargain bits

COLEFAX AND FOWLER

ADDRESS 39 Brook Street, W1Y 2JE
TEL 0171 493 2231   **FAX** 0171 355 4037
Perhaps the most famous name in English decorating, influencing

upper-class taste for over 50 years. John Fowler was in partnership first with Lady Colefax, and then with Nancy Lancaster. They originated and refined the English country house style with its emphasis on elegance and comfort – and have, of course, been widely copied. Traditional, exclusive chintzes are their forte. Also damasks, weaves and trimmings. Furniture and unusual elegant antiques. Wallpapers from hand-blocked originals, decorative borders.
TUBE Bond Street • **OPEN** Mon–Fri 9.30am–5.30pm • **SERVICES** Samples/ brochure. Full interior decorating service; interior decorating consultancy from the North Room. Advice on buying antiques • **ALSO AT** 110 Fulham Road, SW3 6RL (0171 244 7427); open Sat 10am–4pm

THE DECORATIVE FABRICS GALLERY
ADDRESS 278–280 Brompton Road, SW3 2AS
TEL 0171 589 4778   **FAX** 0171 589 4781
The fabric shop with the glamour and excitement of a fashion store. Stylish windows, airy interior, and displays over two floors of six famous fabric brands: G P & J Baker (innovation backed by extensive archives), Monkwell (crisply contemporary), Parkertex (useful selections) Design Archives (subtle update on old patterns, including toiles), Firifiss and Fardis (modern). It's a trade showroom, but there's a warm welcome for the public. Inspirational trimmings and furnishing accessories.
TUBE South Kensington • **OPEN** Mon–Fri 9.30am–5.30pm. Sat 10am–5pm • **SERVICES** Free samples

DESIGNERS GUILD
ADDRESS 275–277 King's Road, SW3 5EN
TEL 0171 351 5775   **FAX** 0171 243 7710
Tricia Guild is the lady to thank for bringing colour to London. Lime, purple, pink, scarlet, cobalt and any combinations thereof were beyond the capital's comprehension before she trail-blazed her unique look for home decoration. All through the eighties her window-displays stopped traffic and made people leap off buses, and now of course everyone's copying. Tricia, however, is consistently out ahead, evolving new looks and new merchandise, and writing books to put the message across: 'Colour is beautiful. Don't be afraid. Mix it up with wonderful shapes, natural materials and hand-made products'. See a huge range of papers, fabrics, borders, trimmings, plus designs for children.
TUBE Sloane Square + 11, 19, or 22 bus • **OPEN** Mon Tues 9.30am–5.30pm. Wed Thurs Fri Sat 9.30am–6pm • **SERVICES** Interior design and soft furnishings; samples, brochures

JANE CHURCHILL
ADDRESS 151 Sloane Street, SW1X 9BX
TEL 0171 730 9847   **FAX** 0171 259 9189
The name over the door is Jane Churchill (who still practises as an interior decorator), but she was bought out years ago by Colefax and Fowler, whose design director is Ann Grafton. Simple, isn't it? It's Ann who has been the driving force behind the formidable number of freshly-styled Jane Churchill collections which are distributed worldwide. See them at this, the flagship store – distinctive easy-to-use designs which sell from around £21. From chinoiserie and vegetable prints through florals to stripes and ginghams, the appeal is wide-ranging. Plus the back-up of carefully-

selected paints (made by Farrow & Ball), bedlinen, upholstered furniture, lighting, accessories and gifts.

TUBE *Sloane Square* • **OPEN** *Mon–Sat 10am–6pm. Late night Wed 7pm*
• **SERVICES** *Curtain making. Samples/brochures. Interior design advice*

MRS MONRO

ADDRESS 16 Motcombe Street, SW1X 8LB
TEL 0171 235 0326   **FAX** 0171 259 6305
Miss Jean Monro – the original English rose of chintz – is semi-retired from the decorating business her mother founded in 1926. Now in her eighties, she was the first woman to receive an OBE for her contributions to interior design worldwide. Her traditional chintzes in original old colourings – glorious glazed cottons and linen unions – are loved the world over. Prices from £35.40 a metre plus VAT.

TUBE *Knightsbridge* • **OPEN** *Mon–Thurs 9.30am–5.30pm. Fri 9.30am–5pm*

MULBERRY HOME

ADDRESS 219 King's Road, SW3 5EJ
TEL 0171 352 1937   **FAX** 0171 823 3886
Mulberry make a complete statement for the home, and draw deep on feelings for the past. It's very English, with its leather and tapestries, but with a hint of continental abandon in the rich Baroque velvets, figured chenilles and heavy fringing. Sumptuous and supremely decorative, this could be a look that's as addictive – and expensive – as those famous handbags.

TUBE *Sloane Square + 11, 19, 22 bus* • **OPEN** *Mon–Sat 10am–6pm. Late night Wed 7pm* • **SERVICES** *Interior design – portfolio of two schemes for £100 refundable against purchase of merchandise*

NICHOLAS HASLAM

ADDRESS 12–14 Holbein Place, SW1W 8NL
TEL 0171 730 8623   **FAX** 0171 730 6679
Celebrity decorator Nicholas Haslam pioneered the linen trend. His glazed version comes from a special mill in Ireland – natural, white, grey, black and brown – £50 a metre, 129 cm wide. But simple basecloth (a natural-coloured linen/cotton union) is £25 a metre. Glorious archive fabrics cost from £35 a metre upwards. Particularly popular is Moleskin, a mock suede, in seven colours, including cream, gold and a pretty lovat green, £45 a metre, 150 cm wide. Also furnishing corduroys, silks, fine wools, and a textured jute/linen weave.

TUBE *Sloane Square* • **OPEN** *Mon–Fri 10am–6pm. Some Saturdays 12 noon–5pm (please phone to check)*

NINA CAMPBELL

ADDRESS 7 Milner Street, SW3 2QA
TEL 0171 589 8589   **FAX** 0171 589 2369
Complete range of Nina Campbell's famous papers and fabrics – traditional themes updated with subtle colourings very liveable-with. Wallpapers from £23.50 to £25 a roll, printed cottons from £22 a metre. Orders placed before 2pm are ready the next day. Manager Paul von Fullman gives on the spot decorating advice. Plus Nina Bis antiques and accessories.

TUBE *South Kensington/Sloane Square/Knightsbridge* • **OPEN** *Mon–Fri 9.30am–5.30pm. Sat 10am–4pm* • **SERVICES** *Cushions, upholstery, headboards and a limited curtain-making service*

OSBORNE & LITTLE
ADDRESS 304–308 King's Road, SW3 5UH
TEL 0171 352 1456 **FAX** 0171 351 7813
It all began in 1968, with wallpapers for the swinging sixties – Antony Little was the designer and his brother-in-law Peter Osborne pitched in with marketing expertise. A winning combination, and now a formidable international success story, with collections for a multitude of furnishing needs – silks, linens, cottons, weaves, prints, plains, often embellished with co-ordinating trimmings. No particular set look – the range on offer caters for most everyone with interior design aspirations. Wallpapers are just as good as the fabrics. O & L pioneered the concept of the showroom shop, and celebrated their thirtieth anniversary with a complete revamp for the now-famous King's Road emporium, which is also a showcase for gracious Liberty and elegant Nina Campbell. Go and browse – you won't regret it (and you can walk to Designers Guild, Thomas Dare, Timney Fowler and Anna French on the same day – a dose of decorating strong enough to satisfy all but the terminally addicted).
TUBE *Sloane Square + 11, 19 or 22 bus* • **OPEN** *Mon–Fri 9.30am–6pm. Sat 10am–5.30pm*

PIERRE FREY
ADDRESS 251–253 Fulham Road, SW3 6HY
TEL 0171 376 5599 **FAX** 0171 352 3024
Leading upmarket French fabric house with around 4000 exclusive, sophisticated designs – tapestries, weaves, hand-prints, for curtains and upholstery. Trimmings and furniture, plus fabric accessories such bags and luggage.
TUBE *South Kensington* • **OPEN** *Mon–Fri 9am–6pm. Sat 10am–5pm*
• **SERVICES** *Free cuttings*

SANDERSON
ADDRESS 112–120 Brompton Road, SW3 1JJ
TEL 0171 584 3344 **FAX** 0171 584 8404
Sanderson: bedrock of English decorating for generations. This huge showcase pays fitting tribute to such a world-famous brand, with good room-settings for an affordable English style (constantly updated) with impeccable design traditions. Eminently usable patterns, in a feast of pattern books, backed by extensive plains, textured weaves, stripes and checks. Fabrics from around £12 a metre. Dressage velvet in 40 colours, £20 a metre. Lovely voiles, including new linens. Wallpaper from £17 a roll. The William Morris Room is a practical sample-filled shrine – a separate little enclave – for this famous Victorian artist-craftsman. Persevere downstairs, for a huge selection of paper and fabric sample books for all top makes. Annual sale (discontinued fabrics and seconds) is usually on one of the May bank holiday weekends at the Uxbridge factory shop – phone for details.
TUBE *Knightsbridge* • **OPEN** *Mon–Sat 10am–6pm* • **SERVICES** *Free samples. Full interior design service. Curtain making plus all soft furnishings*

TIMNEY FOWLER

ADDRESS 388 King's Road, SW3 5UZ
TEL 0171 352 2263 **FAX** 0171 352 0531

Husband and wife team Graeme Fowler and Sue Timney founded this
distinctive Chelsea furnishing landmark in 1979, and soon became known
for the ultimate black and white fabric show – classical and baroque prints
covered with imposing heads of Roman emperors and fragments of Greek
columns – these designs are still unique, and as popular today as ever, at
£34.50 a metre. Wallpapers and borders to match, with some designs
now in neutral and pale colourways. Plus changing modern collections in
a variety of colours, including voiles and velvets. The Aesthetic range has
useful checks and stripes. Also fabrics by Christian Fischbacher, Pallu and
Lake, and Interior Selection. And delightful accessories with the Timney
touch – mugs, plates, boxes, scarves, throws and so on.
TUBE *Sloane Square + 11, 19, 22 bus* • **OPEN** *Mon–Sat 9.30am–6pm*
• **SERVICES** *Brochure, samples, mail order. Borrowing service for sample
lengths – just leave credit card number*

FABRIC SHOPS

*'Good taste is better than bad taste,
but bad taste is better than no taste.'*
Arnold Bennett (1867–1931), British novelist.

Fabric is the big decorating success story of the late nineties, the
key to looks galore. Themes/collections proliferate – one moment
the plain-Jane homespuns of early New England, next the exotica
of Morocco, or the mysteries of oriental script. A plethora of fibres
– silks, linens, cottons and up-dated synthetics are made into
prints/weaves with an ever increasing twist on texture – chenille,
velvet, velour, metallic. You could spend a year making a choice
and who wants to do that? Go for what you like. Your home is not
a fashion forum. Remember an expensive pair of curtains may
have to last you seven years or more. On the other hand, use
fabrics for quick and fashionable room-lifters such as cushions,
throws or wall-hangings. Look out for wide widths – less sewing
and often extra value. Use prints as a basis for a colour scheme –
they are after all the work of trained designers, and increasingly
collections express a look in a nutshell. If a fabric is very expensive,
try and borrow a sample length, or buy a metre before committing
yourself. And make sure you have someone good to make it up.

ALEXANDER FURNISHINGS 🐷

ADDRESS 51–61 Wigmore Street, W1H 9LF
TEL 0171 935 2624/7806/8664/1678 **FAX** 0171 224 3275

Over 50 years, this business has grown into a warren of interconnecting
shops – tucked conveniently behind Oxford Street – with a friendly but
slightly chaotic atmosphere. There's a huge choice of curtain and
upholstery fabrics at keen or discount prices. Browse books for co-
ordinated collections plus wallpapers. Plus many other essentials – tracks,
poles, cushions, trimmings, nets. Definitely worth a detour from Europe's
busiest shopping street, with a promise of discounts of up to 50 per cent on
certain ranges. Even the BBC's 'Changing Rooms' goes shopping here.

TUBE *Bond Street* • **OPEN** *Mon–Sat 9am–6pm. Late night Thurs 7pm*
• **SERVICES** *Samples. Curtains: measure, make, fit and hang. Made-to-measure blinds. Loose covers, re-upholstery. Bedcovers, headboards, quilting to order*

AYRSHIRE TIME LINES ✉

ADDRESS Greenhead Mills, Union Street, Newmilns, Ayrshire, KA16 9BA
TEL 01560 321205   **FAX** 01560 322033
Mail-order supplier of exquisite cotton lace panels and valances, natural white or ivory, in archive designs (including The Stag by CFA Voysey) and modern checks.
SERVICES *Will shorten panels to any length. Free brochures*

B BROWN

ADDRESS 79–89 Pentonville Road, N1 9LW
TEL 08705 340340   **FAX** 08705 329610
Predominantly sells to the trade, but the public can buy a minimum of 1 metre at the trade counter. For example they have super felt in 80 colours, 183 cm wide, £5.24 a metre plus VAT. You can cut this without fraying – good for heavy instant curtains, but they will need dry-cleaning. Their muslins in 20 colours cost £1.65 plus VAT, and their satins are £4.22 a metre, 137 cm wide, plus VAT. Also coated PVC and many other amazing novelty fabrics, including designs featuring newsprint, musical notes, bookcases, leaves, woodgrain, brick, and sky. Plus holographics, metallic silks, mesh and net, foil cloth and crushed velvet. Extras include rolls of wired-edge ribbon, and water-based metallic paints by the litre (gold, silver and copper).
TUBE *Kings Cross/Angel* • **OPEN** *Mon–Fri 8am–5.30pm* • **SERVICES** *Mail order*

BELINDA COOTE TAPESTRIES

ADDRESS Unit 3, 14 Chelsea Harbour Design Centre, Lots Road, SW10 0XE
TEL 0171 351 0404   **FAX** 0171 352 9808
Painstakingly Belinda Coote (formerly an antique dealer) has built up her collection of tapestry wall hangings, tapestry fabrics by the metre, and tapestry borders, taking inspiration from old sources, but re-colouring where necessary to suit today's trends. Some fabrics are double-width, and the collection now includes paisley designs. Plus fringed or piped cushions, and fringed throws, and hand-painted furniture, plus wooden firescreens.
TUBE *Earls Court + C3 bus/Sloane Square + 11, 22 bus* • **OPEN** *Mon–Fri 9am–5pm* • **ALSO AT** *Harvey Nichols, Knightsbridge (0171 584 0011)*

BENNISON FABRICS

ADDRESS 16 Holbein Place, SW1W 8NL
TEL 0171 730 8076   **FAX** 0171 823 4997
Antique-looking 'tea-stained' linen unions, from around £80 a metre (used in numerous period dramas), plus printed silks.
TUBE *Sloane Square* • **OPEN** *Mon–Fri 10.30am–5.30pm*

BROADWICK SILKS

ADDRESS 9–11 Broadwick Street, W1V 1FN
TEL 0171 734 3320   **FAX** 0171 734 3476
Trade prices and friendly service. Silky selections are glorious, from

plain linings and dupions to fashionable sand-washed and tie-dye effects, from sheer chiffons and glamorous metallic organzas to chunky tweeds. Prices from £1.10 to £350 a metre.

TUBE *Piccadilly Circus/Oxford Circus/Tottenham Court Road* • **OPEN** *Mon–Fri 9am–6pm. Sat 9am–5pm* • **SERVICES** *Free samples; mail order*

CATH KIDSTON

ADDRESS 8 Clarendon Cross, W11 4AP
TEL 0171 221 4000   **FAX** 0171 229 1992

For Cath Kidston, the future is rosy: 'I think I'm rose obsessed. Daisies are a bit spiky, tulips have awkward stalks, and poppies just haven't the same graphic appeal.' Rose-sprigged papers and fabrics, based on rescued fifties patterns, are also made up into dozens of delicious accessories that cram this little emporium – aprons, coathangers, covered boxes, napkins. Latest venture is bedlinen, selling in department stores, too. Particularly good for gifts. Prices are reasonable, with intriguing selections of old curtains and china, plus freshly-machined cushions from old fabric pieces. Wallpapers, from £17.70 a roll, including blowsy roses (of course) and woodgrain effects.

TUBE *Holland Park* • **OPEN** *Mon–Fri 10.30am–6pm. Sat 11am–6pm*
• **SERVICES** *Mail-order catalogue*

CIEL DECOR

See LOOKS FROM ABROAD, page 60. Distinctive Provençal block-printed fabrics in rich vivid colours.

CORCORAN AND MAY 🐷

ADDRESS 161 Lower Richmond Road, SW15 1HH
TEL 0181 788 9556   **FAX** 0181 780 2178

Bargains in top-make furnishing fabrics – 'overstocks' (ends of lines and surplus) and seconds from Malabar, Monkwell, Jane Churchill, Anna French *et al*, sold from the roll. From an incredible £1 a metre. Huge choice of voiles and muslins, from £1.99 to £6.99 a metre.

TUBE *Putney Bridge* • **OPEN** *Mon–Sat 10am–5.30pm* • **SERVICES** *Samples. Full making-up service for soft furnishings including curtains and blinds*
• **ALSO AT** *Vast 8,000 sq ft showroom at 31–35 Blagdon Road, New Malden, Surrey (0181 949 0234); and at Sevenoaks*

THE CURTAIN FABRIC FACTORY 🐷

ADDRESS 236a North End Road, W14 9NU
TEL 0171 381 1777   **FAX** 0171 381 8879

Factory shop for designer-style fabrics at prices from around £3.50 a metre, including traditional florals, classic stripes, prints and geometrics. Quilted bedspreads to match the fabrics.

TUBE *Fulham Brodway* • **OPEN** *Mon–Sat 9.30am–5.30pm* • **SERVICES** *Curtain-making*

THE CURTAIN MILL 🐷

ADDRESS 2 The Vale, Acton, W3 7SB
TEL 0181 743 2299   **FAX** 0181 749 4341

A warehouse feel, with vistas of huge rolls of fabric – but don't be put off.

Bargain fabrics, from mills in Britain, the continent and America – all in stock and off the roll. They keep up with fashion trends, at up to half the price of the big stores. Nothing is much over £6.99 a metre, and prices go down to 99p for a lightweight floral. Brilliant choice of good basics at brilliantly basic prices: plains, stripes, checks, linings, interlinings, calico, and muslin. Plus upholstery cloth, nets, and plastic-coated fabric. Ranges change weekly, but ongoing 'classics' are kept in stock.
TUBE *Shepherds Bush + 207 bus* • **OPEN** *Mon–Sun 9am–5.30pm*
• **SERVICES** *Samples. Curtain-making – takes around two weeks. Own car park* • **ALSO AT** *46–52 Fairfield Road, E3 2QB (0181 980 9000), 21 Greycaine Road, Watford, Herts WD3 4PS (01923 220339)*

FABRIC AFFAIR 🐷
ADDRESS 290 Battersea Park Road, SW11 3BT
TEL 0171 585 0125   **FAX** 0171 585 0475
Well-priced furnishing fabrics include their own brand, plus designer clearance lines from other leading makers. Prices from around £3.99 to £25 a metre. Also useful accessories, such as curtain rails, tie-backs, and hooks. Sofas, sofabeds, footstools, and chairs, made to order from four to six weeks.
RAIL *Battersea Park/Clapham Junction* • **OPEN** *Mon–Sat 10am–5pm*
• **SERVICES** *Curtains made and fitted in three weeks, including Roman and festoon blinds. Full design service. Parking bay for four cars in front of shop*

FABRIC WORLD 🐷
ADDRESS 6–10 Brighton Road, South Croydon, CR2 6AA
TEL 0181 688 6282   **FAX** 0181 680 0950
Well-established family business with clearance and discontinued designer fabrics at around £6 to £13 a metre (normal price, around £15 to £50 a metre). Customers flock from all over London; huge stocks (around 4000 to 6000 rolls at any one time).
RAIL *South Croydon/East Croydon* • **OPEN** *Mon–Sat 9am–5.30pm*
• **SERVICES** *Samples, plus mail order including postal cuttings* • **ALSO AT** *287–289 High Street, Sutton, Surrey SM1 1LL (0181 643 5127)*

GREAT LENGTHS
ADDRESS 72 Crouch End Hill, N8 8AG
TEL/FAX 0181 340 6600
Useful source of plain, striped and checked furnishing fabrics, plus coloured muslins and ginghams. Trimmings, plus poles and rails.
TUBE *Finsbury Park + W7 bus* • **OPEN** *Tues–Sat 11am–6pm. Sun 11am–4pm* • **SERVICES** *Curtain and blind making*

IAN MANKIN
ADDRESS 109 Regents Park Road, NW1 8UR
TEL 0171 722 0997   **FAX** 0171 722 2159
Ian Mankin transmuted simple ticking stripes into furnishing fashions in up-to-date colourways everyone can afford. Often copied but never outclassed. Good value plains, stripes and checks that don't date and last for years. 'We simply sell the best and the cheapest.' Butter muslin £1.85 a metre; Indian cotton from £11.80 a metre; ticking from £10 a metre;

gingham £3.25 a metre. Linen sheeting, 240 cm wide, £34 a metre; linen 140 cm, £18 a metre – both these are pure white.
TUBE *Chalk Farm* • **OPEN** *Mon–Fri 10am–5.30pm. Sat 10am–4pm*
• **SERVICES** *Free samples. Colour mail-order catalogue £3* • **ALSO AT**
271 Wandsworth Bridge Road, SW6 2TX (0171 371 8825)

JAVA COTTON CO
See LOOKS FROM ABROAD, page 62. Authentic Indonesian batik fabrics.

JOHN LEWIS
See UNDER ONE ROOF: DEPARTMENT STORES, page 14
I never buy fabrics until I've checked out this famous department store – nor does most of London, so allow time for choosing/measuring/cutting/paying. Masses of fabrics to take away – no tedious ordering from warehouses. Jonelle own-brand prints and weaves: good quality, and fine design at very reasonable prices in a vast well-displayed colour range. Lots of inspirational ideas for making-up. Fabrics marked Duracolour will be replaced if they fade. Curtaining, upholstery and loose-cover fabrics, plus own-brand coloured linings.

P N JONES TRADING 🐷
ADDRESS 18 Holly Grove, SE15 5DG
TEL/FAX 0171 639 2113
Karen Jones, whose great-grandfather imported silks, continues the family tradition with a warehouse packed with Indian natural-fibre fabrics at trade prices. Bargains include cheesecloths, Madras checks and stripes, voiles, heavy Masook cottons, and handwoven Noil silks. Gopi lightweight cotton for linings, plus cotton/silk mixtures and Dupion silk. But please phone and discuss what you need before visiting: they will send suitable cuttings. 'We're not geared up for casual browsing.'
RAIL *Peckham Rye* • **OPEN** *Mon–Thurs 2–4pm* • **SERVICES** *Samples/mail order*

JUST FABRICS ✉
ADDRESS The Bridewell, Dockacre Road, Launceston, Cornwall, PL15 8YY
TEL 01566 776279   **FAX** 01566 773239
Comprehensive showroom in the West Country with hundreds of fabrics is backed by popular mail order service. 'Can make soft furnishings for anywhere in Britain.' Top name fabrics and papers. Bargain prices for plain chintz and calicos. Also sheetings: polycottons and cottons, super percale. Plus linings, interlinings, tapes, piping cord, cushion pads, sheers. Ring for details/samples.
SERVICES *Making-up/quilting*

K A INTERNATIONAL
ADDRESS 68 Sloane Avenue, SW3 3DD
TEL 0171 584 7532   **FAX** 0171 589 9534
Spanish company, with a steadily-expanding range of home furnishings at reasonable prices for designer merchandise. Rolls of fabrics are colour-grouped in baskets – just pull one out and unravel to see how it looks. Good value double-width voiles. Plus upholstered furniture. Part of a growing network of 200 shops worldwide.
TUBE *South Kensington* • **OPEN** *Mon–Sat 10am–6pm. Late night Wed 7pm*
• **SERVICES** *Making-up service for blinds and curtains*

KNICKERBEAN FURNISHING FABRICS

ADDRESS 11 Holywell Hill, St Albans, Herts, AL1 1EZ
TEL 01727 866662 **FAX** 01727 866453

One of five shops spread around the country, offering excellent value in furnishing fabrics, accessories and making-up services. Well-known for bargain buys – often ends-of-range from well-known designers. Also import their own fabrics from leading houses in Europe and the USA. Literally hundreds of different fabrics, including printed voiles, loose natural cotton weaves, checks, stripes, damasks, trad chintz and heavyweight upholstery qualities. Everything in stock, ready to go – no tedious ordering. Prices range from £4.95 to £19.95 a metre.

RAIL *St Albans* • **OPEN** *Mon–Sat 9am–5.30pm* • **SERVICES** *Making-up for blinds, curtains, bedcovers and loose covers, with home visits to measure and advise 'however modest the project'*

LE SHOP

ADDRESS 229c Chiswick High Road, W4 2DW
TEL 0181 400 1433 **FAX** 0181 400 1434

The British have remained strangely ignorant of the benefits of double-width fabrics – less sewing and more cost-effective. This shop has bolt upon bolt of fabrics 280 cm wide (double-width). Around 200 rolls have been imported from the continental makers Stof and PTA, in plains and prints, naturals, neutrals and brights. Prices start at around £13.50 a metre. Using clips or other quick aids, you could get your windows screened in a day.

TUBE *Turnham Green* • **OPEN** *Mon–Sat 10am–6pm* • **SERVICES** *All soft-furnishings made to order, including curtains and loose covers. Re-upholstery*

MATERIALISTIC

ADDRESS Curtain Studio, 60 Hampton Road, Twickenham, Middx, TW2 5QB
TEL 0181 898 2212 **FAX** 0181 296 0715

Kay Wood and her husband have been running this endlessly helpful shop for 15 years. They'll sort out any problem from a small blind to a whole room. Around 100 rolls of furnishing fabrics in stock, with masses more to order. Lots of wallpaper books to browse through, too. Plus all tapes, tracks etc. for DIY, and they can fit tracks etc. 'at well below West End prices'. Furniture, carpets, wooden floors.

RAIL *Strawberry Hill* • **OPEN** *Mon–Sat 10am–5pm* • **SERVICES** *Curtain making, loose covers and all soft furnishings. Samples. Interior design advice* • **ALSO AT** *169B High Street, Hampton Hill, Middx TW12 1NL (0181 979 8425)*

NASSERI FABRICS

See LOOKS FROM ABROAD, page 58. Authentic African fabric designs.

NEW RAINBOW TEXTILES

See LOOKS FROM ABROAD, page 58. Best selection of Indian silks, cottons, prints and embroideries in London.

RUSSELL AND CHAPPLE

ADDRESS 23 Monmouth Street, WC2H 9DE
TEL 0171 836 7521 **FAX** 0171 497 0554

A busy shop catering mainly for artists and the theatrical trade – but the clever furnisher can use many of their fabrics to money-saving advantage.

Three qualities of natural hessian, 180 cm wide. Fourteen shades of dyed hessian, £2.64 a metre. Fine artists linen, £11.07 a metre,180 cm wide. Plus fire-retardant gauzes for filmy drapes, butter muslin, cotton duck, calico.
TUBE *Leicester Square/Covent Garden* • **OPEN** *Mon–Fri 8.30am–5pm. Sat 10am–5pm* • **SERVICES** *Samples, price list. Mail order*

THOMAS DARE

ADDRESS 341 King's Road, SW3 5ES
TEL 0171 351 7991 **FAX** 0171 351 4150
Mix-and-match is a doddle in this smart friendly shop. Exclusive fabrics hand-woven in pure cotton in India are shown in colour 'families', from tropical mango to New England navy, including earth tones and soft, appealing naturals. See immediately which plains, checks, plaids, stripes and spots work well together, and then choose trimmings dyed to match... ropes, braids, cords, tie-backs and tassels. Prices from £15 a metre.
TUBE *Sloane Square + 11, 19 or 22 bus* • **OPEN** *Mon–Fri 9.30am–5.30pm* • **SERVICES** *Buy by phone*

WARRIS VIANI

ADDRESS 85 Golborne Road, W10 5NL
TEL 0181 964 0069 **FAX** 0181 964 0019
A mix of dress and furnishing fabrics – beautiful unusual weaves in heavy cotton, wool and linen. Silk damasks, dupions, organzas, brocades; brushed cottons, woollen paisleys. Some are unusual 'limited editions' – bolts of one-off, often rare fabrics bought directly from mills in India, Thailand and Europe, at prices from around £15 to £85 a metre.
TUBE *Ladbroke Grove* • **OPEN** *Mon–Sat 10am–6pm*

WHALEYS ✉ 🐷

ADDRESS Harris Court, Great Horton, Bradford, West Yorks, BD7 4EQ
TEL 01274 567718 **FAX** 01274 521309
Heaps of undyed bargains, including white linen scrim, £5.58 a metre and natural brown 'loomstate' linen, 158 cm wide, £9.08 a metre. Plus silks, cottons, and jutes – 400 types in all, they say.
SERVICES *Free individual samples plus mail order. Full set of sample books, £19*

SOFT FURNISHING SHOPS AND SERVICES

Most big London stores will make up curtains if you buy the fabric from them. See UNDER ONE ROOF: DEPARTMENT STORES, page 13. For example Liberty of Regent Street have a two tier service – 'Over the Counter' or 'Measuring and Estimating Service'. The drawback is usually the waiting list, which can be four to six weeks. Prices will be quoted by the width. Having your curtains made by the shop from which you buy the fabric means you will get a better deal financially and usually better quality.

USEFUL CONTACTS

THOMAS FRENCH
TEL 0161 998 1811   **FAX** 0161 945 1123
An invaluable free guide to DIY curtain making from the Rufflette people.

THE ASSOCIATION OF MASTER UPHOLSTERERS
TEL 01633 215 454
Can recommend members for all soft-furnishing and upholstery services.
WEBSITE www.upholsterers.co.uk

DEANGUARD DRAPES

ADDRESS 62a–66a Choumert Road, SE15 4AX
TEL 0171 252 8264   **FAX** 0171 639 5653
These soft-furnishing experts (established for over 30 years) specialise
in 'fabricated walling' (tradespeak for covering walls in fabric) using
traditional methods with battens and interlining, with flat or pleated fabric.
RAIL Peckham Rye • **OPEN** Mon–Fri 9am–5.30pm

DEVON HOUSE INTERIORS

ADDRESS 3–4 Devon House, Hermon Hill, Wanstead, E11 2AW
TEL 0181 518 8112   **FAX** 0181 518 8093
Large triple-fronted showroom, over 35 years in the soft-furnishing business,
own workrooms. Full samples of fabrics and papers, plus lighting, furniture,
carpets and accessories.
TUBE Snaresbrook • **OPEN** Mon Tues Wed Fri Sat 9am–5.30pm. Closed
Thurs Sun • **SERVICES** full interior design service

DE WINTER

ADDRESS 223 Kensington Church Street, W8 7LX
TEL 0171 229 4949/1918   **FAX** 0171 221 5635
The De Winter family have been Kensington curtain-makers for over 50
years: they've sorted out furnishing problems all over the Royal Borough.
This is the quintessential family business, now run by Mr Howard Berger,
who is married to the original Mr and Mrs De Winter's daughter. All soft
furnishings are made on the premises from a simple blind to elaborate
swags and tails for more stately homes. They also supply carpets and
furniture. They're stacked to the ceiling with bales of fabric, all top makes,
with bargains in seconds (eg Sanderson) – 'never knowingly understocked!'
TUBE Notting Hill Gate • **OPEN** Mon–Fri 9am–6pm. Sat 9am–4.30pm
• **SERVICES** All soft furnishings and full interior design service. Your own
tapestries stretched and made into cushions/rugs – 'we've done around
20,000 over the past 12 years'. I've tried this service and it's terrific

THE FABRIC MERCHANT

ADDRESS 27 London Road, Twickenham, TW1 3SX
TEL 0181 744 9219   **FAX** 0181 296 9219
Alice Watts promises 'personal friendly service – for one roll of wallpaper
or the whole house.' See a huge selection of sample books plus decorative
accessories.
RAIL Twickenham • **OPEN** Mon Tues Thurs Fri Sat 10am–5.30pm. Closed
Wed Sun • **SERVICES** Measure, make, install all soft furnishings. Interior

design advice. Full interior design service charged at £45 an hour,
refundable against an order. Samples/deliveries

FIONA CAMPBELL

ADDRESS 259 New Kings Road, SW6 4RB
TEL 0171 731 3681 **FAX** 0171 736 7436
This reliable workroom has been established for over 30 years. In the well-stocked showroom you can get professional help on all aspects of curtain and carpet design, and see lots of examples of past work. They can supply fabrics, trimmings, wallpapers, blinds, and lamps. Plus all the necessary tracks and poles, along with selections of furniture and headboards.
TUBE *Parsons Green* • **OPEN** *Mon–Fri 9.30am–5.30pm. Sat 10am–4pm*
• **SERVICES** *Tracks and poles fitted*

THE FINAL CURTAIN COMPANY

TEL 0181 699 3626 **FAX** 0181 291 7937
Susan McMullen gives a new and imaginative twist to window dressing. She visits with natural fabric samples (cream, grey and black) which can be dyed to any colour or effect. Curtains can be hung anywhere in the country. She also has ideas for unusual poles and trimmings. Her fabrics also include a variety of linens, from linen velvet in 20 colours, £50 a metre to a heavy natural linen at £18 a metre, plus linen and jute trimmings.
SERVICES *Curtain-making from £20 a width*

INTERIORS

ADDRESS 454–458 Chiswick High Road, W4 5TT
TEL 0181 994 0073 **FAX** 0181 994 4144
Behind the traffic-stopping windows in Chiswick High Road – guaranteed to lift your spirits on the dreariest of days – is a soft-furnishing business that's been going for 20 years, building its reputation on colour and design. All leading fabric and wallcovering collections, with plenty of experienced advice to help ease painful decision-making. Plus specialist paints, stencils, unusual curtain poles, and a trend-setting carpet department. 'Whatever your style – sumptuous or minimalist, traditional or contemporary, we'll help.'
TUBE *Chiswick Park* • **OPEN** *Mon–Sat 9am–6pm. Late night Thurs 8pm*
• **SERVICES** *Home visits, curtain-making and track-fitting, re-upholstery, loose covers, interior design*

JUDY ST JOHNSON

ADDRESS 46 Markham Street, SW3 3NR
TEL 0171 352 2169 **FAX** 0171 352 7596
A friendly, personal service from a highly-experienced curtain maker who offers high-class, handmade designer curtains.
TUBE *South Kensington* • **OPEN** *By appointment only*

PAINE AND CO

ADDRESS 49–51 Barnsbury Street, Islington, N1 1TD
TEL 0171 607 1176 **FAX** 0171 609 6201
Melanie Paine is an innovative force in the world of curtain-making and has expressed her ideas in stimulating books on fabrics and soft furnishings. See an excellent and ever-changing selection of fabrics,

trimmings, wallpapers and paints, which express Melanie's ongoing passion for texture, pattern and colour. Discuss a complete design project or order a simple pair of curtains in a typically pared-down Paine style. Melanie is guaranteed to express the mood of the moment.

TUBE *Angel* • **OPEN** *Tues–Fri 10am–6pm. Sat 10am–3pm* • **SERVICES** *Complete design/architectural service, mainly for private houses. All soft furnishings made to measure*

PAM BALLARD DESIGNS

ADDRESS 5 Heathfield Court, Heathfield Terrace, W4 4LR
TEL/FAX 0181 995 4465
Pam Ballard, who has years of experience in the decorating trade, now runs an advisory service for soft furnishings. She will visit, measure and make up, and can supply all well-known makes of fabric.
OPEN *By appointment only*

PENBRICE INTERIORS

ADDRESS 63a Cricklewood Broadway, NW2 3JR
TEL 0181 450 6696   **FAX** 0181 452 6870
Come here for personal and enthusiastic service from Mrs Penny Dixon, who has a lifetime's experience in soft furnishings. Stuck for ideas? – then go through her style scrap-book brimming with window pictures. Her studio and workshop is full of designs from traditional to ultra-modern, and she'll show you all the latest samples. Furniture restoration. Poles and tracks.
RAIL *Cricklewood* • **OPEN** *By appointment only* • **SERVICES** *Full interior design service. Poles and tracks fitted*

PICKWICK PAPERS AND FABRICS

ADDRESS 6 Nelson Road, Greenwich, SE10 9JB
TEL 0181 858 1205   **FAX** 0181 858 5252
South of the River, Pickwick is flying the flag for quality and detail – 'We'll see a job right through to the end, personally'. This well-established company has well-trained staff who'll guide you through numerous fabric and paper pattern books, and then supervise your order as it passes through their on-site workrooms. They also stock Sanderson, Zoffany and Designers Guild paints.
RAIL *Greenwich* • **OPEN** *Mon Tues Wed Fri Sat 9.30am–5pm. Thurs 9.30am–3.30pm* • **SERVICES** *Curtain-making, fitting and measuring*

PORTOBELLO CURTAIN SHOP

ADDRESS 245 Portobello Road, W11 1LT
TEL/FAX 0171 221 4277
You can use fabric from this friendly shop, or bring in the material yourself, then they'll make up virtually any soft furnishings you can imagine. Because 'Service is the name of the game' they say.
TUBE *Ladbroke Grove* • **OPEN** *Mon–Sat 9.30am–5.30pm*

L POSNER CONTRACTS

ADDRESS 98 George Lane, South Woodford, E18 1AD
TEL 0181 530 4677 **FAX** 0181 530 2228
Established for 54 years, this small family business stocks samples from all
top makes of fabric. Curtains, blinds, tracks, poles, upholstery.
TUBE *South Woodford* • **OPEN** *Mon–Sat 9am–5.30pm* • **SERVICES** *Visit,
advise and estimate. Fit tracks and poles, make and hang curtains*

PRET A VIVRE ✉

ADDRESS 26 Bassett Road, W10 6JJ
TEL 0181 960 6111 **FAX** 0181 964 0123
Specialist mail order company for made-to-measure curtains and blinds.
Browse through their comprehensive brochure, then owner Jo Cassabois
and her staff will talk you through every step of ordering by telephone –
from how to measure windows, to putting your curtains up. They have a
wide selection of fabrics to suit all budgets including cotton plains in good
colours, printed voiles, and fashionable prints, linens, checks and silks.
Voile shower curtains can be lined with plastic. Fabric range is continually
updated – finished product ready in three weeks.
WEBSITE *www.pretavivre.com* • **SERVICES** *Made-to-measure curtains, blinds,
pelmets, valances, swags, tails, bedcovers, shower curtains, poles and
tracks; fabric by the metre. Colour catalogue. Samples. Measuring and
installation if required* • **ALSO AT** *(Showroom) Grove House, 320 Kensal
Road, W10, by appointment only*

RUFFLE & HOOK

ADDRESS 34 ½ Florence Street, Islington, N1
TEL 0171 226 0370 **FAX** 0171 226 5285
Unusual combinations of fabrics and trimmings create a unique yet
affordable style. That's the philosophy behind this innovative window
dressing shop, where hessian could be lined with taffeta and tied back
with coloured rope. See ideas galore for fabrics, poles, finials, rings,
tapes. Smooth ratchet-free roll-up blinds in silks and taffetas are a speciality.
TUBE *Highbury & Islington* • **OPEN** *Mon–Fri 10am–5.30pm. Sat 10am–
4.30pm* • **SERVICES** *Curtain and blind-making* • **ALSO AT** *122–124 St John
Street, EC1 (0171 490 4321)*

TAYLOR AND MARR

ADDRESS 60 White Hart Lane, SW13 0PZ
TEL 0181 878 1984 **FAX** 0181 876 1279
This busy workroom has just celebrated 50 years in business. Good
selection of samples for fabrics, papers and carpets – and they pride
themselves on excellence of their fitters. All curtain-making and re-
upholstery. They make up headboards and blinds; supply beds and sofas.
RAIL *Barnes Bridge* • **OPEN** *Mon–Fri 9.30am–5.30pm* • **SERVICES**
All interior design/soft-furnishing services

READY-MADE AND SECOND-HAND CURTAINS

For those who just can't wait, the good news is a vast improvement in selections, thanks to clever tab tops and loop tops, and smart pencil-pleat tapes. Width is easier to adjust than length these days but it's acceptable – fashionable even – for curtains to trail the floor. Second-hand curtains are a growing option thanks to shops that now specialise in their re-sale.

THE CURTAIN EXCHANGE

ADDRESS 129–133 Stephendale Road, Fulham, SW6 2PG
TEL 0171 731 8316 **FAX** 0171 610 6844
Wall-to-wall curtains, in a warren of interconnecting rooms and passages. From informal gathers through to classic French pleats, on to ornate swags and tails. Often pelmets or valances and tie-backs are included in the deal. Most curtains are lined, and many interlined. Prices from £30 to £1000; average spend is around £300. Good fabrics: Sanderson, Colefax, Warners, J P & J Baker, Designers Guild and their ilk. Stock comes from private sellers; uncollected or wrongly-made professional orders; from showhouses and from re-furbished hotels; 'Many people actually prefer the softer look of old fabrics,' says director Susie Maynard. 'They blend in better with traditional interiors, and are particularly sympathetic with antiques.'
TUBE *Fulham Broadway* • **OPEN** *Mon–Sat 10am–5pm* • **SERVICES** *Dry-cleaning. Alterations. Track-fitting* • **ALSO AT** *56 Ledbury Road, W11 2AB (0171 229 4923). 80 Park Hall Road, SE21 8BW (0181 670 5570)*

THE CURTAIN SHOP

ADDRESS 54 Abbey Gardens, St John's Wood, NW8 9AT
TEL/FAX 0171 372 1044
Jackie Horsford (interior decorator and furniture restorer) was the lady who first had the second-hand curtain brain-wave. She has around 100 pairs of good-quality second-hand curtains, from around £100 to £600 a pair. Also a budget made-to-measure curtain service, in an exclusive range of plain fabrics (or bring your own), and five curtain styles. Plus decorative accessories.
TUBE *Maida Vale/St John's Wood* • **OPEN** *Tues–Sat 10am–5pm* • **SERVICES** *Alterations. Curtain making – takes up to three weeks*

CURTAIN TRADING CENTRE

ADDRESS 24 Baker Street, W1M 1DF
TEL 0171 224 2006
Good stocks of second-hand curtains, mostly interlined and made from designer fabrics. Plus roller, Austrian and Roman blinds, bedspreads, covered headboards, cushions and tie-backs.
TUBE *Baker Street/Marble Arch* • **OPEN** *Mon–Sat 10am–6pm* • **SERVICES** *Curtain alterations*

THE FUTON COMPANY

See BEDROOMS AND BEDS: FUTONS, WATERBEDS AND BEDS FOR BAD BACKS page 145. Sumptuous velvets, and pretty voiles in ready-mades – excellent for instant furnishing.

HABITAT

See UNDER ONE ROOF: FURNISHING SPECIALISTS, page 11. They have shelves stashed high with loop-headed and eyelet-top curtains in neutral fabrics in various weights/textures, ready for immediate hanging. Plus filmy coloured voiles.

IKEA

See UNDER ONE ROOF: FURNISHING SPECIALISTS, page 11. Good choice of well-priced ready-mades.

JOHN LEWIS

See UNDER ONE ROOF: DEPARTMENT STORES, page 14. Large department with plain and patterned ready-mades in big selection of widths/drops.

THE LONDON CURTAIN AGENCY

ADDRESS 298 Sandycombe Road, Kew, TW9 3NG
TEL 0181 940 5959   **FAX** 0181 977 4415
Hundreds of pairs of second-hand curtains. Also general curtain-making service, with fabric swatches. Or will make curtains from your own fabric.
TUBE/RAIL *Kew Gardens* • **OPEN** *Tues–Fri 10am–4pm. Sat 10am–5pm*
• **SERVICES** *Alterations. Curtain making*

CURTAIN TRIMMINGS, TRACKS AND POLES

ARTISAN ✉

ADDRESS Unit 4A, Union Court, 20 Union Road, SW4 6JP
TEL 0171 498 6974   **FAX** 0171 498 2989
Mail-order service for innovative range of iron curtain poles with fashionable finials in iron, wire, glass, or wood. Plus hooks and portiere rods.
TUBE *Stockwell* • **SERVICES** *Inspirational catalogue. Showroom open by appointment*

BYRON AND BYRON

ADDRESS 2–4 Thane Works, Thane Villas, N7 7NU
TEL 0171 700 0404   **FAX** 0171 700 4111
Chunky poles with wonderful wooden finials: fleur-de-lys, arrow heads and tails, stately home designs. Plus colourful modern ranges.
TUBE *Finsbury Park* • **OPEN** *Mon–Fri 9am–1pm; 2pm–5.30pm*

MCKINNEY & CO

ADDRESS Studio P, The Old Imperial Laundry, 71 Warriner Gardens, SW11 4XW
TEL 0171 627 5077 **FAX** 0171 627 5088
London's most original poles and finials in wood, glass, brass and other
metals, and resin plus a leather collection of poles, finials, rings, tie-backs,
pelmets and leather fringing. Also large selections of antique curtain
fittings. Special poles made for bay windows. Pelmets and coronas
in wood, gilt or painted finishes.
RAIL *Battersea Park* • **OPEN** *Mon–Fri 10am–5pm*

V V ROULEAUX

ADDRESS 54 Sloane Square, SW1W 8AX
TEL 0171 730 3125 **FAX** 0171 730 3468
'Ribbons aren't just for tying hair,' declared Annabel Lewis back in 1990.
She built a successful business to prove her point, writing a book along the
way. Ribbons are for tying parcels, decorating trees, trimming sheets,
curtains, and tablecloths, making tie-backs and so on and so forth. You'll
find literally thousands to choose from in this busy shop, starting with fun
paper ribbons at 28p a metre, and going up to antique ribbons at £85 a
metre. In between, there's organdie, wire-edged, velvet, and grosgrain,
with collections based on antique originals. Fresh and up-to-date are the
linen bands, some with embroidered patterns. Real rabbit fur makes a
cosy edging, with fake fur trims for the faint-hearted. Lots of lavish feather
edgings, too. Find also cords, braids, and fringes, including chenille
bullion (a wide heavy fringe) in fun shades. Plus exotic tassels. 'The most
extensive collection in Europe,' says Annabel proudly.
TUBE *Sloane Square* • **OPEN** *Mon–Sat 9.30am–6pm. Late night Wed
6.30pm* • **SERVICES** *Samples and mail order*

TEMPTATION ALLEY

ADDRESS 359–361 Portobello Road, W10 5SA
TEL 0181 964 2004 **FAX** 0171 727 4432
Here's a corner shop filled with trimmings of every description, from
fringes, feathers, ribbons and tassels to buttons, beads and bows.
Everybody pops in, from theatre designers to dressmakers, from craft
teachers to decorators. And – tucked away somewhere – Sam Sawdon
has just what they need. And if you're lucky, you may catch some bargains
on his wife's Saturday morning Portobello Market stall.
TUBE *Ladbroke Grove* • **OPEN** *Mon–Fri 10am–5.30pm. Sat 9.30am–5.30pm*

WENDY CUSHING TRIMMINGS

ADDRESS G7 Chelsea Harbour Design Centre, Lots Road, SW10 0XE
TEL 0171 351 5796 **FAX** 0171 351 4246
Passementerie is the posh word for curtain trimmings, and here you'll find
it *partout*. Wendy Cushing is queen of the genre. She bought an old
factory in 1983 and revived many traditional techniques. In this little
showroom, luxuriate in an abundance of braids, fringing, tassels, ropes,
tie-backs and rosettes. Historical ranges for the period look, or an
increasingly adventurous selection of modern modes – brilliant colours
and natural neutrals, animal prints, and glass beads.
TUBE *Earls Court + C3 bus/Sloane Square + 11, 22 bus* • **OPEN** *Mon–Fri
10am–5pm* • **SERVICES** *Trimmings made to special order*

BLINDS AND AWNINGS

*'Mr Pritchard: I must dust the blinds and then I must raise them.
Mrs Pritchard: And before you let the sun in, mind it wipes its shoes.'*
Dylan Thomas (1914–1953), Under Milk Wood

CITY BLINDS
ADDRESS 273 Hackney Road, E2 8NA
TEL 0171 739 6206   **FAX** 0171 256 0415
Londoners flock here for off-the-peg wood venetians, in pecan, pine or
walnut with a 50 mm or fashionbly narrow 25 mm slat in a wide range of
sizes, from £30. They have huge stocks, and most people find something
suitable to take away and put up themselves. Reeded Pinoleum blinds are
also very popular. Other types of blinds include rollers, verticals, venetians,
and micro venetians with narrow slats.
TUBE *Bethnal Green/Liverpool Street* • **OPEN** *Mon–Fri 9.30am–5.30pm.
Sat 10am–5pm. Sun 10am–2pm* • **SERVICES** *Measuring and fitting available*

DEANS BLINDS AND AWNINGS
ADDRESS Unit 4, Haslemere Industrial Estate, Ravensbury Terrace,
Earlsfield, SW18 4SE
TEL 0181 947 8931   **FAX** 0181 947 8336
This company is one of London's oldest awning and blind makers. The
familiar curvy segmented external blind you see outside restaurants and
shops is a Dutch canopy. However, for homes, flat awnings are more
popular, projecting at an angle from the wall to shade a patio and shield a
room. Prices start from around £300. Orders take from four to six weeks.
Their first awning was in South London in 1894 for a Victorian lady who
wanted to stay fashionably pale whilst embroidering outside her parlour.
They also do all kinds of other blinds, including rollers and blackouts.
RAIL *Earlsfield* • **OPEN** *Mon–Fri 9am–5pm* • **SERVICES** *Measure, make, install*

FLAMINGO BLINDS AND FABRICS
ADDRESS 2 Chaseville Park Parade, Winchmore Hill, N21 1PG
TEL 0181 364 1902   **FAX** 0181 245 8323
Soft-furnishing specialist established for nearly 20 years – extensive
range of blinds and curtain poles, with a good selection of fabrics and
wallpapers. Supplies and installs canopies, awnings and conservatory blinds.
TUBE *Oakwood/Southgate* • **OPEN** *Mon–Fri 9am–5.30pm. Sat 9.30am–5pm*
• **SERVICES** *Measure, make, install all types of blinds and curtains*

PUTNEY BLINDS
ADDRESS 4 Thornsett Road, SW18 4EN
TEL 0181 874 6001/3127   **FAX** 0181 874 6229
Traditional specialist manufacturers of all types of awnings, exterior blinds
and canopies. Also rollers, venetians, vertical louvres and blackouts.
Factory prices.
RAIL *Earlsfield* • **OPEN** *Representative will call by appointment*
• **SERVICES** *Measure, make, install*

SHADES BEAUTIFUL BLINDS
ADDRESS 2b Chingford Road, Bell Corner, Walthamstow, E17 4PJ
TEL 0181 527 3991   **FAX** 0181 523 4476
A wide choice of blinds is available from this well-established specialist,
including roller blinds (stiffened lace is particularly pretty), venetians
(including wood), verticals, pleated romans, and cane. They can add
a pelmet if you wish. They can also make conservatory blinds, in your
material or theirs.
RAIL *Walthamstow Central* • **OPEN** *Mon–Sat 9.30am–5pm*

THOMAS SANDERSON
CONSERVATORY BLINDS ✉
ADDRESS Sanderson Buildings, Waterbury Drive, Waterlooville,
Hants, PO2 7XN
TEL 01705 232600   **FAX** 01705 232700
This family-owned firm say they are the world's biggest supplier of custom-
made conservatory blinds. They have a huge range of special fabrics that
cut heat and reduce glare. They supply virtually every major conservatory
company.
WEBSITE *www.thomas-sanderson.co.uk* • **SERVICES** *Nationwide installations.
Freephone 0800 220603*

TIDMARSH AND SONS ✉
ADDRESS 32 Hideway, Welling Garden City, AL7 3AW
TEL 01707 886226   **FAX** 01707 886227
Here are the blinds with the Royal Warrant. Established since 1828, until
recently this company was in Islington. Traditionally, it's THE place for
wood venetians, though many other companies have now taken up this
idea. Their 'Timbershade' has 17 colours and grain effects. 'Chain lathe'
blinds are for skylights and conservatories. Sophisticated electrical controls
are available. Phone for leaflet and samples.
OPEN *Mon–Fri 9am–5.30pm* • **SERVICES** *Mail order. Measure, make, install*

ANTIQUE TEXTILES

ANDREW BEWICK
ADDRESS 287 Lillie Road, SW6 7LL
TEL 0171 385 9025
The old quilts and bedhangings in this shop are mainly from the North of
England. 'Modern printing techniques just can't copy the vegetable dyes of
old designs,' says Andrew Bewick. 'And patchwork is very labour-intensive
– people haven't the time today.' His quilts illustrate various techniques from
whole cloth (all one piece of fabric) to strip work, medallions, appliqué
and quilting. They have a mellow much-loved feeling and cost from around
£150. Also antique furniture – 'as unrestored as possible, in sympathy with
the fabrics.'
TUBE *Barons Court/West Brompton* • **OPEN** *Mon–Sat 10.30am–5.30pm*

CLASSIC FABRICS

ADDRESS 37 Bourbon Hanby, The Chelsea Courtyard,
151 Sydney Street, SW3 6NT
TEL/FAX 0171 349 9110

Antique fabric dealer Robin Haydock is known for meticulous and scholarly attention to detail. He collects mainly 18th-century fabrics for his shop from all over Europe and the Middle East – rich pieces of silk, embroidery and needlepoint, with the provenance lovingly explained. Antique backing fabrics and trimmings – for example, 18th-century gold and silver braids – are used for cushions, from £28 to £1500 a pair – average spend on a cushion is £300. Says Haydock: 'I think the thrill is having something so completely unique – it's like having an old oil painting. These fabrics were made by hand and with great imagination. They bring personality into a room.'

TUBE *Sloane Square* • **OPEN** *Mon–Sat 11am–6pm. Sun 11am–5pm*

GALLERY OF ANTIQUE COSTUME AND TEXTILES

ADDRESS 2 Church Street, NW8 8ED
TEL/FAX 0171 723 9981

A friendly attitude towards browsing – so wander at will around the muffled depths of this delightful shop. The walls are swathed in antique fabrics (mostly pre-1920) which can usually be taken on approval. They have cushions, curtains, pelmets, tapestries, hangings, and quilts. Also very special clothing and costumes (mostly pre-1940).

TUBE *Marylebone* • **OPEN** *Mon–Sat 10am–5.30pm*

JANE SACCHI

ADDRESS 7 Markham Street, SW3 3NP
TEL 0171 589 5643   **FAX** 0171 581 3564

Several times a year, Jane Sacchi takes her big Volvo over to France and loads it up with fabrics gleaned from *brocantes* (French antique shops) and other zealously discovered – and jealously guarded – sources. Her finds include old sheets in heavy hemp or unbleached linen (from £55) which make marvellous instant curtains – put them up with curtain clips, turning over the top as necessary to adjust the length. Fragments of ancient toiles and other prints, bits of ticking and old pattern books are rescued, and transformed into cushion covers (some with monograms) which sell from around £48, and look marvellous massed into a heap on sofa or bed.

TUBE *Sloane Square* • **OPEN** *Strictly by appointment* • **WEBSITE** *www.janesacchi.com* • **SERVICES** *Wedding gifts*

LUNN ANTIQUES

ADDRESS 86 New Kings Road, SW6 4LU
TEL 0171 736 4638   **FAX** 0171 371 7113

'We're just a sea of lace', enthuses Stephen Lunn, who has run this delightful boutique with his wife Anne since 1976. They have all types of old lace. Single linen antique sheets cost from around £25; linen damask tablecloths from £20 to £150. A good pair of old double linen sheets costs £150. They also do reproduction designs.

TUBE *Parsons Green* • **OPEN** *Mon–Sat 10am–6pm* • **SERVICES** *Laundry and restoration service for old lace*

PAVILION TEXTILES ✉

ADDRESS Freshford Hall, Freshford, Bath, BA3 6EJ
TEL/FAX 01225 722 522
Elizabeth Baer has a stash of antique linens, with rough textured sheets
from £50. Plus French mattress tickings, bedhangings and old curtains,
trimmings and period haberdashery, and much more. A vast stock, all
waiting for cunning transformation into curtains, cushions and so on.
Send for her brochure.
OPEN *By appointment*

PETA SMYTH ANTIQUE TEXTILES

ADDRESS 42 Moreton Street, SW1V 2PB
TEL 0171 630 9898   **FAX** 0171 630 5398
Old velvets, tapestries, silks, and damasks made into cushions, hangings,
curtains and trimmings 'for that lived-in look.'
TUBE *Pimlico* • **OPEN** *Mon–Fri 9.30am–5.30pm*

DECORATING AND RE-FURBISHING

- **DIY superstores** *page 88*
- **General decorating suppliers** *page 90*
- **Wallpaper specialists** *page 92*
- **Paint specialists** *page 95*
- **Specialist decorating suppliers** *page 97*
- **Specialist painting and decorating services** *page 101*
- **Plaster mouldings and restorations** *page 103*
- **Wooden mouldings and panelling** *page 104*
- **Unusual materials** *page 105*

'I will make a palace fit for you and me
Of green days in forest and blue days at sea.'
Robert Louis Stevenson (1850–1894)

DIY SUPERSTORES

B & Q

TEL 0181 466 4166 for nearest store
B & Q Supercentres stock 15,000 DIY and garden products, including
kitchens and bathrooms. B & Q Warehouses have 40,000 lines, and a
much wider range of heavy building products – 'everything you need to
build a house and decorate it.'

STAR STORE
ADDRESS 1 Dearsley Road, Enfield, Middx, EN1 3FF
TEL 0181 366 0366
OPEN *Mon–Sat 7am–9pm. Sun 10am–4pm* • **WEBSITE** *www.diy.co.uk*
• **SERVICES** *Timber cutting, paint mixing. Advice from trade experts: interior designers, horticulturists, plumbers, electricians, builders, decorators, joiners. Kitchen and bathroom design service, with home visits. Installation service, with two-year guarantee. 20-year guarantee for kitchens. Regular project demos – for example fitting a smoke detector, laying laminate flooring, coving, paint effects, and tiling. Cafe. Free delivery for goods over £250. Van hire for taking home heavy goods* • **ALSO AT** *(nearest stores to central London) Gunnersbury Avenue, W4 (0181 995 8028). 524 Old Kent Road, SE1 (0171 252 0657). Smugglers Way, Wandsworth, SW18 (0181 875 1099)*

FOCUS DO IT ALL

TEL 0800 436436 for nearest store
Do It All, now part of the Focus Group, stock some 20,000 products for DIY, decoration and home improvement, gardening, kitchens and bathrooms. Many products are exclusive or own-brand. All staff are well-trained.

STAR STORE
ADDRESS Unit 4, Staples Retail Park, Edgware Road, NW2 6LW
TEL 0181 208 4588
OPEN *Mon–Sat 9am–8pm. Sun 10am–4pm* • **TUBE** *Kilburn* • **SERVICES** *Deliveries free over purchases of £100. Free paint-mixing. Free timber and board-cutting. Free 'How To' leaflets. In-store demos by DIY experts on request. 10 per cent discount for pensioners on Fridays* • **ALSO AT** *89 South Ealing Road, W5 4QS (0181 840 0669). 52 Capitol Industrial Park, Edgware Road, Kingsbury, NW9 0EQ (0181 205 6066). 1 Gallions Road, off Woolwich Road, SE7 7SA (0181 858 3212)*

HOMEBASE

TEL 0645 801 800 for nearest store
Very good for indoor and outdoor plants and horticultural accessories, plus massive range of pots, both glazed and terracotta. Electrical and hand tools. Shelving and well-designed storage (autumn is best season for this). Lighting and security. Cookshop – in selected stores. Building materials. Decorative products – particularly strong in paint, with several specialist range, including Farrow & Ball, and Casa Mediterranean range. Historic dead flat matt paint. Some stores stock Jane Churchill and Designers Guild paint. Bathrooms and accessories – 25-year guarantee on some bathroom suites. Good for Christmas trees and decorations (in season), and for garden furniture and accessories (in season). Blinds and curtain accessories, with textile shops in selected stores. Laura Ashley boutiques in many stores. Gift wrapping service at Christmas and for Mother's Day. Free 'How To' leaflets, with around 50 titles.

STAR STORE
ADDRESS 255 Finchley Road, NW3 6LU
TEL 0171 435 3457 **FAX** 0171 433 3270
OPEN *Mon–Sat 8am–9pm. Sun 11am–5pm* **WEBSITE** *www.homebase.co.uk*
• **SERVICES** *Made-to-measure curtains. Free timber cutting. Glass cutting.*

*Customer advice on power tool selection and use. Dulux interior design service. Paint mixing. Cookshop. In-store demos. Garden design. Bathroom installations. Free delivery for bulky items. Special order desk for nearly 5,000 extra lines • **ALSO AT** (nearest store to central London) 195 Warwick Road, Kensington* W14 8PU *(0171 602 5125)*

WICKES BUILDING SUPPLIES
TEL 0500 300 328 for nearest store
Extensive selection of competitively-priced building materials – over 90 per cent of products are own-brand. Everything for home improvements – kitchens, bedrooms, bathrooms, conservatories, doors and windows, timber and sheet materials, showers, paint, wallcoverings, fencing, gates and so on.

STAR STORE
ADDRESS 53 Plough Lane, Wimbledon, SW17 0BW
TEL 0181 947 9818 **FAX** 0181 947 9819
OPEN *Mon–Sat 7.30am–8pm. Sun 10am–4pm* • **SERVICES** *Free computer-aided design for kitchens, bedrooms, and conservatories, with home visits if necessary. Free deliveries for goods over £200. Free 'Good Idea' leaflets and Project Guides. Paint mixing. Help with colour schemes and paint effects. Building advisor for practical home improvement advice and technical queries* • **ALSO AT** *734–736 Seven Sisters Road,* N15 5NL *(0181 800 9966). 317 Cricklewood Broadway,* NW2 6JN *(0181 450 9025). Quill Street, Hanger Lane, Ealing* W5 1DP *(0181 810 6793)*

GENERAL DECORATING SUPPLIERS

At first sight the big 'sheds' may seem cheaper – especially for large quantities of white paint. However you may not get the same covering power as a quality paint, so you'll need more and the job will take longer. And the 'sheds' are not automatically cheaper for all the 'sundries' – filling knives, brushes, fillers and so on. It could be worth making friends with one of London's many big decorating merchants, who although busy supplying 'the trade' are always remarkably willing to help the amateur painting punter, and spend hours dispensing knowledge of products and skills. Lookout for the 🐷 tag.

ASKEW PAINT CENTRE
ADDRESS 103 Askew Road, W12 9AS
TEL 0181 743 6612 **FAX** 0181 746 2368
Helpful and knowledgable staff. This small and lively shop has recently been refitted, and has a large and useful range of paint mixing machines, backed by some small specialist ranges.
TUBE *Stamford Brook + 266 bus* • **OPEN** *Mon–Fri 7am–5pm. Sat 7.30am–1pm*

DIRECT BARGAIN CENTRE 🐷

ADDRESS 69–79 Mile End Road, E1 4TT
TEL/FAX 0171 790 1094
Constantly changing stock. Decorating materials usually include: paint,
wall coverings, ceramic tiles etc. Also large range of carpets and furniture
TUBE *Stepney Green* • **OPEN** *Mon–Fri 9am–6pm. Sun 10am–4pm.
Early closing in winter on Fri at 3pm*

LEYLAND

ADDRESS 371–373 Edgware Road, W2
TEL 0171 723 8048
Own-brand paints, good colours. Wallpaper discounts: up to 35 per cent
off. Cut-price Bosch power tools. Very good selection of specialist products
including Craig and Rose varnishes, Liberon waxes and polishes, Le Franc
artists' oil colours. 'Probably the best paint shop for miles and miles!'
TUBE *Edgware Road* • **OPEN** *Mon–Fri 7am–7pm. Sat 7am–6pm. Sun
9am–3pm* • **SERVICES** *Computerised paint mixing: over 4000 colours*
• **ALSO AT** *9 branches across London*

LOMAX WALLPAPERS AND PAINTS 🐷

ADDRESS 283–285 New North Road, Islington, N1 7AA
TEL 0171 226 1516/2569   **FAX** 0171 226 1516
Good paint prices for Leyland, Dulux etc. Large shop with 2500 wallpapers
in stock, some discounted up to 50 per cent. Enormous pattern book bar.
Free paste on all wallpaper sales over one roll; refunds on unused stock rolls.
Friendly, knowledgeable advice from family business trading for over 25
years. Ceramic tile showroom. Marble inserts for fire surrounds (cut to size).
TUBE *Essex Road/Highbury & Islington* • **OPEN** *Mon–Fri 8am–5.30pm.
Fri 8am–6pm. Sat 8.30am–5.30pm* • **SERVICES** *Curtain-making and blinds*

LORDS TRADE AND DIY

ADDRESS 119–121 Westbourne Grove, W2 4UP
TEL 0171 221 4756   **FAX** 0171 792 9513
Good stocks and helpful assistants at this traditional DIY plumbing and
paint shop.
TUBE *Bayswater/Queensway* • **OPEN** *Mon–Fri 8am–6.30pm.
Sat 9am–6.30pm*

MYLANDS

ADDRESS 80 Norwood High Street, West Norwood, SE27 9NW
TEL 0181 670 9161   **FAX** 0181 761 5700
Good stocks, leading brands, and some specialist ranges at reliable
old-fashioned shop with expert help and attentive service.
RAIL *West Norwood* • **OPEN** *Mon–Fri 9am–1pm; 1.30pm–4.45pm*

S AND S HOME SUPPLIES

ADDRESS 389–391 Honeypot Lane, Stanmore, Middlesex, HA7 1JJ
TEL 0181 905 0667   **FAX** 0181 905 0776
Good range of all leading paints, plus smaller interesting ranges, at this
large shop with enthusiastic staff.
TUBE *Stanmore* • **OPEN** *Mon–Fri 8am–6pm. Sat 8.30am–5pm* • **ALSO AT**
16–18 Hayle Lane, Mill Hill NW7 3NX (0181 201 0281)

SIMPSONS PAINTS
ADDRESS 122–124 Broadley Street, NW8 8BB
TEL 0171 723 3762 **FAX** 0171 706 4662
When this old family business started in 1815, paint was mixed by
'colourmen' with a bucket of this and pinch of that. Now computers control
mixing machines for nearly 2,000 shades from the Dulux Colour Palette
(£12.50 for 2.5 litres of vinyl matt). They also have Sanderson machines
and are distributors for Farrow & Ball's National Trust range. Inspirational
selection of paints and varnishes for decorator effects including water-
based 'scumbles', frosting varnish, and Craquelure. A new American
primer enables you to paint over tiles or old melamine kitchen cabinets.
Plus wallpapers, decorative mouldings and ceiling roses. Radiator covers
made to measure, or buy decorative panels to make your own. Most items
in stock, or within 24 hours (except radiator covers).
TUBE *Edgware Road* • **OPEN** *Mon–Fri 7.30am–5.30pm. Sat 7.30am–4pm*
• **SERVICES** *Deliveries in London area; can recommend decorators. Parking
bay outside shop*

WALLPAPER SPECIALISTS

You should also refer to FABRICS AND SOFT FURNISHINGS: FABRIC
MANUFACTURERS WITH SHOWROOM SHOPS, page 66, as many of these
big 'fabric houses' are strong in wallpaper, too. If money's an object,
watch out for the MONEY SAVER tag. You will also find wallpaper books
heaped high in the INTERIOR DESIGN specialists, page 16.

USEFUL CONTACTS

DULUX SELECT DECORATOR SERVICE
TEL 0345 697668
Will recommended painters and paperers.

THE VICTORIAN SOCIETY
ADDRESS 1 Priory Gardens, Bedford Park, London, W4 1TT
TEL 0181 994 1019 **FAX** 0181 995 4895
Helpful A4 colour leaflet on restoring/replacing Victorian wallcoverings,
price £3.00.

BAER AND INGRAM WALLPAPERS
ADDRESS 273 Wandsworth Bridge Road, SW6 2TX
TEL 0171 736 6111 **FAX** 0171 736 8581
This is my favourite wallpaper shop. It's small but perfectly stocked, with
endless friendly service. Specialist suppliers of traditional and hand-printed
papers. Toile de Jouy is their forte, with their own exclusive designs: six
toile papers (£22.50 a roll), plus checked co-ordinates and matching
fabrics – blue is by far the favourite, says Caroline Ingram. Also exclusive
stocks of Wallace and Gromit papers and borders. Hundreds of pattern
books. Damasks, moires, stripes, flowers, special effects.
TUBE *Fulham Broadway* • **OPEN** *Mon–Fri 10am–5.30pm.
Sat 10.30am–4.30pm*

BELLEVUE INTERIORS

ADDRESS 1 Bellevue Parade, Bellevue Road, SW17 7EQ
TEL 0181 767 6659　**FAX** 0181 682 4055
Extensive wallpaper and fabric selections. Specialises in children's ranges.
Good paint selections: Sanderson Spectrum and Dulux Colour Palette
paint mixing.
TUBE *Tooting Bec* • **OPEN** *Mon–Sat 8.30am–5.30pm*
• **SERVICES** *Curtain-making with instant computerised quotes*

CATH KIDSTON

See FABRICS AND SOFT FURNISHINGS: FABRIC SHOPS, page 73
Brilliant selection of 'rescued' wallpaper designs, including candy stripes,
blowsy rose bouquet floral, muted Sussex Rose, sophisticated Fernleaf, and
go anywhere Spot. From £17.50 to £23.50 a roll. Matching lampshades
(to order) and A4 box files make pretty accessories/presents.

DAVE'S DIY 🐷

ADDRESS 294–296 Firs Lane, Palmers Green, N13 5QQ
TEL 0181 807 3539　**FAX** 0181 803 3818
Friendly family business providing quality wallpapers at discount prices
(400 books). 40 per cent off thousands of stock designs. 50 per cent off
12 rolls of the same design and Anaglyptas (embossed wallpapers).
Dulux computerised paint-mixing machines.
RAIL *Winchmore Hill* • **OPEN** *Mon–Wed 8.30am–5pm. Thurs Sat
8.30am–1pm. Fri 8.30am–8pm*

HAMILTON WESTON

ADDRESS 18 St Mary's Grove, Richmond, Surrey, TW9 1UY
TEL 0181 940 4850　**FAX** 0181 332 0296
Those bulky layers of wallpaper so dreaded by amateur decorators thrill
building conservator Robert Weston. ('My record was 22'). Carefully peeled
apart, they're the fragile base for delightful period paper copies, and have
starred on the small and large screen in numerous period revivals. He and
his wife Georgina patiently share with customers their inexhaustible fount of
specialist knowledge on period homes. Their own collections of 18th- and
19th-century document papers are taken from London townhouses. Their
restored Victorian corner shop also sells period fabric, plus compatible
papers and borders from other suppliers, and historical paint. Friendly and
accessible: required visiting for the dedicated home restorer.
TUBE/RAIL *Richmond* • **OPEN** *Mon–Fri 9.30am–6pm. Sat 10am–4pm*
• **SERVICES** *Scholarly period advice. Reference books/leaflets. Curtain-
making/upholstery. Copying of clients' own designs. Lists of craftsmen*

JOHN OLIVER

See DECORATING AND REFURBISHING: PAINT SPECIALISTS, page 97
Well-known for unusual selections of wallpaper, with books from all over
the world. Special effects include ceramic chips, glitter, seagrass, silk
strands and so on. Still have famous large-scale designs from the sixties –
these have to be hand-painted with a nine-roll minimum order design.
SERVICES *Can paper-back fabrics for use as wallpaper (some are not suitable,
so discuss this with the shop). Can turn images such as monograms, logos
etc into wallpaper designs*

OTTILIE STEVENSON
ADDRESS 4 Charlotte Road, EC2A 3DH
TEL 0171 739 7321   **FAX** 0171 739 7371
Designer showroom for eminently usable modern wallpapers in soft
contemporary colours which nevertheless evoke *le temps perdu* – floral
sprigs, trailing florals, sprays of roses. There are matching fabrics.
All papers are £20.50 a roll. A new paint collection completes the
decorating palette and includes gold and silver.
TUBE *Old Street* • **OPEN** *Mon–Fri 9am–5.30pm*

PAINT LIBRARY
See DECORATING AND REFURBISHING: PAINT SPECIALISTS, page 97.
Subtle, of-the-moment range of wallpapers by decorator Emily Todhunter in
chic chocolates and bland beige.

PAPER MOON
ADDRESS 53 Fairfax Road, NW6 4EL
TEL 0171 624 1198   **FAX** 0171 372 5659
Specialists in exclusive USA and Canadian designs – always something a
bit different. Contemporary, classic and country styles in wallcoverings,
co-ordinated fabrics and borders, including good choice of tartans. Strong
in fabrics, too, and consistently innovative – superb Oceanes collection
from France, for example, with linen weights from voile to upholstery, in
neutrals of pewter grey, cream, beige and chocolate plus strong bright
colours; from £34.66 to £42.90 a metre, widths from 140 to 160 cm.
Also striking wallpaper designs by Paloma Picasso – 'different rooms need
different dresses' she says, with velvet paisleys, animal prints, jazzy
tweeds, and metallics from £26.67 a metre, papers from £35.00 a roll.
TUBE *Finchley Road or Swiss Cottage* • **OPEN** *Mon–Sat 10am–5pm*
• **SERVICES** *Interior design advice and curtain-making*

PETER TOPP WALLCOVERINGS
ADDRESS 343 Fulham Palace Road, SW6 6TD
TEL 0171 736 4821   **FAX** 0171 731 5322
For top service, it's friendly Peter Topp – his family have been trading in
Fulham and Chelsea since 1853. As one of London's few wallcovering
specialists, he has heaps of samples and display panels from all top
makes. Special paint colours mixed to order, including Sanderson
Spectrum. 'Most of our customers just keep on coming back'. I'm not
surprised.
TUBE *Putney Bridge* • **OPEN** *Mon–Fri 9.30am–5pm. Sat 10am–1pm*
• **SERVICES** *Wallpapers trimming for hand-prints. Fabrics and soft
furnishings to order*

G THORNFIELD
ADDRESS 321 Gray's Inn Road, WC1X 8PX
TEL 0171 837 2996/2771   **FAX** 0171 278 2515
See many a beaming bargain hunter here; wallpapers are up to 50 per
cent off, with up to 30 per cent off co-ordinating fabrics. All best brands:
phone to check prices. Delivery from stock or within a few days of order.
Plus experienced advice from a family firm trading over 35 years.
TUBE *King's Cross* • **OPEN** *Mon–Fri 10am–6pm. Sat 9am–2pm* • **SERVICES**
Extensive picture framing department. Deliveries within the London area

WALL TO WALL
ADDRESS 549 Battersea Park Road, SW11 3BL
TEL 0171 585 3335 **FAX** 0171 228 5080
Miles O'Donovan, who pioneered the now-familiar concept of designer fabric
sale shops has applied the notion to wallpapers. He has designer papers all
at £7.95 a roll. The shop is also a centre for designer fabric clearance, with
12,000 in stock at prices from £9.95 to £13.95 a metre, all top names.
RAIL *Clapham Junction* • **TUBE** *Sloane Square + 319 bus* • **OPEN** *Mon–Sat
10am–6pm. Sun 11am–4pm* • **SERVICES** *Curtain-making and fitting*

ZUBER AND CIE
ADDRESS 42 Pimlico Road, SW1W 8LP
TEL 0171 824 8265 **FAX** 0171 824 8270
Come here for an instant mural. They have panoramic landscapes ready to
paste on the wall, taken from designs dating back to the early 19th-century.
Also smaller Rose Garden and Atrium *trompe l'oeil* panels. Plus stick-on
columns for around £200. Classical statues are £280, plus plinths, and
balustrading.
TUBE *Sloane Square* • **OPEN** *Mon–Fri 10am–6pm*
• **SERVICES** *Can recommend paper-hangers*

PAINT SPECIALISTS

How do you change a look in a weekend? With paint, the modern
wonder-worker. Modernist white (chic and cheap), Mediterranean
terracotta, historic drab, contemporary brights – paint is the
passport. At first a huge selection evokes euphoria, but it's often
easier to choose from a well-pruned palette. Be warned, however.
Specialist paint ranges can be expensive – perhaps three times as
much as something from your local DIY Superstore. Colours from
Dulux and Crown have vastly improved, taking on board new
trends such as metallics and special effects. It's worth studying their
paint charts carefully – they have been radically re-arranged to
take the agony out of choosing. A shop's own brands may be
even cheaper. Paint mixed to order from a machine is still a lot
cheaper than the more rarefied suppliers. So do your sums if you
have a budget at stake.

USEFUL CONTACTS

DULUX ADVICE CENTRE
TEL 01753 550555
Leaflets and brochures on all Dulux products plus practical help with
painting problems. Calls cost 49p per minute.
OPEN *Mon–Fri 8.30am–5pm* • **WEBSITE** *www.dulux.com*

DO IT ALL HELPLINE
TEL FREEPHONE 0800 436436
Expert personal advice on all DIY and decorating problems.
OPEN *Mon–Sat 9am–8pm. Sun 10am–4pm*

BRATS

ADDRESS 281 King's Road, SW3 5EW
TEL 0171 351 7674 **FAX** 0171 349 8644

Relive your holiday through the Mediterranean Palette, a vivid expanding selection of chalk-based authentic shades from Turkey, from mellow creams and terracottas to Grecian blues, emeralds and aqua. A 3.4 kilo pot of paste dilutes with water to 3 1/2 litres and costs £28. A smaller pot dilutes to 1 litre (£8.50). Samples, £2; shade cards, £1.50. Brushes give the best finish.

TUBE *Sloane Square + 11, 19, 22 bus* • **OPEN** *Mon–Sat 10am–6.30pm. Sun 1pm–6pm* • **ALSO AT** *624c Fulham Road, SW6 5EW (0171 731 6915)*

FARROW & BALL

ADDRESS 249 Fulham Road, SW3
TEL 0171 351 0273 **FAX** 0171 351 0221

For that authentic costume drama look, history meets paint at Farrow & Ball, whose reputation and colours come from meticulous restoration of Britain's most stately of homes. There are 57 National Trust colours and an additional 38 shades from F & B's archives. Pedigrees are fascinating – for example Eating Room Red was 'popular around the middle of the 19th-century, with the discovery of new pigments.' Sample pots, approx 100 ml, £2.99. Estate emulsion, £16.99; casein or soft distempers, £20.99; dead flat oil, £23.99; all for 2.5 litres. Limewash is £13.69 for 5 litres. Hand-painted colour card, £6.00; printed colour chart, free. Apply by brush – orange-peel effect of roller ruins beautiful matt finish. Also striped and brush-dragged papers to match paints – £26.95 a roll.

TUBE *South Kensington* • **OPEN** *Mon–Fri 10am–6pm. Late night Wed 7pm. Sat 10am–5pm* • **WEBSITE** *www.farrow-ball.co.uk* • **SERVICES** *Dorset factory can send/deliver (01202 876141)*

FIRED EARTH

See TILES, page 106. Free hand-painted paint chart shows historic colours researched at the Victoria & Albert Museum. 'Drabs' were originally for the servants, rich tones to complement fine paintings in living-rooms, and more subtle blues and greys for bedrooms. Plus Morris with that wonderful green and Pugin, glowing with unexpected brilliance. Emulsion, from £16.80 for 2.5 litres; sample 100 ml pot, £2.90; distemper in selected colours, £32.95 for 5 litres.

FRANCESCA'S LIME WASH

ADDRESS Unit 2A Battersea Business Centre, 99/109 Lavender Hill, SW11 5QL
TEL 0171 228 7694 **FAX** 0171 228 8067

Authentic limewash finishes in modern colours brought to London by Francesca Wezel, who learned the recipes in Sydney where she worked for five years as manager and colour consultant for Porter's Paints, traditional paint specialists. Product comes ready-mixed and dries to a chalky streaky finish. Send £4.50 for current shade card.

GRAND ILLUSIONS (MAISON)

See ACCESSORIES: SHOPS WITH FURNITURE, page 24. For that special chalky look, 41 colours that copy the look of 19th-century milk paints, for walls or wood – from muted earth tones to brights. £8.95 a litre; £2.75 for a 110 ml sample pot. Colour card, £1. Seal with their acrylic dead flat varnish.

JOHN OLIVER

ADDRESS 33 Pembridge Road, W11 3HG

TEL 0171 221 6466/727 3735   **FAX** 0171 727 5555

John Oliver himself has retired but the great paint show goes on. Hand-painted swatch of this year's 40 shades costs £2. Matt emulsion with dull 'distemper' finish is £23.21, 2.5 litres; also vinyl silk, flat oil, eggshell, gloss and floor paints. Stone and creams always popular – more racy is vivid Betty II Blue, Imperial Chinese Yellow, or the inimitable Kinky Pink. Colour matching a speciality – John even matched paint to 'knickers, loo seats...and an aubergine.'

TUBE *Notting Hill Gate* • **OPEN** *Mon–Sat 9am–5.30pm*

PAINT LIBRARY

ADDRESS 5 Elystan Street, SW3 3NT

TEL 0171 823 7755   **FAX** 0171 823 7766

Artist David Oliver is the decorator's delight for his mouth-watering colours in *outré* finishes such as glitter and pearl – but you pay for the privilege. Also fabrics, and subtle contemporary wallpapers by interior decorator Emily Todhunter, whose Nudes design is elegantly classic – no page three stuff here.

TUBE *Sloane Square/South Kensington* • **OPEN** *Mon–Fri 9am–5.30pm. Sat 10am–2pm* • **SERVICES** *Mail order. Delivery*

PAPERS AND PAINTS

ADDRESS 4 Park Walk, SW10 0AD

TEL 0171 352 8626   **FAX** 0171 352 1017

Tireless enthusiasm and scholarship makes Patrick Baty London's historical paint buff. His old-established family firm sell Traditional Colours (64 shades), from the mid-17th to the mid-19th-century. Historical Colours (112 shades) are inspired by decorative antiques such as tapestries and pottery. Matt and silk emulsion, £12.57 a litre; eggshell and gloss, £15.28 a litre. Set of hand-painted colour cards, £7.52, Varnishes, brushes, tools, pigments, books.

TUBE *Gloucester Road* • **OPEN** *Mon–Fri 8.30am–5.30pm* • **SERVICES** *Hand-painted mail-order colour cards*

SPECIALIST DECORATING SUPPLIERS

This section includes stencils, materials for paint effects, print rooms, varnishes etc, although some of these are also stocked by more adventurous DECORATING AND REFURBISHING: GENERAL DECORATING SUPPLIERS, page 90, and by DIY SUPERSTORES, page 88.

USEFUL CONTACTS

The best way to learn crafty decorating techniques is hands on and straight from the horse's mouth – here are numbers to ring for details of courses:

HARRY LEVINSON
TEL 0181 348 2811   **FAX** 0181 348 4293
WEBSITE *www.decorart.co.uk*

KLC
TEL 0171 602 8592

PAINT MAGIC ISLINGTON
TEL 0171 359 4441

PAINT MAGIC RICHMOND
TEL 0181 940 9799

STENCIL STORE
TEL 0171 730 0728

ARC

ADDRESS 103 Wandsworth Bridge Road, SW6 2TE
TEL 0171 731 3933   **FAX** 0171 610 6591
Classic narrow border patterns, plus 'embellishments': swags, ropes, ribbons, chains, designed for you to create your own print room. Sold on sheets to cut out. Use to frame their black and white copies of 17th- to 19th-century prints – in 1987 they started with just 26 images, and now their collection exceeds 700, with exports worldwide. Exclusive and unusual. Christopher and Denise Outlaw have also designed print-room fabrics for chairs, curtains and screens.
TUBE *Fulham Broadway* • **OPEN** *Mon–Fri 10am–6pm. Sat 11am–5pm*

J W BOLLOM AND J T KEEP

ADDRESS 15 Theobalds Road, WC1 8SN
TEL 0171 242 0313   **FAX** 0171 831 2457
Old-established professional marblers and grainers have used Keep's scumble glaze for years. Unlike water-based emulsions, it stays 'open' keeping a wet edge for an even effect. Traditional Keep's glaze (£19.27, 2.5 litres) tends to yellow which enhances warmer shades. But for fashionable cooler pastels, there's newer Transparent glaze (£22.67, 2.5 litres). Tint the glaze with Super fine Colour in Oil (30 mixable colours, 250 ml tubes from £5 to £10). Plus trade prices, books, specialist advice, and all brushes/tools (stipplers, floggers, draggers, grainers etc).
TUBE *Holborn* • **OPEN** *Mon–Fri 7.30am–5pm. Sat 8am–noon*
• **ALSO AT** *314 Old Brompton Road, SW5 (0171 370 3252)*

BRODIE & MIDDLETON ✉

ADDRESS 68 Drury Lane, WC2B 5SP
TEL 0171 836 3289   **FAX** 0171 497 8425
For that *coup de théâtre*, shop with stage designers and scenery makers busy buying materials for backdrops etc. Many people mix the jazzy pigments available here with PVA to make their own paint for ultra-brilliant walls/furniture. This old established company also sells glitter, luminous paint, and ultra-violet powder. Special enamel varnishes can create the look of a stained glass window. Plus a range of fabrics, including canvas, cotton duck, calico, and Bolton twill, and fire-proofing materials.

TUBE *Holborn/Covent Garden* • **OPEN** *Mon–Fri 8.30am–5pm*
• **SERVICES** *Catalogue (please send stamp). Mail order (no credit cards)*

L CORNELISSEN AND SON

ADDRESS 105 Great Russell Street, WC1B 3RY
TEL 0171 636 1045   **FAX** 0171 636 3655

Creative home decorators buy high-quality pigments to tint their own paints from these specialist supplier of materials for artists. Also find materials for gilding and scumble glazing and a wide selection of brushes.
TUBE *Tottenham Court Road* • **OPEN** *Mon–Fri 9.30am–5.30pm.*
Sat 9.30am–5pm • **SERVICES** *Full price list and 'magnificent mail-order service – though we do say it ourselves'*

THE ENGLISH STAMP COMPANY ✉

ADDRESS Worth Matravers, Dorset, BH19 3JP
TEL 01929 439117   **FAX** 01929 439150

They took the simple rubber stamp and gave it a whole new decorating dimension. Selection is huge (stars, shells, flowers, leaves, animals, folk and ethnic motifs) for decorating walls, ceilings, furniture, fabrics and so on – plus their rollers and special paints.
WEBSITE *www.englishstamp.com* • **SERVICES** *Colour catalogue*

FOXELL & JAMES

ADDRESS 57 Farringdon Road, EC1M 3JB
TEL 0171 405 0152/2487   **FAX** 0171 405 3631

The City's trade specialist paint supplier – 'a lot of craftsmen work in this area'. By their own admission 'not the tidiest of shops' but full of everything you could need from general painting to specialist polishes, varnishes, lacquers, restoration products, and gilding materials. Messrs Foxell and James are as charmingly prepared to sort out an individual crisis as to supply a large contract. Recommended.
TUBE *Farringdon* • **OPEN** *Mon–Fri 7am–5pm. Sat 7am–12.30pm*

GREEN AND STONE

ADDRESS 259 King's Road, SW3 5EL
TEL 0171 352 0837   **FAX** 0171 351 1098

Established as picture framers in 1927, the emphasis is now on fine art materials. But it's a good source for paints, tools and books for special effects, and for crafts.
TUBE *Sloane Square + 11, 19, 22 bus* • **OPEN** *Mon Tues Thurs Fri 9am–6pm. Wed 9am–7pm. Sat 9.30am–6pm. Sun 12 noon–5pm*

HARRIS FINE ART ✉

ADDRESS 712 High Road, North Finchley, N12 9QD
TEL 0181 445 2804   **FAX** 0181 446 0640

Artist's supplies with a good range of materials for special paint effects. Thousands of ready-made picture frames in stock, plus framing to order, and a good selection of prints.
TUBE *Woodside Park* • **OPEN** *Mon–Sat 9am–5.30pm* • **SERVICES** *Mail order*

LONDON GRAPHIC CENTRE

ADDRESS 16–18 Shelton Street, WC2H 9JJ

TEL 0171 240 0095   **FAX** 0171 831 1544

A comprehensive stock of all arts and graphics materials right in the centre of town, including pigments, dyes, stencils and so on.

TUBE *Covent Garden/Leicester Square* • **OPEN** *Mon–Fri 9.30am–6pm. Sat 10.30am–6pm* • **ALSO AT** *254 Upper Richmond Road, SW15 (0181 785 9797)*

PAINT MAGIC ISLINGTON

ADDRESS 34 Cross Street, Islington, N1 2BG

TEL 0171 359 4441   **FAX** 0171 359 1833

Jocasta Innes – self-styled 'duchess of DIY' – was the first to do dragging, stippling, sponging with emulsion paints, rather than old-fashioned oil-based scumble glazes. It was about 20 years ago and was revolutionary. Jocasta doesn't stand still – she's ever inventing new products, finishes, and colours, and now appears on TV. Her many books are filled with personal anecdotes – this woman is DIY incarnate. Emulsions in lovely colours (£18.80 for 2.5 litres, sample jar, £3.10 for 60 ml) and paints for colourwashing. Plus textured finishes, like Marmorino which you trowel on for a polished plaster finish. Apply water-based Frosting Medium through stencils on to glass for an old-fashioned etched effect – £3.10 for 16 ml. Free leaflets on techniques: colour and wood washing; gilding; distemper; limewash; Marmorino; stencilling; liming; and metallic effects. Stencils, blank objects to decorate, mosaic equipment. Inspiration everywhere – if you didn't do it before, you will now.

TUBE *Highbury & Islington/Angel* • **OPEN** *Mon–Sat 10am–6pm* • **ALSO AT** *Paint Magic Richmond (0181 940 9799); open 7 days and at 48 Golborne Road, Notting Hill, W10 (0181 960 9910), where Jocasta Innes is now based* • **SERVICES** *Phone 0171 354 9696 (head office) for full product details/free mail-order pack. Hand-painted emulsion colour chart: £7.50 refundable on purchase. Weekly courses in paint effects and other crafts – phone branches for details. Also design and decoration service – £65 for a room scheme refundable upon acceptance – phone 0181 960 9960 for details*

E PLOTON

ADDRESS 273 Archway Road, N6 5AA

TEL 0181 348 0315   **FAX** 0181 348 3414

Well-known for artist's supplies including pigments – also gilding materials and other specialist paints/varnishes.

TUBE *Highgate* • **OPEN** *Mon–Sat 10am–3.45pm*

THE STENCIL LIBRARY ✉

ADDRESS Stocksfield Hall, Stocksfield, Northumberland, NE43 7TN

TEL 01661 844844   **FAX** 01661 843984

Particularly good for architectural stencils – huge and inspiring range – send £5 for a vast inspirational catalogue, refundable against order. For example, Victorian Poppy frieze, 8¾ in by 16 in, costs £23.95.

THE STENCIL STORE

ADDRESS 89 Lower Sloane Street, SW1W 8DA

TEL 0171 730 0728

Good selection of decorative stencils, from trailing ivy to Greek columns.

Brushes and paints for various surfaces including fabrics. Pre-tinted glazes. Materials for cutting your own stencils.
TUBE *Sloane Square* • **OPEN** *Mon–Sat 10am–5.30pm. Late night Thurs 6.30pm. For catalogue (£2.50), ring 01923 285577* • **SERVICES** *Stencil cutting. Workshops for stencilling and marbling*

REEVES
ADDRESS 178 Kensington High Street, W8 7NX
TEL 0171 937 5370
This vast emporium of art supplies is brilliant for all specialist craft paints – add your own decorative touches to glass, metal or ceramics. Also have fabric paints, crayons and dyes, for that touch of the TV makeovers.
TUBE *High Street Kensington* • **OPEN** *Mon–Fri 9am–5.30pm. Sat 9.30am–5.30pm. Sun 12 noon–5pm*

SPECIALIST PAINTING AND DECORATING SERVICES

BERY DESIGNS
ADDRESS 157 St John's Hill, SW11 1TQ
TEL 0171 924 2197   **FAX** 0171 924 1879
Hand-painted fabrics, wall-hangings, rugs and pelmets in large-scale flowing Baroque designs. Their special technique uses a minimum of eight colours plus gold highlights to give their signature shadowed effect. Ex-exhibition rugs and cushions are on sale at good prices at the studio
RAIL *Clapham Junction* • **OPEN** *Mon–Fri 9.30am–5.30pm. Sat by appointment*

BRUSHSTROKES
TEL 0171 737 6876
Well-established partnership of two design graduates – murals and specialist paint finishes. Professional and practical advice, free estimates.

CATHERINE LOVEGROVE MURALS
TEL 0171 371 7814
'Plagiarism a speciality'. Unique method of painting on to canvas panels, which can be taken with you when you move. Special techniques for painting with gold.

CHRIS WESTALL
TEL 01268 570323
Murals and *trompe-l'oeil*. Gentle classical and rustic scenes, paint effects and children's rooms. Extensive portfolio.
WEBSITE *www.westalls.demon.co.uk*

COLIN FAILES
TEL/FAX 0171 274 2093
Trompe-l'oeil murals and frescos.

CRAWLEY STUDIOS
TEL 0181 516 0003   **FAX** 0181 516 0002
Their speciality is classical murals and Italian designs. Also gilding and lacquer work. Painted furniture and modern commissions.

DIANA FINCH
TEL 0171 352 0131
Specialist mural and stencil designer. Also furniture painting and fabric stencilling. Paint finishes and gilding.

DOUGLAS DRUCE
TEL 0171 722 4581
Murals, *trompe-l'oeil*, interior wall paintings. Also portraits and marbling.

FIONA LATTA
TEL 0171 585 3035
This experienced artist (20 years) can paint *trompe-l'oeil* on to walls or moveable panels. Arcadian vistas, jungles. Furniture and blinds.

KATIE BEREFORD
TEL 0171 486 4770
Murals, *trompe-l'oeil,* paint effects.

LOOK INTERIORS
TEL/FAX 0181 943 1401
Magic and fantasy in rooms for children and grown ups – murals, *trompe-l'oeil* and decorative finishes.

MARTIN JARVIS
TEL/FAX 0181 567 1331
'From the subtle to the fantastical' – murals, *trompe-l'oeil* and other paint effects for interiors and furniture.

MCJ
TEL 0181 399 3685
A varied portfolio of styles to suit your whim – from classical to comical to personal.

PAINTED ILLUSIONS LTD
TEL 0171 727 1595
A team of artists directed by Sophia Barratt. Murals, *trompe-l'oeil* and decorative paint effects including woods and marbles.

SARAH TISDALL & ARTURO REYES
TEL/FAX 0171 394 0250
A partnership of fine artists for murals, *trompe l'oeil*, portraits, subtle colour washes, and faux marble.

TOUCHSTONE DESIGNS (TIM BIZLEY)
TEL 0181 349 0195
Stencils, murals, frescos. Graining and marbling

WALLIS-TOZER
TEL 0171 652 3313
Eye-catching murals and paint finishes.

PLASTER MOULDINGS AND RESTORATIONS

> `Without a cornice, no room can have a finished appearance.'
> J C Loudon, Encyclopedia of Cottage, Farm and Villa Architecture, 1833

H AND F BADCOCK
ADDRESS Unit 9, 57 Sandgate Street, Old Kent Road, SE15 1LE
TEL 0171 639 0304 **FAX** 0171 358 1239
Large, specialist workshop. Fibrous plastering and mouldings. Can restore any moulded plasterwork. Also solid plastering and screeding. Prestige jobs have included the Foreign Office, Westminster Abbey and Liz Hurley and Hugh Grant's house.
TUBE *New Cross/Elephant and Castle* • **OPEN** *Mon–Fri 8am–5pm*

BUTCHER PLASTERING SPECIALISTS
ADDRESS 8 Fitzroy Road, Primrose Hill, NW1 8TX
TEL 0171 722 9771 **FAX** 0171 586 2953
Forty-year old family business. Specialists in decorative mouldings for walls, arches, ceilings, cornices etc. Able to match existing mouldings.
TUBE *Chalk Farm* • **OPEN** *Mon–Thu 8am–4.30pm. Fri 8am–3.30pm*
• **SERVICES** *Brochure available*

LONDON FINE ART PLASTER
ADDRESS 8 Audrey Street, E2 8QH
TEL 0171 739 3594 **FAX** 0171 729 5741
The majority of their work is matching existing mouldings, but they'll use their existing patterns to keep costs down if possible.
OPEN *Mon–Fri 7am–4.30pm. Sat by appointment*

LONDON PLASTERCRAFT
ADDRESS 314 Wandsworth Bridge Road, SW6 2UF
TEL 0171 736 5146 **FAX** 0171 736 7190
See samples of their work in an attractive corner showroom. Restoration is a speciality. They can supply and fit – and they own all the old moulds from J D McDonough, until recently in the New King's Road.
TUBE *Parsons Green* • **OPEN** *Mon–Fri 8am–5pm. Sat 8.30am–2.30pm*

PLASTERWORKS
ADDRESS 38 Cross Street, N1 2BG
TEL 0171 226 5355   **FAX** 0171 288 0218
Plaster specialists who can make/restore all types of architectural
mouldings and cornices. Also sell decorative plaster figures and wall-hung
masks – you might find a film star sharing shelf space with a Roman bust or
a Pharoah's head. Plus decorative architectural features such as corbels
and capitals for sale.
TUBE *Angel* • **OPEN** *Mon–Sat 10am–6pm* • **SERVICES** *Commissions*

WOODEN MOULDINGS AND PANELLING

CHARLES HURST
See FURNITURE: STORAGE AND BUILT-IN FURNITURE, page 171. Can
panel out a whole room with 6-in wide Victorian-style tongue-and-grooved
panelling – or can simply supply boards for DIY.

COURT DAVIS JOINERY
ADDRESS 38a Highgate Road, NW5 1NS
TEL 0171 485 8538   **FAX** 0171 284 3375
Manufacturer of specialist and standard joinery. Victorian mouldings.
Stairs and handrails made to order; established over 10 years.
TUBE *Kentish Town* • **OPEN** *Mon–Thurs 8am–5pm. Fri 8am–4.30pm.
Sat 9am–1pm*

CROWTHER OF SYON LODGE
ADDRESS Busch Corner, London Road, Isleworth, Middx, TW7 5BH
TEL 0181 560 7978   **FAX** 0181 568 7572
Top quality bespoke panelled rooms – the Rolls Royce of the business.
Oak, pine, mahogany etc made up by a team of skilled joiners into
imposing period styles: Tudor linenfold, Jacobean, Queen Anne,
Georgian. Choice of finishes, including hand beeswaxing.
TUBE *Boston Manor* • **RAIL** *Syon Lane* • **OPEN** *Mon–Fri 9am–5pm. Sat Sun
11am–4pm* • **SERVICES** *Design, make, install*

GENERAL WOODWORK SUPPLIES
ADDRESS 76–80 Stoke Newington High Street, N16 7PA
TEL 0171 254 6052   **FAX** 0171 254 7223
Established since 1946. Wide range of timber and mouldings cut to order.
RAIL *Rectory Road* • **OPEN** *Mon–Fri 8am–6pm. Thu 8am–4pm.
Sat 8.30am–6pm*

LONDON'S GEORGIAN HOUSES
ADDRESS 291 Goswell Road, EC1V 7LA
TEL/FAX 0171 254 2254
Ray Wheeler, dedicated to preserving London's fine architectural
woodwork, has a specialist workshop for restoring/making authentic
Georgian- and Victorian-style panelling, windows, shutters, doors, fitted
cupboards, alcoves and so on. 'We use the same old-style materials –

Baltic pine almost without exception – and techniques to produce perfect imitations.'
SERVICES *Brochure available. Phone to discuss a site visit*

ROY BLACKMAN ASSOCIATES ✉

ADDRESS Bryant Avenue, Gallows Corner, Romford, Essex, RM3 0AP
TEL 01708 373708 **FAX** 01708 373709
Simulated oak linenfold and Jacobean wall panelling. Reproduction oak beams, fireplaces. Decorative plate-racks, carved friezes, cornices. Lightweight, durable, convincing – unless you touch them!
OPEN *Mon–Fri 9am–5.30pm* • **SERVICES** *Colour brochure*

VICTORIAN WOOD WORKS

See FLOORS: WOOD FLOORS: NEW AND RECLAIMED BOARDS, page 181. Wall and dado panelling, and all bespoke joinery (including libraries) in antique timber. Hand-finishing and French polishing.

UNUSUAL MATERIALS

For all kinds of sheet glass, see entries under WINDOWS: GENERAL GLASS MERCHANTS, page 206. For various craft supplies, see entries under CRAFTS AND DESIGNER-MAKERS: CRAFT SUPPLIES, page 56.

B.BROWN

See FABRICS AND SOFT FURNISHINGS: FABRIC SHOPS, page 72. Felt in wide widths, metallic gauzes and other unusual fabrics.

THE CANE STORE

See CRAFTS AND DESIGNER-MAKERS: CRAFT SUPPLIES, page 57. Bamboo rods, and reed screening panels of woven cane which can be used for screens and radiator covers.

DANICO BRASS

See DOORS: DOOR FURNITURE AND SPECIALIST IRONMONGERY, page 203 Huge selection of decorative metal grilles in brass, gold anodised aluminium, chrome or white, supplied cut to size. Also sheets of solid brass, rod and sections.

JALI ✉

TEL 01227 831710 **FAX** 01227 831950
Vast selection of decorative grilles, edge trims, pelmets and brackets, fretwork screens, shutters, decorative pelmets, wallpanels and so on, all cut from MDF. Despite the plethora of scallops and curlicues, the basic diamond trellis is the biggest seller.
SERVICES *Catalogue*

LONDON METAL CENTRE

ADDRESS 10 Titan Business Estate, Finch Street, SE8 5QA
TEL 0181 694 6022 **FAX** 0181 694 2666
All kinds of aluminium, steel, galvanised, and stainless steel sheet cut to

sizes as little as one square foot. Plus mesh sheet, chrome plating, and metal cladding. Recently, for example, they clad a customer's kitchen unit doors in stainless steel.

RAIL *Deptford* • **OPEN** *Mon–Fri 9am–5.30pm, but please phone before calling*

LUXCRETE
ADDRESS Premier House, Disraeli Road, Harlesden, NW10 7BT
TEL 0181 965 7292   **FAX** 0181 961 6337
Glass blocks (clear, coloured and patterned) for screens, dividing walls, and shower enclosures etc. A block 190 by 190 by 80 mm costs around £5, but the right fixing materials (such as strengthening steel rods and special mortar) increases the price to around £8.
TUBE *Harlesden* • **OPEN** *Mon–Fri 9am–1pm; 2–4pm*

MARCHMADE
ADDRESS 79 Dean Street, W1V 6HY
TEL 0171 437 6241   **FAX** 0171 437 6244
Acrylic sheet cut to size, plus rods and tubes. Holes drilled, boxes made.
TUBE *Tottenham Court Road* • **OPEN** *Mon–Fri 8.30am–4.30pm*

TILES

USEFUL CONTACT

THE VICTORIAN SOCIETY
ADDRESS 1 Priory Gardens, Bedford Park, London, W4 1TT
TEL 0181 994 1019   **FAX** 0181 995 4895
Helpful A4 colour leaflet on restoring/replacing Victorian decorative tiles costs £3.

CASTELNAU TILES
ADDRESS 175 Church Road, SW13 9HR
TEL 0181 741 2452   **FAX** 0181 741 5316
Friendly service from efficient tile specialists. Fine handmade wall/floor tiles: many from 'undiscovered' factories overseas. Specialists in repro Victorian and Deco wall tiles. Stone and terracotta tiles. Custom-designed panels and murals.
TUBE *Hammersmith + bus* • **OPEN** *Mon–Fri 9am–5.30pm. Sat 9.30am–4pm* • **SERVICES** *Plan, design and fix*

CORRES MEXICAN TILES
ADDRESS 1a Station Road, Hampton-Wicks, Kingston, KT1 4HG
TEL 0181 943 4142   **FAX** 0181 943 4649
Terracotta floor and wall tile specialists with huge selections in many shapes and sizes. Over 100 different coloured and decorated glazed tiles, cut and painted by hand. Brochure.
RAIL *Hampton-Wicks* • **OPEN** *Mon–Fri 9am–5pm*

CRITERION TILES

ADDRESS 196 Wandsworth Bridge Road, SW6 2UF
TEL 0171 736 9610   **FAX** 0171 736 0725

Attractive showroom, with airy conservatory extension for daylight viewing. Specialists in British tiles and decorative tiling techniques; exclusive and bespoke designs. Manager Tom Sedgwick is no tile tyro – witness his impressive file of past commissions. 'A lot of the work here is one-offs. Each tile in the shop is there for a reason, nothing is selected without careful thought.' Small, flexible British ceramicists can make special designs and colours to order. Dados, borders, painted panels. Enthusiastic service.
TUBE *Parson's Green/Fulham Broadway* • **OPEN** *Mon–Fri 9.30am–5.30pm. Sat 9.30am–5pm* • **ALSO AT** *2a Englands Lane NW3 4TG (0171 483 2608)*

ELON TILES

ADDRESS 66 Fulham Road, SW3 6HH
TEL 0171 460 4600   **FAX** 0171 460 4601

Stunning, hand-decorated floor and wall tiles from Mexico and France. Naive motifs in rich colours that never date. Delicate flower tiles and murals from Provence. Hand-stencilled tiles from Normandy. Catalogue. Plus ceramic sinks.
TUBE *South Kensington* • **OPEN** *Mon–Sat 10am–5.30pm*

FIRED EARTH

ADDRESS 117–119 Fulham Road, SW3 6RL
TEL 0171 589 0489   **FAX** 0171 225 3671

Today, a sophisticated furnishings-buying public knows all about the beauties of handmade tiles in terracotta. But this wasn't the case fifteen years ago, when Nicholas Kneale started selling them from an Oxfordshire farmyard. It's a tribute to his zeal, enthusiasm and imagination that from this small beginning he has grown his company into a national chain, with four shops in London and an inspirational colour brochure. Now terracottas come from all around the Mediterranean and Mexico, together with reclaimed older tiles. They've been joined by selections of slate and other stones, and mosaics – see innovative ideas for mixing these floorings on the showroom floors. Wall tiles are equally seductive with handmade selections from kilns all around the world – including a dazzling rainbow of 100 glazed colours on handmade squares from Provence; Delft blue and whites; vivid Islamics and continuous innovations from British craft potters. To this ceramic mix have been added a Fired Earth paint range; a selection of natural floorings and rugs; and a range of fabrics, including embroidered crewel work, rich chenilles and velvets, and country checks.
TUBE *South Kensington* • **OPEN** *Mon–Sat 9.30am–6pm. Late night Wed 7.30pm. Sun 12 noon–5.30pm* • **SERVICES** *A thick free colour brochure – phone 01295 814300. Free samples and mail order – phone 01295 814315. Tiling service and service for fitting natural floorcoverings – details from installation department, 01295 814310* • **ALSO AT** *102 Portland Road, W11 4LX (0171 221 4825). 174 Chiswick High Road, W4 1PR (0181 994 5355). 41 Heath Street, NW3 6UA (0171 435 1473)*

JUST TILES 🐷

ADDRESS 142–144 Kenton Road, Harrow, Middx, HA3 8BL
TEL 0181 907 3020   **FAX** 0181 907 1687

'Unbeatable on price' is the claim – substantial discounts on ceramic tiles

for walls and floors because they buy direct from wholesalers and hold very large stocks.
TUBE *Harrow on the Hill* • **OPEN** *Mon Tues Thurs Fri Sat 9am–5.30pm. Sun 10am–4pm. Wed closed all day*

LANGLEY LONDON LTD

ADDRESS Harling House, 47–51 Great Suffolk Street, SE1 0SR
TEL 0171 803 4444   **FAX** 0171 803 4428
Import exclusive decorative tiles for kitchens and bathrooms; plus sanitaryware.
TUBE *Waterloo* • **OPEN** *Mon–Fri 9am–5.15pm* • **SERVICES** *Design service for tiles/mosaics*

QUALITY MARBLE

ADDRESS Unit 1, Fountayne House, Fountayne Road, Tottenham, N15 4QL
TEL 0181 808 1110   **FAX** 0181 885 2455
Polished marble tiles for walls and floors. Also granite and terrazzo. Marble and granite slabs for kitchen worktops or vanity tables.
TUBE *Seven Sisters/Tottenham Hale* • **OPEN** *Mon–Fri 8am–5pm*
• **SERVICES** *Installation, cleaning*

THE REJECT TILE SHOP

ADDRESS 178 Wandsworth Bridge Road, SW6 2UQ
TEL 0171 731 6098   **FAX** 0171 736 3693
Ceramic tile seconds (usually only sold from factory shops) with minute faults, imported from around the world, as well as choice of fine English tiles. Also discontinued first-quality tiles. Come here for plains, patterns, borders, dados, including Victorian reproductions and some floor quarries. They're an offshot of The Criterion Tile Shop down the road, and have the same helpful attitude to customers. Prices from about £8 per square metre to around £47.50 per square metre. Bags of second quality loose mixed coloured glass mosaic cost £4 each plus £2 p&p per bag. Fixing/grouting materials.
TUBE *Fulham Broadway* • **OPEN** *Mon–Fri 9.30am–5.30pm. Sat 9.30–5pm*
• **SERVICES** *Sample tiles for sale individually – money refunded on return*

RYE TILES

ADDRESS 12 Connaught Street, W2 2AS
TEL 0171 723 7278
London showroom for celebrated Sussex tile specialists. Tarquin Cole (ex-RCA) put art into British tiles in the early sixties. Exciting screen prints, geometrics/abstracts. Infinitely charming, handpainted images of English birds, flowers, boats, landscapes. You'll never tire of these miniature works of art.
TUBE *Marble Arch* • **OPEN** *Mon–Fri 9.30am–1pm; 2.15pm–5pm*
• **SERVICES** *Commission your own hand-painted tiles*

TERRA FIRMA

ADDRESS 70 Chalk Farm Road, NW1 8AN
TEL 0171 485 7227   **FAX** 0171 485 7203
Here the speciality is all those appealing natural materials – handmade and glazed terracotta floor tiles, slate from India and China, and limestone

and marbles. Also encaustic (inlaid) patterned tiles and mosaic borders.
There's also a selection of wall tiles.
TUBE *Chalk Farm* • **OPEN** *Mon–Fri 10am–5pm. Sat 10.30–5pm*
• **SERVICES** *Local deliveries. Can recommended tilers*

THE TILE GALLERY

ADDRESS 1 Royal Parade, 247 Dawes Road, Fulham, SW6 7RE
TEL 0171 385 8818   **FAX** 0171 381 1589
Stanley Cohen has more than 4,500 wall and floor designs, from
handmade handpainted tiles, through Victorian and Edwardian copies
to modern British and continental patterns. Separate section for currently-
fashionable marble and granite. Special 'white' collection, from cream
through ivory to polar, in satin, gloss and textures.
TUBE *Fulham Broadway* • **OPEN** *Mon–Fri 8.30am–5.30pm.*
Sat 9.30am– 4pm. Sun 9.30am–12.30pm • **SERVICES** *Made-to-measure*
worktops and vanitory units

TILES & BATHS DIRECT 🐖

ADDRESS 60 The Broadway, West Hendon, NW9 7AE
TEL 0181 202 2223   **FAX** 0181 202 2517
Huge showroom for importers/wholesalers with ceramic, marble and
granite wall and floor tiles in spacious settings along with bathroom fittings
from major UK and European makers – baths, taps, showers, bathroom
furniture. Also limestone, slate and antique marble at 'unbeatable prices'.
RAIL *Hendon* • **OPEN** *Mon–Fri 9am–6pm. Sat 10am–4pm. Sun 10am–2pm*
• **SERVICES** *Customers' car park. Manufacturers of marble and granite tops.*
Can recommend bathroom installers

TILES GALORE 🐖

ADDRESS Astoria Buildings, Gracefields Gardens, SW16 2ST
TEL 0181 677 3035/6068   **FAX** 0181 677 3038
Discount prices for ceramic tiles mainly imported from Spain and Italy,
where they're bought direct from the makers.
RAIL *Streatham Hill* • **OPEN** *Mon–Sat 8am–5.30pm*

WARD AND STEVENS 🐖

ADDRESS 248 High Street North, E12 6SB
TEL 0181 472 4067   **FAX** 0181 470 9091
Budget range of ceramic tiles, with interesting good-quality seconds. Low-
cost quarry floor tiles, for that rustic look, at prices from around £6.80 a
square metre plus VAT. Wall tile prices start at around £2 a square metre
and go up to £25 a square metre. Budget wallcoverings, plus a vast range
of paints (more than 5,000 colours, they say) at prices 'lower than trade'.
TUBE *East Ham* • **OPEN** *Mon–Sat 9am–5.30pm*

WORLD'S END TILES

ADDRESS British Rail Yard, Silverthorne Road, Battersea, SW8 3HE
TEL 0171 819 2100   **FAX** 0171 819 2101
Tile fanatic Paul Portelli, trading for over 25 years, has fulfilled his ultimate
fantasy. He's turned an old warehouse into a 4,000 sq ft tile palace, with
inspirational cameos and sets every whichway you turn. Ceramic wall
and floor tiles, mosaics, glass, porcelain, terracotta, limestone, marble

and accompanying borders and trims – all are set out in beguiling patterns and designs. Friendly staff help you work out how it all will look scaled down to your flat or semi, and provide technical back-up.

RAIL *Queenstown Road* • **OPEN** *Mon–Fri 8.30am–5.30pm. Late night Thurs 7pm. Sat 9am–5.30pm. Sun 11am–5pm* • **WEBSITE** *www.worldsendtiles.co.uk* • **SERVICES** *Deliveries. Children's TV and play area, plus baby-changing facilities. Italian-style cafe*

KITCHENS

- **Complete kitchens** *page 111*
- **Appliances, sinks and worktops** *page 119*
- **Kitchenware** *page 123*

> '*A design does not come from nothing but from a long history of shapes, functions and sensations.*'
> Renzo Piano, internationally-known modern architect

In times past, the kitchen was a mis-matched assembly of table, cooker, sink and dresser, homely but the site of drudgery. Then came the great fitted revolution, the most mammoth domestic make-over of modern times. Relatively rapidly the kitchen evolved into a line or 'L' shape of uniform boxes with flat tops, concealing all manner of modern appliances, from sink to hob to oven to dishwasher. Hygienic? Undoubtably. Easy to work in? Usually. Visually stimulating? Rarely.

Now new ideas about style and function are shaping the capital's kitchens. Designers still claim 'fitted' benefits – standard units save space, cut costs and provide lots of worktop – but they give the concept a fresh twist for a livelier look.

The box syndrome takes a battering from the new kitchen geometry. Heights for worktops are varied for functional efficiency and visual relief. Curves snake around sinks, island units, and table tops. Chic shapes are added with handles, cooker hoods, unusual cupboard tops, and open shelving. Materials, natural and manmade, are combined with uninhibited vigour – MDF, melamine and laminates, moulded resins, natural wood, ceramic tiles, granites, limestone, marble. Metals make their mark – stainless steel, copper, brass, wrought iron, chrome, zinc. And even glass and mirror are included, as the kitchen cognoscenti noticeably lighten up. Colour joins in joyfully – acid yellow, cobalt blue, forest green, double-decker red; texture, too – rough stone, smooth granite, pebbly concrete, grainy timber.

Most of today's kitchens are still built-in and fitted (although the unfitted movement is gaining ground). But the design and planning exercise has become more complex and subtle, and much harder to achieve without professional guidance. Luckily, in London we're spoilt for choice, with a kitchen showroom in virtually every main street.

Militant modernists yearn for the shock of the new, but love of the past remains deep-rooted in the British psyche. Consumers however, have become more demanding. No longer are kitchens sold under the woolly catch-all phrase of 'traditional'. Now there is a multitude of looks, each carefully detailed, if not necessarily totally accurate. Did William Morris own a microwave? Did Mrs Beeton use a freezer? When it comes to such niceties, the 'traditional' kitchen invariably sacrifices history to convenience.

PLANNING POINTERS

- List what your family does in the kitchen – add entertaining, homework, chatting etc to the more obvious chores of cooking, laundry and washing-up.
- Make a hate hit-list for your present kitchen – this concentrates the mind wonderfully.
- The most travelled route is between sink and cooker or hob, for safety's sake, keep it free of through traffic.
- The famous 'work triangle' is the path that links sink, cooker or hob and fridge – if these are cramped together you can't move, but big gaps mean unnecessary walking.
- Don't cram your cooker/hob into a corner – you need working space on either side. Don't interrupt a run of worktop with a tall appliance – for example site big fridge-freezers at the end of a run.
- To find comfortable worktop heights, stand with elbows flexed; a convenient height for chopping etc is 5 cm (2 in) lower; a convenient height for cooking is 7.5–10 cm (3–4 in) lower. A comfortable height for the bottom of the sink is 25 cm (10 in) lower.
- Seek professional advice – but remember this can only be as good as the briefing you supply. Always check plans and dimensions carefully before finalising an order.

COMPLETE KITCHENS

You'll be looking at a minimum of £5,000 and in most cases £10,000, £15,000 or £20,000 (to include designing, appliances and installation). This is a huge amount of money so make sure your lifestyle warrants it, and that you do a lot of cooking. Of course, if you've plumped for loft-living, all up-front and in-your-face, everything will be on show and the kitchen has at least to look convincing.

USEFUL CONTACT

THE KITCHEN SPECIALISTS ASSOCIATION
ADDRESS 4 Barbourne Terrace, FREEPOST WR716, Worcester, WR1 3JS
TEL 01905 726066 (helpline)   **FAX** 01905 726469
The KSA is a nationwide body of independent kitchen retailers, with rigorous quality standards for membership. They operate ConsumerCare, an insurance-backed deposit protection scheme. Ring or write for further details of the advantages of using a KSA member. In our listings of kitchen specialists in the London area, we have indicated KSA membership.
WEBSITE www.ksa.co.uk

ALTERNATIVE PLANS
ADDRESS 9 Hester Road, SW11 4AN
TEL 0171 228 6460   **FAX** 0171 924 1164
With unstinting enthusiasm, they'll concoct futuristic mainly continental
designs that match your lifestyle. Says owner Laurence Pidgeon: 'I like to
allow plenty of time for the best new kitchen possible'. He'll happily spend
two to three weeks at the planning stage, using computer-aided design
(CAD) to re-think and re-draw. Established over 15 years. Speciality: Boffi,
an imaginative state-of-the-art Italian brand.
TUBE *Sloane Square* • **OPEN** *Mon–Fri 9am–5.30pm. Sat 10am–4pm*
• **SERVICES** *Plan, design, supply, install. Own parking bay*

ANDREW MACINTOSH
ADDRESS 462–464 Chiswick High Road, London, W4 5TT
TEL 0181 995 8333   **FAX** 0181 995 8999
Designer Andrew Macintosh brings a breath of fresh air to kitchen design
with clean lines and subtle colours for his Shaker, Mackintosh and Country
ranges, plus Skylon with a fifties feel. Friendly and enthusiastic: 'we treat all
customers as individuals and don't force square pegs into round holes'.
TUBE *Chiswick Park* • **OPEN** *Mon–Fri 9am–5.30pm. Sat 10am–5.30pm*
• **SERVICES** *Colour brochure. Plan, design, make, install*

AVANT GARDE INTERIORS 🚗
ADDRESS 14 High Street, Kingston-upon-Thames, Surrey, KT1 1EY
TEL 0181 546 2921   **FAX** 0181 546 2010
It's worth a journey to see this airy new kitchen showroom with its riverside
terrace at the back. Forget the fitted box – here it's all seductive curves and
changes of level, plus exciting ideas in Corian, granite, stainless steel, and
wood, from Alno and Miele. The emphasis is very much on cooking with
stunning new appliances and friendly demos. Star of the show is the built-in
steam oven. KSA member.
RAIL *Kingston* • **OPEN** *Mon–Sat 9am–5.30pm* • **SERVICES** *Plan, design,
supply, install. On-going cookery demos*

BRUTON KITCHENS
ADDRESS 122 Brompton Road, SW3 1JD
TEL 0171 225 2999   **FAX** 0171 225 0445
'Experience is our forte.' Up-market classy foreign brands: Poggenpohl,
Pronorm, allmilmo, and Goldrief.
TUBE *Knightsbridge* • **OPEN** *Mon–Fri 9am–6pm. Sat 10am–5pm*
• **SERVICES** *Plan, design, supply, install. 'We do everything.'*

BULTHAUP
ADDRESS 37 Wigmore Street, W1H 9LD
TEL 0171 495 3663   **FAX** 0171 495 0139
Bulthaup, a top German make, were showing domestic kitchens in stainless
steel when this metal was confined to catering. They have remained
suitably avant-garde – ideal for lofts. They've added a series of unfitted
units to their famous work-bench look.
TUBE *Bond Street* • **OPEN** *Mon–Fri 9.30am–5.30pm. Sat 10am–4pm*
• **SERVICES** *Plan, design, supply, install*

CHALON

See FURNITURE: CANE, PINE, COUNTRY AND PAINTED, page 162
Handmade country-style kitchens in wood or painted distressed finishes,
with free-standing dressers and cupboards, and work surfaces in marble,
limestone, granite or hardwood.
SERVICES *Plan, design, make, install*

CLASSIC KITCHENS

ADDRESS 12 St Georges Road, E7 8HY
TEL 0181 5034498   **FAX** 0181 503 4673
'Anything and everything', in two showrooms side by side – one ultra
modern, the other more traditional with pine and maple. KSA member.
RAIL *Forest Gate* • **OPEN** *Mon–Sat 10am–6pm* • **SERVICES** *Plan, design,
supply, install, plus all ancillary services*

COMPLETE KITCHENS AND BATHROOMS

ADDRESS 56–58 Springbank Road, SE13 6SN
TEL 0181 852 5926   **FAX** 0181 244 0907
Pleasant family business, trading for over 25 years – fitted kitchens,
bathrooms and bedrooms, in the middle price bracket.
RAIL *Hither Green* • **OPEN** *Mon–Fri 10am–6pm. Sat 10am–3pm*
• **SERVICES** *Plan, design, supply, install*

CONNAUGHT KITCHENS

ADDRESS 2 Porchester Place, W2 2BS
TEL 0171 706 2210   **FAX** 0171 706 2209
Exclusive lacquered MDF cabinets in huge choice of colours are softened
with elegant panels, aluminium lattice-work, and Georgian-style wired
glass panes – traditional with a modern twist.
TUBE *Marble Arch* • **OPEN** *Mon–Thurs 9am–5pm. Fri 9am–5pm.
Sat 10am–5pm* • **SERVICES** *Plan, design, supply, install*

CRABTREE KITCHENS

ADDRESS The Twickenham Centre, Norcutt Road, Twickenham, TW2 6SR
TEL 0181 755 1121   **FAX** 0181 755 4133
John Crabtree, his son Patrick, and daughter Alex have a reputation for
quality and design stretching back 20 years. Their look is subtly different –
witness their burgeoning Mackintosh range. 'We led the trend towards a
less fitted approach.' KSA member.
RAIL *Twickenham* • **OPEN** *Mon–Fri 9am–5.30pm. Sat 10am–2pm.
By appointment at other times* • **SERVICES** *Plan, design, make, install.
Full project management – architectural problems, building works, lighting,
flooring. Own car park*

THE DANISH KITCHEN

ADDRESS 4 Eton Street, Richmond, Surrey, TW9 1EE
TEL 0181 332 2298   **FAX** 0181 332 2297
For that blonde Scandinavian look, The Danish Kitchen import attractive
pale kitchens in maple, birch, ash and beech. Designs feature lots of
storage, with all plumbing under the plinth. KSA member.
TUBE *Richmond* • **OPEN** *Mon–Sat 10am–5pm* • **SERVICES** *Plan, design, supply,
instal. Plus tiling, flooring, electrics and plumbing. Nationwide delivery*

FULHAM KITCHENS
ADDRESS 19 Carnwath Road, SW6 3HR
TEL 0171 736 6458 **FAX** 0171 371 9289
Trained chefs like Mark Parmenter, co-owner of this innovative outfit,
come up with kitchens that really work when the heat's on. This company
consistently provides original solutions mixing traditional materials – wood,
laminates, marble – with ultra-tech materials, such as stainless steel or
Pyrolave – a new coloured worktop based on volcanic lava. KSA member.
TUBE *Parsons Green* • **OPEN** *Mon–Fri 10am–5.30pm. Sat 10am–5pm.
Sun 11am–3pm* • **SERVICES** *One-off designs; all making and installing.
Kitchen solutions for unusual locations*

HARVEY JONES
ADDRESS 57 New Kings Road, SW6 4SE
TEL 0171 731 3302 **FAX** 0171 371 0735
The budget approach. 'Highest quality, lowest prices' promises Roy
Griffiths, a mover and Shaker in the kitchen trade, with his Simple brand.
His claim: to cut the cost of a typical kitchen by around 40 per cent by
restricting free advice and planning (just one two-hour showroom session
and a single site visit). Two styles: Victorian with traditional panels; and
plain-Jane Shaker. Choice of woods and painted finishes, or primed and
ready to paint yourself.
TUBE *Fulham Broadway/Parsons Green* • **OPEN** *Mon–Fri 9.30am–6pm.
Sat 9.30am–5.30pm* • **SERVICES** *Price includes delivery. Fitting service
available* • **ALSO AT** *172 High Road, Byfleet, Surrey, KT14 (01932 341385)*

HAYLOFT WOODWORK
ADDRESS 3 Bond Street Chiswick, W4 1QZ
TEL 0181 747 3510 **FAX** 0181 742 1860
No standard sizes or set styles here – Cole and Janet Manson are
endlessly inventive and very obliging, making kitchens and other furniture,
mainly in wood and MDF, for over 20 years. They work around needs and
wants. 'I'm a lateral thinker' says Cole, 'an obstacle is a challenge not a
problem'.
TUBE *Turnham Green* • **OPEN** *By appointment* • **SERVICES** *Plan, design,
make, install. Back-up* **SERVICES** *include plumbers, electricians, tilers*

HYGROVE
ADDRESS 152–154 Merton Road, SW9 1EH
TEL 0181 543 1200/6520 **FAX** 0181 543 6521
A painted look is their strong point for custom-built kitchens – from primaries
to subtle washes. 'No limits,' says director Vic Grayson, who has been
designing and making kitchens for over 15 years.
TUBE *South Wimbledon* • **OPEN** *Mon–Fri 10am–6pm. Sat 10am–5pm
or by appointment* • **SERVICES** *Plan, design, make, install* • **ALSO AT**
45 Fairfax Road, NW6 4EL (0181 624 6616)

IKEA
See UNDER ONE ROOF: FURNISHING SPECIALISTS, page 11. Ikea's
kitchen are sleek and good looking – many architects use them as
components to save money. Demand, however, is great, and supply
does not always run smoothly.

IN-TOTO KITCHENS AT FINCHLEY

ADDRESS 869 High Road, North Finchley, N12 8QA
TEL/FAX 0181 445 7499

Cleo Matsukis runs this large display of Wellman kitchens – 11 kitchens on show. Huge choice of door fronts, including country-style wood and the Shaker look. 'Excellent quality at very reasonable prices – you can tell by the well-engineered drawer runners.'

TUBE *Woodside Park* • **OPEN** *Mon–Fri 9.30am–5pm. Sat 9.30am–4pm*
• **WEBSITE** *www.intoto.co.uk* • **SERVICES** *Plan, design, supply, install*

IN-TOTO KITCHENS AT TEDDINGTON

ADDRESS 10–12 The Causeway, Teddington, TW11 0HE
TEL 0181 943 2293   **FAX** 0181 943 2294

The In-Toto chain sell the German Wellman brand – one of the largest in Europe. Peter Ward has around ten kitchens and two bedrooms on display. Mainly modern, wide choice of door fronts, plus appliances by Smeg, Bauknecht, Whirlpool, AEG, and sink/taps by Blanco. KSA member.

RAIL *Teddington* • **OPEN** *Mon–Sat 9.30am–5pm* • **WEBSITE** *www.intoto.co.uk*
• **SERVICES** *Plan, design, supply, install*

JAMES MEYER FURNITURE 🐷

ADDRESS 160 Fazeley Street, Birmingham, B5 5RS
TEL 0121 643 8349   **FAX** 0121 643 6690

Made-to-measure replacement kitchen doors in MDF from £16.10. Also built-in wardrobes and dado panelling.

SERVICES *Brochure (£2): 0121 643 8344*

JOHN LEWIS OF HUNGERFORD 🚙

ADDRESS Park Street, Hungerford, Berks, RG17 0EF
TEL 01488 682066   **FAX** 01488 686660

'A kitchen shouldn't be stark, bare and merely functional, but warm, friendly and practical.' John Lewis of Hungerford, a self-taught carpenter, is famous for his bespoke kitchens – country-style with a wash of colour. But there's also the affordable Artisan range, with two door styles in 14 painted finishes; chairs, tables and dressers to match. Artisan is delivered but not fitted. 'See it, touch it, smell it' information pack, £2.

RAIL *Hungerford* • **OPEN** *Mon–Fri 9am–5.30pm. Sat 9.30am–5pm*
• **SERVICES** *Fitting service available. Nationwide deliveries* • **ALSO AT**
Liberty's, 210–220 Regent Street W1R 6AH (0171 734 1234)

J U KITCHEN CONSULTANTS

ADDRESS 160–162 Notting Hill Gate, W11 3QG
TEL 0171 221 0257   **FAX** 0171 229 4382

Top quality Miele units plus their splendidly robust appliances. This well-established business flourishes on word-of-mouth recommendations. KSA member.

TUBE *Notting Hill Gate* • **OPEN** *Mon Tues Thurs Fri 9.30am–5.30pm. Sat 10am–5pm* • **SERVICES** *Plan, design, supply, install. Full interior design service, including flooring and tiling. Fitted bathrooms*

JUST KITCHENS

ADDRESS 172 Brompton Road, SW3 1HW
TEL 0171 584 2022/460 2301 **FAX** 0171 584 2160
Edward Hallatt founded his kitchen company in 1972. He shows the
modern hi-tech German SieMatic brand, and his own Osborne & Hallatt
range, made in England and adaptable to virtually any design, including
new-look curves. 'We have an interior design approach – kitchens that
really work, but at the same time have all the decorative details – flooring,
lighting, blinds and curtains, and so on.' One person oversees your order
from start to finish. They can do unfitted kitchens, with units that go with
you if you move.
TUBE *Knightsbridge* • **OPEN** *Mon–Fri 9am–6pm. Sat 9am–5.30pm*
• **SERVICES** *Plan, design, supply/make, install. Interior design* • **ALSO AT**
206–208 Upper Richmond Road, East Sheen SW14 8AH (0181 876 6106)

KITCHENS ETCETERA

ADDRESS 62–63 High Street, Wimbledon Village, Wimbledon, SW19 5EE
TEL 0181 946 3855 **FAX** 0181 288 0204
Stocking Poggenpohl and Scottwood, this friendly shop offers a variety of
looks, from modern through to country or traditional, including granite
worktops. KSA member.
TUBE/RAIL *Wimbledon* • **OPEN** *Mon–Sat 9am–5.30pm* • **SERVICES** *Plan,
design, supply, install. Full interior design service, including tiling and
flooring*

KITCHEN WORLD

ADDRESS 311–313 Bethnal Green Road, E2 6AH
TEL 0800 783 1713
Established for over 25 years, this reliable firm displays British brands in
attractive showrooms.
TUBE *Bethnal Green* • **OPEN** *Mon–Fri 10.30am–6.30pm.
Sat 11.30am–3.30pm* • **SERVICES** *Plan, design, supply, install*

MARK WILKINSON

ADDRESS 126 Holland Park Avenue, W11 4JA
TEL 0171 727 5814 **FAX** 01380 850184
Mark Wilkinson is prominent in the who's who of British kitchens – a
co-founder of Smallbone and designer of the original country kitchen
with that much-copied fishtail frieze. He is above all a woodworker par
excellence, restlessly on the move, experimenting and perfecting new
designs in his Wiltshire design studio and workshop. Come here for
kitchens with a life of their own – the Provence, the Arts and Crafts,
the Santa Fe, with quirky details down to the last catch, latch and tile.
Also bedrooms and bathrooms, and an endearing range of Goldilocks
children's furniture. Such originality, however, does not come cheap.
TUBE *Holland Park* • **OPEN** *Mon–Fri 9am–5.30pm. Sat 10am–5pm*
• **SERVICES** *Plan, design, make, install. Inspirational colour brochure*

MOGGS OF GREENWICH

ADDRESS Unit 511, 49 Greenwich High Road, SE10 8JL
TEL 0181 694 2113 **FAX** 0181 694 2116
Film-set fantasy or at least something a bit different – designer Trevor
Morgan used to work for the big screen (*Passage to India, Little Dorrit*),

and he'll twist the most unusual materials into arresting shapes, including over-the-top Art Deco and Gothic.

RAIL *Greenwich* • **OPEN** *7am–5.30pm Mon–Sat* • **WEBSITE** *www.moggs.co.uk* • **SERVICES** *Plan, design, make, install*

THE NEW ENGLAND KITCHEN CO

ADDRESS 78a Waldegrove Road, Teddington, Middx, TW11 8LG (office address)
SHOWROOMS AT Norbert Levingston Interiors, 101 High Street, Teddington, Middx; and The House of Treasures, 22 Hill Street, Richmond
TEL 0181 977 0948   **FAX** 0973 201931

Anthony James does Shaker kitchens, with simple doors, willow baskets and wooden worktops, teamed with latest appliances. 'We're very environmentally friendly – we use no solvent-based paints, for example.'
SERVICES *Plan, design, make, install. All interior design, plus any necessary building works, including extensions/conservatories*

NICHOLAS ANTHONY

ADDRESS 40 Wigmore Street, W1H 9DF
TEL 0171 935 0177   **FAX** 0171 935 1887

A friendly personal welcome at this convenient showroom in the heart of London, with top-brand fitted kitchens, bedrooms and bathrooms in styles from ultra-modern through to country, including painted finishes. KSA member.
TUBE *Bond Street* • **OPEN** *Mon–Fri 9.30am–6pm. Sat 10am–4pm*
• **SERVICES** *Plan, design, supply, install. Flooring, lighting, plumbing, electrics – 'the complete service'*

THE PAINTED KITCHEN CO

ADDRESS 245 Munster Road, SW6 6BS
TEL/FAX 0171 385 3020

Robert Malston is a wizard with paint finishes, and his partner Barry Higginson is a cabinet maker. The result is Gustavian and Shaker-inspired bespoke kitchens in natural wood and specialist paint effects. 'The emphasis here is heavily on service – we tailor all our designs to the client's specifications.' Special cabinetry is made in workshops in Greenwich; other less expensive units are bought in. They are the only London agents for the Alpha range oil- or gas-fired cooker – a jet-burner system which comes up to temperature very quickly. Demo model in the showroom
TUBE *Fulham Broadway* • **OPEN** *Tues–Fri 10.30am–6pm. Sat 10.30am–5pm* • **SERVICES** *Plan, design, make, install. Full interior design service, with all tiling, flooring, plumbing, electrics*

RHODE DESIGN

ADDRESS 137–139 Essex Road, Islington, N1 2NR
TEL 0171 354 9933   **FAX** 0171 354 1006

Rhode Design pioneered the Shaker approach – look, no fuss – and painted their simple flat doors in deep blue-greens, rusty reds and chalky blues. London loved the look, which has been widely copied. Change of ownership now gives a choice of three brands: Harvey Jones (qv), Rhode Design and Mertzbau. Also furniture to paint and fit yourself.
SERVICES *Plan, design, make, install. Ideas modified to suit*

ROOMS

ADDRESS 49 Mottingham Road, SE9 4QZ
TEL 0181 857 5699   **FAX** 0181 857 7425
Tony Witcombe has run this friendly company for 19 years, selling mostly small manufacturers (Ultima, La Cuisine and Rooms own brand) 'to provide the unusual'. KSA member.
RAIL *Mottingham* • **OPEN** *Mon–Sat 9am–5pm* • **SERVICES** *Plan, design, supply, install. Free local delivery*

ROUNDHOUSE DESIGN

ADDRESS 25 Chalk Farm Road, NW1 8AG
TEL 0171 428 9955   **FAX** 0171 267 1035
This partnership of architects and furniture designers describe their 'signature look' as 'clean, fresh and contemporary'. Specialising in hand-built kitchens and other bespoke furniture, they have several standard ranges as well as individually-designed wooden and hand-painted cabinets.
TUBE *Chalk Farm/Camden* • **OPEN** *Mon–Fri 9.30am–6pm. Sat Sun 11am–5pm* • **SERVICES** *Plan, design, make, install* • **ALSO AT** *857 Fulham Road, SW6 5HJ (0171 736 7360) – closed Sun*

SMALLBONE

ADDRESS 105–109 Fulham Road, SW3 6RL
TEL 0171 581 9989   **FAX** 0171 581 9415
Behind the hyped-up image Smallbone is indeed a trend-setter – it introduced the first kitchens in old pine, then the painted finishes, followed by the unfitted kitchen. Now the mood is smooth and metropolitan. However for all this, expect to pay substantially. The magic name of Smallbone in posh property ads ups the value of a house. The imposing showrooms are a very palace of interior design and well worth a browse, even if – just for the time-being – such excellence is beyond your finances. The service is a total cocoon, and includes fitted bathrooms, bedrooms and panelled rooms.
TUBE *South Kensington* • **OPEN** *Mon–Fri 9am–5.30pm. Sat 10am–5pm. Some Sundays 12 noon–6pm – please phone to check* • **SERVICES** *Plan, design, make, install. Expert in painted finishes. Interior design. Inspirational brochure – 0171 589 5998*

SMITH AND SONS

ADDRESS Anvil House, Matthias Road, N16 8NU
TEL 0171 254 1200   **FAX** 0171 249 6988
This old-established firm – it dates back to 1865 – has earned the nickname 'the professionals' professional'. It's an upmarket builders merchant, specialising in kitchens and bathrooms with extensive displays, including sink, taps, tiles and appliances.
RAIL *Dalston Junction* • **OPEN** *Mon–Fri 8am–5pm. Sat 8am–4pm* • **WEBSITE** *www.smithgroup.co.uk* • **SERVICES** *Planning*

WOODSTOCK FURNITURE

ADDRESS 4 William Street, Knightsbridge, SW1X 9HL
TEL 0171 245 9989   **FAX** 0171 245 9981
For the look and feel of solid wood, go to the people that pioneered it. Famous for solid timbers such as oak, maple and cherry, they also offer

pretty painted finishes. Plus furniture, panelling, worktops and joinery for any room from their Winchester workshops.

TUBE *Knightsbridge* • **OPEN** *Mon–Fri 9am–5.30pm. Sat 10am–4pm (viewing only)* • **SERVICES** *Plan, design, make, install. Nationwide deliveries*

APPLIANCES, SINKS AND WORKTOPS

> *'Shirley Williams is a member of the upper-middle class and can achieve that kitchen-sink-revolutionary look that one cannot get unless one has been to a really good school.'*
> Dame Rebecca West, in an interview with journalist Jilly Cooper in *The Sunday Times*

These are the kitchen bits that take all the strain, yet often people are more concerned about the look of their cupboards than choosing these vitals. Get the appliances to suit the life you live. And ditto the sink – which needs to cope with the washing-up rather than simply look beautiful. You could say the same for worktops, too. And the whole lot need fixing at heights which are comfortable for you and partner/family to use. Then you can think about filling the gaps with cupboards – or with simple shelves and under work-top trollies if money is tight.

For cut-price/discounts, look for MONEY SAVERS. When buying discounted electrics, please ask about servicing/parts/guarantee. Re-conditioned appliances can be real money-savers – again ask about guarantees, and if possible buy from a source reasonably close to home so you can go back if anything goes wrong.

AMERICAN APPLIANCE CENTRE
ADDRESS Larkshall Business Centre, 52 Larkshall Road, E4 6PD
TEL 0181 529 9665 **FAX** 0181 529 9666
Showroom for luxury American fridge freezers, range cookers, vast sinks, ice-makers and so on. Definitely the top end of the market, and if for you, biggest is best, this is where you'll find it. They'll then recommend a stockist, which in London will probably be Harrods.
TUBE *Woodford Green* • **RAIL** *Chingford* • **OPEN** *Mon–Fri 9am–5pm*
• **WEBSITE** *www.american-appliance.co.uk*

APPLIANCE DIRECT
ADDRESS 66 Westbourne Grove, W2 5SH
TEL/FAX 0171 221 1144
Ex-display and discounted washing machines, dishwashers, and cookers, plus some small electrical goods.
TUBE *Notting Hill Gate* • **OPEN** *Tues Thurs 9.30am–7pm. Sat 10am–5.30pm*

ARCHITECTURAL WALL AND FLOOR
ADDRESS Unit 3, Premier Mill, Begonia Street, Darwin, Lancs, BB3 2DR
TEL 01254 873994 **FAX** 01254 702243
Sanitaryware handmade by local craftsmen using 100-year-old methods. Belfast sinks, combination sinks, gamekeepers, French farmhouse, cleaners'

sinks, waste-disposal Belfast are all available. Also fire-clay drainers, plus
co-ordinated taps and wastes.
OPEN *Mon–Fri 9am–5pm. Sat 9am–2pm* • **SERVICES** *Nationwide deliveries*

BORDERCRAFT ✉

ADDRESS Old Forge, Peterchurch, Herefordshire, HR2 0SD
TEL 01981 550 251   **FAX** 01981 550 552
Specialist makes of bespoke hardwood worktops

BUYERS AND SELLERS

ADDRESS 120–122 Ladbroke Grove, W10 5NE
TEL 0171 229 1947/8468   **FAX** 0171 221 4113
Cynthia Coyne, wheeler-dealer par excellence and domestic appliance
doyenne, offers 'best prices' on all white and a burgeoning choice of
coloured goods. Some tall fridge-freezers are even patterned with huge
cityscapes or giant fruits. All stock is brand new and guaranteed. Major
brands – Electrolux, Zanussi, Philips, Ariston *et al*; discounts up to 20 per cent.
TUBE *Ladbroke Grove* • **OPEN** *Mon–Fri 9.30am–5.30pm. Sat 9.30am–4.30pm*
• **SERVICES** *Armchair shopping: Cynthia and helpers give advice and/or
take orders over the phone. Deliveries*

CARTERS

ADDRESS 1 Thesiger Road, SE20 7NQ
TEL 0181 778 2165   **FAX** 0181 778 5002
Buy stainless steel trollies, tables and even ranges second-hand to save
money. Trollies are around £90, and a 5ft table is £140.
RAIL *Kenthouse* • **OPEN** *Mon–Fri 9.30am–6pm. Closed for lunch 1–2pm*
SERVICES *Can make up stainless steel worktops to order*

CITY DOMESTIC APPLIANCES 🐷

ADDRESS 131 Essex Road, N1 2SN
TEL 0171 837 6668   **FAX** 0171 359 7202
Hoover machines; full guarantee. Spare parts. Repairs.
RAIL *Essex Road* • **OPEN** *Mon–Fri 9am–5pm. Sat 9.30am–4.30pm*

CLASSIC GRANITES ✉

TEL/FAX 01777 710366
Full range of granites for custom-designed worktops, supplied and
installed nationwide.

CRAFTSHIP WORKTOPS ✉

TEL 01444 232234   **FAX** 01444 246706
Quality hardwood made-to-measure worktops with sink cut-outs, drainers,
granite inserts and so on.
SERVICES *Made to measure – takes three to four weeks. Nationwide deliveries*

DAVID EMERSON ✉

ADDRESS King's Close, Yapton, Arundel, W. Sussex, BN18 0EX
TEL 01243 552966   **FAX** 01243 553324
Made-to-measure worktops (takes seven days). Hard-wearing Duropal
laminates in huge colour range and textures. Cut-outs for sinks, hobs etc.
OPEN *Mon–Fri 8am–5pm* • **SERVICES** *Nationwide deliveries*

DISCOUNT COOKERS 🐷

ADDRESS 97 Rushey Green Road, Catford, SE6 4AF
TEL 0181 461 5273   **FAX** 0181 695 0046

The freestanding cooker and fridge is still much in demand, and here's where you'll find them – and at a bargain price. New and reconditioned models from all top makes, with around 2,000 in stock at any one time. Buying in bulk means keener prices. Their speciality is those covetable big American appliances – range cookers and fridge-freezers.

RAIL *Catford Bridge* • **OPEN** *Mon–Sat 9am–6pm. Sun 10am–3pm*

J D DOMESTIC APPLIANCES 🐷

ADDRESS 988–994 Harrow Road, NW10 5NT
TEL 0181 968 8722   **FAX** 0181 968 7041

Reconditioned fridges, cookers, washing machines. Also service/repairs.

TUBE *Kensal Green* • **OPEN** *Mon–Sat 9am–5pm*

G D EVANS 🐷

ADDRESS 331–333 High Street, Slough, Berks, SL1 1TX
TEL 01753 524188   **FAX** 01753 572029

Ex-exhibition, ex-display, built-in or freestanding ovens, hobs, cookers, washing machines, fridges, freezers, all colours. Handsome discounts. Over 2000 appliances in stock. Mainly Neff, AEG and Siemens. Friendly service from family firm trading since 1956. Phone for current offers.

RAIL *Slough* • **OPEN** *Mon–Sat 9–5.30pm* • **SERVICES** *Nationwide deliveries*

FREDERICK

ADDRESS 387–9 High Road, Wood Green, N22 8JA
TEL 0181 881 5509   **FAX** 0181 889 8443

Made-to-measure or cut-to-size laminated worktops in pastels, bright colours and speckled effects. Also solid wood worktops in oak, cherry, maple, sycamore, ash or pine. Plus complete kitchens and appliances.

TUBE *Wood Green* • **OPEN** *Mon–Fri 8.15am–5pm. Sat 9am–1pm*
• **SERVICES** *Mitreing, and cut-outs for sinks and hobs*

GEC ANDERSON 🚐

ADDRESS Oakengrove, Shie Lane, Hastoe, Herts, HP23 6LY
TEL 01442 826999   **FAX** 01442 825999

For many years, this firm beavered away at stainless steel sinks for hospitals and schools, and loos for prisons. Suddenly, industrial chic is top of the looks, and now they're flooded with domestic demands, mostly channelled through architects. Stainless-steel sinks and worktops are made to measure, including cut-outs for hobs. Bowls available separately, with flat flanges for mounting under granite or marble. Also stainless-steel shelves, drawers and cupboards to finish the job. Not cheap, but 'the best possible price'.

RAIL *Tring* • **OPEN** *By appointment only* • **SERVICES** *Nationwide deliveries*

HANSENS KITCHEN EQUIPMENT

ADDRESS 306 Fulham Road, SW10 9ER
TEL 0171 351 6933   **FAX** 0171 351 5319

These catering suppliers are specialists in range cookers. In an impressive basement display kitchen, you can put a working Lacanche range through its paces. 'Men in particular get really enthusiastic,' they say. But it doesn't come cheap. These cookers must be fitted with professional-style hoods, so supplied and installed it costs around £5000. Other brands include Viking. **TUBE** *Fulham Broadway* • **OPEN** *Mon–Fri 9am–5.30pm. Sat 10am–5pm* • **WEBSITE** *www.hansens.co.uk* • **SERVICES** *Saturday cooking demos. Site surveys and installations. Stainless steel fabrication*

HOT AND COLD INC 🐖

ADDRESS 13–15 Goldborne Road, W10 5NY
TEL 0181 960 1300   **FAX** 0181 960 4163
Very British despite the name. In a smallish, jam-packed shop, owner Richard Fuchs tirelessly controls sale and despatch of hundreds of appliances on display. Around 90 brands – all discounted. You're virtually certain of a bargain, and a pretty posh one at that. Miele, Scholtes, Neff, Gaggenau, Bosch etc. New perfect but superseded models from half-price.
TUBE *Westbourne Park* • **OPEN** *Mon–Sat 10am–6pm*

ICETECH APPLIANCES

ADDRESS 1–3 Baron's Court Road, W14 9DP
TEL 0171 381 2303/3119   **FAX** 0171 381 9090
All makes of freestanding/built-in appliances from budget to top range. 1000 lines in stock, including sinks, taps, waste disposers. Very competitive prices. Also Bosch appliances with slight 'cosmetic' faults (eg small chip or scratch).
TUBE *West Kensington* • **OPEN** *Mon–Fri 9.30am–6pm. Sat 9am–5pm*

JOHN STRAND

ADDRESS 12–22 Herga Road, Wealdstone, Harrow, Middx, HA3 5AS
TEL 0181 930 6006   **FAX** 0181 930 9008
Specialise in complete mini-kitchens which shut away into cupboards – for example sink with drainers, two hotplates, fridge, cupboard space and a microwave for around £940 plus VAT.
TUBE *Harrow & Wealdstone* • **OPEN** *Mon–Fri 9am–5pm*

KIRKSTONE

ADDRESS 128 Walham Green Court, Moore Park Road, SW6 4DG
TEL 0171 381 0424   **FAX** 0171 381 0434
New London showroom for Kirkstone and Brathay green Cumbrian slates found only in the Lake District, and quarried since Roman times – plus limestones, granites, travertines and slates from abroad.
TUBE *Fulham Broadway* • **OPEN** *Tues–Fri 9.30am–5.50pm. Sat 10am–4.30pm* • **SERVICES** *Design advice and cut-outs for sinks, hobs etc*

LACY GAS 🐖

ADDRESS 22 Lacy Road, SW15 1NL
TEL 0181 785 7126   **FAX** 0181 789 3080
New merchandise and all major brands with discounts from 10–40 per cent. Common appliances are readily available but boilers, fires etc may need a few days.
TUBE *Putney Bridge* • **OPEN** *Mon–Fri 9am–5pm. Sat 9am–3pm* • **SERVICES** *Can order anything that is not standard stock*

QUALITY MARBLE

See TILES, page 106. Marble and granite slabs for kitchen worktops.

RUISLIP APPLIANCES

ADDRESS 114 Pembroke Road, Ruislip Manor, Middx, HA4 8NW
TEL 01895 633837   **FAX** 01895 674551
Most models of Neff and De Dietrich in stock. Service some appliances.
TUBE *Ruislip Manor* • **OPEN** *Mon–Fri 9am–5.30pm. Sat 9am–5pm*

SOUTH LONDON HARDWOODS

ADDRESS 12 Belgrave Road, SE25 5AN
TEL 0181 771 6764   **FAX** 0181 771 5555
Specialists in hardwood worktops – 'basically anything customer wants'.
Popular woods include cherry, red elm, iroko, oak, beech, maple and ash.
Takes about three weeks. They also do flooring and make up doors.
RAIL *Norwood Junction* • **OPEN** *(factory shop) Mon–Fri 8am–5.30pm.
Sat 8am–1pm* • **SERVICES** *Installations in London area*

TRADITIONAL KITCHENS ✉

ADDRESS The Pound, Kinthall Lane, Broadheath, Tenbury Wells, WR15 8QR
TEL 01886 853421
The sink you can take with you – Belfast sink with brass taps built into free-
standing unit in reclaimed pine, hardwood or painted. Matching furniture
to order.

VICTORIA KITCHENS 🐖

TEL 0181 648 7773
Bob Hornsby (in the fitted kitchen business for 20 years) will advise
on all built-in appliances and then supply at 'lowest prices', boxed and
guaranteed – ovens, hoods, dishwashers, sinks, fridges, freezers and so
on. No showroom, but he will visit in the London area and discuss needs.

WOODSTOCK

See KITCHENS: COMPLETE KITCHENS, page 111. Experts in wooden
worktops.

ZARKA MARBLE

ADDRESS 41a Belsize Lane, NW3 5AU
TEL 0171 431 3042   **FAX** 0171 431 3879
Marble and granite worktops in any size or shape. Also marble vanity
tops, table tops, bath surrounds, flooring, wall lining and so on.
TUBE *Belsize Park/Swiss Cottage* • **OPEN** *Mon–Fri 8am–5pm, but please
phone first* • **SERVICES** *Supply and fix*

KITCHENWARE

Good cooks avoid pot luck. They choose pans with deadly
discrimination. Top chefs love copper, not for its seductive golden
glow, but because it gets hot quickest. A popular alternative is
robust stainless steel, easy to keep squeaky clean and shiny, but

needing a 'sandwich' bottom of another metal such as copper to cook well. Other possibilities are aluminium, colourful enamel, or even glass for see-through cooking. Make sure your pans and cooker enjoy a good relationship: for example, fussy new-tech ceramic and halogen hobs demand quality pans with super-flat bases. Knobs and handles should be comfortable to hold and heatproof: wood is pleasant, but hates the dishwasher, or even a long soak in the sink. A hole or ring for hanging high is useful. PS: don't cry over burnt pans. Soak them overnight in a solution of biological washing powder.

BODUM

ADDRESS 24 Neal Street, WC2H 9PS
TEL/FAX 0171 240 9176
'Good design should not be expensive,' declares Jorgen Bodum, the man from Denmark who's the force behind this delightful shop. He's not a puritan, though, and there's a fun element as well. Designs have become classics, but are more affordable than Alessi. Glass, plastics and metal combine in witty and useful coffee-makers, teapots, vacuum flasks and other essentials. The range just keeps on growing, and staff are friendly.
TUBE Covent Garden • **OPEN** Mon–Sat 10am–7pm. Sun noon–5pm.
ALSO AT Whiteley's Shopping Centre, Queensway W2 (0171 729 1213).
71 King's Road, SW3 (0171 376 3825)

DAVID MELLOR

ADDRESS 4 Sloane Square, SW1W 8EE
TEL 0171 730 4259   **FAX** 0171 730 7240
One of London's first 'designer' shops, and a perennial favourite. David Mellor, who's just – and justly – had a retrospective at the Design Museum, is internationally famous – particular for cutlery. Come here for full displays of his modern classics. Also find English crafts such as baskets, ceramics and woodware to soften the effect of gleaming metal pans and knives. A high degree of excellence, with pleasant, friendly service.
TUBE Sloane Square • **OPEN** Mon–Sat 9.30am–6pm • **SERVICES** Mail-order catalogue

DISCOUNT HOUSE

ADDRESS 148 Kilburn High Road, NW6 4JD
TEL 0171 328 4306   **FAX** 0171 625 6306
Happy hunting-ground for bargain kitchen and tableware.
TUBE Kilburn/Kilburn Park • **OPEN** Mon–Thurs 9am–5.30pm.
Fri Sat 9am–6pm. Sun 10am–4pm

DIVERTIMENTI

ADDRESS 139–141 Fulham Road, SW3 6SD
TEL 0171 581 8065   **FAX** 0171 823 9429
Their specialist cookware makes even advanced cooking seem easy. Plus the very best for everyday tasks. Luscious tableware in shiny, plain glazes and hand-decorated patterns. Also cookbooks, baskets, herbs and spices. Beguiling and beautiful: batten down your wallet.
TUBE South Kensington • **OPEN** Mon–Sat 10am–6pm.
Sun 12 noon– 5.30pm • **SERVICES** Mail order (0181 246 4300)
• **ALSO AT** 45–47 Wigmore Street W1H 9LE (0171 935 0689)

ELIZABETH DAVID

ADDRESS 3 North Row, The Market, Covent Garden, WC2E 8RA
TEL 0171 836 9167   **FAX** 01264 354403

The spirit of the most famous cook pre-Delia lives on – ED was the first to give Britain a blast of the Mediterranean, complete with herbs and garlic. There's everything here to keep even the most demanding cook happy, in porcelain, earthenware, copper, stainless steel and aluminium. From basic knives and pans to specialist equipment and gadgets, with woodware and baskets as a softening touch. Especially good for colourful Le Creuset. Personal service and friendly advice.

TUBE *Covent Garden* • **OPEN** *Mon–Sat 10.30am–6.30pm. Sun 12 noon–5pm* • **SERVICES** *Cake tin hire*

GILL WING COOKSHOP

ADDRESS 190 Upper Street, N1 1RQ
TEL/FAX 0171 226 5392

Opening on Sundays has earned this small crowded shop a loyal following amongst cooks with a busy lifestyle. Atmosphere is friendly. 'We have all those tricky bits of equipment that are hard to find elsewhere.' How about an oyster knife, for example? Plain white bone-china seconds are a good money-saver.

TUBE *Highbury & Islington* • **OPEN** *Mon–Sat 9.30am–6pm. Sun 10am–6pm*

LA CUISINIERE

ADDRESS 81–83 Northcote Road, SW11 6PJ
TEL/FAX 0171 223 4487

Annie Price and Anne Blackie cram their inspirational shop with utensils and gadgets of all kinds, packed on to shelves and even hanging overhead. Service, they promise, is 'sincere, knowledgeable and friendly.' Here you can hire jam pans, fish kettles or cake tins, and they can carry out wedding lists, or supply by mail order. 'If we haven't got something in stock, then we'll try and get for you.'

RAIL *Clapham Junction* • **OPEN** *Mon–Sat 9.30am–6pm* • **WEBSITE** *www.la–cusiniere.com* • **SERVICES** *Wedding lists. Pan hire. Mail order*

LEON JAEGGI AND SONS

ADDRESS 77 Shaftesbury Avenue, W1V 7AD
TEL 0171 631 1080   **FAX** 0171 494 3591

Caters for caterers, but individual shoppers are welcome. The stacks of burnished copper which stand beacon-like in the window are made in their own Staines workshops. Most pans are lined with tin (re-tinning service available). But for very high temperatures (crêpes, omelettes) linings are silver. Also own-make black iron omelette and frying pans. Season on first use: sprinkle with salt, and heat gently for half an hour. Wipe out with kitchen paper and rub over with cooking oil and more salt; heat again. Wipe out and never wash again – suits me!

TUBE *Leicester Square* • **OPEN** *Mon–Sat 9am–5.30pm* • **SERVICES** *Re-tinning for copper pans*

MRS SYKES KITCHENRY
ADDRESS 146 High Street, Teddington, TW11 8HZ
TEL 0181 943 2951   **FAX** 0181 977 5160
In the environs of Teddington, the name of Mrs Ginny Sykes is nearly as
well-known as Mrs Beeton. Shop here both for basics and specialist items.
A double-fronted Victorian façade leads into a charming interior full of
unexpected corners and original fireplaces. In the centre: a long refectory
table weighed down with gleaming pans, scales, fish kettles, steamers and
smokers, above which hang racks full of sieves, graters, heat diffusers and
chapatti pans.'We are idiosyncratic and friendly,' Ginny promises, 'with
a helpful and knowledgeable staff of housewives and cooks: they won't
look blank if you ask for a dariole mould.' Always in stock: sugar cake
decorations.
RAIL *Teddington* • **OPEN** *Mon–Sat 9.30am–5.30pm* • **SERVICES** *Hire service
for cake moulds (numbers, letters, shapes, wedding cake tiers), plus fish
kettles/preserving pans*

RICHARD DARE
ADDRESS 93 Regents Park Road, NW1 8UR
TEL 0171 722 9428   **FAX** 0171 625 7639
The original Mr Dare has retired, but the shop – a local byword for kitchen
necessities – goes on, providing essential and attractive kitchenware
including iron racks and willow baskets. Kit yourself out with a complete
batterie de cuisine (serious saucepans from £50 to £100), or buy a small
gift for a £1.
TUBE *Chalk Farm* • **OPEN** *Mon–Fri 9.30am–6pm. Sat 10am–6pm*

SUMMERHILL AND BISHOP
ADDRESS 100 Portland Road, W11 4LN
TEL 0171 221 4566   **FAX** 0171 727 1322
Here old is mixed with new, continental with British, in a mix that spreads
down narrow twisty stairs into a deep basement. This is where fashionable
foodies get their home equipment fix, and prices are not cheap. Boxwood-
handled cutlery from France's oldest makers, Nontron and Laguiole, costs
from £145 for a set of six knives with stainless steel blades. French baker's
shelves in any size to order. Olive wood from the South of France is
popular – salad bowls from £53 to £150; pestle and mortar from £39.
Much-prized are American maple chopping boards, from £90 to £200.
Equipment for the professional cook includes the complete range of
American Calphalon and Italian Paderno pans, and knives from Henkel of
Germany, plus items from Japan. Also basketware, terracotta, wirework
and old French enamel from markets and *brocantes* (French antique
shops) – cafetieres from £45. A fleeting visit is no good – you've got to
browse.
TUBE *Holland Park* • **OPEN** *Mon–Sat 10am–6pm* • **SERVICES** *Solid French
oak furniture made to measure – tables and cupboards in colourwashed
finishes. Takes four weeks*

BATHROOMS

> *'The biggest waste of water in the country by far.*
> *You spend half a pint and flush two gallons.'*
> The Duke of Edinburgh

The bathroom's lot is not a spacious one in most cases, so space-saving is top priority. Look out for new ideas in storage furniture that fit around basins and loos.

By contrast, some London homeowners decide to sacrifice a spare bedroom to bathroom conversion. Then the trend is to make the bathroom a comfy living area, with extras that might include an armchair or even an open fire.

White is still the preferred colour for over half the purchasers of new sanitaryware – however, like paint, it comes in numerous guises, including cream, ivory and stone. Brighter colours are creeping back – aquamarine and yellow are in demand.

You wouldn't think your basic bath could change much. But research and innovation is relentless. Latest space-saving shapes taper off at the tap/feet end. Period-loving punters can peruse a fresh influx of cast-iron repro, getting prettier and cheaper all the time. Meanwhile modern materials improve – acrylics such as Lucite are smooth, warm to the touch, strong, and chip-proof.

Plumbing is getting cleverer. Ducted designs conceal snaky pipework behind shallow partitions. New back-to-the-wall designs for loos have concealed cisterns. The result is sleeker and easier to clean. Basin shapes are wilder – chic ceramic ovals or circles set in slabs of glass, marble, granite or resin. Underframes replace dreary pedestals providing more sculptural potential.

The modern bathroom is a haven of water therapy, with pulsating power showers, steam cabinets, baths with massage jets. Or just a traditional tub for a good old long hot soak. The British still don't favour bidets – 'we'd only buy one to fill a space,' said the majority of respondents in a recent survey.

USEFUL CONTACTS

THE BATHROOM SHOWROOM ASSOCIATION
TEL 01782 747123
For your nearest member and planning hints.

ARMITAGE SHANKS
TEL 0800 866966
Bathroom Book including design and layout advice.

MIRA
TEL 01242 221221
For shower facts and free booklet.

DOULTON
TEL 01270 879 777
Free inspirational bathroom magazine.

IDEAL STANDARD
TEL 01482 499414
Bathroom planning advice and latest design news.

BATHROOM SPECIALISTS

BRITISH BATHROOM CENTRE
ADDRESS 35–41 Market Place, Hampstead Garden Suburb, NW11 6JT
TEL 0181 201 8811   **FAX** 0181 207 8831
Large showroom with four shops knocked into one, showing all major brands.
TUBE *East Finchley* • **OPEN** *Mon-Fri 9am–6pm. Sat 10am–4pm* • **SERVICES**
Complete design and installation service for the whole bathroom, including plumbing and tiling

COLOURWASH
ADDRESS 63-65 Fulham High Street, SW6 3JJ
TEL 0171 371 0911   **FAX** 0171 371 9670
David Jones promotes affordable designer bathrooms – both top-name products and own-label ranges. He promises friendly expert customer service and technical advice. Showrooms have small room-settings with good design ideas.
TUBE *Putney Bridge* • **OPEN** *Mon–Fri 9.30am–5.30pm. Sat 10am–5pm*
• **SERVICES** *Free site visits locally, to advise and plan. Free local delivery*
• **ALSO AT** *165 Chamberlyne Road, NW10 3NU (0181 459 8918)*

DURANTE INTERNATIONAL BATHROOMS
ADDRESS 266 Brompton Road, SW3 2AS
TEL 0171 589 9990   **FAX** 0171 589 9955
Paula and Aubrey Durante are Jacuzzi junkies – they've been promoting them for 21 years. Together with technical advisor Andy Reynolds, they provide the 'active bathroom', complete with Jacuzzi whirlpool baths, and/or spas and steam enclosures. They specialise in contemporary, very minimalist shower enclosures and sanitaryware, with glass and stainless steel tops from makers like Megius, Bolan, Triade and Pyram, as well as traditional designs, including popular Art Deco. 'We scour the USA and Europe for these unusual products.' They're particularly good at cutting and fitting marble and granite.
TUBE *South Kensington* • **OPEN** *Mon–Fri 9.30am–5.30pm.*
Sat 10.30am– 5pm • **SERVICES** *Full interior design – colour schemes. Cut/fit marble, granite and other stones*

C P HART AND SONS

ADDRESS Newnham Terrace, Hercules Road, SE1 7DR
TEL 0171 902 1000   **FAX** 0171 902 1001

One moment, the Waterloo wastelands, the next a glowing glassy modern shopfront spread out literally underneath the arches, a landmark in South East London for more than 30 years. Hart's pioneered a designer look for the old trade-type showrooms, and were one of the first to welcome the public as well as builders and plumbers. Now displays spread out over 25,000 sq ft – 'largest showrooms in the UK', they say – seemingly endless vistas of inspirational bathrooms and kitchens, both mod and trad. Handy information boards set out costs, with staff trained in design and practicalities. Extensive Siematic kitchens displays. Good stocks, value for money, exclusive lines, and design pioneers in their own reliable way. They get my vote.

TUBE *Lambeth North/Waterloo* • **OPEN** *Mon–Sat 9am–5.30pm* • **SERVICES** *Free immediate delivery within the London area. Free colour bathroom brochure – a bathroom bible. Kitchen planning. Can recommend plumbers/fitters. Ample free parking* • **ALSO AT** *103–105 Regent's Park Road, Primrose Hill, NW1 8UR (0171 586 9856). Here's the place for Philippe Starck and other avant-garde ablutionaries – Jasper Morrison, Dieter Sieger, and Phoenix Design*

MAX PIKE

ADDRESS 4 Eccleston Street, SW1W 9LN
TEL 0171 730 7216   **FAX** 0171 730 3789

Top Max: the man that elevated bathroom fittings into objects of desire – a larger than life character who has infinite expertise in the provision of timeless luxury bathrooms, claiming the widest and most exclusive range in Europe. He is tireless in his exploration of new materials and technology. A trawl around his showroom, with its arresting window displays, will uncover traditional and modern shapes for basins, bidets and taps. And baths, of course, from the coolest white to the hottest red, from a small hip bath to a family tub. Hydrotherapy, power showers, glazed lava worktops, and an exclusive stainless steel collection called The Kan are also on the Pike agenda.

TUBE *Victoria* • **OPEN** *Mon–Fri 10am–6pm*

ORIGINAL BATHROOMS

ADDRESS 143/145 Kew Road, Richmond, Surrey, TW9 2PN
TEL 0181 940 7554   **FAX** 0181 948 8200

The Pidgeons are the oldest UK bathroom family – five generations since 1876. Great-uncle Frederick was apprenticed in 1871 to Thomas Crapper, the celebrated inventor of the WC (and enricher of the English language). 'We offer unparalleled depth of knowledge and experience, plus the very best of service.' Around 20 displays of modern and traditional bathrooms in a well-lit showroom. Fittings at the cutting edge of bathroom design, imported exclusively from Italy: basins created from minimal slabs of glass, stainless steel or wood; taps that work like a joystick. Soak up the benefits of pulsating Jacuzzis and thrill to the power of the pumped shower.

TUBE/RAIL *Richmond* • **OPEN** *Mon-Fri 9am–5.30pm. Sat 9am–5pm* • **SERVICES** *Design/planning*

PIPE DREAMS OF KENSINGTON

ADDRESS 72 Gloucester Road, SW7 4QT
TEL 0171 225 3978   **FAX** 0171 589 8841

Luxury room-settings abound in this up-market bathroom company, established for ten years, with an 'anything you want' attitude. Tailor-made steam shower rooms, luxury baths, and hydro-massage systems. Skilled artists can paint ceramic basins and so on with your own designs. They make limestone, granite and marble for vanity tops, splashbacks, bath surrounds and floors.

TUBE *Gloucester Road* • **OPEN** *Mon–Fri 9.30am–5.30pm. Sat 10.30am–5pm* • **WEBSITE** *www.pipedreams.co.uk* • **SERVICES** *Design, supply and install. Hand-painting. Cabinet-making. Marble, granite, mosaic*

TSUNAMI

ADDRESS 27 Wigmore Street, W1H 9LD
TEL 0171 408 2230   **FAX** 0171 408 2210

In case you're wondering, Tsunami (a Japanese word) is a scientific tag for a seismic sea wave. This particular Tsunami has moved from the King's Road, where they were called, more prosaically, Chelsea Interiors (no need to explain that). Luxury bathrooms and kitchens are sourced from all over Europe. Teuco Italian whirlpool baths and steam shower units, Showerlux German baths and shower enclosures, Hans Grohe German taps and showers, and French specialist baths and taps. They also show Rapsel and Vola – ultra-modern glass basins and taps, together with Vcosan baths and shower enclosures, Koralle showers and baths, and Selles sanitaryware. Kitchens by Zeyko and Rivendell, with quality appliances. Granite and marble is a speciality (plus Corian and Pyrolave) for worktops, bathroom counters, bath surrounds, and wall cladding. 'We listen carefully, we're very conscious of design, and we pay attention to detail.'

TUBE *Bond Street* • **OPEN** *Mon–Fri 9.30am–5.30pm. Sat 10am–4pm*
• **SERVICES** *Complete interior design service for bathrooms and kitchens*

WEST ONE BATHROOMS

ADDRESS 130–138 Garratt Lane, SW18 4EE
TEL 0181 870 2121   **FAX** 0181 874 4141

Well-known for their pretty showroom in the heart of Mayfair, with its selections of French hand-painted basins, West One Bathroom (established in 1978) have opened a 'state-of-the-art' Wandsworth showroom covering 10,000 sq ft. Around 30 bathroom displays, with sanitaryware and tiles by Villeroy & Boch. Also Hans Grohe, Vola, Jado, Sanitan, Vernon Tutbury, Margot, Pom D'Or and many more. Working displays show trade and public alike the best way to install sophisticated continental models. Jacuzzi whirlpool and steam baths, and lots of ideas for different tile layouts. Bathroom accessories down to the last wastebin, light, crystal pot and so on.

RAIL *Earlsfield* • **OPEN** *Mon–Sat 9am–6pm* • **SERVICES** *Bathroom planning/ design. Children's play area with TV and video. Deliveries* • **ALSO AT** *45–46 South Audley Street, W1Y 5DG (0171 499 1845) Well-established Mayfair branch for luxury bathroom fittings. And at 60 Queenstown Road, SW8 3RY (0171 720 9333)*

TRADITIONAL BATHROOMS

*'The next thing he saw was a washstand with ewers and basins and soap
and brushes and towels; and a large bath, full of clean water – what a
heap of things and all for washing!...Tom for the first time in his life found
out that he was dirty, and burst into tears with shame and anger.'*
Charles Kingsley (1819–75), *The Water Babies*

However hi-tech the world of water becomes, there are still those
that yearn for the reassuring solidity of a roll-top cast-iron bath, or
a loo with a cistern on high that you pull with a clunking chain.

BATHING BEAUTIES
ADDRESS 43 Muswell Hill Road, N10 3JB
TEL 0181 365 2794   **FAX** 0181 444 2383
Set in a fairly ordinary suburban parade of shops, this pretty little
showroom glows with polished wood, shiny ceramics and burnished brass.
They are specialists in fitted period-style bathrooms in solid, richly-coloured
hardwoods (from sustainable sources), and offer the expertise of a business
that's been going for 12 years. 'We're not interested in veneers, substitutes
or fakes.' They supply fully re-furbished French and English roll-top baths –
sample price for a double-ended French roll-top, £850. They also do a
range of re-cast Victorian basin stands and high level cisterns – a stand
and basin costs around £475 plus VAT. They can also offer marble
surrounds for basins and baths.
TUBE *Highgate + 134 bus* • **OPEN** *Mon–Fri 9am–5.30pm. Sat 9am–4pm*
• **SERVICES** *In-situ bath enamelling. Plan, design, install*

CZECH & SPEAKE
ADDRESS 39C Jermyn Street, SW1Y 6DN
TEL 0171 439 0216   **FAX** 0171 734 8587
Letting luxury loose in the bathroom is what this firm is all about, from
elegant old-style taps and shower fittings to the popular roll-top bath which
boasts all the style and stability of cast iron but in a man-made material
which is warm to the touch, won't chip, and helps keep the water hot
longer. The finishing touch is an exclusive range of aromatic fragrances –
bath oils, colognes and room sprays, made from high quality essential oils
and in agonisingly elegant packaging.
TUBE *Green Park/Piccadilly* • **OPEN** *Mon Wed Thurs Fri 9.30am–6pm.
Tues 10am–6pm. Sat 10am–5pm* • **ALSO AT** *125 Fulham Road, SW3 6RT
(0171 225 3667)*

SITTING PRETTY
ADDRESS 131 Dawes Road, SW6 7EA
TEL 0171 381 0049   **FAX** 0171 385 9621
James and Janice Williams pioneered the traditional bathroom revival over
20 years ago. This is the company that's still tops for bottoms – when
plastic was ubiquitous, they brought back the wooden loo seat, friendly,
comfortable, and, correctly treated and cleaned, perfectly hygienic.
The loo seats are made from joined sections of solid timber to save trees,
using mahogany and English hardwoods such as oak, elm, ash and
cherry. They cost from around £125 plus VAT. Add your coat of arms –

yes, people do – for an extra £80. Also reproduction sanitaryware,
including Gothic styles, with a wide range of taps.
TUBE *Fulham Broadway* • **OPEN** *Mon–Fri 10am–5pm. Sat 10am–1pm*
• **SERVICES** *Will recommend plumbers*

THE WATER MONOPOLY
ADDRESS 16–18 Lonsdale Road, NW6 6RD
TEL 0171 624 2636   **FAX** 0171 624 2631
Fine English and French antique sanitaryware. Free-standing roll-top baths
lined with acrylic can be given an outer coating of matt polyurethane in
virtually any colour. China basins are set in curlicues of wrought iron, whilst
wooden loo seats are bleach and stained. Baths range from a tiddly 2 ft
long to a giant 7 ft – in cast iron, with double ends, in copper, porcelain,
marble, or fireclay. These can be co-ordinated with porcelain basins, loo
pans and floral bidets. Capacious canopy baths can wrap you all around
in zinc, glass or copper hoods. They have photographs of their stock,
so phone and discuss needs, and they'll send ideas. Also reproduction
sanitaryware, with baths starting at £1,800.
TUBE *Queens Park* • **OPEN** *By appointment* • **SERVICES** *Own shotblasters,
metalplaters, recasters, engineers, enamellers and plumbers*

GENERAL
BATHROOM SUPPLIERS

The bathroom merchant has come up in the world, abandoning a
trade-only approach in favour of a consumer welcome, with bright
displays and friendly service. In some cases, the firms listed below
will take care of installation too; otherwise, they'll mostly have
a list of local plumbers they can recommend. And some of them
are even open on Sundays which shows the times really are
a-changing for the bathroom trade. Not long ago, you wouldn't
get a peep out of them beyond Saturday lunch time.

ABACUS
ADDRESS 681–689 Holloway Road, N19 5SE
TEL 0171 281 4136   **FAX** 0171 272 5081
Good display of major brands, including Sottini, plus kitchens. Unusual
items include small deep soaking tubs which fit into a very limited space.
TUBE *Archway* • **OPEN** *Mon–Fri 9am–5.30pm. Sat 9am–5pm. Sun
10.30am–1pm* • **SERVICES** *Design and plan bathrooms and kitchens*

ASTON-MATTHEWS
ADDRESS 141–147a Essex Road, Islington, N1 2SN
TEL 0171 226 7220   **FAX** 0171 354 5951
Established in Islington since 1823, this company has a huge range of
products – many exclusive – at keen prices. Ceramic shower trays, high-
quality taps, mixers and showers, over 100 styles of wash-basins and
WCs, double Belfast sinks and so on. Large stocks with speedy deliveries
on most lines. Large selection of new cast-iron baths (26 models, 16 sizes)
– for example repro Victorian roll-top baths with claw feet from around
£575. The Astonian contemporary stone slab basin is £198 – sharp

BATHROOMS 133design, at a sharp price. Also sleekly of the moment is the Astonian
stainless steel basin in beech or glass surround. Astonian ToTo chrome taps
are £104. Knowledgeable, enthusiastic staff do their best to de-mystify the
bathroom business – so walk right in and ask for John, David or Howard.
TUBE *Highbury and Islington* • **OPEN** *Mon–Fri 8.30am–5pm.
Sat 9.30am–2pm*

BATHWISE
ADDRESS 265–267 Northfield Avenue, W5 4UA
TEL/FAX 0181 840 5313
Established for four years this showroom covers two floors, and has
up-market brands such as Villeroy and Boch and Hans Grohe.
TUBE *Northfields* • **OPEN** *Mon–Fri 9am–5pm. Sat 9am–4pm. Sun 10am–
1pm* • **SERVICES** *Plan, design, and can install or recommend installers*

BURGE AND GUNSON
ADDRESS 13–27 High Street, Colliers Wood, SW19 2JE
TEL/FAX 0181 543 5166
Established for 30 years, this large 'working' showroom (power showrooms,
Jacuzzis) with over 50 displays, shows well-known brands, including Ideal
Standard, Sottini, and Villeroy & Boch.
TUBE *Colliers Wood* • **OPEN** *Mon–Fri 8am–5.30pm. Sat 8am–4pm*
• **SERVICES** *Customer car parking*

EMPRESS BUILDING CENTRE
ADDRESS 137 Long Lane, Finchley, N3 2HY
TEL 0181 346 6669 **FAX** 0181 346 4653
'Working' showroom (Jacuzzis, steam showers), established 12 years, and
with around 20 displays of well-known brands, including Sottini, Imperial,
Trent and Armitage Shanks.
TUBE *Finchley Central* • **OPEN** *Mon–Fri 8am–5.30pm. Sat 8.30am–5pm*
• **SERVICES** *Design and supply*

K D A HOMETEAM
ADDRESS 254–258 Watford Way, Hendon, NW4 4UJ
TEL 0181 202 4162 **FAX** 0181 203 5657
Well-established showroom (20 years) with wide selection of brands,
including Ideal Standard and Sottini – around ten bathroom and eight
kitchen displays.
TUBE *Hendon* • **OPEN** *Mon–Fri 8.30am–5pm. Sat 10am–5pm*

MISCELLANEA OF CHURT 🚗
ADDRESS Crossway, Churt, near Hindhead, Surrey, GU10 2JA
TEL 01428 714014 **FAX** 01428 712946
Huge selections – over 1,000 suites always in stock for immediate
collection or delivery, from major continental and British makers, including
Imperial, Sanitan, and Chatsworth. All latest colours, features and styles,
including saunas, Jacuzzis, steam enclosures, and pumped showers.
Also tiles and marble for sink and worktops, along with fitted kitchens
and bedrooms. Useful stock of rare and discontinued colours.
OPEN *Mon–Fri 8.30am–5pm. Sat 8.30am–4pm*
• **SERVICES** *Design and planning*

T PATTON

ADDRESS 588 Leabridge Road, Leyton, E10 7DN
TEL 0181 539 4942   **FAX** 0181 558 3578
Well-established firm of bathroom merchants – going for around 40 years –
with large showroom with around 20 displays: Armitage, Ideal Standard,
Vernon Tutbury and Sottini.
TUBE *Walthamstow Central/Leyton* • **OPEN** *Mon–Fri 8am–5pm.*
Sat 8am–12 noon

POTTER PERRIN

ADDRESS 412 Streatham High Road, SW16 6EX
TEL 0181 677 5321   **FAX** 0181 677 5326
Expect reliable personal service from a bathroom, shower and kitchen
specialist in business for over 50 years. Experienced in-store design service
is backed by huge stocks, including fireclay imported direct from France.
RAIL *Streatham* • **OPEN** *Mon–Sat 8.30am–5.30pm. Late night Thurs 8pm*

VENEZIA BATHROOMS

ADDRESS 1–5 Hampden Square, Osidge Lane, Southgate, N14 5JP
TEL 0181 368 6463   **FAX** 0181 361 3641
Around 50 displays in a smart showroom, established for 13 years.
Villeroy & Boch, Sottini, Sanitan, and Vernon Tutbury.
TUBE *Southgate* • **OPEN** *Mon–Sat 9am–5pm* • **SERVICES** *Design and install,*
including all plumbing and tiling

BATHROOM RENOVATION SERVICES

BATHROOM RENOVATIONS

ADDRESS 20 Moxon Street, W1M 3JE
TEL 0171 935 6590   **FAX** 0171 486 7639
Remove limescale, iron stains etc from enamelled cast-iron baths and then
re-coat in virtually unlimited choice of colours. Discoloured basins/loos
cleaned. Also do marble polishing.
TUBE *Baker Street* • **OPEN** *Mon–Fri 8.30am–5.30pm*

RENUBATH

ADDRESS 248 Lillie Road, SW6 7QA
TEL 0171 381 8337   **FAX** 0171 381 8907
Established now for over 30 years, Renubath supply a quick and efficient
re-surfacing bath treatment nationwide – no job is too small, or too large,
they say.
OPEN *Mon–Fri 9am–5pm, Sat by appointment*
• **WEBSITE** *www.weaveworld.co.uk/renubath*

BEDROOMS AND BEDS

The Romans used a 'lectus genialis' for their wedding night: then it was moved to the other side of the room and called a 'lectus adversus'
Plus ça change, plus c'est la même chose.

Something to sleep on is a basic necessity – along with a cooker and a way to keep warm. You spend a third of your life in bed – if you're lucky. Yet industry research reveals a huge proportion of younger people sleeping in second-hand beds. Not a good idea for reasons both of health and comfort. Standard width for a double bed is 135 cm (4 ft 6 in), but that's only 68 cm (2 ft 3 in) each – about the same as a cot. Buy wider if you can. And a bed should be at least 10–15 cm (4–6 in) longer than the tallest partner. A single bed should be at least 90 cm (3 ft) wide.

There are numerous types of mattress and base. Mattresses include springs of various kinds, and foam. Base types include sprung, mesh, and wooden slats. Golden rule 1. Buy mattress and base together as a unit, the way they were designed to be used. Try to avoid new mattress/old base. Antique bedsteads can be fitted with a new base/mattress combination. Golden rule 2. Lie before you buy, in the shop, together with your partner. Take off coat and shoes and stretch out, and change positions. Lie back and slide the flat of your hand into the small of your back. If there's an empty hollow, the mattress may be too hard; if full, it may be too soft.

Recently beds have come back into the design limelight becoming very much part of the look of a room. Particularly popular is slim black iron (modern minimalist) and antique or repro continental (French chateau), with pine (modern country) and brass (Victorian revival) holding their own. There's even a thriving new breed of designer beds. Looks are lovely but comfort still remains paramount – remember you can't actually see your bed when you're in it.

USEFUL CONTACT

THE SLEEP COUNCIL (an industry-sponsored promotional body)
ADDRESS High Corn Mill, Skipton, North Yorkshire, BD23 1NL

For helpful leaflets, send sae. Leaflets include *The Bed Buyer's Guide; Sleep Good, Feel Good; Goodnight Guide for Children;* and *Back to Bed* (produced with the National Back Pain Association).

BEDROOM SPECIALISTS

Many of the large furniture stores listed in FURNITURE, page 149, have extensive departments for continental fitted furniture, including fitted wardrobe systems, beds and accessories.

AND SO TO BED
ADDRESS 638–640 King's Road, SW6 2DU
TEL 0171 731 3593   **FAX** 0171 371 5272
In 1973, Keith and Lorraine Barnett found their lovingly-restored bedstead was too big for their room. So they advertised it for sale in the local paper. The response was massive, and prompted them to start the business which has grown into one of the country's best-known bed specialists. They still have original brass beds, plus reproductions made in their own workshops. Now, however, wood beds have taken over – a huge selection, in styles from many periods – everything from an elaborate hand-carved lit bateau to a splendid four-poster. Plus all bedroom accessories, including linens from France and Italy, and up-market fabrics from Titley & Marr and Zoffany.
TUBE *Fulham Broadway* • **OPEN** *Mon–Sat 10am–6pm* • **SERVICES** *All bedhangings and soft furnishings. Interior design service for bedrooms*

DUXIANA
ADDRESS 46 George Street, W1H 5RF
TEL 0171 486 2363   **FAX** 0171 935 8080
Ultra-stylish Swedish bedrooms; slimline Dux beds, with double layer springs for firm but resilient support. All-cotton bed linens. Down-filled pillows and duvets. Headboards include upholstered models and stained cane. Bedside tables to match overall scheme.
TUBE *Baker Street* • **OPEN** *Mon–Fri 10am–1pm; 2pm–6pm. Sat 10am–1pm; 2pm–5pm* • **WEBSITE** *www.duxbed.com* • **SERVICES** *Nationwide delivery*

HULSTA
ADDRESS 22 Bruton Street, W1X 7DA
TEL 0171 629 4881   **FAX** 0171 409 2417
Modern fitted storage and beds from Germany. Also furniture for living and dining rooms. Wood veneers and lacquers. Sophisticated, flexible, high-quality systems. You'll also find Hulsta furniture at many of the large shops listed in the FURNITURE page 149.
TUBE *Green Park* • **OPEN** *Mon–Fri 9am–5.30pm*
• **SERVICES** *Nationwide delivery*

OLAF AHRENS
ADDRESS 128 Malden Road, New Malden, Surrey, KT3 6DD
TEL 0181 949 9226   **FAX** 0181 395 7170
Trading over 30 years, here you'll find 4000 sq ft of showroom with accessorised room-settings. Specialist in 'system storage', including sleek continental brands, with individual planning for the best permutations and

combinations. Bedrooms, living and dining rooms; studios, children's rooms, and the home office. Electrically adjustable beds and fold-down wallbeds. Hinged and/or sliding wardrobes. Custom-made furniture.
RAIL *New Malden* • **OPEN** *Mon–Sat 9.30am–5.30pm*
• **SERVICES** *Plan, install. Comprehensive delivery service*

ROYAL AUPING
ADDRESS 35 Baker Street, W1M 1AE
TEL 0171 935 3774   **FAX** 0171 935 3720
These Dutch Royal Warrant holders arrived in London four years ago. Their prestigious Komfortable Royal is billed as the world's first self-airing and climate-controlled adjustable bed. Custom-made for weight and height, and adjusted at the touch of a button into a myriad of different sleeping and sitting positions. Also sells suitably luxurious duvets, pillows, and sheets. Fabrics from peaceful neutrals to vibrant individualist modern designs. Duvets made with an innovative 'thermofix' process claimed to minimise spread of dust-mites – a boon to asthma sufferers. Bed surrounds and bedroom furniture in modern and traditional styles.
TUBE *Baker Street* • **OPEN** *Mon–Fri 9.30am–5.30pm. Sat 10am–5.30pm*
• **SERVICES** *Interest free credit. Interior design*

BED SHOPS

BEAUMONT BEDS
ADDRESS 238–240 High Street, Lewisham, SE13 6JU
TEL 0181 852 4515   **FAX** 0181 852 1949
Good stocks, with same day or 24 hour deliveries. Mattresses and divans sold separately. Custom-made beds. Special and odd sizes.
RAIL *Lewisham* • **OPEN** *Mon–Sat 9am–6pm. Sun 11am–5pm* • **SERVICES** *Nationwide deliveries* • **ALSO AT** *Woolwich, Stratford, Tooting, Walthamstow, Croydon, Orpington, Dagenham*

BEDS ARE UZZZ
ADDRESS 490–494 Greenford Road, Greenford, Middx, UB6 8SH
TEL 0181 578 2883   **FAX** 0181 575 2953
Specialist family business: large range, including custom-made. 1000–3000 beds always in stock. All major brands; Relyon, Dunlopillo, Sealy. 'We'll refund the difference if you can find it cheaper.'
RAIL *Greenford* • **OPEN** *Mon–Sat 9am–5.30pm. Sun 10am–4pm*
• **SERVICES** *Same day delivery/installation. Free removal of old bed*
• **ALSO AT** *140 Station Road, Harrow, Middx (0181 427 5137)*

BEDS, BEDS, BEDS
ADDRESS 220 North End Road, W14 9NX
TEL 0171 385 4550/7711   **FAX** 0171 385 7711
Large selections, with frequent sales. Good for a bed in a hurry.
TUBE *Fulham Broadway/West Brompton/West Kensington* • **OPEN** *Mon–Fri 9.30am–6.30pm. Sat 9.30am–6pm. Sun 11am–4pm* • **SERVICES** *Same day deliveries in many cases* • **ALSO AT** *313–321 North End Road, SW6 1NN (0171 381 2726)*

BEDWORLD BEDDING CENTRE

ADDRESS 95 Fore Street, N18 2TW
TEL 0181 807 3331
Family business, going for over 15 years. 2000 sq ft of showroom, all top makes, including bunks and storage beds. Headboards, pillows, duvets.
RAIL *Dalston Junction* • **OPEN** *Mon–Sat 9am–5pm. Thurs 9am–1pm*
• **SERVICES** *Nationwide delivery* • **ALSO AT** *Harrow Weald, Barnet*

C W BURROWS

ADDRESS 79 Leonard Street, EC2A 4QY
TEL 0171 739 1410   **FAX** 0171 729 3057
Family business, going for over 50 years. 'Friendly, old-fashioned service.' 4000 sq ft warehouse. Leading brands, full range of styles and prices.
TUBE *Old Street* • **OPEN** *Mon–Fri 9am–5pm* • **SERVICES** *Free local delivery. Custom-made beds*

CITY BEDS

ADDRESS 15a Kennard Road, E15 1AH
TEL 0181 534 9000   **FAX** 0181 519 8450
Discount warehouse for all branded makes. Divans. Brass, wood, four-posters, bunks. Orthopaedic beds. 1500 beds in stock for immediate delivery. 5 per cent discount for Senior Citizens who pay in cash.
TUBE *Stratford* • **OPEN** *Mon–Sat 8.30am–5pm. Sun 10am–4pm*
• **SERVICES** *Free old bed disposal. Nationwide delivery*

DREAMS

ADDRESS 180 Tottenham Court Road, W1P 9LE
TEL 0171 323 1066   **FAX** 0171 637 4560
Conveniently central selection of beds in all price brackets crammed into two floors – from £69 for a single divan to around £3000 for a handmade 6 ft bed for that luxury lie. Friendly atmosphere takes the embarrassment out of stretching out. Part of a chain of around 40 stores in the South East.
TUBE *Tottenham Court Road/Goodge Street* • **OPEN** *Mon Tues Wed Sat 9am–6pm. Thurs Fri 9am–8pm. Sun 11am–5pm* • **SERVICES** *Speedy deliveries. Price promise: will refund difference if you find same merchandise anywhere cheaper. Comfort guarantee on divan sets – will exchange within 40 days if bed is uncomfortable* • **WEBSITE** *www.dreams.plc.uk*
• **ALSO AT** *Phone 01628 535353 for other branches*

FOAM DIRECT

ADDRESS 30–34 Eden Grove, N7 8EJ
TEL 0171 609 2700   **FAX** 0171 700 5995
Director Jack Craig boasts that his grandfather and father were 'in rubber' before him. From a sales counter in a large modern factory, this company sells handmade mattresses made from high-quality latex foam or reflex fire-resistant foam, with coverings of Belgian damask or straightforward English cotton tickings. Order a mattress in the morning and pick it up the same day and 'genuine latex mattresses are cheaper than any competitor.' Mattresses made to any size or any shape, eg round mattresses. Also foam cushions cut to any size and thickness; plus a service for loose covers and upholstery. Cushions can be filled with foam while you wait. Range of bean bags and inexpensive foam seating – plus polystyrene beads for your

own fillings. Soft overlays for a bed that's too hard. Black polyether foam cut to size for camera cases.

TUBE *Holloway Road* • **OPEN** *Mon–Fri 9am–5.30pm. Sat 10am–4pm*
• **SERVICES** *London deliveries by own vans; nationwide by 48-hour carrier*

MYERS WAREHOUSE

ADDRESS 39–51 The Broadway, Crouch End, N8 8DT
TEL 0181 340 9488
Discounts for branded beds: Relyon, Myers, Sleepeezee. Orthopaedic and pine beds; king sizes. Large pine showroom; pine bedroom furniture. Sofabed specialists.

TUBE *Finsbury Park* • **OPEN** *Mon–Sat 9am–5.45pm. Sun 12 noon–4pm*
• **SERVICES** *Deliver within the M25*

TULLEYS OF CHELSEA

ADDRESS 289–297 Fulham Road, SW10 9PZ
TEL 0171 352 1078   **FAX** 0171 352 5677
Ground floor bedding department with 35 beds on show. Brass beds, pine beds, folding beds, sofabeds, bunks, storage beds, ottomans, headboards, firm beds, mattresses, pillows. Wide range of sizes and prices; hundreds in stock for immediate delivery

TUBE *South Kensington/Gloucester Road* • **OPEN** *Mon–Sat 9am–5.30pm*
• **SERVICES** *Nationwide delivery*

TRADITIONAL BEDS

AMAZING EMPORIUM

ADDRESS 249 Cricklewood Broadway, Edgware Road, NW2 6NX
TEL 0181 208 1616   **FAX** 0181 450 4511
Spacious showroom (10,000 sq ft) with around 25 variations on the popular French lit bateau, in solid cherry, oak, walnut, mahogany and pine, including day beds. Plus wardrobes with various interior fittings for clever storage. Also iron beds, and furniture from new and reclaimed pine, or distressed French-polished oak. Well-known brands include Vi-Spring, Hypnos, and Staples for mattresses, and Brigitte Forestier and Simmon for furniture. 'Unbeatable prices guaranteed.'

RAIL *Cricklewood Broadway* • **OPEN** *Mon–Sat 10am–6.30pm.
Sun 11am–6pm* • **SERVICES** *Custom-made service for beds. Free parking for 200 cars. Interest-free credit, and monthly special offers*

THE ANTIQUE BEDSTEAD COMPANY

ADDRESS Baddow Antique Centre, The Bringy, Church Street, Great Baddow, Chelmsford, Essex, CM2 7JW
TEL 01245 471137
Huge antiques showroom (over 7000 sq ft) with around 350 antique bedsteads, all painstakingly restored – from £300 to £400, single, from £600 to £800 for a double. Proprietor Mr Rabin can supply traditional 'lay-on' metal bedsprings ('we consider no other support suitable') and quality Hypnos mattresses. Alternatively, he'll modify a bedstead to suit your own divan. Choice ranges from sturdy workaday models to over-the-top glamour – black iron, stove-enamelled white, and brass of all descriptions. Some have inlaid mother-of-pearl, painted porcelain plaques,

and cut-glass mirrors. Many come from Birmingham – peak period was
1860–1880. Four-posters and half-testers cry out for pretty drapes.
RAIL *Chelmsford* • **OPEN** *Mon–Sat 10am–5pm. Sun 11am–5pm* • **SERVICES**
*Restoration. Collection from station (please book in advance). Large free
car park. Coffee Shop*

BEAUDESERT
ADDRESS Old Imperial Laundry, Warriner Gardens, Battersea, SW11 4XW
TEL 0171 720 4977 **FAX** 0171 720 4970
Traditional four-poster bed specialists, with a huge variety of styles
available, all made up to order, which takes from eight to ten weeks. Prices
from £2,250, plus VAT (double size), plus around £1,800 for mattress and
base. Fabric 'bed dressings' are designed on an individual basis, as there
are so many possibilities. 'External dressings' take around 20–25 metres of
fabric, while the interior can take up to 45 metres for a sunray pleated
canopy roof.
RAIL *Clapham Junction* • **OPEN** *By appointment* • **WEBSITE**
www.beaudesert.co.uk • **SERVICES** *Design service for special beds to
order. All bed soft-furnishings made to order. Full interior design service.
Fine curtain-making*

LA MAISON
ADDRESS 410 St John's Street, EC1V 4NJ
TEL/FAX 0171 837 6522
A huge selection of antique French beds, fruitwood armoires and fireplaces,
imported directly from France by Guillaume Bacou, with prices starting at
around £500.
TUBE *Angel* • **OPEN** *Mon–Sat 10am–6pm or by appointment*

LULLABY HANDMADE MATTRESSES
ADDRESS 28 Scrubs Lane, NW10 6RA
TEL/FAX 0181 968 0182
Using natural materials, and keeping waste to a minimum, this showroom/
workshop was voted Islington's greenest business in 1992. Mattresses
made to any size or shape, within two days to a week – 'unusual shapes
are not a problem for us'.
TUBE/RAIL *Willesden Junction* • **OPEN** *Mon–Sat 10.3am–5.30pm*
• **SERVICES** *Personal and friendly; home visits to measure, make templates
and advise (small charge). Deliveries*

NORRIS BEDDING
ADDRESS 88 Coldharbour Lane, Camberwell, SE5 9PU
TEL/FAX 0171 274 5306
Trading for 53 years, their famous customers include Julie Andrews,
Tom Cruise, and Kensington Palace. 'Best prices and quickest delivery'
for made-to-order divan sets in any size and shape. Springs plus layers
of natural materials. For example, £310 for divan set 4 ft 4 in by 6 ft.
TUBE *Oval* • **RAIL** *Loughborough Junction/Denmark Hill* • **OPEN** *Mon–Fri
8.30am–4.30pm. Sat 9am–3pm*

SAVOIR BEDS

ADDRESS Unit 1A, Claudia House, Old Oak Common Lane, NW10 6DX
TEL 0181 838 4838   **FAX** 0181 838 6660

Sleep on a Savoy Hotel bed without leaving home. 'Supreme comfort and quality and an exceptional lifespan'. Customers have included Emma Thompson, Lisa Minelli, and the Rothschild family – the King of Morocco bought 24. Beds are made to 1905 standards by hand on workshop benches crammed with springs, horsehair, lambswool, and linen ticking. From around £2,000 for a single to just over £4,000 for king size.

TUBE *East Acton/North Acton* • **OPEN** *By appointment*
• **SERVICES** *Deliver and install*

SIMON HORN

ADDRESS 117–121 Wandsworth Bridge Road, SW6 2TP
TEL 0171 736 1279   **FAX** 0171 736 3522

Simon Horn, trading since 1982, introduced London to the curvy wooden 'lit bateau' – also known as a sleigh bed – now so widely copied. Now you'll find around 60 different French and classical wooden bed designs in a large jam-packed showroom, many based on European originals and sized up for today's bigger people. Also a cot that grows to child's bed to sofa, plus adaptable nursery furniture/accessories. Bedside tables, armoires, desks and dressing tables. Plus antiques, including splendid old armoires. Inspirational colour brochure. Beds from around £1,500 to around £7,000. Bedside tables from £300. Cot from £1,475. Antique armoires, from £1,500.

TUBE *Parsons Green* • **OPEN** *Mon–Sat 9.30am–5.30pm* • **SERVICES** *Making bed-hangings. Designing one-offs. Restoring antique beds and furniture. Copying designs to order. Decorative hand-painting for furniture*
• **WEBSITE** *www.simonhorn.com*

PINE AND IRON BEDS

ART IN IRON

ADDRESS Unit F, Bridges Wharf, Bridges Court, off York Road, Battersea, SW11 3AD
TEL 0171 924 2332   **FAX** 0171 924 2744

Modern slimline iron beds at factory prices are the attraction at this successful workshop, founded in 1993. Wide range of styles – from dead simple to plenty of curly bits, including four posters in kit form. Finishes include clear lacquer for a rustic look; matt black; a matt silver; and a pale cream. Beds have springy beech slatted wood bases plus quality Hypnos mattresses. Attractive colour brochure, and selections of colourful Turquaz bed linens. Singles from around £260; doubles from around £350; super king size (6 ft by 6 ft 6 in), from around £460 to £750.

RAIL *Clapham Junction* • **OPEN** *Mon–Fri 10am–6pm. Sat–Sun 11am–5pm*
• **SERVICES** *Deliveries nationwide. Assembly service within Greater London area*

BIG TABLE

ADDRESS 56 Great Western Road, W9 3NT
TEL 0171 221 5058   **FAX** 0171 229 6032

Get one thing straight – this friendly furniture co-operative makes straightforward pine beds. They started out with tables in 1983, weren't successful, turned to beds but never changed the name. Everything is made on site in honest, undating designs with sprung beech slats, and mattresses (also made on site) in three degrees of firmness – plus a friendly invitation to come and try before you buy. Orders take about a week. Take beds home and assemble them yourself. From around £145 for a double bed, plus mattresses from £160.

TUBE *Westbourne Park* • **OPEN** *Mon–Sat 10am–6pm. Sun 12 noon–5pm. Late night Thurs 10pm* • **SERVICES** *Deliveries. Assembly service in Greater London*

THE IRON BED COMPANY

ADDRESS 584 Fulham Road, SW6 5NT
TEL/FAX 0171 610 9903

Anne and Simon Notley are a go-ahead young couple who have popularised the current cult of the modern iron bed, with a nationwide group of shops. They stay ahead of the field with new designs/looks/finishes. Prices start from around £289 for a 3 ft bed, £359 for 4 ft 6 in bed, £399 for a 5 ft bed. Four-poster versions are popular, and finishes include bright paintwork as well as black, white and stainless steel. Accessories complete the contemporary bedroom, from bright bedlinens in plains and checks to iron bedside tables, lighting, and mirrors – and even alarm clocks and hotwater bottles. Even if you don't want to buy big with a bed itself, you could find a snoozy gift.

TUBE *Parsons Green* • **OPEN** *Mon–Sat 10am–6pm. Sun 11am–4pm*
• **WEBSITE** *www.ironbed.co.uk* • **SERVICES** *Free mail-order brochure*
• **ALSO AT** *Guildford, Chichester, and Tonbridge Wells – for more details phone 01243 778999*

LITVINOFF & FAWCETT

ADDRESS 281 Hackney Road, E2 8NA
TEL 0171 739 3480   **FAX** 0171 739 1018

Back in 1979, when pine beds were a novelty, Julian Litvinoff and Mel Fawcett set up their workshop. Fawcett subsequently left to start his own joinery company, but Litvinoff stayed to build the business to its present strength, perfecting his own construction method – easy to assemble yet very strong. Currently, 15 models – optional extras include fitted drawers, matching bedside cabinets, and chests of drawers. In stock: eight sizes of the two best-selling and simplest beds, plus six types of mattress, from basic to luxury. Other beds to order – takes two to three weeks – in a choice of colours and finishes. The platform bed is good value – 3 ft base, £90; Gothic 4 ft 6 in bed is £295. Plus furniture from England, India, Eastern Europe and Indonesia – eg rush seat ladderback chair, £80 – or £70, for four or more.

TUBE *Old Street/Bethnal Green* • **OPEN** *Mon–Fri 10am–6pm. Sat 10am–5pm. Sun 10.30am–2.30pm* • **SERVICES** *Evening and Saturday deliveries – average cost is £14. Assembly service, £7.50. Workshop car park* • **ALSO AT** *238 Grays Inn Road, WC1X 8HB (0171 278 5391)*

MORIARTI'S WORKSHOP ✉

ADDRESS High Halden, near Ashford, Kent, TN26 3LY
TEL 01233 850214   **FAX** 01233 850524
Master craftsman Ian de Fresnes (alias 'Moriarti') masterminds this country
showroom and workshop: he's a designer-maker par excellence. Thirty-
eight bed styles, each in up to eight sizes. Solid pine, slatted bases.
Space-saving pine storage bed specialists – with drawers and cupboards.
Exclusive mattresses.
OPEN Mon–Sat 9am–5pm • **SERVICES** Brochure, mail order

REDHOUSE

ADDRESS 105c Commercial Street, Old Spitalfields Market, E1 6BG
TEL 0171 392 2010
For a popular modern look, a slimline well-priced range of black iron
bedsteads with pine slats, starting at around £299 for single size. Sprung
bases optional; range of orthopaedic mattresses. Plus all kinds of iron
furniture, and table tops, frames and mirrors in rough-hewn natural wood.
Plus lighting.
TUBE Liverpool Street • **OPEN** Mon–Sat 11am–5pm. Sun 10am–6pm
• **ALSO AT** 43 Brushfield Street, E1 6AA (0171 375 0516)
• **SERVICES** Designs modified to order

TAURUS PINE BEDS

ADDRESS 242 Kilburn High Road, NW6 2BS
TEL 0171 624 3024
Small family business producing handmade solid pine bed frames direct
from workshop. Self-assembly, but they can put them together for you on
demand. Quality mattresses.
TUBE Kilburn • **OPEN** Mon–Sat 10am–6pm. Sun 11am–4pm
• **SERVICES** Nationwide delivery

WARREN EVANS

ADDRESS 158a Camden Street, NW1 9PH (front entrance),
3a Proust Place, NW1 9PA (back entrance)
TEL 0171 284 1132   **FAX** 0171 267 6604
Workshop/showroom for quality pine beds. Various styles and finishes.
Futons, futon sofabeds, pine furniture, orthopaedic mattresses. Also
bedroom and kitchen furniture – handmade to order within four days.
TUBE Camden • **OPEN** Mon–Sun 10am–6pm. Late night Wed 9pm
• **SERVICES** Delivery in London area. National deliveries by arrangement

FUTONS, WATERBEDS, FOLDING BEDS AND ORTHOPAEDIC BEDS

USEFUL CONTACT

THE NATIONAL BACKPAIN ASSOCIATION
ADDRESS The Old Office Block, 16 Elmtree Road, Teddington, Middx, TW11 8ST
TEL 0181 977 5474 **FAX** 0181 943 5318
Send a sae for information

7+7 FUTONS AND INTERIORS

ADDRESS 109 Balham High Road, SW12 9AP
TEL 0181 675 6727 **FAX** 0181 673 6396
Futons with easily-converted frames in a wide choice of materials (metal, pine, hardwood, exotic timbers) from America, Canada, Denmark and Sweden. This group started in Copenhagen in 1980 and also sell in Amsterdam. Plus gifts, rugs and candles.
TUBE *Balham* • **OPEN** *Mon–Sat 10am–6pm. Sun 12 noon–4pm* • **SERVICES** *Non-standard sizes made to measure* • **ALSO AT** *91 Northcote Road,* SW11 6PL *(0171 924 1753)*

BACK 2 (ANATOMIA)

ADDRESS 28 Wigmore Street, W1H 9DF
TEL 0171 935 0351 **FAX** 0171 935 5293
Swedish Lattoflex beds. Anatomically designed pillows for an ideal neck position. Snore-stop pillows (I am assured they work). Ergosleep beds, Balans chairs and ergonomic furniture; from desks to hand massage units. Office chairs, recliners.
TUBE *Bond Street/Oxford Circus* • **OPEN** *Mon–Fri 9am–5.30pm. Late night Thurs 8pm. Sat 9.30am–5pm. Sun 12 noon–5pm*

BACK IN ACTION 🚗

ADDRESS 3 Quoiting Square, Oxford Road, Marlow, Bucks, SL7 2NH
TEL 01628 477177 **FAX** 01628 477188
David Newbound and Linda Pearce run a popular consultancy service for back-pain sufferers and carers. Postural training. Bed and chair selection. Chiropractor-designed King Koil beds with strengthened middle section. Hydrobeds. Also trade as 'The Children's Seating Centre', whose aim is to 'keep kids comfy from day one.'
OPEN *Tues–Fri 9.30am–5pm. Sat 10am–2pm. Or phone for appointment*

THE BACK SHOP

ADDRESS 14 New Cavendish Street, W1M 7LJ
TEL 0171 935 9120 **FAX** 0171 224 1903
'We're a comfort shop'. Beds tailored to height and weight of partners, plus pillows and ergonomically designed chairs and desks. Lumbar wedges for cars and chairs.

TUBE *Bond Street/Baker Street* • **OPEN** *Mon–Fri 10am–5.45pm. Sat 10am–2pm* • **SERVICES** *Free posture assessment service – phone for appointment. Catalogue*

THE BACK STORE

ADDRESS 330 King Street, Hammersmith, W6 0RR
TEL 0181 741 5022   **FAX** 0181 741 0683
Chairs, desks, children's products. Pillows and mattress toppers. Advisers will visit.
TUBE *Stamford Brook* • **OPEN** *Mon–Fri 9am–5pm. Sat 10am–4pm*

EVER-REDDY BEDS

ADDRESS 125 Essex Road, Islington, N1 8LU
TEL 0171 226 1207/354 4044   **FAX** 0171 226 1207
'London's leading specialist bedmakers' promise same-day deliveries. Back care specialists offering 12-year guarantee.
TUBE *Highbury and Islington* • **OPEN** *Mon–Sat 9am–5pm* • **SERVICES** *Home visits with advice. 30-day satisfaction guarantee*

THE FUTON COMPANY

ADDRESS 138 Notting Hill Gate, W11 3QG
TEL 0171 727 9252   **FAX** 0171 792 1165
Managing director Robert Pearce was covered in cotton fluff the first time I met him – he was making futons himself in a co-operative with friends. That was 1980. Now his company has 22 shops nationwide and is the largest futon maker in the UK. He doesn't do the making anymore but he constantly sources new products, and improves old ones. Futon means mattress in Japanese and The Futon Company still handmakes them using traditional methods. 'The Japanese have been sleeping on futons for centuries and back problems are virtually unheard of there,' says Robert. Most futons are made to order, in a choice of coloured coverings. £89 buys a five-layer natural Woolmix single futon. They also sell beds (good, clean-lined designs), sofabeds, mattresses, bedding, curtains, cushions, storage, tables and lighting. Pine bed frames from £58 (single) and £199 (double).
TUBE *Notting Hill Gate* • **OPEN** *Mon–Sat 10am–6pm. Late night Thurs 7pm. Sun 11am–5pm* • **SERVICES** *Mail-order catalogue – write to FREEPOST FUTON COMPANY. Or ring 0171 727 9252* • **ALSO AT** *169 Tottenham Court Road, W1P 9LH (0171 636 9984). 654 Fulham Road, SW6 5RU (0171 736 9190). 60 Sloane Avenue, SW3 3XB (0171 581 3626) and in Battersea, Finchley, Chiswick and Muswell Hill – phone 0171 586 7444 for details*

THE FUTON FACTORY AND NATURAL FURNITURE COMPANY

ADDRESS 192 Balls Pond Road, N1 4AA
TEL 0171 226 4477   **FAX** 0171 704 0544
Factory showroom for a firm founded 20 years ago. Futons and mattresses made to order in pure cotton and wool layers. Bases which 'anyone can convert with ease.' Plus baby cot mattresses. Prices: cot mattresses, £39; two-seater sofabed, £198; three-seater sofabed, £517. Also bedspreads and fitted sheets, and Cloud Nine pure lambswool comforter, £134. They

supply futon cot mattresses to the Natural Childbirth Trust. Orders take
around two weeks.

TUBE *Highbury & Islington* • **OPEN** *Mon–Sat 10am–6pm* • **WEBSITE**
www.futon-factory.co.uk • **SERVICES** *Any size mattress to order*

THE LONDON WALL BED COMPANY
ADDRESS 430 Chiswick High Road, W4 5TF
TEL 0181 742 8200   **FAX** 0181 742 8008
Established for 15 years, their folding beds go in homes, schools, colleges
and even fire stations. All kinds of wall beds for every-night use – they fold
away complete with bedding. Over 40 different finishes, in mattress sizes
up to 6 ft 6 in long. Send a room plan – they'll suggest a suitable bed.
Prices from £1074 for a single wall bed, and from £1231 for a double,
fitted by their own team. If you want to make your own cabinets, there's a
simple pivoting bed frame and mechanism (single vertical) for £385, and
a double vertical, from £495. Prices include delivery and VAT.
OPEN *Mon–Fri 9.30am–6pm. Sat 10am–5pm* • **TUBE** *Chiswick Park*
• **SERVICES** *Design and installation*

LONDON WATERBED COMPANY
ADDRESS 99 Crawford Street, W1H 1AN
TEL 0171 935 1111   **FAX** 0171 723 5846
Waterbeds are widely misunderstood, says Maureen Pope, trading for
around 10 years. They're very good for bad backs and allergy sufferers.
Floors don't need strengthening because weight is evenly distributed.
Heaters are separated by safety liners. Softside beds look like ordinary
beds; hardsides are cradled in wooden frames. Prices from around
£495, for a bed 5 ft wide.
TUBE *Baker Street* • **OPEN** *Tues–Fri 10am–5.30pm. Sat 10am–5pm*
• **SERVICES** *Install and fill beds with hose; can also move waterbeds to
new premises*

WALLBEDS DIRECT (GOLDEN PLAN) ✉
ADDRESS 622 Linen Hall, 162–168 Regent Street, W1 R5TB
TEL 0171 434 2066   **FAX** 0171 287 2329
Beds fold (fully made-up) flat against wall vertically (on end) or horizontally
(widthways). Beds have firm bases with proper mattresses to take standard
bedding. Five-year guarantee.
SERVICES *Catalogue*

BED LINEN, QUILTS
AND DUVETS

BOUTIQUE DESCAMPS
ADDRESS 197 Sloane Street, SW1X 9QX
TEL 0171 235 6957   **FAX** 0171 235 3903
Showcase for this old-established, but thoroughly modern, French company
(founded in 1888). Exclusive bed linens and towelling collections feature
new designs every season to reflect latest designs and colours. The 'Petit

Descamps' collections includes nursery bedlinen, towelling and accessories for babies to the age of two.
TUBE *Knightsbridge* • **OPEN** *Mon–Sat 10am–6.30pm. Late night Wed 7.30pm* • **WEBSITE** *www.descamps.com* • **SERVICES** *Made-to-order baby furniture*

CARRE BLANC

ADDRESS Ground Floor, The Bentall Centre, Kingston-upon-Thames, KT1 1TR
TEL 0181 549 2246   **FAX** 0181 549 2238
This is the first UK branch for a famous continental bedlinen company that has 140 branches in every corner of France – they started with one shop in Lyon in 1983. Designs are bright, original and contemporary, and merchandise is well-priced, with new ranges every six months. Sheets, duvet covers etc are all 100 per cent cotton. Plus towels, bathrobes, shower curtains, soaps, roomsprays by Guerlain, tablecloths, mats, napkins, china and gifts.
RAIL *Kingston* • **OPEN** *Mon–Sat 9.30am–6pm. Late night Thurs Fri 9pm. Sun 11am–5pm* • **SERVICES** *Mail-order catalogue, monogramming, free gift wrapping, bridal book* • **ALSO AT** *Guildford (01483 301300) and Debenhams, Oxford Street W1*

COLOGNE & COTTON

ADDRESS 791 Fulham Road, SW6 5HD
TEL 0171 736 9261   **FAX** 0171 736 6862
For ten years, sisters Jenny Deeming and Vicky Shepherd have pioneered the return of old-fashioned bed linen – lovely crisp designs in 100 per cent cotton, with plain hem-stitched edging, cream or white, and sometimes trimmed with lace. Also candystripes and dog-tooth checks. Plus delicious scents based on old recipes.
TUBE *Parsons Green* • **OPEN** *Mon–Sat 9.30am–7pm* • **ALSO AT** *39 Kensington Church Street, W8 4LL (0171 376 0324). 88 Marylebone High Street, W1M 3DE (0171 486 0595)*

DAMASK

ADDRESS 3 & 4 Broxholme House, New King's Road (junction with Harwood Road), SW6 4AA
TEL/FAX 0171 731 3553
Fresh cotton bed linen and nightwear with embroidered patterns of ribbons, shells, hearts, and leaves. The same motifs decorate sheets, pillows, cushions and all kinds of small accessories. Anything from a small gift to a whole bottom drawer. Patchwork quilts are exclusive – from £295, matching cushions £30. Scalloped jacquard bedspreads from £95, cushions from £21. Hand-embroidered curtain panels, £49; organdie cushions £26. Children's appliqué cot covers and bed linen. Household accessories include French decorated enamelware, wirework sculptures, glass vases, bread baskets and scented candles.
TUBE *Fulham Broadway* • **OPEN** *Mon–Sat 10am–6pm. Late night Thurs 7pm* • **SERVICES** *Mail order*

THE LINEN CUPBOARD

ADDRESS 21–22 Great Castle Street, W1N 7AA
TEL 0171 629 4062   **FAX** 0171 491 4576
Small, but well-stocked. Bed linen, towels, table linen at very reasonable prices. Specialists in baby linen.
TUBE *Oxford Circus* • **OPEN** *Mon–Sat 9.30am–6.30pm*

THE MONOGRAMMED LINEN SHOP

ADDRESS 168 Walton Street, SW3 2LJ
TEL 0171 589 4033   **FAX** 0171 823 7745
Far more special than its name: they can of course monogram most linens – from £9.50 for three initials. But owner Anne Singer, with French flair, has ravishing collections of her own designs, including wonderful extra-wide linen 3 metre in 100 colours, from naturals to deep dyes at £68 a metre, to use for sheeting, curtains or table linen. Plus wide range of bed and table linen (eg £49.50 for table cloth 170 cm square). Bed linen from £89 a set. The MLS has been trading for 20 years.
TUBE *South Kensington* • **OPEN** *Mon–Fri 10am–6pm. Sat 10am–5pm*
• **SERVICES** *Embroidery from simple monograms to reproducing complete images, such as a child's picture. Bed furnishings in client's choice of fabrics. Eiderdowns renovated and re-covered*

PATCHWORK QUILTS BY TERESA BELL ✉

ADDRESS Top House Farm, West Lane, Burn, Selby, N.Yorks, YO8 8LR
TEL 01757 270343
Charming traditional square-blocked designs, with wadded/quilted backings in 100 per cent cotton fabrics, including all top names: Warner, Colefax and Fowler, Osborne and Little etc. Definitely heirlooms.

PUPPY

ADDRESS 26 Portobello Green Arcade, 281 Portobello Road
(under Westway), W10 5TZ
TEL/FAX 0181 964 1547
Big bold modern designs – huge roses, or scripted love poems. Sheets and towels can be dyed to a vast choice of over 450 colours – for example double duvet, dyed to order, costs £55 and takes about three weeks.
TUBE *Ladbroke Grove* • **OPEN** *Mon–Sat 10am–6pm*

FURNITURE

GENERAL

*'It's unwise to pay too much, but it's unwise to pay too little.
When you pay too much, you lose a little money. That is all.
When you pay too little, you sometimes lose everything.'*
John Ruskin (1819–1900)

CHAPLINS
ADDRESS 477–507 Uxbridge Road, Hatch End, Pinner, Middx, HA5 4JS
TEL 0181 421 1779 **FAX** 0181 421 3872
Spacious 20,000 sq ft showroom has exclusive furniture and furnishings,
lighting, and kitchens. Includes one of the widest ranges of the famous
German Hulsta make of fitted furniture for bedroom, living-room or office.
RAIL *Hatch End* • **OPEN** *Tues–Sat 10am–6pm* • **SERVICES** *Large free car
park. Colour brochure. Interior design*

CHARLES PAGE
ADDRESS 61 Fairfax Road, Swiss Cottage, NW6 4EE
TEL 0171 328 9851 **FAX** 0171 328 7240
Specialists in quality modern furniture for more than 60 years – see
the results in a showroom which spreads over 10,000 sq ft. Friendly
atmosphere – 'We'll help with a single lamp or a complete interior'.
Governing principle is good design, high quality and value for money,
implemented with a vast selection of continental and British brands.
Furniture by Molteni, Fendi, Grange and Hulsta, plus their own exclusive
pieces. Fabrics by Ralph Lauren, JAB, Kravet, and more.
TUBE *Finchley Road/Swiss Cottage* • **OPEN** *Mon–Sat 9.30am–5.30pm*
• **SERVICES** *Full interior design service. Design and make furniture using
own upholsterers, blacksmiths, stonemasons, and cabinetmakers.
'We relish a challenge'*

FURNITURE CRAFT INTERNATIONAL
ADDRESS Rays House, North Circular Road, NW10 7XP
TEL 0181 961 7780 **FAX** 0171 561 5787
Spacious showrooms (11,000 sq ft) for top European modern names;
using room-settings show Hulsta (bedroom studio), Ligne Roset, Kesterport
and others. Established for 15 years.

TUBE *Hanger Lane* • **OPEN** *Mon–Sat 10am–6pm. Sun 11am–5pm*
• **SERVICES** *Plan, design, supply, install a wide range of fitted furniture for living-rooms and bedrooms. Full interior design service, including all soft furnishings*

THE FURNITURE GALLERY
ADDRESS 17 Church Road, NW4 4EB
TEL 0181 202 0525   **FAX** 0181 203 2523
Uncluttered showroom with personal service. Sleek modern continental sofas, dining-room furniture, fitted bedroom furniture, picture frames, mirrors etc from friendly family firm. Fabric-covered Italian 'designer' three-piece suite, £1,599.
TUBE *Hendon Central/Golders Green* • **OPEN** *Mon–Thurs 11am–5.30pm. Fri 11am–2pm. Closed Sat. Sun 10.30am–4.30pm* • **SERVICES** *Evening and Sunday deliveries. Planning and fitting for bedroom furniture. Furniture design and planning with home visits. Local delivery same day*

FURNITURE VILLAGE
ADDRESS Hurlingham Retail Park, Fulham, SW6 2TZ
TEL 0171 610 6111   **FAX** 0171 610 6624
Here you get the size of an out-of-town superstore on the fringes of Fulham – vast selections of top brands, for furniture, upholstery, carpets and beds including Tetrad and Collins & Hayes, plus sections for ethnic Indian and one-off Chinese pieces, all put together in attractive groupings. Claim to be the biggest bedding retailer in London – major stockist for Vi-Spring, Hypnos and Slumberland. Friendly helpful advice, and even free coffee and cookies.
TUBE *Fulham Broadway + 295 bus* • **OPEN** *Mon–Fri 10am–6pm. Late night Thurs 8pm. Sat 9am–6pm. Sun 11am–5pm* • **SERVICES** *Interior design and curtain-making. Own car park* • **ALSO AT** *Maples House, 145 Tottenham Court Road, W1P PLL*

IFEX
ADDRESS Unit 21, Capitol Park Industrial Estate, Capitol Way, Colindale, NW9 0EQ
TEL 0181 205 7711   **FAX** 0181 205 7722
This large showroom – 20,000 sq ft – reflects the growing interest in modern furniture – it only opened last year. Huge selection of Europe's top contemporary furniture – Hulsta of Germany, Ligne Roset of France, C & J2 of Spain, Morex of Italy. Flooring, curtains, upholstery fabrics, lighting and good quality wood, glass and marble-topped tables. Also bedroom and kitchen furniture, and sofas in fabric and leather, plus smaller accessories.
TUBE *Colindale* • **OPEN** *Mon–Sat 10am–6pm. Sun 11am–5pm* • **SERVICES** *Large car park. Full interior design service*

LIGNE ROSET
ADDRESS 418–422 Chiswick High Road, W4 5TF
TEL 0181 995 7722   **FAX** 0181 995 7733
Large new showroom for one of Europe's favourite brands of modern furniture made in France. Also accessories – vases, bowls and lamps.
TUBE *Chiswick Park* • **OPEN** *Mon–Sat 9.30am–6pm. Sun 12–4pm* • **SERVICES** *Interior design. Free comprehensive catalogue. Phone 0845 602 0267 for catalogue*

SOUTHWAY INTERIORS

ADDRESS 964 North Circular Road, NW2 7JR
TEL 0181 452 8011   **FAX** 0181 450 9295

Eurostyle is streamlined, luxurious, efficient, and modern. Here's where to find leading brands shown in room-settings. Ground floor: living-room and dining-room furniture from Hulsta, Interlubke and B & B Italia, along with sofas and chairs from Saporiti, B & B Italia, Desiree, and Seven Salloti, and occasional pieces from Tonelli, Sica and Fiam. Upstairs: bedroom displays from Hulsta, Interlubke, and Zalf. The kitchen showroom is modern Poggenpohl, with top-brand fitted appliances – Gaggenau, Miele and Neff plus double ovens and Dacor range cookers. Plus limestone, slate, marble and granite for worktops – exclusive stones sourced directly from quarries in Europe, the Middle East and India.

TUBE Brent Cross/Neasden • **OPEN** Mon–Fri 10am–5.30pm. Sat 10am–5pm • **SERVICES** Full interior design and room planning services. Own car park (entrance in Waterloo Road)

WHARFSIDE DANISH FURNITURE

ADDRESS 66 Buttesland Street, N1 6BY
TEL 0171 253 3206   **FAX** 0171 253 1500

Huge showrooms packed full of high-quality solid wood (teak, cherry, oak, beech) sourced from Scandinavia and Italy by director Jonathan Stewart (in business for over 40 years). 'No plastics, no laminates, no compromise.'

TUBE Old Street • **OPEN** Mon–Thurs 9am–5pm. Fri 9am–3pm. Sat 10am–4pm. Sun 10am–2pm • **WEBSITE** www.wharfside-furniture.co.uk

UPHOLSTERY INCLUDING LOOSE COVERS AND SOFABEDS

'I love it, I love it, and who shall dare
To chide me for loving that old arm chair...
Would ye learn the spell, a mother sat there,
And a sacred thing is that old arm chair.'
Eliza Cook (1818–1889)

You can pay from around £300 to £2000 upwards for a sofa – puzzling for the average punter. As a benchmark, John Lewis (see UNDER ONE ROOF: DEPARTMENT STORES, page 13) sofa prices range from around £700 to £2500, including cover. Why the huge price variation? It's difficult to be specific, as it's tricky to compare like with like – lots of sofas are unbranded or specials for a particular store. Various factors may push up the price. Firstly, there's the intrinsic quality of materials and construction – very difficult to assess. A good sofa has a hardwood frame, glued, screwed and dowelled; some slimline designs may have metal frames. Hand-crafted upholstery, hand-stitched trimmings, hand-buttoning, coil springing, sprung arms, and feather-and-down fillings are quality extras that may increase cost. Price of fabric makes a huge difference – you can pay from £10 to £40 a metre and upwards. Average is around £25 a metre. A three-seater can need as little as 7 metres or as much as 18 metres. So there's an add-on of perhaps £150 to £600 if prices do not include fabric. Confusingly, some shops give inclusive prices, others give price plus fabric, quoting quantity required. Then there's the all-important question of The Look – cheaper sofas tend to be boxy and conventional, with fabric down to the floor. A modern designer sofa (slimline with legs on view) will cost on average £1,500 to £2000. Don't buy a sofa that's too big for your room – a common mistake. Make sure you have access up stairs or in lifts. Allow plenty of time – ideally sit for about half an hour to allow for compression of fillings. Push your hand into cushions upholstery cushions: they should have resilient filling that spring back quickly. On a strongly patterned sofa, check motifs are centred properly.

THE CONRAN SHOP
See UNDER ONE ROOF: FURNISHING SPECIALISTS, page 10
Excellent selections of modern sofas. Furniture catalogue, £2.50.

DELCOR FURNITURE
ADDRESS 65 Tottenham Court Road, W1P 9PA
TEL/FAX 0171 580 7900
Sofas and chairs are made in classic designs to order in the firm's workshops. Allow six to eight weeks. They can assemble on site if access is difficult – because of narrow stairs, for example. Standard sizes can be altered to meet individual needs. Huge choice of fabrics.
TUBE *Goodge Street* • **OPEN** *Mon–Sat 9.30am–6pm. Late night Thurs 7.30pm* • **SERVICES** *Colour brochure and fabric samples*
• **ALSO AT** *279c King's Road, SW3 (0171 352 5551)*

GEORGE SMITH
ADDRESS 587–589 King's Road, SW6 2EH
TEL 0171 384 1004   **FAX** 0171 731 4451
English upholstered furniture handmade in their own workshops to order. Exclusive fabrics include printed linens based on authentic old designs, velvets, chenilles and woven damasks. Also hand-blocked wallpapers. Specialists in hand-coloured leathers and kilim upholstered furniture.
TUBE *Fulham Broadway* • **OPEN** *Mon–Fri 9am–6pm. Sat 10am–5pm*
• **SERVICES** *Brochure*

HABITAT
ADDRESS 1 Drury Crescent, Purley Way, Croydon, Surrey
TEL 0181 649 9312
Slightly damaged Habitat goods and end of lines, including sofas, at discounts between 20 to 40 per cent. Best time to visit is Friday afternoon.
OPEN *Mon–Fri 9.30am–6pm. Late night Thurs 8pm. Sat 9am–6pm. Sun 11am–5pm*

HIGHLY SPRUNG
ADDRESS 185–186 Tottenham Court Road, W1P 9LE
TEL 0171 631 1424   **FAX** 0171 636 7987
Neil Brown and Ian MacGuffog have an upholstery factory at High

Wycombe and a down-to-earth sales policy: 'No sales, no interest-free credit, no buy-now-pay-later, no promotions... these gimmicks inflate prices.' Most popular model (a three-seater sofa) costs £895 plus 18 metres of fabric. Other sofas from £895. £48 to add bun feet, and £25 plus 1½ metres of fabric for armcaps. Loose covers are £50 extra (but many models feature loose covers as standard) and a sofabed is an extra £170.

TUBE *Goodge Street/Warren Street* • **OPEN** *Mon–Sat 10am–6pm. Late night Thurs 7.00pm. Sun 1–5pm* • **SERVICES** *Deliveries £30, including evenings. Standard dimensions can be altered. Loose covers for existing furniture. Re-upholstery. New cushions. Headboards and screens to order.* • **ALSO AT** *310 Battersea Park Road, SW11 3BU (0171 924 1124; head office number for all enquiries)*

INTERMURA
ADDRESS 27 Chalk Farm Road, NW1 8AG
TEL 0171 485 6638   **FAX** 0171 284 4564

Asymmetrical shapes and sweeping curves are the signature theme for upholstery that's startling bright and modern, down to the legs (spirals with a silver finish, for example). Avant-garde but with a sound background – they've been trading for nearly 20 years, with their own factory in Hackney. The company is run by Christopher and Ann Hymers – he's a furniture designer, and she comes from fashion and textiles. It's a mix that has produced some of the most innovative sofas on the market – expect to pay around £1000.

TUBE *Chalk Farm/Camden Town* • **OPEN** *Tues–Fri 10am–5.30pm. Sat Sun 10.30am–5.30pm* • **SERVICES** *Brochure*

JILL SAUNDERS
ADDRESS 46 White Hart Lane, SW13 0PZ
TEL 0181 878 0400   **FAX** 0181 395 8454

This shop specialises in selling old upholstered furniture. Re-upholstery and furniture repairs along with re-caning and re-rushing. Other services include making curtains, blinds and other soft furnishings. Also a wide selection of haberdashery, and materials for DIY re-upholstery, together with curtain accessories, poles, tassels, and tapestry kits.

RAIL *Barnes* • **OPEN** *Mon–Sat 10am–5.30pm*

KINGCOME SOFAS
ADDRESS 302–304 Fulham Road, SW10 9EP
TEL 0171 351 3998   **FAX** 0171 351 1444

This firm pioneered the concept of made-to-measure upholstery. Each piece is handmade to the highest standards, and 'truly bespoke'. Contemporary or traditional styles.

TUBE *Earls Court/Fulham Broadway* • **OPEN** *Mon–Fri 9.30am–5.30pm*

LET IT LOOSE
TEL 0171 928 8300

Julia O'Dowd has perfected a service for loose covers. They are cut on site, made up and usually returned within a week. Curtains can be made in two weeks.

MELISSA KAY ✉

TEL/FAX 01430 449499
Velvet-covered furniture in funky shapes at reasonable prices — phone for brochure.

MULTIYORK

ADDRESS 95 Tottenham Court Road, W1P 9HF
TEL 0171 255 1677   **FAX** 0171 255 1682
Over 25 sofa designs, in choice of around 10,000 fabrics. All have tailored removable covers – many can be washed, the rest dry-cleaned. Solid hardwood frames and steel coil spring construction guaranteed for ten years. Most large models can be dismantled for ease of access (up narrow stairs or through narrow doorways, for example). Matching curtains and other soft-furnishings to order. Plus dining and occasional furniture in mahogany, pine, oak and cherry veneers. Accessories, including rugs, mirrors, lamps and pictures.
TUBE *Warren Street* • **OPEN** *Mon–Fri 10am–6pm. Late night Thurs 7pm. Sat 9am–6pm. Sun 1–5pm* • **WEBSITE** *www.multiyork.co.uk*
• **SERVICES** *All upholstery can be Scotchgarded – costs about £150 a suite. Templates for every order kept on file for replacement covers* • **ALSO AT** *555 King's Road, SW6 2EB (0171 371 5029). 25/28 Thurloe Place, SW7 2HQ (0171 589 2303). Triangle House, 309–311 Green Lanes, N13 4YB (0181 886 7514). 13 Harben Parade, Finchley Road, NW3 6JP (0171 722 7810). Bromley, Kingston, Loughton, Sutton. For general store information, telephone 0990 273747*

PETER DUDGEON

ADDRESS 1a Brompton Place, Knightsbridge, SW3 1QE
TEL 0171 589 0322   **FAX** 0171 589 1910
Come here for the top end of the trade – a company that's been making quality handmade upholstery since 1947. Over 30 styles – 'no foam' is their proud boast. Hand-tied springs with horsehair and cane seat edges; beech frames with dowelled joints. Distinguished classic and traditional designs, for example wing and leather chairs straight out of a gentlemen's club. Plus simple modern shapes.
TUBE *Knightsbridge* • **OPEN** *Mon–Fri 9am–5.30pm. Sat 10am–5pm*
• **SERVICES** *Colour catalogue available*

POETSTYLE 🐷

ADDRESS Unit 1, Bayford Street Industrial Centre, Mare Street, E8 3SE
TEL 0181 533 0915   **FAX** 0181 985 2953
Sofas/sofabeds made on the premises by traditional methods from £450 upwards, including fabric. They also sell off ex-display models (not damaged but perhaps grubby) at half-price under the trading name Sofa to Bed.
RAIL *London Fields/Hackney Central* • **TUBE** *Bethnal Green*
• **OPEN** *Mon–Fri 7am–6pm. Sat 10am–5pm. Sun 10am–3pm*

PURVES & PURVES

See UNDER ONE ROOF: FURNISHING SPECIALISTS, page 12. Modern sofas from mainland Europe and Britain.

RECLINE & SPRAWL

ADDRESS 604 King's Road, SW6 2DX
TEL 0171 371 8982   **FAX** 0171 371 8984

Aim is relatively low prices for elegant quality traditional upholstery (made in their own factory). Large selection of fabric books from leading makers. Most popular model is Brigadier three-seater, £1495 plus 16 metres of fabric. Two seaters start at £1395, plus 11–13 metres of fabric. Popular in-between size is the '2.5 seater sofa'.

TUBE *Fulham Broadway* • **OPEN** *Mon–Sat 10am–6pm* • **SERVICES** *Deliveries. Standard dimensions can be altered*

THE SOFABED FACTORY

ADDRESS 258–260 Lavender Hill, SW11 1LJ
TEL 0171 228 4588

Custom-made sofas, chairs and sofabeds. Choose your own fabric and size. Customise your furniture if you wish – for example, order a higher back, change of fillings and so on. Very flexible – lots of styles and patterns.

RAIL *Clapham Junction* • **OPEN** *Mon–Sat 10am–6pm. Late night Thurs 7.30pm. Sun 11am–5pm* • **ALSO AT** *334–340 Caledonian Road N1 1BB (0171 607 3096)*

SOFAS AND SOFABEDS

ADDRESS 82 Tottenham Court Road, W1P 9HD
TEL 0171 813 1489   **FAX** 0171 813 1956

Over 80 models of sofas, sofabeds and chairs, available immediately or made to measure in top-name fabrics at reasonable prices. 'Great products, great value, great service'. Very flexible – a variety of cushion fillings, loose or tight covers, a choice of over 10,000 fabrics. Nominated best sofabed supplier in a recent Which? survey.

TUBE *Goodge Street* • **OPEN** *Mon–Sat 10am–6.30pm. Late night Thurs 7pm, Sun 12 noon–5pm* • **WEBSITE** *www.sofabeds.co.uk* • **SERVICES** *Fabric samples, brochure* • **ALSO AT** *296 Upper Richmond Road, Putney; and Woolwich*

THE SOFA WORKS 🐷

ADDRESS 5–7 Tottenham Street, W1 9BB
TEL 0171 580 8444   **FAX** 0171 580 8666

London factory shop for Welsh direct-sell upholstery firm (established 1981) – traditionally-constructed made-to-measure upholstery takes from four to six weeks, in wide choice of covering materials. Trade prices, including fabrics. Sample price: large sofa with loose covers from £766

TUBE *Goodge Street* • **OPEN** *Mon–Sat 10am–6pm. Late night Thurs 7pm. Sun 12 noon–5pm* • **SERVICES** *Catalogue, expert advice. Deliveries from £25*

SOFA WORKSHOP

ADDRESS 84 Tottenham Court Road, W1P 9HD
TEL 0171 580 6839   **FAX** 0171 580 6847

They say: 'There is no such thing as an ideal sofa, only your ideal sofa.' A popular policy which has led to 30 stores nationwide in 14 years. Over 60 models of sofas, sofabeds and chairs, which can be altered to suit individual requirements. Over 1,500 plain and patterned fabrics for tight or loose covers, many of them machine washable. Off the Peg is a less expensive range – seven set styles in a selected collection of fabrics.

TUBE *Goodge Street/Warren Street* • **OPEN** *Mon–Sat 9.30am–6pm. Late night Thurs 7.30pm. Sun 12 noon–6pm* • **SERVICES** *'Access check' to make sure sofa will fit (chargeable)* • **ALSO AT** *32–38 Battersea Rise, SW11 1EE (0171 924 3967). 147 Chiswick High Road, W4 4DT (0181 742 0159). 8 High Street, Ealing Broadway Centre, W5 5DB (0181 579 0693). 419–423 Upper Richmond Road West, SW14 7PJ (0181 876 8254). 99–101 Golders Green Road, NW11 (0181 905 5982). 324–326 King's Road, SW3 5UH (0171 352 1945). Kingston and Bromley*

SUCCESSION

ADDRESS 179 Westbourne Grove, W11 2SB
TEL 0171 727 0580   **FAX** 0171 229 2588
Nick Plant makes to order by traditional methods a choice of around 20 upholstery styles with beech frames, webbing, springs and feather fillings. Sofas costs from around £1,200 plus VAT and 14–16metres of fabric. Elegant designs include chunky art deco look. Coverings include leathers in jewel colours, and animal hide effects. Also leather-covered storage cubes, coffee tables and bookcases handmade to order.
TUBE *Notting Hill Gate* • **OPEN** *Tues – Sat 11am–6pm*

TULLEYS OF CHELSEA

ADDRESS 153–155 Wandsworth High Street, SW18 4JB
TEL 0181 870 9809   **FAX** 0181 874 6244
Part of the Chelsea landscape for generations (trading for over 100 years), they've now moved across the river. Over 20 classic designs of sofas and chairs made to traditional standards in the firm's workshops. Choose from over 8000 covering fabrics or buy 'in the white' (unbleached calico) and make your own loose covers – some of these models are available immediately. Promotional fabrics (50 per cent discount) take six to eight weeks. Other fabrics and tight upholstery need 10 to 12 weeks, loose covers take 12 to 14 weeks.
TUBE *East Putney* • **RAIL** *Wandsworth Town* • **OPEN** *Mon–Sat 9.30am–5.30pm* • **SERVICES** *Immediate delivery of sofas/beds from display*

VIADUCT

See CUTTING EDGE AND TWENTIETH-CENTURY CLASSICS, page 161. Good selections of slim-line minimal continental sofas at reasonable starting prices.

WESLEY-BARRELL

ADDRESS 60 Berners Street, W1P 3AE
TEL 0171 580 6979   **FAX** 0171 580 6984
Cotswold craftsmanship comes to London through the family firm of Wesley-Barrell, who, in three generations have grown from a small shop in the Oxfordshire village of Witney to a furnishings company with 16 showrooms nationwide, selling not only their own largely handmade upholstery (named after Cotswold villages), but also cupboards, chests/tables, accessories, co-ordinated soft furnishings.
TUBE *Goodge Street* • **OPEN** *Mon–Sat 9.30am–6pm* • **SERVICES** *Colour catalogue. Interior design. Full soft-furnishing making* • **ALSO AT** *409 Upper Richmond Road West, SW14 7NX (0181 878 4001). And in Bromley, St Albans and Tonbridge Wells*

CUTTING EDGE AND 20TH-CENTURY CLASSICS

'The golden rule is that there are no golden rules'.
George Bernard Shaw (1856–1950)

The great designers of the first half of this century – Eames, Le Corbusier, Aalto, Breuer, *et al* – have an enduring appeal, and much of their work has come to be called 20th-century classics. Their furniture (still in production) is stocked alongside the avant-garde in many of the shops listed below, some of which also specialise in tracking down original older pieces of classic furniture. Very modern designs and 20th-century classics are also stocked by some of the shops listed in UNDER ONE ROOF: FURNISHING SPECIALISTS, page 10, and by shops listed under FURNITURE: GENERAL, page 149.

AERO
ADDRESS 357–359 King's Road, SW3 5ES
TEL 0171 351 0511   **FAX** 0171 351 0522
The Aero experience is a fresh wind through the world of design hype, powered by no-nonsense design dynamo Paul Newman. He says: 'Our aim is to create functional, affordable and stimulating home products and we're fuelled by customer-feedback and passionate enthusiasm. We're not into design education.' Clean-lined useful of-the-moment furniture that looks good and is made from a wide range of materials. Steel and glass shelving units, sleek sofas, kitchen and bedroom storage with clever solutions to everyday problems, and a host of neat accessories. Also sells classic pieces from Fritz Hansen and B & B Italia. The smaller Westbourne Grove store has become an essential destination for all serious design devotees and this second larger store opened in December 1998.
TUBE *Sloane Square + bus* • **OPEN** *Mon–Sat 10am–6.30pm. Sun 12 noon–5pm* • **WEBSITE** *www.aero-furniture.com* • **SERVICES** *Mail-order catalogue* • **ALSO AT** *96 Westbourne Grove, W2 5RT (0171 221 1950)*

ARAM DESIGNS
ADDRESS 3 Kean Street, WC2B 4AT
TEL 0171 240 3933   **FAX** 0171 240 3697
Fin de siècle and time for reappraisal. The best place to buy great 20th-century furniture classics is this mini-museum of modern design. Formidable founder (32 years ago) is Zeev Aram, ex-Israeli naval officer who trained at London's Central School of Art. A life-long fight for public recognition has been not for himself, but for the great moderns: Eileen Gray, Le Corbusier, Marcel Breuer, Charles Eames, Mies van der Rohe, Alvar Aalto, Arne Jacobsen *et al.*
TUBE *Covent Garden/Temple/Holborn* • **OPEN** *Mon–Fri 9.30am–5.30pm*

ATRIUM

ADDRESS 22–24 St Giles High Street, WC2H 8LN
TEL 0171 379 7288 **FAX** 0171 240 2080
Stylish modern European furniture and lighting in spacious well-arranged showroom. Also sell washable imitation Novasuede.
TUBE *Tottenham Court Road* • **OPEN** *Mon–Fri 9am–6pm*

BOWWOW

ADDRESS 70 Princedale Road, W11 4NL
TEL 0171 792 8532 **FAX** 0171 792 8351
A small gallery in an old poodle parlour, with solid sculptural furniture by designer-maker Ahmed Sidki in re-claimed elm, bronze or tautly-stretched hide over tables, stools and benches. Also cushions in calfskin, kid and Mongolian lamb by Samson Soboye. Plus an impressive selection of collectable fifties glass.
TUBE *Holland Park* • **OPEN** *Tues–Sat 10am–6pm*

CENTURY

ADDRESS 68 Marylebone High Street, W1M 3AQ
TEL 0171 487 5100 **FAX** 0171 265 9845
20th-century classic furniture by Charles and Ray Eames, Saarinen and Knoll – both older pieces and re-editions. Cushions made from fifties fabrics, plus contemporary ceramics and fabrics. Design books. Handmade Danish Le Klint pleated and moulded white lampshades in stunning sculptural forms.
TUBE *Baker Street* • **OPEN** *Tues–Fri 11am–7pm. Sat 10am–6pm*
• **SERVICES** *Search service. Interior design*

CO-EXISTENCE

ADDRESS 288 Upper Street, N1 2TZ
TEL 0171 354 8817 **FAX** 0171 354 9610
Predominantly a showroom for the contract trade, but you can see individual modern classics by such great 20th-century designers as Alvar Aalto, Charles Eames, Arne Jacobsen *et al*. Plus contemporary lighting and accessories.
TUBE *Angel* • **OPEN** *Mon–Fri 9–6pm (but please phone for an appointment)*

FURNITURE UNION

ADDRESS Bankside Lofts, 65A Hopton Street, SE1 9LR
TEL 0171 928 5155 **FAX** 0171 928 5253
Large new space for modern Euro-furniture for large new spaces – including their own range of upholstery.
TUBE *Blackfriars* • **OPEN** *Mon–Fri 10am–6pm* • **SERVICES** *Interior design*

HAUS

ADDRESS 23–25 Mortimer Street, W1N 7RJ
TEL 0171 255 2557 **FAX** 0171 255 1331
'I'm just a furniture freak,' sighed the man on the modern sofa, lovingly stroking the suede. Haus, a newish enterprise, brings design into the heart of the West End – a brave venture. It's popular with Londoners who love 20th-century furniture and know their Bauhaus from their terraced house. Browse among stock by fresh young talent (Michael Young, Procter:Rihl)

augmented by established classics from Knoll in particular – Haus have
exclusive rights in Central London on their Studio range (Mies van der
Rohe, Ero Saarinen, Harry Bertoia). Fine art on the walls, lots of smaller
pieces on shelves and tables. Knowledgeable and enthusiastic staff.
TUBE *Goodge Street* • **OPEN** *Mon–Fri 9am–6pm. Sat 11.30am–6pm*
• **WEBSITE** *www.haus.co.uk* • **SERVICES** *Interior design – 'problem solving
is our speciality'*

NOEL HENNESSY FURNITURE
ADDRESS 6 Cavendish Square, W1M 9HA
TEL 0171 323 3360   **FAX** 0171 323 3361
It's a brave man that sets up shop behind John Lewis, that giant ant-heap
of furnishing activity. But this is more of a gallery than a department store –
an eclectic individualistic selection of modern European design over two
floors. Cabinets from Tratina of Sweden, and textiles by Alcove of France
plus selected Italian pieces. British furniture includes the quirky Oxo seating
system, with its dinky interlocking cubes (by architect Nigel Coates), and
the Cato rocker by Tony Portus. Room groups give a domestic feel, with rugs
and sculptures, and fine art on the wall. All a trifle intimidating, perhaps to
the initiated, but worth seeing nonetheless. Prices on the steep side.
TUBE *Bond Street/Oxford Circus* • **OPEN** *Mon–Fri 10am–6pm. Sat
10am–4.30pm* • **SERVICES** *Full interior design service 'however big or
small the project'*

PLACES AND SPACES
ADDRESS 30 Old Town, SW4 0LB
TEL/FAX 0171 498 0998
Paul Carroll and Nick Hannam show new design alongside classics from
the fifties and sixties (Charles Eames and Verner Panton). Furniture, lighting,
ceramics, glass, and artwork. Plus a small range of their own designs.
TUBE *Clapham Common* • **OPEN** *Tues–Sat 10.30am–6pm. Sun 11am–5pm*

PURE CONTEMPORARY DESIGNS
ADDRESS Ground Floor, 1–3 Leonard Street, EC2A 4AQ
TEL 0171 250 1116   **FAX** 0171 250 0616
Orianna Fielding-Banks shows her distinctive range of upholstery and
cabinets and an ever-changing selection of sixties and seventies classics.
She says: 'I aim for an eclectic mix of materials from velvet, leather, vinyl and
Novasueade to resins, Perspex and natural.' Her loft packs (from £4,950)
provide a stimulating mix of furniture with the modern London loft in mind.
TUBE *Old Street* • **OPEN** *Mon–Fri 10am–6pm* • **WEBSITE** *www.puredesign.uk.com*
• **SERVICES** *Interior design. Furniture to commission*

SAME
ADDRESS The Bridge, 146 Brick Lane, E1 6RU
TEL 0171 247 9992   **FAX** 0171 247 9993
Piers Roberts and Rory Dodd, who met while studying furniture design at
college, have filled an atmospheric space (once a Trumans brewery) with
an international selection of modern design. Work from Germany, Holland,
Scandinavia, Spain and Italy mingles with such homegrown talents such as
Jam, Babylon, Inflate, Tom Dixon and Michael Sodeau.
TUBE *Aldergate East/Liverpool Street* • **OPEN** *Tues–Sun 10am–6pm.
Late night Thurs 8pm* • **WEBSITE** *www.same.uk.com*

SCP

ADDRESS 135–139 Curtain Road, EC2A 3BX
TEL 0171 739 1869   **FAX** 0171 729 4224

Britain has many fine modern furniture designers but lamentably few manufacturers prepared to back them. So the designers go abroad (to Italy mainly) to get their goods made. Sheridan Coakley (SC) is the entrepreneurial exception that proves the rule. Since 1985, he's been making British modern furniture with bulldog tenacity, and even taking it to the Milan furniture fairs. 'It'll never sell in Britain,' said the gloom-mongers. But it did – from a showroom-cum-shop set up in a disused Shoreditch factory. Now SCP's design stable includes Jasper Morrison, Matthew Hilton, Terence Woodgate and Konstantin Gric. In retailing, design has started to ring the tills, and the East End has become fashionable. This two-floor 6,000 sq ft shop houses a huge consumer-friendly selection of contemporary furniture, lighting, ceramics, glass and accessories, plus books and stationery. Cappellini, Artek, Flos and Alessi join the home team, along with an extensive range of 20th-century classics.
TUBE *Old Street* • **OPEN** *Mon–Sat 9.30am–6pm*

SPACE

ADDRESS 214 Westbourne Grove, W11 2RH
TEL 0171 229 6533   **FAX** 0171 727 0134

Notting Hill became fashionable and Space was born. Cool clean gallery atmosphere (glass, concrete, white walls) for a modern melange of furniture in arresting shapes by Edra, Michael Sodeau, and Michael Young, with the shop's own range of sheepskin loungers and big leather bean bags. Jeremy Lord's Chromawall moulded light boxes hypnotically ripple with colour. Candles by artist Anne Severine Liotard are giant wax sculptures. Prices extend to a scary £12,000, but you can still browse – you could just buy an exquisite porcelain vase for £16, or a candle, or Japanese incense. The aim, says owner Emma Oldham, is beauty and desirability. She adds: 'I want to mix the affordable with the limited edition.'
TUBE *Notting Hill Gate* • **OPEN** *Mon–Sat 10am–6pm* • **SERVICES** *Interior design consultancy*

THEMES AND VARIATIONS

ADDRESS 231 Westbourne Grove, W11 2SE
TEL 0171 727 5531   **FAX** 0171 221 6378

The best of post-war Italian and Scandinavian furniture and glass, plus pieces from the European avant-garde. Always worth a design delve.
TUBE *Notting Hill Gate* • **OPEN** *Mon–Fri 10am–1pm; 2pm–6pm. Sat 10am–6pm*

TWENTYTWENTYONE

ADDRESS 274 Upper Street, N1 2UA
TEL/FAX 0171 288 1996

Trading initially as 20th Century Design, Simon Alderson and Tony Cunningham were the first people in London to take second-hand 20th-century classic furniture away from provincial attics and market stalls, give it a good clean-up (with restoration and re-upholstery where necessary) and show it to proper advantage in a gallery setting. Older pieces are supplemented with re-editions. The icing on the cake is a changing programme of exhibitions of the very best of our new designers for the next century.

TUBE *Angel* • **OPEN** *Tues–Sat 10am–6pm* • **WEBSITE**
www.twentytwentyone.com • **SERVICES** *Search service* • **ALSO AT**
*18c River Street, EC1R 1XN (warehouse – open by appointment only,
0171 837 1900)*

VIADUCT

ADDRESS 1–10 Summer's Street, EC1R 5BD
TEL 0171 278 8456   **FAX** 0171 278 2844

For ten years, architect James Mair has been introducing the crisp-lined
glamour of modern European furniture to the notoriously traditional British
public. His recently-expanded showroom is now known for one of the best
contemporary furniture selections in London. This is the place to enjoy the
Euro-look for the new millennium. Leading brands and designers include
Driade, B&B Italia, Montis, Pallucco, Zeus, Foscarini, Philippe Starck, Ingo
Maurer. Smaller items are designer tableware and other accessories, plus
lighting. Prices from £3 to £5000. Enthusiastic and helpful service.
TUBE *Farringdon/Chancery Lane* • **OPEN** *Mon–Fri 9.30am–6pm.
Sat 10.30am–4pm* • **SERVICES** *Delivery and installation*

CANE, PINE, COUNTRY AND PAINTED

Pine was a seventies fashion that has just gone on and on. The
perennial appeal is that it remains very good value for money.
In the early days, old pine pieces were stripped of their original
painted finishes. These are rare now, and most pine furniture
is made up from old or new wood. Start your searches in
Wandsworth Bridge Road – claimed to have the largest
concentration of pine shops in Europe!

Cane is a stalwart standby of the budget furnisher — it's
inexpensive, yet pretty enough for living-rooms. Later on, move it
to a bedroom – or even to the conservatory, if you get rich enough
to build one. Specialists in painted furniture are also listed in the
chapter devoted to CHILDREN'S ROOMS, page 174. Many of the
artists listed in DECORATING AND RE-FURBISHING: SPECIALIST PAINTING AND
DECORATING SERVICES, page 101 can also undertake commissions
for painted furniture.

AT THE SIGN OF THE CHEST OF DRAWERS

ADDRESS 281 Upper Street, N1 2TZ
TEL/FAX 0171 359 5909

Tony Harms has been selling pine since 1986. Stock from small workshops
in various parts of the country, with pieces of old furniture at good prices in
amongst the new. Tables in old wood are popular and good value: they
look convincingly old. Smaller sizes are around £280. A table 7 ft by
35 in is £320. Beech library steps, £99. Slim Jim bookcases will usefully
fit about 100 books into a narrow space of 18 in wide. Wardrobes can
be made in runs of up to 15 ft: a good alternative to built-ins.
TUBE *Highbury & Islington* • **OPEN** *7 days 10am – 6pm*
• **SERVICES** *Special sizes to order*

BISHOPS PARK ANTIQUES
ADDRESS 53–55 Fulham High Street, SW6 3JJ
TEL/FAX 0171 736 4573

Partners Jo Collin and Paula Ottignon, specialists in antique pine, travel abroad frequently to bring back unusual pieces—sleigh beds, armoires, chests. They also sell inexpensive pieces of well-finished reproduction pine, some carved and made from old wood. Reproduction chairs cost around £45, or £60 with arms. A farmhouse table 72 in by 36 in costs about £325. Artists can paint furniture to customers' orders in a variety of styles from bold stencils to intricate garlands; it takes from around 10 days to two weeks.
TUBE *Parsons Green/Putney Bridge* • **OPEN** *Mon–Sat 10am–6pm*
• **SERVICES** *Painted furniture and repro and antique pine to order. Free delivery within the M25*

CANE CONNECTION
ADDRESS 57 Wimbledon Hill Road, SW19 7QW
TEL 0181 947 9152   **FAX** 0181 947 4291

Mike and Jackie Grafton have devoted themselves to cane for over 21 years – 'if you want it in cane, we've got it.' Their newer branch at Ashstead has room-settings over two floors, with around 80 per cent of stock available immediately. Three-piece suites for inside, outside and conservatories, plus furniture for bedrooms, dining-rooms, and bathrooms, and a wide range of basketware. Three-piece suite from £399. Chairs from £39.95.
TUBE *Wimbledon* • **OPEN** *Mon–Sat 9.30am–5.30pm. Sun 10.30am–2.30pm.* • **SERVICES** *Furniture made to order and painted any colour. Upholstery in customers' own fabrics. Bookcases to order* • **ALSO AT** *Bramely Corner, Epsom Road, Ashtead, Surrey* KT21 1JG *(01372 273590)*

CHALON UK
ADDRESS The Plaza, 535 King's Road, SW10 0SZ
TEL 0171 351 0008   **FAX** 0171 351 0003

Atmospheric kitchen room-settings display country-style furniture, hand-crafted at The Old Hambridge Mill in Somerset using solid Quebec yellow pine and Canadian maple. Chalon's signature is paint ageing and distressing – their techniques are a company secret. Extensive palette of traditional colours-soothing greens and blues, dusty pinks, warm reds, soft ochres and timeless greys. Painted floral or naif motifs can be added. For the bedroom, prices range from £1,250 for a single bed, to £3,150 for a large fitted wardrobe (shoe racks, tie pulls, and drawers). Dressers from £1,850. Tables from £950, chairs from £275. Bookcases from £2,350. Plus chandeliers, wineracks, and mirrors.
TUBE *Fulham Broadway* • **OPEN** *Mon–Fri 9am–5.45pm. Sat 9am–5pm*
• **WEBSITE** *www.chalon.com*

CHISWICK COUNTRY PINE
ADDRESS 158 High Road, W4 1PR
TEL 0181 747 0734   **FAX** 0181 742 1183

Large range in mellow reclaimed pine and new wood plus traditional furniture in French oak, Italian hardwoods, and French cherrywood, for bedrooms, dining-rooms, and studies.
TUBE *Turnham Green* • **OPEN** *Mon–Sat 10am–6pm. Sun 12 noon–5pm*
• **SERVICES** *Special designs, sizes and finishes to order. Deliveries*

THE PINE AND CANE FURNITURE CENTRE

ADDRESS 1–3 and 10 Chingford Road, E17 4PW
TEL/FAX 0181 531 8369
Friendly service from a well-established family firm with good prices. Spread over three floors, with selections for every room. Cane conservatory suite from £299. Pine bedroom furniture from five different makers.
TUBE *Walthamstow Central* • **OPEN** *Mon–Fri 10am–4.30pm. Sat 9.30am–5.30pm. Sun 11am–2pm* • **SERVICES** *Free parking for 10 cars*

PINE GROVE

ADDRESS 186 Wandsworth Bridge Road, Fulham, SW6 2UF
TEL 0171 731 7673   **FAX** 0171 736 3847
Friendly service for a huge range of pine furniture from around 25 small country workshops including dressers, wardrobes, tables, chairs, chests and so on. Bookcases (very popular), can be made to order in any size. Coffee tables 3 ft by 2 ft cost £100; blanket boxes are £110; bedside cabinets, £74. Useful smaller items (good for presents) include folding wooden plateracks (£58 and £89), a variety of wall and dressing-table mirrors, small cabinets, shelf units and plant stands.
TUBE *Fulham Broadway* • **OPEN** *Mon–Sat 10am – 6pm. Sun 11am–5pm*
• **ALSO AT** *Pine Warehouse, 86 Wandsworth Bridge Road, SW6 2TF (0171 371 8476)* • **SERVICES** *Furniture made to size in old wood (very popular). Finishing to order*

PINE MINE

ADDRESS 100 Wandsworth Bridge Road, SW6 2TF
TEL 0171 736 1092   **FAX** 0171 736 5283
David Crewe-Read founded Pine Mine in 1972, and has a worldwide reputation for antique furniture. His shop has large stocks of Victorian and Georgian pieces, with antique tables, from £450 to £3000, old wardrobes from £500, and old chairs from £110. 'Increasingly our business is making up furniture to order in old woods,' says Caspian Crew-Read. Tables from £200 to £800. New pieces include chests at £310, single wardrobes at £570, and double at £760.
TUBE *Fulham Broadway* • **OPEN** *Mon–Sat 9am–6pm. Sun 10.30am– 5pm*
• **SERVICES** *Restoration*

THE PINE SHOP

ADDRESS 176–184 West End Lane, West Hampstead, NW6 1SG
TEL 0171 435 4462/1044
Well-established in the pine trade – 'better quality furniture backed by personal service is the secret of our success.' Faithful customers return to add to their furniture: 'pine is very collectible, and we maintain continuity of stock.' Ranges by Ducal are ever popular.
TUBE/RAIL *West Hampstead* • **OPEN** *Mon–Fri 9.30am–6pm. Sat 9am–6pm. Sun 11am–5pm* • **ALSO AT** *311/323 Muswell Hill Broadway, N10 1BY (0181 444 6055/9856). 2 Chequer Street, St Albans, AL1X 3X2 (01727 812345). 2/3 St Onge Parade, Southbury Road, Enfield EN1 1YU (0181 366 6339)*

SOPHISTO-CAT
ADDRESS 188–192 Wandsworth Bridge Road, SW6 2UF
TEL 0171 731 2221   **FAX** 0171 731 0802
Jennifer Taylor can tell you how she started the pine boom in Chelsea nearly 20 years ago. Now she has three adjoining shops with loads of furniture in old or new wood, including the newly-fashionable oak. Particularly good value for dining tables.
TUBE *Parsons Green/Fulham Broadway, + 28, 92, 295 bus* • **OPEN** *Mon–Fri 10am–6pm. Sat 9.30am–5pm* • **SERVICES** *Furniture made to order*

STEWART LINFORD 🚗
ADDRESS Kitchener Works, Kitchener Road, High Wycombe, Bucks, HP11 2SJ
TEL 01494 440408   **FAX** 01494 451555
Stewart Linford has been re-creating original Windsor chairs in Buckinghamshire since 1977. He now has a small team of highly-skilled wood carvers, turners, chairmakers and polishers, who use only solid woods.
OPEN *Mon–Sat 9am–5pm. Sun 11am–4pm* • **SERVICES** *Colour brochure*

SUSSEX WINDSORS 🚗
ADDRESS Dormer's Farmhouse, Windmill Hill, Herstmonceaux, East Sussex, BN27 4RY
TEL 01323 832388
Barry and Mary Murphy make traditional Windsor chairs with deeply-saddled seats carved from solid elm; other parts are steam-bent from best selected young ash; legs and spindles are turned by hand. Barry's contemporary Windsors include his Apple Pickers Rocker, unique Writing Arm Windsor, and his elegant four-seater settee. Certain to be family heirlooms.
OPEN *By appointment*

THIS AND THAT
ADDRESS 50–51 Chalk Farm Road, NW1 8AN
TEL 0171 267 5433   **FAX** 0171 916 4720
Big attraction here is the solid oak Provençal country-style furniture – tables to seat 12 people cost about £1095; bookcases for about £700. They have some Mexican pieces too – chunky three-door sideboards (around £820), chests and small bedside cupboards. Plus big squashy sofas, attractive wood and iron bedsteads, and furniture made to measure in reclaimed pine. 'We sell the same things as the posher department stores but at much lower prices.'
TUBE *Chalk Farm* • **OPEN** *Mon–Fri 10am–6pm. Sat–Sun 10.30am–6pm*
• **SERVICES** *Simple furniture restorations. Deliveries*

VOGUE SUPERSTORES
ADDRESS 12 Spring Bridge Road, Ealing Broadway, W5 2AA
TEL 0181 579 4414   **FAX** 0181 579 2395
'We're furniture people,' says Bob Walker who has been in his father Ray's furniture business since he was 13. Vast selections of pine/repro furniture. All major makes stocked at good prices. Cabinet furniture is their speciality; bookcases can be made in special sizes. They also sell beds.
TUBE/RAIL *Ealing Broadway* • **OPEN** *Mon–Sat 9am–5.30pm. Sun 10am–4pm* • **SERVICES** *Bookcases to order. Facilities for the disabled* • **ALSO AT** *MFI Building, 333 The Hyde, Edgware Road, Colindale, NW9 6TD; and at High Wycombe and New Denham*

SPECIALITY SHOPS

These are the furniture shops that wouldn't fit neatly into any category.

AFRICAN TRACKWOODS ✉

ADDRESS MBC House, Crown Lane, Marlow, Bucks, SL7 3HL
TEL 01628 481086 **FAX** 01628 481087
Family business based in Zimbabwe making furniture from old teak sleepers. 'Exotic hardwoods are scarce today,' says director Anne Brown. 'We are utilising a valuable resource without depleting the environment any further – but the supply is finite and one day the wood will run out.' In the meantime, immaculate finishing gives this furniture a smooth silky feel that just has to be touched. Coffee tables from £660 to £1000; diningtables from £1550; plus chairs, sideboards, bureaux and so on.

BEYOND THE SEA ✉

TEL 01736 360980
Rescuing driftwood from Cornish beaches, this company turns it into an attractive range of distinctive and individual furniture – no two pieces are the same. 'We get our best wood supplies off the beach after a storm,' says director Demelza Prettejohn. Extra appeal comes from hand-applied colourwashes and decorative details, making each piece exclusive. Prices for coffee tables start at around £150; cabinets from £95 to £150. Also filing cabinets, trunks and clocks. Ring for brochure.

CHANNELS

ADDRESS 3 New Kings Road, SW6 4SB
TEL 0171 371 0301 **FAX** 0171 371 0021
Furniture designer Samuel Chan has refined the clean lines of traditional Chinese pieces into sparse elegant designs in light oak, ash or cherry, with fastenings of stainless steel.
TUBE *Fulham Broadway* • **OPEN** *Mon–Sat 10am–5.30pm*

THE DINING CHAIR COMPANY

ADDRESS 4 St Barnabas Street, SW1W 8PE
TEL 0171 259 0422 **FAX** 0171 259 0423
A wide range of upholstered dining chairs in styles from Georgian to slimline modern designs. Prices start at around £236 plus cost of fabric (average is 1.5 metres). Orders take from six to eight weeks.
TUBE *Sloane Square* • **OPEN** *Mon–Fri 10am–1pm; 2pm–6pm. Sat by appointment* • **SERVICES** *Variations in style/fabric/trimmings to order. Interior design advice*

FREUD

ADDRESS 198 Shaftesbury Avenue, WC2H 8JL
TEL 0171 831 1071 **FAX** 0171 831 3062
The striking geometric designs of Glasgow architect Charles Rennie Mackintosh (those tall, tall chairs) – immaculate reproductions made in England.
TUBE *Covent Garden/Tottenham Court Road* • **OPEN** *Mon–Fri 10.30am–6.30pm. Sat 11am–6pm* • **SERVICES** *Brochure*

FRONTIERS
ADDRESS 37–39 Pembridge Road, W11 3HG
TEL 0171 727 6132 **FAX** 0171 229 4835
Beneath displays of ethnic jewellery and pottery, a basement with an original selection of modern Italian versions of Lloyd Loom and elegant Biedermeir styles for tables, chairs and chests.
TUBE *Notting Hill Gate* • **OPEN** *Mon–Sat 11am–6.30pm. Sun 12 noon–4pm*

INTERIORS BIS
ADDRESS 60 Sloane Avenue, SW3 3DD
TEL 0171 838 1104 **FAX** 0171 838 1105
An eclectic mix of contemporary Italian and French furniture (including new pieces in carved wood and leather) plus unusual antique pieces from the continent, and a range of stylish accessories that include table linens, throws, cushions and so on.
TUBE *South Kensington* • **OPEN** *Mon–Sat 10am–6pm*

JARABOSKY ORIGINAL
RAILWAY SLEEPER FURNITURE ✉
ADDRESS Old Station Yard, Exley Lane, Elland, W Yorks, HX5 0SW
TEL 01422 311922 **FAX** 01422 374053
Railway sleepers take on a new look under the skilled hands of Yorkshire woodworkers. Oak comes from France, Jarrah wood from Australia, and four other types from Africa. The reclaimed wood is fashioned into coffee tables, dining-tables and chairs, sideboards, dressers, CD holders, TV units and sea chests. A dining table to seat eight costs around £1,885.
SERVICES *Designs made to measure*

PEW CORNER
ADDRESS Artington Manor Farm, Old Portsmouth Road, Guildford, Surrey, GU3 1LP
TEL 01483 533337 **FAX** 01483 535554
Mark Groes has an intriguing collection of mainly Victorian original church pews which he sells from around £250. They make wonderful seats for kitchens, dining-rooms and halls, and no two are the same.
RAIL *Guildford* • **OPEN** *Mon–Sat 10am–5pm* • **SERVICES** *Pews cut to size. Furniture made to order from reclaimed timber*

THE SHAKER SHOP
ADDRESS 25 Harcourt Street, W1H 1DT
TEL 0171 724 7672 **FAX** 0171 724 6640
'Put your hands to work and your hearts to God', said the Shakers, an early American religious sect, whose simple faith permeated every aspect of their daily life. The result: the furniture and artifacts that became design classics. Their motto 'beauty rests on utility' preceded the modernist diktat 'form follows function' by around a hundred years. And when Liz Shirley and Tim Lamb opened this the first Shaker shop in 1989, the furniture was so plainly elegant and timeless, customers thought they were visiting an outlet for new contemporary design. Here you will find genuine Shaker sewing and coffee tables, benches and steps. Plus classic finely-balanced rocking chairs with rush seats – the Shakers believed an angel might sit on them. Famous Shaker pegged wall rails take small hanging cupboards,

shelves, mirrors and even chairs. Trestle tables in solid American cherry are superbly practical and undating. Not so much a furniture shop as an affirmation of faith. Plus all the accessories for a loving home – beeswax candles, tin sconces, copper pans, and homespun textiles.

TUBE *Edgware Road* • **OPEN** *Mon–Sat 10am–6pm* • **ALSO AT** *322 King's Road, SW3 5UH (0171 352 3918); and (newest branch) 72–73 Marylebone High Street, W1M 3AR*

SOMERSET DESIGN ✉

ADDRESS Laurel Farm, Westham, Wedmore, Somerset, BS28 4UZ
TEL 01934 712416   **FAX** 01934 712210
Rainforest tables and benches from rescued South American hardwood pallets. Plus oak and elm beds from salvaged beams.

WALTER CASTELAZZO

ADDRESS 84 Highgate High Street, N6 5XH
TEL/FAX 0171 263 5945
Gothic bookshelves, spaceship cupboards, heart-shaped storage units – the imagination of this talented furniture-maker knows no bounds, and his fantasy shapes can be enhanced with shiny coats of paint in brilliant colours. Also screens, mirrors and smaller pieces.

TUBE *Archway/Highgate* • **OPEN** *Tues–Sun 11am–6pm* • **SERVICES** *All kinds of fanciful furniture and screens made to order*

GLASS, METAL AND LEATHER

ALMA HOME

ADDRESS Unit D, 12–14 Greatorex Street, E1 5NF
TEL 0171 377 0762   **FAX** 0171 375 2471
One of the best places in London to seek your hides is Alma, old-established East End skin suppliers, who have a complete home collection created by furniture designer Ou Baholyodhin and Ilse Crawford, ex-Elle Deco editor now in New York designing homewares for Donna Karan. Here, cushions cost from £57, bean-bags from £400, and modular leather seating is from £700. There's also floor and wall tiles, and they'll sell you a complete hide for around £300.

TUBE *Aldgate East* • **OPEN** *Mon–Fri 9am–5pm*

CHELSEA METALWORKS

ADDRESS Unit 6, Parson's Green Depot, 33–39 Parson's Green Lane, SW6 4HS
TEL 0171 731 3673/2529   **FAX** 0171 384 3250
Metal is the medium in this thriving workshop, where a team of artists from different parts of the world fashion, not only iron, but copper, aluminium, brass and stainless steel into one-off decorative and functional pieces for the home. 'There's nothing in metal we cannot do.'

TUBE *Parson's Green* • **OPEN** *Mon–Fri 8am–5pm. Sat–Sun telephone first* • **SERVICES** *Free estimates and surveys*

DISTINCTION
ADDRESS Bishops Park House, 25–29 Fulham High Street, SW6 3JH
TEL 0171 731 3460 **FAX** 0171 384 2048
Mark Elliot designs and makes inventive all-glass designs for dining, coffee
and console tables, plus wrought iron and glass cabinets, and bedroom
furniture. Also clocks, mirrors, shelving, and bathroom accessories.
TUBE *Putney Bridge* • **OPEN** *Mon–Fri 9am–6pm. Sat Sun 11am–4pm*
• **SERVICES** *Brochure. Interior design*

FORGE AHEAD
ADDRESS 59 Patcham Terrace, SW8 4BP
TEL 0171 622 5514 **FAX** 0171 622 6761
Flamboyant fanciful metal chairs, tables, beds and so on designed and
made by Jamie Hart. All handmade – takes four to six weeks.
RAIL *Battersea Park* • **OPEN** *By appointment* • **WEBSITE**
www.forgeahead.co.uk • **SERVICES** *Commissions*

HOUSE OF STEEL
See HEATING: FIREPLACES, page 216. Metal suprema Judy Cole designs
and makes reasonably-priced ranges of metal furniture in a variety of styles
in her North London workshops. Dining chairs from £135 to £200. Simple
X-frame for a dining table costs from £250 – tops are extra and can be
glass, marble, or metal grille. Also coffee tables.

MUFTI
ADDRESS 789 Fulham Road, SW6 5HA
TEL 0171 610 9123 **FAX** 0171 384 2050
Supple calf leathers and suede are combined with re-claimed Burmese teak
for unusual seating – for example, safari chair, £285. Plus hand-woven
Indian silks, cottons and cashmeres and good value in leather cushions.
TUBE *Parsons Green* • **OPEN** *Mon–Sat 10am–6.30pm* • **SERVICES** *Mail
order. Interior design. Furniture made to order any style, any size.*

ORE DESIGN COMPANY
ADDRESS 563–565 Battersea Park Road, SW11 3BL
TEL 0171 801 0919 **FAX** 0171 801 0912
Design graduate Caroline Musson shows imaginative wrought-iron
furniture at her lively pleasant shop – dining-tables, chairs and beds.
Smaller pieces and accessories are great fun – witty, colourful and
handmade, including papier mâché, ceramics, textiles, and glass for
mirrors, lighting, frames, cushions, mugs, fruit bowls and so on. Good for
unusual gifts from London's zanier designer-makers.
RAIL *Clapham Junction* • **OPEN** *Mon–Sat 10am–6pm* • **SERVICES** *All kinds
of wrought iron made to order, including furniture, beds, window grilles
and so on. Interior design*

J H PORTER & SON
See WINDOWS: SHUTTERS, AWNINGS AND GRILLES, page 212.
Metal furniture made to measure by old-established forge in Battersea.

SIX SMITHS

ADDRESS Arch 11, Culvert Place, Battersea, SW11 5BA
TEL/FAX 0171 498 2977

Brilliant modern metalworking talent in a brick-vaulted workshop under a
Battersea railway arch. Originally, there were six graduates of Camberwell
School of Art – hence the name. The team is now down to three
experienced faithfuls – Cefyn Jones, Felicity Evans and Stephen Edwards.
Available for all kinds of decorative metalwork – anything from a single
candlestick or shelf bracket to a set of sculptural chairs, or an off-beat
garden gate or intricate security grille with wavy sunflower shapes.
Originality and flair guaranteed.

RAIL *Queenstown Road/Battersea Park* • **OPEN** *Mon–Fri 10am–6pm,*
but phone first • **SERVICES** *Delivery*

SUZANNE RUGGLES

ADDRESS 436 Kings Road, SW10 0LJ
TEL 0171 351 6565   **FAX** 0171 351 7007

This designer uses the skills of British blacksmiths to produce elegant
furniture in a modern idiom. Hand-blown glass and rich contemporary
fabrics soften the look. Also a gallery for other young contemporary artists
with special exhibitions for paintings, photography and glass.

TUBE *Sloane Square/South Kensington* • **OPEN** *Mon–Sat 10am–5.30pm*
• **WEBSITE** *www.i-i.net/suzanneruggles* • **SERVICES** *Special commissions.*
Project management

SPECIAL COMMISSIONS

For makers of special furniture to commission you can consult the
CRAFTS COUNCIL Photostore Index, and the commissioning service
of CONTEMPORARY APPLIED ARTS. Details are in CRAFTS AND DESIGNER-
MAKERS: GALLERIES, STUDIOS AND WORKSHOPS, page 52. You will also
find craftsmen/women making to special commission in the section
on FURNITURE: GLASS, METAL AND LEATHER, page 167.

ADAM MARLING FURNITURE

ADDRESS 461 Rathgar Road, SW9
TEL 0171 639 8349

Attractive furniture for the home and office made to order-often the work
has a distinctive arts and crafts feel.

OPEN *By appointment*

DAVID LINLEY & CO

ADDRESS 60 Pimlico Road, SW1W 8LP
TEL 0171 730 7300   **FAX** 0171 730 8869

If you can't afford to commission a beautiful piece of cabinetwork in
ebonised wood with inlays of rhodium-plated silver from the royal
woodworker and his team, you'll still be welcome to browse – and maybe
purchase a pair of bookends, a door stop, or an egg in a rare timber.

TUBE *Sloane Square* • **OPEN** *Mon–Fri 10am–6pm. Sat 10am–5pm*
• **WEBSITE** *www.davidlinley.com*

ECHO DESIGN AGENCY
TEL 0171 251 6990
Director Naiomi Cleaver can put you in touch with some of London's finest avant-garde furniture makers.
TUBE *Old Street* • **OPEN** *By appointment* • **SERVICES** *Can also find unusual artist-designers, architects and interior designers*

GUY MALLINSON FURNITURE
ADDRESS 7 The Coachworks, 80 Parsons Green Lane, SW6 4HU
TEL 0171 371 9190 **FAX** 0171 371 5099
Rare wood veneers with beautiful colours and figuring such as ripple sycamore, burr maple and lacewood are the speciality of this RCA graduate, who went on to train at Parnham. His special craft is veneering by hand. Design, however, is innovative and modern, incorporating metals, plastic and stone.
TUBE *Parsons Green* • **OPEN** *By appointment* • **SERVICES** *Plan, design, make and install*

LILLI CURTIS DESIGNS
ADDRESS 401½ Workshops, 401½ Wandsworth Road, SW8
TEL 0171 627 2728/0850 200552
Golden girl Lilli Curtis makes curvy gilded metal furniture, ornate mirrors, and elegant lamps. From around £200 for lamps, and £400 for mirrors.
RAIL *Wandsworth Road* • **OPEN** *By appointment*

OAKEY & OAKEY
ADDRESS 240 Brompton Road, SW3 2BB
TEL 0171 589 7795 **FAX** 0181 840 3161
Grahame Oakey and his wife Vaanita use their elegant shop as a showcase for the fine work you can commission from their Hanwell workshop. They can offer up to 200 species of timber plus a collection of rare veneers (myrtle, pippy yew, burr cherry). Cabinet-making, custom joinery, bespoke kitchens, wood turning, marquetry, all are possible, in styles from contemporary to classic. Curved work is a speciality. Small wood accessories and gifts, plus a range of interior furnishings are also on sale.
TUBE *Knightsbridge/South Kensington* • **OPEN** *Mon–Sat 10.30am–6pm*

SHELLEY THOMAS
ADDRESS The Forge, Kew Bridge Steam Museum, Green Dragon Lane, Brentford, Middx, TW8 0EN
TEL 0181 569 7386
Steel is twisted into infinitely intricate spirals and curlicues to make spectacular chaise longues and chairs, which are softened with sumptuous velvet upholstery and adorned with finials in beaten brass, crystal or whatever – use your imagination or hers. Also curtain-poles, mirrors, screens and so on.
TUBE *Gunnersbury* • **RAIL** *Kew Bridge* • **OPEN** *By appointment*
• **WEBSITE** *www.giraffe.u-net.com/shelley/index.htm*

TABLE MAKERS
ADDRESS The Studio, 155 St Johns Hill, SW11 1TQ
TEL 0171 223 2075   **FAX** 0171 223 7296
Choose a base from the modern styles on show, and then combine it with
a top in solid wood (oak, cherry, walnut, maple), or steel or slate for a
handsome custom-made table for the dining-room or kitchen. They also do
low tables and consoles. Average price is around £1,000, and orders take
from four to six weeks.
RAIL *Clapham Junction* • **OPEN** *Mon–Sat 9.30am–5pm*
• **SERVICES** *All tables made to measure*

STORAGE AND
BUILT-IN FURNITURE

ALCOVE DESIGNS
ADDRESS 109 Lavender Hill, Battersea, SW11 5QL
TEL 0171 585 1481   **FAX** 0171 924 4186
Built-in alcove cupboards/shelving. Wardrobes, studies, replacement
kitchen doors. Choice of styles and finishes.
RAIL *Clapham Junction* • **OPEN** *Fri–Sat 10.30am–5.30pm or by appointment*
• **SERVICES** *Design and install. Fitted in one day, depending on size of job*

CHARLES HURST
ADDRESS Unit 21, Bow Triangle Business Centre, Eleanor Street, Bow, E3 4NP
TEL/FAX 0181 981 8562
Experienced designer-maker – established for 20 years – will build
anything from a set of bookshelves to a complete kitchen in hardwoods
such as oak, teak or tulipwood, which can be varnished or painted.
OPEN *By appointment*

CUBESTORE ✉
ADDRESS Charlwoods Road, East Grinstead, West Sussex, RH19 2HL
TEL 01342 310033 (24 hours)   **FAX** 01342 310099
Versatile, practical, inexpensive storage system for shelves, wardrobes,
desks and even beds. Tried and tested. Finishes include beech veneers.
Free brochure.
SERVICES *Phone for appointment to visit. Factory and showroom at Brandon
Industrial Estate, Suffolk IP27 0NZ (appointments through E. Grinstead phone
number).*

HAYLOFT WOODWORK
See KITCHENS: COMPLETE KITCHENS, page 114. Experienced, creative
woodworkers with wide range of ideas for built-in shelving, cupboards and
so on, in solid wood or MDF.

HOWDLE BESPOKE FURNITURE

ADDRESS 9 Marylebone High Street, W1M 3PB
TEL 0171 224 6453   **FAX** 0171 224 1516

Clive Howdle (trained furniture and interior designer) makes fine furniture including fitted kitchens in materials from MDF to best hardwoods, such as cherry, oak and maple. Strong architectural feel with clean lines and good proportions.

TUBE *Baker Street/Bond Street/Oxford Circus* • **OPEN** *Mon 12 noon–5pm. Tues–Thurs 10am–5pm. Fri 10am–4pm* • **SERVICES** *Large-scale joinery such as staircases and doors*

PETER LEER FURNITURE

ADDRESS 2 Vicar's Road, NW5 4NL
TEL/FAX 0171 267 0211

Trained as an architect, Peter Leer does fitted cabinetwork 'in the main to suit traditional Victorian housing stock.' Fitted cupboards, bedrooms and some kitchens, with special paint effects if required. Commissions take around three to four weeks to complete.

OPEN *Home visits by appointment*

SHELFSTORE

ADDRESS Frognal Parade, 158 Finchley Road, NW3 5HH
TEL 0171 794 0313   **FAX** 0171 435 3927

First invented in Sweden in 1947, and continuously updated, this reliable, flexible storage system is made from sanded and varnished Swedish pine. The large number of components means the system can change and grow with your needs. Starter Pack, £339, includes bed 80 cm wide, small desk area, and some high level storage. This can be converted into bunk beds later on.

TUBE *Finchley Road* • **OPEN** *Mon–Sat 10am–5pm. Sun 11am–5pm*
• **WEBSITE** *www.shelfstore.co.uk* • **SERVICES** *Free computer-aided space planning and design service available by post or in store*

THE HOME OFFICE

ANDREWS OFFICE FURNITURE

ADDRESS 97–101 Hackney Road, E2 8ET
TEL 0171 256 1269   **FAX** 0171 613 1399

One of London's largest suppliers of second-hand office furniture, coming mainly from bankruptcies. Filing cabinets from £25. Computer desks from £35.

TUBE *Old St/Liverpool St* • **OPEN** *Mon–Fri 7.30am–5.30pm. Sat 7.30am–2pm* • **ALSO AT** *299 Camden Road, N7 (0171 609 0737). 64 Shepherds Bush Road, W6 (0171 602 6767). 112 Hoe Street, E17 (0181 509 0623). 51–53 Fulham High Street, SW6 (0171 610 6113)*

BUDGET FURNITURE

ADDRESS St Jude's Church, Dulwich Road, SE24 0PB
TEL 0171 737 1371   **FAX** 0171 274 2023

'Don't let the name put you off – we've got top quality furniture here.' Everything you need, including desks, filing cabinets and posture chairs.

RAIL *Herne Hill* • OPEN *Mon–Fri 8.30am–5pm* • SERVICES *Mail-order catalogue*

BACK 2 (ANATOMIA)

See BEDROOMS AND BEDS: FUTONS, WATERBEDS AND ORTHOPAEDIC BEDS, page 144. If you have a persistent back problem you can get advice on a special chair from these shops.

DESK DEPOT

ADDRESS 274 Queenstown Road, SW8 3NP
TEL/FAX 0171 627 3897
A useful shop for reconditioned and reproduction desks, plus filing cabinets and tables.
RAIL *Queenstown Road/Battersea Park* • OPEN *Mon–Sat 9am–5pm*
• SERVICES *Re-leathering. Made-to-order bookcase and alcove units*

DORKING DESK SHOP 🚗

ADDRESS 41 West Street, Dorking, Surrey, RH4 1BU
TEL 01306 883327   FAX 01306 875363
This narrow shop opens into a large warehouse. 'The best selection of antique desks and writing furniture in the country,' says owner Jan Elias, who has been collecting and restoring for over 20 years. Types of desk on show include rolltops, secretaires, bureaux and knee holes. And usually she has over 30 of those impressive partners' desks, which give access on both sides.
RAIL *Dorking* • OPEN *Mon–Fri 8am–5.30. Sat 10.30am–5.30pm*
• WEBSITE *www.thesaurus.co.uk/dorkingdeskshop/* • SERVICES *'Finding' service for odd sizes or rare types. Local/international deliveries*

THE HOLDING COMPANY

See ACCESSORIES: SHOPS WITH FURNITURE, page 24. Special sections are devoted to the Home Office.

IKEA

See UNDER ONE ROOF: FURNISHING SPECIALISTS, page 11. IKEA have a new department which has excellent reasonably-priced office furniture, with suggestions for layouts.

JUST DESKS

ADDRESS 20 Church Street, NW8 8EP
TEL 0171 723 7976   FAX 0171 402 6416
On three floors of showrooms in a 150-year-old building are antique and repro desks, chairs, filing cabinets, writing tables, and bookcases, plus computer desks with 'wire management'. Good quality, keen prices, quick deliveries.
TUBE *Edgware Road* • OPEN *Mon–Fri 9.30am–6pm. Sat 9.30am–5pm*
• SERVICES *Commissions. Restoration. Re-leathering including DIY postal kit with full instructions*

CHILDREN'S ROOMS

'I have a big house and I hid a lot'.
Mary Ure, British actress (1933–1975), explaining how
she coped with her large family of children

The problem with furnishing for children is their rapid rate of
growth. Small babies are probably very much less aware of decor
than their fond parents. Toddlers and young children however are
very appreciative of furnishings chosen specially for them, but
change their mind very rapidly about what they prefer. I don't think
there are any universal answers to these problems; every family
finds their own solutions, according to the needs/demands of their
children, the amount of space available, and the overall budget. A
robust low table and small-scale chairs can be a good investment –
they give children a separate space to eat and play, and can be
handed down. But children soon grow out of small-scale beds –
and the same is true of little wardrobes and chests. Better, perhaps,
to subdivide something bigger. Simply adding a border, or a
stencilled frieze is one way to make a room child-friendly – it's not
expensive and can be changed later.

ANNA FRENCH
See FABRICS AND SOFT FURNISHINGS: FABRIC MANUFACTURERS
WITH SHOWROOM SHOPS, page 67. Papers, borders and fabrics for
children—imaginative rather than twee.

BUNDLES ✉
TEL/FAX 0151 236 8727
A delightful range of nursery fabrics, papers, bed linen and accessories,
ranging from marching soldiers to safari animals. Plus wardrobes, chests,
toyboxes, shelves etc, hand-painted to match fabric designs.
SERVICES *Colour catalogue, samples. Interior design. Furniture painting*

DESIGNERS GUILD
See FABRICS AND SOFT FURNISHINGS: FABRIC MANUFACTURERS
WITH SHOWROOM SHOPS, page 68. Good selections of children's
fabrics, papers and borders.

DRAGONS
ADDRESS 23 Walton Street, SW3 2HX
TEL 0171 589 0548   **FAX** 0171 584 4570
Rosie Fisher is the loveliest of ladies – mother, granny, author and
wonderful artist. She started her range of hand-painted children's furniture
over 15 years ago because there were no suitable designs for her own
children. Now it includes chests, tables, miniature chairs with rush seats

(hand-painted with names to order), toy chests and so on. Also scaled-down upholstery for nurseries. She has the licence to the Beatrix Potter designs, which she reproduces on the furniture, wallpapers and fabrics.
TUBE *Knightsbridge* • **OPEN** *Mon–Fri 9.30am–5.30pm. Sat 10am–5pm*
• **WEBSITE** *www.classicengland.co.uk/dragons.html* • **SERVICES** *Full interior design service. Murals a speciality. Catalogue £3*

ENGLISH STAMP COMPANY
See DECORATING AND RE-FURBISHING: SPECIALIST DECORATING SUPPLIERS, page 99. Lots of jolly stamps suitable for decorating children's walls, furniture and fabrics.

IKEA
See UNDER ONE ROOF: FURNISHING SPECIALISTS, page 11. Excellent selections of reasonably priced furnishings for children – they take the subject very seriously in Sweden, as indeed we all should.

LITTLE BRIDGE
ADDRESS 56 Battersea Bridge Road, SW11 3AG
TEL 0171 978 5522   **FAX** 0171 978 5533
Brigid Courtney and her team of artists promise 'a realistic service at a realistic price.' This charming shop takes familiar shapes for chests, chairs, beds and so on, and paints them in virtually any colour you choose, adding names and motifs that are only limited by your imagination. A single bed costs from around £250; a two-over-three chest of drawers is around £395. Orders take around six weeks.
TUBE *South Kensington or Sloane Square plus bus* • **RAIL** *Clapham Junction* • **OPEN** *Mon–Fri 10am–5pm. Sat 10am–5pm* • **WEBSITE** *www.littlebridge.force9.co.uk* • **SERVICE** *Hand-painted furniture to order*

NURSERY WINDOW
ADDRESS 83 Walton Street, SW3 2HP
TEL 0171 581 3358   **FAX** 0171 823 8839
Children's tastes in decorating are increasingly sophisticated and extend far beyond fluffy bunnies and comic characters. Nursery Window's paper and fabrics have a depth of detail that appeals to imaginative children and adults alike. Scheherazade, for example, draws inspiration from the fantasy world of the Russian ballet (£27.50 a metre), and New World is based on old-time sea charts, complete with galleons in full sail. Plus a range of useful stripes and checks. Fabrics, papers, bed linens, and lots of pretty accessories. Baby Direct has re-assuring essentials for a new mother.
TUBE *South Kensington* • **OPEN** *Mon–Sat 10am–5.30pm*
• **SERVICES** *Mail-order catalogue. Gift wrapping*

POPPY ✉
ADDRESS 44 High Street, Yarm, North Yorks, TS15 9AE
TEL 01642 790000   **FAX** 01642 788235
Fabrics by the metre, wallpaper and borders in fresh bright exclusive designs – both pastel and primaries, with curtains and bedding made to order including Polartec baby blankets.

THE STENCIL LIBRARY
See DECORATING AND RE-FURBISHING: SPECIALIST DECORATING
SUPPLIERS, page 100. Beatrix Potter stencils, plus Alice in Wonderland,
American football, and other appealing motifs.

FLOORS

CARPETS AND NATURAL FLOORINGS

Carpets are graded according to how they will wear in different
rooms. It is foolish to ignore these grading labels. For example,
a bedroom-grade carpet used in a hall will soon wear and look
shabby. If the carpet you want is outside your budget, look around
for an alternative, or re-think the idea and look for some other way
of creating the same effect.

Never put down a carpet until all building, plumbing and electrical
work is completed. 'Natural' floorcoverings (made from plant
fibres such as sisal, coir, jute, rush, seagrass and so on) have met
a modern demand for fashionable floorings at an affordable cost.
The range of patterns and colours is constantly expanding. Fibres
are now being mixed, to give floorings with a more interesting
look and a better feel. New blends often contain a percentage of
wool – the original natural floorcovering! Ironically, many all-wool
carpets are now made to mimic the look of the so-called naturals,
but with a softer texture.

USEFUL CONTACT

CARPET INFORMATION CENTRE
Excellent site for browsing – around 30,000 people 'visit' each week.
It contains a full list of carpet retailers in the London area, plus carpet
products, details of fibres and so on.
WEBSITE www.carpetinfo.co.uk

ALLIED CARPETS GROUP
ADDRESS 258–264 Goldhawk Road, W12 9PE
TEL 0181 735 0504   **TEL** 0800 192192 for other store addresses
Huge range of carpets, vinyls, wood and laminates, and rugs. Plus beds
and curtains in most stores. Jeff Banks home collection is modern and
affordable, with co-ordinated carpets, fabrics and papers.

TUBE *Hammersmith/Stamford Brook/Turnham Green* • **OPEN** *Mon 10am–6pm. Tues–Sat 9.30am–6pm. Late night Thurs 8pm. Sun 11am–5pm* • **SERVICES** *HomeVision computer shows how floorings look in a room. Free planning and estimating. 14-day exchange guarantee. Curtains/blinds made to order* • **ALSO AT** *90–100 Edgware Road, W2 2HX (0171 402 2233). 64–68 High Street, Camden NW1 0LT (0171 387 3248). New Holloway Arcade, Holloway Road, N7 0RY (0171 609 4143). 377–379 North End Road, SW6 1NP (0171 385 2592). Beckton, Brixton, Charlton, Edmonton, Eltham, Friern Barnet, Lewisham, Peckham, Penge, Putney, Tottenham, Walworth Road, West Ealing, Wembley, Wood Green*

BLENHEIM CARPETS

ADDRESS 41 Pimlico Road, SW1W 8NE
TEL 0171 823 5215   **FAX** 0171 823 5210
Definitely on the A-list, with a branch in Antibes (for the yacht trade) – pop stars come here for something special. Their own mills can make a carpet for any room in any colour or design, from around £45 a metre, 68 cm wide. Also all-wool flatweaves from £17 a square metre, and good strong colours in plain wool Wiltons.
TUBE *Sloane Square* • **OPEN** *Mon–Fri 9am–5pm. Sat 10am–12.30pm* • **SERVICES** *Manufacture any design, colour and fit*

BOWERS AND CO

ADDRESS 111 The High Road, East Finchley, N2 8AG
TEL 0181 444 9911   **FAX** 0181 365 3791
Elegant upmarket showroom for all flooring, except ceramics. Amtico specialists.
TUBE *East Finchley* • **OPEN** *Mon–Sat 8am–4pm* • **SERVICES** *Fitting with own workforce*

CAPITOL CARPETS

ADDRESS 98–100 Northcote Road, Battersea, SW11 6QW
TEL 0171 228 7167   **FAX** 0171 228 4154
Family business trading for nearly 40 years: 'service is our priority.' Showrooms (backed by a large warehouse in Croydon) display all major carpet brands, (including special colours and extra wide widths), carpet tiles, linos and vinyls, including Amtico. They belong to the Metro buying group, which secures extra-keen prices by bulk buying.
RAIL *Clapham Junction* • **OPEN** *Mon–Sat 9am–5.30pm* • **SERVICES** *Fitting* • **ALSO AT** *437–439 Upper Richmond Road West, SW14 7PJ (0181 878 2051). 104 Beddington Lane, Croydon, Surrey CR0 4TB (0181 688 6209)*

CARPET AND RUG WAREHOUSE

ADDRESS 1 Alexandria Road, West Ealing, W13 0NP
TEL 0181 566 4022   **FAX** 0181 566 1014
Keen prices from carpet specialists now in 25th year. Fitted carpets from leading makers, plus vinyls, laminated and wood flooring. Weekly half-price factory clearance of roll ends and large remnants. Oriental rugs from India, China, Afghan, Turkey and Persia.
RAIL *West Ealing* • **OPEN** *Mon–Sat 9am–6pm* • **SERVICES** *Own fitters – service is free in many cases*

THE CARPET LIBRARY

ADDRESS 148 Wandsworth Bridge Road, SW6 2UH
TEL 0171 736 3664 **FAX** 0171 736 7554
Martin Long, in the trade since he was 15, turns carpet laying into a
decorative art: the windows of The Carpet Library are a perfect picture.
Borders are his forte. Some come as strips of carpet 68 cm wide, split
down the middle for fitting; other are narrow strips of tapestry which can
be stitched onto any carpet, including a huge range of natural floorings.
Decorative stair rods in iron, steel or gleaming brass, many exclusive, are
another option.
TUBE *Fulham Broadway/Parsons Green* • **OPEN** *Mon–Fri 10am–1pm;
2pm–5pm. Sat 10am–1pm; 2pm–4pm* • **SERVICES** *Fitting, borders*

E J CARPETS

ADDRESS 1–5 Perry Vale, Forest Hill, SE23 2NE
TEL 0181 699 9300 **FAX** 0181 699 4999
Family business trading for over 23 years. Member of the Greendale
buying group, so prices are competitive. Samples from most leading
manufacturers, including Ryalux, Tomkinsons, BMK and Sanderson.
Room-sized remnants. Plus vinyls and laminate flooring.
RAIL *Forest Hill* • **OPEN** *Mon Tues Thurs Fri 8.30am–5.30pm. Wed 8.30am–
1pm. Sat 9am–5pm* • **SERVICES** *Own fitters – service is usually free*

THE CARPET TILE CENTRE

ADDRESS 227–229 Woodhouse Road, N12 9BD
TEL 0181 361 1261 **FAX** 0181 361 3147
Wide range of Heuga seconds as well as end of lines, seconds and
specials and trial lines. Plus wide range of other flooring including
carpets, wood, vinyl and lino.
RAIL *New Southgate* • **OPEN** *Mon–Fri 9am–5pm. Sat 9am–1pm*

GILT EDGE CARPETS

ADDRESS 255 New King's Road, SW6 4RB
TEL 0171 731 2588/3368 **FAX** 0171 736 3042
Brian Nangle – 'all my life in carpets' – is king of colour at his Chelsea
carpet boutique—there is every shade imaginable. Wool carpets from £12
a square metre; synthetic fibres from £6. Over 100 designs in popular
wool weaves that imitate natural fibres, from £10 a square metre. Also all
leading makes of hardwood flooring.
TUBE *Parsons Green* • **OPEN** *Mon–Fri 9am–5.30pm. Sat 10am–2pm*
• **SERVICES** *Own fitters. Can lay within 48 hours if necessary. Any colour
dyed to order – takes around two to three weeks and costs from £25
a square metre*

INTERFURNISH

ADDRESS 77 Haverstock Hill, NW3 4SL
TEL 0171 722 2621 **FAX** 0171 483 0968
Jerry Whelan and Tom Hennighan have 80 years combined carpet
experience – 'inevitably, we're known as Tom and Jerry.' All carpet needs,
from tiny bathroom to luxury through lounge. Emphasis is on service –
they'll work through the night to get jobs done, and have travelled as

far as Wiltshire, Norfolk and the South Coast. Samples from over
40 manufacturers. Lino, vinyl and wood floors.
TUBE *Chalk Farm/Belsize Park* • **OPEN** *Mon–Fri 9am–6pm. Sat 9am–5pm*
• **SERVICES** *Own fitters. Home visits*

JOHN LEWIS

See UNDER ONE ROOF: DEPARTMENT STORES, page 14. John Lewis
is an antidote to carpet confusion, with racks of plains arranged in
convenient tonal order. Good value are over 300 colours in own-brand
Jonelle ranges. For example, 'New Homes' (over 50 colours) aimed at first-
time buyers comes in three textures: twist pile at £11.50 a square metre;
velvet pile at £12 a square metre; and plush pile at £10.50 a square
metre. Cuttings are available to take away, with larger samples for loan.

NATURAL FLOORING DIRECT

ADDRESS Unit 38, New Lydenburg Street, SE7 8NF
TEL 0800 454721   **FAX** 0181 293 7123
Coir, jute, sisal, seagrass and wood floorings supplied and fitted with all
relevant underlays, doorbars and so on. Send £5 for full set of samples.
Prices from around £26 a metre.
SERVICES *Finance and fitting*

S AND M MYERS 🐖

ADDRESS 100–106 Mackenzie Road, N7 8RG
TEL 0171 609 0091   **FAX** 0171 609 2457
Bargain carpet-baggers in the know have long beat a path to this family
business (established 1819!), to take advantage of discontinued or slightly
imperfect ranges (mostly plains, around 200 rolls). Carpets are displayed
warehouse-style at cut prices. For example, 80/20 wool/nylon pile carpets
at around £7.99. A friendly courteous welcome and professional advice.
TUBE *Caledonian Road* • **OPEN** *Mon Wed Fri 10am–5.30pm. Tues
Thurs 10am–5pm. Sat 9.30am–5pm* • **SERVICES** *Samples; expert fitting*
• **ALSO AT** *81–85 East End Road, East Finchley, N2 (0181 444 3457)*

SINCLAIR TILL

See SMOOTH FLOORINGS: LINO, RUBBER, VINYL AND CORK,
page 183. Full selection of all natural floorings, in sisal, jute, coir and rush.

WEST END CARPET CO

ADDRESS 1e Baker Street, W1M 1AA
TEL 0171 224 6635   **FAX** 0171 224 6104
'Quality with economy.' Top-grade carpets plus wood, vinyl (Amtico stockist)
and cork.
TUBE *Marble Arch* • **OPEN** *Mon–Fri 9am–5.30pm* • **SERVICES** *Fitting
service and free samples* • **ALSO AT** *922–928 High Road, N12 9RW
(0181 446 5331)*

WOOD FLOORS: NEW AND RE-CLAIMED BOARDS

'The white-washed wall, the nicely sanded floor,
The varnished clock that clicked behind the door;
The chest contrived a double debt to pay,
A bed by night, a chest of drawers by day.'
Oliver Goldsmith (1728–74)

London's smartest board rooms are no longer in the city, but in Islington, Fulham, Notting Hill, Wandsworth and all residential points radiating outwards. 'Take up your carpets!' is the rallying cry for the design equivalent of the chattering classes. Wooden floors, when properly sealed, are easy to keep clean and very durable. Estate agents say they make a property much easier to sell, and may well increase its value. However, a wood floor can be cold, and is not as cosy as carpet – a point to remember if you like to sit on the floor or walk around in bare feet. It can be noisy for people living underneath – particularly relevant if you live in a flat. Newer types of 'floating floor' have an underlay which cuts noise transmission; a special 'silent floor underlay' reduces the problem even further.

CAMPBELL MARSON

ADDRESS 573 King's Road, SW6 2EB
TEL 0171 371 5001 **FAX** 0181 946 9395
The place for pukka parquet (they've been going for 75 years) – elaborate panels and borders in the grand old style. Plus less expensive planks and boards.
TUBE *Fulham Broadway* • **OPEN** *Mon–Fri 10.30am–12.30pm;*
1.15pm–4.30pm. Sat 10.30am–12.30pm; 1.15pm–4pm • **SERVICES**
Parquet restoration. Patching in broken areas, sanding, and re-sealing

FINEWOOD FLOORS

ADDRESS 5 Gibson Business Centre, rear of 800 High Road, N17 0DH
TEL 0181 365 0222 **FAX** 0181 885 3860
Leading maker of wide-planks and parquet with beautiful solid hardwood floors in English or American oak, elm, walnut, maple, and so on, all produced in their own London mill. Oiled finishes are a speciality, and they can also offer bevelled, limed and other special effects. Prices from £25 a square metre.
RAIL *Whitehart Lane* • **OPEN** *Mon–Fri 9am–5pm* • **SERVICES** *Expert fitting if required*

THE HARDWOOD FLOORING COMPANY

ADDRESS 146–152 West End Lane, NW6 1SD
TEL 0171 328 8481 **FAX** 0171 625 5951
They pioneered the wood floor boom around 12 years ago – main brands are Kahrs and Junckers. Unfinished strip flooring from around £23.50 a square metre, plus £30 to £35 a square metre for laying/finishing. Pre-finished products cost from £25 a square metre, plus around £14.50

a square metre for laying. 'We've based our business on quality and
service – around 70 per cent comes from personal recommendations'.
'New timber is certainly not cheaper than carpet,' says director Alan
Peploe, whose large showroom overflows with samples. 'But correctly laid,
fitted and maintained, it will look good for far longer'. Also chromed steel
shelving and hardwood kitchen worktops.

TUBE/RAIL *West Hampstead* • **OPEN** *Mon–Fri 8.30am–5.30pm*
• **SERVICES** *Own floor layers – no sub-contracting*

THE NATURAL WOOD FLOOR CO

ADDRESS 20 Smugglers Way, SW18 1EQ
TEL 0181 871 9771 **FAX** 0181 877 0273

Family business, founded eight years ago by the three enterprising Keane
brothers. Speciality is reclaimed wood turned into flooring in their own
workshop and country mills. Prices from around £18 a square metre –
they'll recommend layers from an extensive London-wide list. If you're
sanding and sealing (see page 182), and have damaged boards, they'll
do their best to match your old ones. They also do new wood floors.

RAIL *Wandsworth Town* • **OPEN** *Mon–Fri 9am–6pm. Sat 9am–4pm*

POSNERS

ADDRESS 35a–37 Fairfax Road, NW6 4EW
TEL 0171 625 8899 **FAX** 0171 625 8866

They claim to be the largest hard floor showroom in London. Plus American
and continental carpets; all backed by huge stocks.

TUBE *Swiss Cottage* • **OPEN** *Mon–Sat 9am–6pm* • **SERVICES** *Free estimates,
samples. Fitting*

SOLID FLOOR

ADDRESS 128 St John Street, EC1 4JS
TEL 0171 251 2917 **FAX** 0171 253 7419

They have around 80 different types of timber flooring, including an
unusual three-layer sandwich of tongue-and-groove glued bamboo strips –
£49 a square metre. Also timbers for the popular wide-board look, in oak,
teak and other dark woods.

TUBE *Farringdon* • **OPEN** *Mon–Fri 10am–5pm. Sat 11am–2pm* • **SERVICES**
Can organise laying • **ALSO AT** *53 Pembridge Road, Notting Hill W11 3HG
(0171 221 9166)*

VICTORIAN WOOD WORKS

ADDRESS International House, London International Freight Terminal,
Temple Mills Lane, E15 2ES
TEL 0181 534 1000 **FAX** 0181 534 2000

The mission is to rescue complete floors – beautiful parquet from all over
Europe and as far as Russia. They restore them to pristine glories and
adapt them to the customer's needs. Established for nine years, the team is
headed by director Declan Malloy. Original oak boards – up to 300 years
old – can be up to 14 in wide. Parquet patterns have romantic names –
Chantilly, Versailles, Parisienne – and glow with a soft waxed patina.
'We'll go anywhere to get the timber we need'. At the other end of the
scale, they sell flooring made from old beams, from around £20 a square
metre. Panelling for walls is another speciality.

TUBE *Stratford* • **OPEN** *Mon–Fri 8.30am–5.30pm. Sat 8.30am–12.30pm*

THE WOODEN FLOOR SPECIALISTS

ADDRESS 302 Cavendish Road, SW12 0PL
TEL 0181 675 2431   **FAX** 0181 675 5100

Over 500 samples of hardwood flooring including unfinished and pre-finished solid and wood laminates. 'Knowledge and expertise to rely on.' Brands include Junkers, Kahrs, Tarkett, Langmoen and Boen Parkett. Sanding machines, stains, joint fillers, varnishes, oils and lacquers plus expert advice for intrepid 'do-it-yourselfers'. Special offers always available.

TUBE/RAIL Balham • **OPEN** Mon–Fri 9am–5pm. Sat 10am–2pm • **SERVICES** Own experienced fitters. Maintenance programmes

WOOD FLOORS: RESTORATION, SANDING AND SEALING

Provided you have boards, the cheapest way to get a wooden floor is sanding and sealing – new water-based lacquers dry paler and in less time than older polyurethanes or two-part lacquers. The result will suit modern and traditional looks alike. You can do-it-yourself with machine like a small lawn mower hired from a local branches of the HSS Group (0800 282828, free catalogue). A floor sander costs around £32 for a weekend but add on around £70 for various extras, including varnish. Techniques are tricky, and you could damage your floor. Many people therefore prefer to hire a professional at a cost of from £15 to £30 a square metre. THE WOODEN FLOOR SPECIALISTS and VICTORIAN WOOD WORKS, (see WOOD FLOORS: NEW AND RE-CLAIMED BOARDS, page 180) will tackle renovations, as will TUDOR FLOORING, listed under SMOOTH FLOORINGS: LINO, RUBBER, VINYL AND CORK, page 183. Other firms specialise in renovations.

USEFUL CONTACTS

ANDREW KEAN
TEL 0181 653 0221
'So many people don't realise that their wooden floorings are perfectly good,' says Andrew, who has around 18 years experience in floor restoration, and charges up to £20 a square metre.

THE FLOOR STORE
TEL/FAX 0181 880 0888
Charles Farrar runs a hire service for DIY floor sanding – 'very user-friendly'. They deliver and collect machines, special plastic 'sandpaper', varnish etc and teach you how to use them. Advice on different finishes and specials colours mixed to order.

WOOD FLOORS
TEL 01628 529200/09761 150434
Mike Wetherall has 20 years experience of sanding, restoring and laying new and re-claimed wood floors. All varnishing, liming etc.

WORLDS END STRIPPING COMPANY
TEL/FAX 0171 281 0875   **MOBILE** 0468 622120
Michael Winette and his team have been established for 15 years, and
are experts in all aspects of floor renovation, including decorative effects
such as liming. They can also supply and lay new wood floors. They can
strip any other timber in situ, and do general carpentry.
WEBSITE *www.wood-floors.freeserve.co.uk*

SMOOTH FLOORINGS, INCLUDING LINO, RUBBER, VINYL AND CORK

DUROLINO
ADDRESS 24 Trinity Road, SW17 7RE
TEL 0181 672 3593   **FAX** 0181 672 7172
Sixty years ago, this firm was laying lino when it was fashionable first
time round. Now the fourth generation of the family is doing the fitting.
Also Amtico, and wood floors.
TUBE *Tooting Bec* • **RAIL** *Wandsworth Town* • **OPEN** *Mon–Fri 8.30am–5pm.
Sat 9.30am–2pm* • **SERVICES** *Own fitters*

FIRST FLOOR
ADDRESS 174 Wandsworth Bridge Road, SW6 2UQ
TEL 0171 736 1123   **FAX** 0171 371 9812
Speciality here is French Dalsouple rubber tiles in a huge range of colours
and finishes, including studs and ribs. Plus upmarket individual designs for
linoleum and vinyl, with inlays and borders. Also cork and wood, plus
bordered carpets and special rugs.
TUBE *Fulham Broadway/Parsons Green* • **OPEN** *Mon–Fri 10am–5.30pm.
Sat 10am–2pm* • **SERVICES** *Brochure. Samples*

SINCLAIR TILL
ADDRESS 791–793 Wandsworth Road, SW8 3JQ
TEL 0171 720 0031   **FAX** 0171 498 3814
Suzie and Alastair Till pioneered the lino revival from their spacious corner
showroom, crammed with inspirational samples and examples of work.
Speciality is inlaid lino. Made from linseed oil, wood flour, and cork, lino
is very 'green'- it's also warm, natural, hard-wearing and practical. Also
innovative designs for wood. Plus good selections of natural-fibre mattings
and wool carpets
TUBE *Clapham Common* • **RAIL** *Clapham Junction/Queenstown Road*
• **OPEN** *Mon–Fri 9.30am–5.50pm* • **SERVICES** *Samples. Design service*

SOUTHSIDE FLOORING
ADDRESS 274 Earlsfield Road, SW18 3DX
TEL 0181 870 5681   **FAX** 0181 875 1678
Lino sheet, tiles and inlaid designs. Amtico specialists, and stockists for
Dalsouple rubber floors.
RAIL *Earlsfield* • **OPEN** *Mon–Fri 9am–5pm. Sat 10am–12.30pm*
• **SERVICES** *Own fitters – speedy service*

TUDOR FLOORING
ADDRESS 2 Avenue Parade, Ridge Avenue, N21 2AX
TEL 0181 360 4242   **FAX** 0181 360 6881
Proprietor Allan Ling was trained in parquet under French and Italian craftsmen and heads a team of specialists – 'prices and service second to none.' Also carpets, Amtico and other vinyls, lino, cork, and wood. Brands: Armstrong, Marley, Nairn, Junkers, Kahrs, Tarkett, Wicanders.
TUBE *Southgate* • **OPEN** *Mon–Sat 9am–5pm* • **SERVICES** *Own fitters*

VICTORIA FLOORING
ADDRESS 4 Croxted Road, SE21 8SW
TEL 0181 670 3322   **FAX** 0181 766 6058
All smooth flooring, including lino (sheet and tiles), Amtico, wood floors and cork, plus good selections of carpet.
RAIL *West Dulwich* • **OPEN** *Mon–Fri 9am–5pm. Sat 10am–4pm*
• **SERVICES** *Own fitters*

STONE, MARBLE, SLATE.

Stone floors are relatively new for London, and can be confusing. Stone comes as tiles of varying sizes and thicknesses. It suits the natural look, and fits minimalist or rural-style rooms. It's a must-have for kitchens, conservatories, halls, and even living rooms. Stone floors can be millions of years old and look a million dollars; some are rescued from old buildings. Granite is very hard, and can be polished to a high shine without wax. Sandstone is normally pale beige, but colours range through grey to yellow and even purple. British is expensive, but cheaper types come from the third world. Use for external paving, but not for kitchens as it stains. Limestone's true colour is white, but can be yellow, beige or bluey grey. Prices vary from affordable to expensive. With proper sealants it won't stain, so use for kitchens, bathrooms, halls etc. Don't use outside. Travertine, though very hard, has holes which must be filled for floors; it can then be used for kitchens if well-sealed; also for outside pool areas. Slate is very affordable – particularly from third world countries such as India, China and Brazil. Use anywhere, outside or in. The huge colour range includes greys and pinks. Quartzite is similar to slate but harder. Marble is limestone hardened by natural pressure and high temperatures within the earth – it's expensive though cheaper types come from Eastern Europe and China; it needs polishing and is mostly used in bathrooms.

Upper floors may need strengthening before a stone floor is laid – consult a reputable supplier and use an experienced installer. Stone floors can be laid onto wood overlaid with external grade 18 mm ply fixed all over with screws at 300mm centres.

ATTICA
ADDRESS 543 Battersea Park Road, SW11 3BL
TEL 0171 738 1234   **FAX** 0171 924 7875
A design service (founded five years ago) for exclusive and different stone floors. Stones are brought in from around the world, including old and

rescued floors. Limestone from around £65 a square metre. Antique
travertine is £78; slate from around £34.

RAIL *Battersea Park* • **OPEN** *Mon–Fri 10am–5pm. Sat 11am–6pm*
• **WEBSITE** *www.attica.co.uk* • **SERVICES** *In-house design team*

FIRED EARTH

See TILES, page 107. Good selections of stone and slate, with inspiring
samples of floor designs in situ. Ring 01295 814300 for special stone
brochure.

KIRKSTONE

See KITCHENS: APPLIANCES, SINKS AND WORKTOPS, page 122.
Inspirational showroom for unusual natural stone. There's the company's
own Cumbrian slates, plus limestones, granites, travertines and slates from
abroad, which can be combined with mosaics and patterned borders,
ceramic or even glass tiles for individual flooring or wall cladding.
Professional service for design, installation and maintenance advice.

PARIS CERAMICS

ADDRESS 583 King's Road, SW6 2EH
TEL 0171 371 7778 **FAX** 0171 371 8395
This superb showroom over three floors is a thrilling destination for all new
stone age worshippers. Very cool. It's the place for new and antique stone
and terracotta for floors and walls. They salvage old floors from historic
sites throughout Europe, including ancient Jerusalem stone. Or there's newly
quarried limestones in a variety of colours depending on local quarries –
in many of them, you can see the fossil remains. Prices: from £68 a square
metre for refined white limestone to £395 a metre for mosaic borders.

TUBE *Fulham Broadway* • **OPEN** *Mon–Fri 9am–5.30pm. Sat 10am–5pm*
• **WEBSITE** *www.parisceramics.com* • **SERVICES** *Individual floors to order.
Beautiful colour brochure*

STEVE CHARLES

ADDRESS 42 Elcho Street, SW11
TEL 0171 228 5785
Pop stars and impresarios (rich ones) go to Steve Charles for imaginative
bespoke stone, terracotta, marble and mosaic pavements using stones
from all over the world – rare Roman marbles and biblical slabs. Works
with own floor layer, Clifford Jones.

RAIL *Battersea Park* • **OPEN** *By appointment*

STONE AGE

ADDRESS 19 Filmer Road, SW6 7BU
TEL 0171 385 7954 **FAX** 0171 385 7956
Ten years ago, director Jo O'Grady was one of the first to realise the
domestic potential for stone floors – he had worked in his uncle's Wiltshire
stone business and 'felt drawn to the material.' Celebrated client architects
have included Eva Jiricna and Foster Associates. Specialises in sandstone
and limestone – 'the biggest range at the fairest price' from Europe, and
Africa, in colours from Irish Black through various beiges and browns, to
Barcelona Green and Vix Blue. From around £33 a square metre for
sandstone and limestone tiles.

TUBE *Parson Green/Fulham Broadway* • **OPEN** *Mon–Fri 9.30am–5.30pm.
Sat by appointment* • **WEBSITE** *www.stone-age.co.uk*

STONELL

ADDRESS 521–523 Battersea Park Road, SW11 3BN
TEL 0171 738 0606 **FAX** 0171 738 0660

Since 1992, Stonell have become the UK's largest stone retailers. They made stone flooring affordable and accessible, halving its price and laying in huge stocks: stone for everyman. Limestone from around £38 a square metre, slate from around £18 a square metre, sandstone from around £36 a square metre. Super brochure; inspirational showrooms.

RAIL *Battersea Park Road* • **OPEN** *Mon–Fri 9.30am–5.30pm. Sat 9.30am–5pm* • **SERVICES** *Special in-house service for cutting skirtings, copings, slabs for seats and so on. Nationwide deliveries* • **ALSO AT** *1197–1199 Finchley Road, NW11 0AA (0181 731 7723). Forstal House, Beltring, Paddock Wood, Kent, TN12 6PY (01892 833500) Fax (01892 833600);* ☞ *head office warehouse – selections of stone floorings – ends of lines. Phone for details*

LIGHTING

- **General lighting** *page 186*
- **Modern lighting specialists** *page 188*
- **Traditional and antique lighting** *page 190*
- **Lighting accessories** *page 192*

GENERAL

CHRISTOPHER WRAY LIGHTING

ADDRESS 591–593 King's Road, SW6 2YW
TEL 0171 736 8434 **FAX** 0171 731 3507

Around 30 years ago, Christopher Wray, then an actor, started the Victorian light-fittings craze and mopped up the market. He was so successful he gave up his night-job. His lighting business has gone from strength to strength, and now encompasses not only all kinds of traditional repro lighting but also a wide range of modern fittings. The showroom, with its huge clock, flashy window displays and hanging baskets is a local landmark. Here you can buy anything from an intricate Tiffany stained-glass copy to a simple Victorian green glass shade. The range of over 6,000 lights, shades and lighting accessories now includes downlighters (low voltage and mains), spotlights, traditional floor lights, table lights (classic and contemporary), wall lights, chandeliers, modern uplighters, desk lights and task lights, bathroom lights, and exterior lighting. Plus all those little extras that complete the job – such as flex (including twisted silk-bound flex in a choice of colours), various styles of switches, and a huge choice of bulbs, which are helpfully displayed on a large board. The catalogue is a veritable bible, weighs a ton, and makes selection a whole lot easier.

TUBE *Fulham Broadway* • **OPEN** *Mon–Sat 9.30am–5.45pm* • **SERVICES** *Lighting repairs for personal shoppers only Mon–Fri 9am–12.30pm; 1.30pm–5.30pm. Free customer parking at rear of premises. Hefty catalogue, price £7.95, mailed with £5 voucher redeemable against first purchase (24-hour catalogue hotline, 0171 384 2888)* • **WEBSITE** *www.christopher-wray.com* • **ALSO AT** *199 Shaftesbury Avenue, WC2H 8JR (0171 836 6869). This branch specialises in modern lighting.*

*Also at Bromley, Caversham, and Enfield (for other branches, phone
0171 736 8434)*

MENOS LIGHTING
ADDRESS 225–227 High Street, Acton, W3 9BY
TEL 0181 993 7013   **FAX** 0181 992 8588
A friendly and infinitely obliging husband and wife team preside over this
large showroom selling from stock and to order. A huge variety of modern
and traditional designs hang from the ceiling, and are grouped around the
walls. See crystal chandeliers, spots, wall lights, table and floor lamps. Plus
low-energy fittings, and height-adjustable lights (good for over dining-tables).
Every type of bulb you could want, and reliable and unstinting advice.
TUBE *Acton Town* • **OPEN** *Mon–Wed Sat 9am–6pm. Thurs Fri 9am–7pm.
Sun 10.30am–4.30pm* • **SERVICES** *Lamp and shade repairs and renovations.
Lamps made from china jars and so on*

MR LIGHT
ADDRESS 275 Fulham Road, SW10 9PZ
TEL 0171 352 7525   **FAX** 0171 376 8034
Mike Piercy is Mr Light. He's been trading since 1975, consistently keeping
ahead of lighting trends, and bringing affordable, attractive and up-to-the-
minute designs to his two London shops. His stock is a mix of modern –
with downlighters, track systems, low-voltage spots, and wall/floor halogen
uplighters – and traditional – with pendants and table lamps. A new range
of English bronze has a finish of darkened brass, and comes in floor and
table lamps and wall fittings – from £60 to £500. Much used for lighting
works of art is a new matchbox-size halogen spot light in English bronze
or brushed nickel at £75. You'll also find cheaper ranges here, with desk
lamps from around £20.
TUBE *South Kensington* • **OPEN** *Mon–Sat 10am–6pm*
• **ALSO AT** *279 King's Road, SW3 5EW (0171 352 8398)*

RYNESS
ADDRESS 45 Old Compton Street, W1V 5PN
TEL 0171 437 8833   **FAX** 0171 734 1243
Ryness is a handy shop – with a branch within reach of most everywhere in
Central London. It's been established for nearly 40 years, and you'll find
knowledgeable service and a wide stock. Ceilings are covered in wired-up
fittings which can be turned on for demo purposes. Contemporary and
traditional lights (low and mains voltage), tungsten halogen suspended
wire systems, downlighters and uplighters, surface and recessed tracks and
spots, exterior and security lighting, wall lights, table lamps, desk lights
and novelty lighting. Plus bulbs, sockets, switches, cables and other fittings.
If you can't see exactly what you want, order from their catalogues. Also
electrical appliances – toasters, kettles, coffee makers and irons, plus the
latest telephones and answering machines.
TUBE *Piccadilly Circus* • **OPEN** *Mon–Sat 9am–6pm* • **SERVICES** *Mail order –
please phone 0171 278 8993* • **ALSO AT** *37 Goodge Street, W1
(0171 636 9681). 326 Edgware Road, W2 (0171 723 5376).
103 King Street, Hammersmith, W6 (0181 741 4398). 211 Kensington
High Street, W8 (0171 937 9830). 84 Victoria Street, SW1 (0171 828
8377). 67 Camden High Street, NW1 (0171 387 4594). 54 Fleet Street, EC4
(0171 353 0575). 17 Market Place, Kingston-upon-Thames (0181 546
6049). 185 High Street, Sutton, Surrey (0181 643 8339)*

MODERN LIGHTING SPECIALISTS

CHELSEA LIGHTING DESIGN
ADDRESS Units 1–3 23a Smith Street, Chelsea, SW3 4EJ
TEL 0171 824 8144 **FAX** 0171 823 4812
Recently expanded showroom shows off special lighting effects, with areas for bathrooms and gardens. See all the most modern ideas, including low-voltage fittings, miniature track systems and concealed cornice lighting. Particularly ingenious are mini-recessed wall/step lights. Plus sophisticated fibre optics and ideas for display lighting. Modern classics are their speciality, with exclusive continental designs including top Italian names such as Fontana Arte and Arte Luce.
TUBE *Sloane Square* • **OPEN** *Mon–Fri 10am–6pm. Sat 10am–5pm*
• **WEBSITE** *www.scoot.co.uk/chelsealightingdesignltd/* • **SERVICES** *In-home consultancy or full lighting design service (chargeable)*

INTO LIGHTING DESIGN
ADDRESS 131 Putney Bridge Road, SW15
TEL 0181 877 1707 **FAX** 0181 877 1506
Good source for modern European lighting with many exclusive lines. Low-voltage models plus 'intelligent' controls.
TUBE *East Putney* • **OPEN** *Mon–Fri 9am–5.30pm* • **SERVICES** *Design, supply, install*

JOHN CULLEN LIGHTING
ADDRESS 585 King's Road, SW6 2EH
TEL 0171 371 5400 **FAX** 0171 371 7799
'So where are the lights?' – a typically bemused response from first-time visitors to John Cullen's attractive stone-floored showroom. You just can't see any obvious table lamps, pendants, spots and so on. John Cullen is all about designing with light (rather than with light fittings) using hidden light sources. This is the ultimate showcase for explaining how it's done. They just lower the blinds and give you your own personal demo – uplighters, downlighters, even starlights: in fact the whole works. And – at last! – the meaning of tungsten halogen and low-voltage will become crystal clear. Led by director Sally Storey, a team of lighting designers provide solutions for every possible lighting situation. Don't miss the best light show in town.
TUBE *Fulham Broadway* • **OPEN** *Mon–Fri 9.30am–5.30pm. Sat 10am–4pm*
• **SERVICES** *Design and install 'discreet' lighting systems for the home and garden*

LONDON LIGHTING COMPANY
ADDRESS 135 Fulham Road, SW3 6RT
TEL 0171 589 3612 **FAX** 0171 581 9652
This is the company that introduced London to the splendours of modern continental light fittings with their arresting shapes in metal, glass and plastics. Others now imitate them, but their modern showroom is still probably the largest in London, filled with high-quality continental and

English fittings. Benefit from their expert advice and see the 'widest range of Italian lighting anywhere'.

TUBE *South Kensington* • **OPEN** *Mon–Sat 9.30am–6pm. Sun 12am–5pm*

MATHMOS

ADDRESS 179 Drury Lane, WC2B 5QF
TEL 0171 405 6990   **FAX** 0171 404 6997
Moving on from the original sixties lava lamps, the new development is colour phasing – a light that changes colour at different speeds or in time to music.

TUBE *Covent Garden* • **OPEN** *Mon–Fri 9am–6pm. Sat 10am–6pm*
• **WEBSITE** *www.mathmos.co.uk* • **ALSO AT** *20–24 Old Street, EC1V 9AP*

MCCLOUD LIGHTING

ADDRESS 3rd Floor, Unit 19–20, Chelsea Harbour Design Centre, SW10 0XE
TEL 0171 352 1533   **FAX** 0171 352 1570
Kevin McCloud is evolving into one of Britain's best known designers, the author of excellent books on decorative finishes and star of the small screen. Fanciful and imaginative metalwork is his forte – fairy-tale chandeliers, sconces, and pendants in a host of romantic finishes – such as verdigris, gilt, rust, and aged leaf. There's also exciting new work in glass and plaster, some with a simple modern feel. Wall sconces start at around £140; chandeliers cost from £750 to £5,950.

OPEN *Mon–Fri 10am–5pm* • **SERVICES** *Colour brochure £5*

SKK LIGHTING

ADDRESS 34 Lexington Street, W1R 3HR
TEL 0171 434 4095   **FAX** 0171 734 0901
Years ago, Shiu-Kay Kan built a house of tin cans as an architectural student, doing his placement in the offices of James Stirling, and that's when I first met him. Now all the big names come to him – he is one of Britain's foremost lighting innovators. He was the first in this country to perfect barewire systems: tensioned parallel silver-plated copper wires carry a safe 12 volt current to take a choice of low-voltage fittings, the ultimate in slender elegance. This is the nineties replacement for old track systems. Motorised robotic systems can be remote controlled by computer and laser technology. The little showroom is deceptive – it conceals a huge talent for lighting design, and a multitude of fitting ideas. Some are architecturally unobtrusive; others are deliberately decorative – like the cube-shaped magic lanterns with their flickering patterns. My favourites are Shiu-Kay's maddest notions – like the dinosaur table lights which emanate a friendly glow. 'My dinosaur is my Anglepoise,' says Shiu-Kay, as always tongue-in-cheek. 'His limbs are fully adjustable.'

TUBE *Piccadilly Circus* • **OPEN** *Mon–Fri 9.30am–6.30pm. Sat 11am–7pm*
• **SERVICES** *Lighting design service*

TRADITIONAL AND ANTIQUE FITTINGS

A fine traditional or period interior deserves to be lit by fittings of similar quality. If your purse can run to it, there are many shops who sell the real thing, suitably adapted to modern-day electricity. Take a stroll down Kensington Church Street, where there's a cluster of traditional lighting shops.

ANN'S LIGHTING
ADDRESS 34A/B Kensington Church Street, W8 4HA
TEL 0171 937 5033   **FAX** 0171 937 5915
Pretty windows filled with fittings lure you inside, to find one of the best ranges of traditional lighting in town.
TUBE *Kensington High Street/Notting Hill Gate* • **OPEN** *Mon–Sat 9am–6pm* • **SERVICES** *Lamp conversions and repairs. Handmade lampshades to order*

THE ANTIQUE LAMP SHOP
ADDRESS 600 King's Road, SW6 2DX
TEL 0171 371 0077   **FAX** 0171 371 3507
Good selections of restored genuine period lighting.
TUBE *Fulham Broadway* • **OPEN** *Mon–Fri 9.30am–6pm*

BESSELINK JONES & MILNE
ADDRESS 99 Walton Street, SW3 2HH
TEL 0171 584 0343   **FAX** 0171 584 0284
Elegant decorator lighting to blend with traditional and antique interiors. Wide choice of table lamps in various materials and styles – column, glass, ceramic, and so on. Picture lights, and floor, table and wall lights made from solid brass in own workshops, with alternative finishes of silver and verdigris. Hanging Gothic-style lanterns, and fine hand-painted lampshades.
TUBE *South Kensington* • **OPEN** *Mon–Fri 10am–5.30pm. Sat 10am–4pm* • **WEBSITE** *www.besselink.com* • **SERVICES** *Make shades to order. Lamp conversions* • **ALSO AT** *4th Floor, Harvey Nichols, Knightsbridge, SW1. Unit 2–24 Chelsea Harbour Design Centre, SW10. 344 Richmond Road, East Twickenham, TW1*

FERGUS COCHRANE – LEIGH WARREN
ADDRESS 570 King's Road, SW6 2DY
TEL 0171 736 9166   **FAX** 0171 736 6687
Genuine lighting antiques, from Regency to Deco – lampbases, lanterns, chandeliers, tablelamps, at prices from £100 to £500.
TUBE *Fulham Broadway* • **OPEN** *10am–5pm Mon–Fri. Sat 10am–5pm*

JONES (ANTIQUE LIGHTING)
ADDRESS 194 Westbourne Grove, W11 2RH
TEL/FAX 0171 229 6866
A glittering shop with one of the largest collections of original light fittings in Europe. They span the period 1860–1960, and include converted Victorian gas fittings, plus Arts & Crafts, Edwardian, Art Nouveau and Art

Deco designs. Around 2,000 lights in stock: table lamps, wall and ceiling fittings, and glass lampshades. 'No reproductions. Our fittings hold their value and become an investment.'

TUBE *Notting Hill Gate* • **OPEN** *Mon–Sat 9.30am–6pm*
• **SERVICES** *Valuations, repairs, polishing, wiring, and lacquering*

KENSINGTON LIGHTING COMPANY

ADDRESS 59 Kensington Church Street, W8 4HA
TEL 0171 938 2405   **FAX** 0171 937 5915
Traditional lighting specialists, with crystal and metal chandeliers, wall fittings, and lamp bases.

TUBE *Kensington High Street* • **OPEN** *Mon–Sat 9am–6pm*
• **SERVICES** *Lighting consultancy*

LIGHTS ON BROADWAY

ADDRESS 6a Greenwich Market, Greenwich, SE10 9HZ
TEL 0181 293 3445   **FAX** 0181 948 2021
Traditional repro lighting – at very reasonable prices – from a small friendly family-run firm, who make their own products. Style is predominantly art nouveau in delicious curvy shapes with shades from delicate opalescent white and apricot to a glowing traditional Edwardian green. Many have rich beaded fringes. Solid brass is distressed to a dark patina that simulates a century of use. Also clocks, frames and candelabra.

RAIL *Greenwich* • **OPEN** *Tues to Fri 11am–5pm. Sat Sun 10.30am–5.30pm*

MRS M E CRICK

ADDRESS 166 Kensington Church Street, W8 4BN
TEL 0171 229 1338   **FAX** 0171 792 1073
At this well-established lighting shop, the speciality is chandeliers, wall lights and candelabra.

TUBE *Notting Hill Gate* • **OPEN** *Mon–Fri 9.30am–5.30pm*

ODDIQUITIES

ADDRESS 20 Sunderland Road, Forest Hill, SE23 2PW
TEL 0181 699 9574
Large antique shop on the South Circular (established for nearly 35 years), with an impressive selection of original lighting for ceilings, walls, table and floor. Candlesticks, converted gas and early electric fittings are mostly dressed with their original shades. All stock is one-offs with no reproductions, plus personal service to advise on size and type of light needed. There are literally hundreds of original fittings all rewired and ready to use. Prices from around £50 (which would buy a converted gas swan-neck fitting) to £4,000.

RAIL *Forest Hill* • **OPEN** *Mon–Fri 10am–5pm. Closed all day Thurs. Sat 10am–2pm*

TULISSIO DE BEAUMONT

ADDRESS 28 Church Street, NW8 8EP
TEL 0171 724 4631
Genuine period lighting dating mostly from 1850 onwards. You'll find chandeliers, lamps, and wall brackets, plus bronzes and decorative pieces. It's opposite Alfie's antiques market.

OPEN *Tues–Sat 10am–6pm* • **SERVICES** *Workshop carries out alterations*

TURN ON LIGHTING
ADDRESS 116/118 Islington High Street, N1 8EG
TEL/FAX 0171 359 7616
Good for genuine antique lighting, from approximately 1840–1940. Wall lamps, chandeliers, table and standard lamps, plus original shades in all sorts of designs and colours. Prices from around £350.
TUBE *Angel* • **OPEN** *Tues–Sat 10.30am–5pm*

LIGHTING ACCESSORIES

J D BEARDMORE
See DOORS: DOOR FURNITURE AND SPECIALIST IRONMONGERY, page 203. Good selections of brass and wood switches, sockets, plates and so on.

CHRISTOPHER WRAY LIGHTING
See LIGHTING: GENERAL LIGHTING, page 186. Vast and comprehensive array of lighting accessories, clearly photographed and described in catalogue and at shop. Includes glass shades (art glass, prismatic, antique-style, modern), choice of lampshades, and all bulbs. Also old-fashioned toggle switches, brass switches, square and round wood wall-mounts, and chrome or brass bathroom pull-switches. Also big selection of accéssories for restoring
oil-lamps, plus 18 different types of chain, suspension kits, galleries (glass shade holders), gimbals (shade carriers) and coloured flexes.

FORBES & LOMAX
ADDRESS 205a St John's Hill, SW11 1TH
TEL 0171 738 0202   **FAX** 0171 738 9224
If you're properly switched on, an ugly white plastic box is unthinkable. The alternatives are here: 'invisible designs' in Perspex, which allow the wallpaper or paint finish to show through. Or there are traditional unlacquered brass switches, or switches in plain white or black Perspex, or elegant silver nickel. Flush-to-the-wall socket outlets have been etch-primed to take any paint finish (2 amp, 13 amp, TV/FM, shaver, telephone points etc). When painted, they almost disappear into the wall or skirting board.
RAIL *Clapham Junction* • **OPEN** *Mon–Fri 9am–5pm*

LOCKS AND HANDLES
See DOORS: DOOR FURNITURE AND SPECIALIST IRONMONGERY, page 205. Excellent selections of brass and chrome switches and socket plates, with special styles and finishes to order, including art deco, colour coated, wrought iron and so on.

OLIVERS LIGHTING COMPANY ✉
ADDRESS Udimore Workshops, Udimore, Rye, TN31 6AS
TEL/FAX 01797 225166
Authentic traditional light switches. Catalogue.

HEATING

USEFUL CONTACTS

THE CENTRAL HEATING INFORMATION COUNCIL
TEL 0845 600 2200
A fact file to explain modern central heating systems, and put you in touch with registered installers.

COUNCIL FOR REGISTERED GAS INSTALLERS (CORGI)
TEL 01256 372 200
By law, all contractors who deal with gas fittings must be registered with CORGI. Avoid the cowboys, and ring them for an installer in your area.
COUNCIL FOR ENERGY EFFICIENCY DEVELOPMENT
TEL 01428 654 011
Can provide help and advice on draught proofing and insulation.
Can suggest contractors.

THE SOLID FUEL ADVISORY SERVICE
ADDRESS 7 Swanick Court, Old Swanick Colliery Road, Alfreton, Derbyshire, DE55 7AS
TEL Freephone 0800 600 000
Advice on solid fuel fires, cookers, boilers and central heating systems, including useful free leaflet on opening up an old fireplace.

RADIATORS

ASTON-MATTHEWS
See BATHROOMS: GENERAL BATHROOM SUPPLIERS, page 132.
Cast-iron column rads a speciality, from around £85, with old-fashioned brass handwheels.

BISQUE
ADDRESS 244 Belsize Road, NW6 4BT
TEL 0171 328 2225   **FAX** 0171 328 9845
Why should radiators be ugly white slabs? Explore alternatives at Bisque, who have a showroom full of exciting ideas. They've been at the cutting edge of radiator design for more than 15 years. Slimline columns and panels can be used vertically or horizontally, or there are low long skirting radiators, or classic boxy shapes. You can order them in a virtually unlimited choice of colour combinations. More like a sculpture gallery than a plumber's merchant! Classic old-style steel radiators (from £275) contrast with the unique Hot Springs coil plug-in heater which has been chosen as a Millennium Product.
TUBE *Kilburn Park* • **OPEN** *Mon–Fri 9am–5pm. Sat 10.30am–1pm*
• **SERVICES** *Unique individually-tailored heating solutions and technical advice*

DIAMOND MERCHANTS
ADDRESS 43–45 Acre Lane, SW2 5TN
TEL 0171 274 6624   **FAX** 0171 978 8370
Large, independent plumbing and heating supplier; very service-conscious
and specialists in combination boilers.
TUBE *Brixton* • **OPEN** *Mon–Fri 8am–5.30pm. Sat 9am–1pm; 2pm–5pm*

THE HOUSE HOSPITAL
See ARCHITECTURAL SALVAGE, page 216. Specialise in cast-iron radiators.

LASSCO RBK
See ARCHITECTURAL SALVAGE, page 216. Huge selection of cast-iron
radiators – choose your finish from simply shot-blasted to powder-coated in
a vast choice of colours.

PRIORITY PLUMBING SUPPLIES
ADDRESS 80b Uxbridge Road, W13 8RA
TEL 0181 579 2288   **FAX** 0181 579 8433
They offer discount prices for a large range of boilers, radiators and
copper tube; they also sell pressed steel baths and lagged cylinders.
Watch out for 'bargain buys': sometimes a bottle of Scotch is thrown in!
TUBE *Ealing Broadway* • **OPEN** *Mon–Fri 7.30am–5pm. Sat 8am–2pm*
• **SERVICES** *A full colour price list is available* • **ALSO AT** *86 Askew Road,
W12 (0181 749 2966). 175 Uxbridge Road, W12 9RA (0181 740 5952).
1373 High Road, Whetstone N20 (0181 445 2945). 62–66 Park Parade,
NW10 (0181 961 9948)*

RADIATING STYLE
ADDRESS Unit 15, Derby Road Industrial Estate, Derby Road,
Hounslow, Middx, TW3 3UQ
TEL 0181 577 9111   **FAX** 0181 577 9222
Individually-designed radiators in a huge choice of shapes, from tall and
slim to chunky cast-iron, plus arresting ideas for sculptural forms. 'Hot seats'
are long low radiators on which the customer fits a marble bench-top.
TUBE *Hounslow Central* • **OPEN** *Mon–Fri 8.30am–5.30pm. Sat 10am–2pm*

FIREPLACES

*'To an Englishman, the idea of a room without
a fireplace is quite simply unthinkable.'*
Hermann Muthesius (1861–1927), The English House

USEFUL CONTACTS

THE NATIONAL ASSOCIATION OF CHIMNEY SWEEPS
AND CHIMNEY LINING ENGINEERS
TEL/FAX 01785 811732
They can provide names of chimney sweeps in your area.

THE NATIONAL FIREPLACE ASSOCIATION
ADDRESS Freepost, PO Box BM2043, B11 2BD
TEL Freephone 0800 521611
They publish the annual Fireplace Year Book, packed with news, ideas, designs and suppliers – it costs £3. Pay by credit card, or send cheque to NFA. Plus a number of technical leaflets on specific fireplace/chimney problems.

THE GEORGIAN GROUP
ADDRESS 6 Fitzroy Square, W1P 6DX
TEL 0171 387 1720   **FAX** 0171 387 1721
Advisory leaflet on Georgian fireplaces costs £2.75 plus 20p postage.

THE VICTORIAN SOCIETY
ADDRESS 1 Priory Gardens, Bedford Park, London, W4 1TT
TEL 0181 994 1019   **FAX** 0181 995 4895
Colour leaflet on restoring/replacing Victorian fireplaces costs £3.00.

ACQUISITIONS
ADDRESS 24–26 Holmes Road, NW5 3AB
TEL 0171 482 2949   **FAX** 0171 267 4361
Can you believe that people used to strip out their traditional old fireplaces? Ken Kennedy was one of the first to help Londoners appreciate the beauty of cast iron, founding this firm in 1974. Now it's hard to get originals so their workshop uses authentic patterns and casting skills to copy original Victorian/Edwardian designs, in silvery burnished steel, or matt black or white primed undercoat (for painting). To finish off, you can use their embossed and/or hand-painted reproduction Victorian or Edwardian tiles in a cast-iron insert. Also fireplaces in wood, stone and marble, and gas wood- and coal-effect fires.
TUBE *Kentish Town* • **OPEN** *Mon–Sat 9am–5pm* • **SERVICES** *Installation*

AMAZING GRATES
ADDRESS 61–63 High Road, East Finchley, N2 8AB
TEL 0181 883 9590   **FAX** 0181 365 2053
Established in 1979, and one of London's original fireplace shops. Fine collection of fireplaces includes originals and sympathetic reproductions, which they make in their own workshop, using materials such as limestone and marble. See settings to suit every kind of house, from traditional through to ultra-modern, as well as accessories which include grates, baskets, fire irons and gas coal fires. Expert advice on choosing and installation. Sample price: a popular flat Victorian fireplace in limestone costs £475.
TUBE *East Finchley* • **OPEN** *Mon–Sat 10am–5.30pm*
• **WEBSITE** *www.amazing-grates.co.uk*

CHESNEY'S ANTIQUE FIREPLACE WAREHOUSE
ADDRESS 194–202 Battersea Park Road, SW11 4ND
TEL 0171 627 1410   **FAX** 0171 622 1078
Largest fireplace displays in London with an impressive run of showrooms. Brothers Paul and Nick Chesney show antique marble and stone British fireplaces from about 1740–1880 (with appropriate iron and/or steel inserts) in their 18,000 sq ft warehouse. They've been established nearly 15 years, and now demand is outstripping supply. So they also make

reproductions – French and English period designs – as correct as possible in every detail, in marble, stone, and pine. Check info on the internet.
RAIL *Clapham Junction* • **OPEN** *Mon–Fri 9am–5.30pm. Sat 10am–5pm*
• **WEBSITE** *www.chesneys.co.uk* • **SERVICES** *Home visits and installations. Reference books for checking period details. Beautiful free colour brochure. Bespoke fireplace design, with unique masonry service. Gas log- and coal-effect fires. Can even recommend a chimney sweep!* • **ALSO AT** *734–736 Holloway Road, N19 3JF (over 3,500 sq ft in an old Victorian candle factory – well over 100 fireplaces on show)*

CHISWICK FIREPLACES
ADDRESS 68 Southfield Road, W4 1BD
TEL 0181 995 4011   **FAX** 0181 995 4012
Restored antiques and popular cut-price package deals for repro models, sold complete with surround, insert, slate hearth, and gas coal fire.
TUBE *Turnham Green* • **OPEN** *Mon–Fri 9.30am–5.30pm. Sat 9.30am–5pm* • **SERVICES** *In-situ fireplace restorations*

THE FIRE PLACE
ADDRESS 257 High Street, Eltham, SE9 1TY
TEL/FAX 0181 850 4887
This family business offers 'quality service', selling Victorian and Edwardian original fireplaces plus handmade wood and marble reproductions, made-to-measure if necessary. They also do gas log and coal-effect fires, and have over 50 fireplaces on display.
RAIL *New Eltham* • **OPEN** *Mon–Sat 9.30am–5pm. Sun 10am–2pm* • **SERVICES** *Installations, own fitters. Brochures*

H AND D FIREPLACE COMPANY
ADDRESS Arches 381–382, 385, Mentmore Terrace, E8 3PN
TEL 0171 359 8179   **FAX** 0171 704 6891
Antique and reproduction fireplaces, along with other architectural items such as leaded lights. This is a rambling 5,000 sq ft complex of showroom, workshops, and warehouse.
DLR *London Fields* • **OPEN** *Mon–Fri 10am–5pm. Sat 10am–4pm* • **SERVICES** *Search service. Restorations/installations. Reclaimed wood flooring. Architectural salvage. Brochure*

FIREPLACE DESIGNERS
ADDRESS 157c Great Portland Street, W1N 5FB
TEL 0171 580 9893   **FAX** 0171 637 2531
Conveniently situated in the heart of town, this firm sell hand-carved and hand-finished traditional mantelpieces fitted out with classical fire grates.
TUBE *Great Portland Street* • **OPEN** *Mon–Fri 9.30am–5.30pm. Sat 9.30am–3.30pm* • **SERVICES** *Individual orders made-to-measure*

FLAMELOG
ADDRESS Unit 6, Chingford Industrial Centre, Hall Lane, Chingford, E4 8HY
TEL 0181 529 1010   **FAX** 0181 524 4350
A display of over 80 fire surrounds in marble, wood, cast iron and so on is

backed by a comprehensive service for installing coal- and log-effect gas
fires – they've been trading since 1978.

TUBE *Walthamstow Central + bus* • **RAIL** *Chingford* • **OPEN** *Mon–Fri
9.30am–5pm. Sat 9.30am–4pm* • **SERVICES** *Own installers, including
gas engineers*

FOCAL POINT ORIGINAL FIREPLACES

ADDRESS 133–135 and 94 Eardley Road, Streatham, SW16 6BB
TEL 0181 769 5496 **FAX** 0181 769 8758

Trading for over 20 years, Ben and Olan Shorten have amassed hundreds
of old fireplaces in marble, wood and cast iron – this is around 90 per cent
of their stock. The rest is a selection of stoves, including modern
Scandinavian designs.

RAIL *Streatham Common* • **OPEN** *Mon–Sat 9am–5.30pm* • **SERVICES**
Recommended installers. Supply of old fireplace spare parts. Restorations

GALLEON CLAYGATE 🚗

ADDRESS 216–230 Red Lion Road, Tolworth, Surbiton, Surrey, KT6 7RB
TEL/FAX 0181 397 3456

They boast the 'largest displays of fireplaces in the South of England', and
have around 80 displays on show, including traditional rustic 'briquettes',
and designs in stone, marble, ceramic tiles and wood, made in their own
workshops at Surbiton. Also grates, fireguards, fenders and coal scuttles.
Galleon – going for over 60 years – have developed an ingenious
'chimney closure plate' to stop draughts when fires aren't burning.
Phone for catalogue and full road directions.

RAIL *Tolworth/Surbiton* • **OPEN** *Mon–Thurs 9am–5pm. Fri 9am–4.30pm
Sat 9am–4pm* • **SERVICES** *Large free car park. Free design service.
Installations. Free colour catalogue*

MARBLE HILL FIREPLACES

ADDRESS 70–72 Richmond Road, Twickenham, Middx, TW1 3BE
TEL 0181 892 1488 **FAX** 0181 891 6591

Experts with nearly 25 years of experience who made their name with fine
selections of carefully-restored antique French marble designs. Now they
have marble and stone reproductions. Workshop also makes pine and
white Adam-style mantels. Pine can be given a wide choice of decorative
finishes – liming or antiquing; staining (oak or mahogany colours and
so on), or marbleising in Victorian style. Or the wood can be dragged,
stippled or sponged for a coloured finish. Also Adam/Regency fire
baskets, fenders, fire irons, screens. Gas coal-effect and electric fires.
Radiator covers.

RAIL *Twickenham/St Margarets* • **OPEN** *Mon–Fri 10am–5.30pm. Sat
9.30am–5pm* • **WEBSITE** *www.marblehill.co.uk* • **SERVICES** *Design. Install*

PECO OF HAMPTON

See DOORS: FRONT AND INTERIOR DOORS, page 202. Large stock of
original restored fireplaces in stock – eg cast iron (from £265) and marble
(from £850) – around 500 to 600 in all. Gas fires made to order.

PETIT ROQUE 🚗

ADDRESS 5a New Road, Croxley Green, Rickmansworth, Herts, WD3 3EJ
TEL 01923 779 291   **FAX** 01923 896 728

Extensive showrooms, established nearly 30 years – particularly cater for DIY enthusiasts. Exclusive fireplace designs each with installation instructions. They have hand-carved mantel surrounds in yew, cherry, lime, mahogany, oak and so on, plus copper, brass, and stainless steel canopies. Also chimney extraction fans, hearths, and fireplace accessories.

TUBE *Rickmansworth/Croxley* • **OPEN** *Tues–Fri 9am–5.30pm. Sat 9.30–5pm* • **SERVICES** *Advisory service on problem chimneys. Individual design and installation within 25 mile radius*

REAL FLAME

ADDRESS 80 New Kings Road, SW6 4LT
TEL 0171 731 2704/3056   **FAX** 0171 736 4625

For the no-hassle open fire, you could consider gas with a log or coal effect. They're amazingly realistic. This company's famous installations include the state rooms at 10 Downing Street. If you already have a grate, they can fill it with gas coals from £200 plus £60 for connecting to a nearby gas point. They can design fire surrounds, and, if you don't have a chimney, they can organise a powered flue. Also a splendid range of decorative fire grates, fireplaces and accessories.

TUBE *Parson's Green* • **OPEN** *Mon–Sat 9am–6pm* • **ALSO AT** *The Gas Log Fire Centre, 232 Fulham Road, SW10 9NB (0171 352 2560). 26 Sydenham Road SE26 5QW (0181 659 5899)*

REALISTIC FIRES

ADDRESS 135 Kingston Road, Wimbledon, SW19 1LT
TEL 0181 543 2170   **FAX** 0181 543 9199

Antique cast-iron and marble fireplaces, plus gas coal-effect fires and fireside accessories.

TUBE *Wimbledon* • **OPEN** *Mon–Thurs Sat 9.30am–5.30pm. Fri and Sun closed* • **SERVICES** *Installations*

TOWNSENDS FIREPLACES

ADDRESS 81 Abbey Road, NW8 0AE
TEL 0171 624 4756   **FAX** 0171 372 3005

A favourite North London showroom for original and reproduction fireplaces in stone, wood, cast iron, and marble. Average spend is around £1000, going up to £2000. All necessary accessories, including reproduction fire grates, firebacks, coal scuttles, plus gas coal- and log-effect fires. Original and new stained and etched glass.

TUBE *Swiss Cottage/St John's Wood* • **OPEN** *Mon–Fri 10am–6pm. Sat 10am–5pm* • **SERVICES** *Installations in London area. Design and make stained and etched glass*

WALTHAMSTOW GAS

ADDRESS 51 Wood Street, E17 3JX
TEL/FAX 0181 520 7005

Friendly family business – founded in 1963 – has a selection of fireplaces on display, and specialises in installing decorative gas and electric fires.

RAIL *Wood Street* • **OPEN** *Mon–Sat 9am–5.30pm* • **SERVICES** *Own installers*

STOVES

Stoves (enclosed heaters which burn coal, smokeless fuel or wood)
are romantic and practical and bring heat out into a room. They
provide a decorative and emotional focal point. Around 95 per
cent of the stoves on the market are multi-fuel so you can burn a
clean fuel in a smokeless zone.

BRENT-WOOD-BURNERS

ADDRESS 3–9 Coxtie Green Road, Pilgrim's Hatch, Brentwood,
Essex, CM14 5PN
TEL 01277 374247 **FAX** 01277 374949
Around 50 stoves on show at this pleasant family-run showroom – the
business goes back 20 years. Many burn smokeless fuel. They even have
some stoves with catalytic converters for wood-burning in a smokeless zone.
RAIL Brentwood • **OPEN** Mon–Sat 9am–5pm • **SERVICES** Chimney lining
and installations

FOCAL POINT ORIGINAL FIREPLACES

See FIREPLACES, page 197. Selection of gas-burning stoves – some for
smokeless fuel.

THE MORLEY STOVE SHOP

ADDRESS Marsh Lane, Ware, Herts, SG12 9QB
TEL 01920 468001 **FAX** 01920 463893
Around 50 stoves on display, many installed and working, and burning
solid fuel, gas or wood. From Britain, America, France, Belgium and
Scandinavia.
RAIL Ware • **OPEN** Mon–Sat 9am–5pm • **SERVICES** Chimney lining and
installations

DOORS

- **Front and interior doors** page 200
- **Door furniture and specialist ironmongery** page 202

> 'A door is what a dog is perpetually the wrong side of.'
> Ogden Nash (1902–71), A Dog's Best Friend Is His Illiteracy

It's an estate agent's cliché that the front entrance – and in
particular the door – can make or break a property sale. But,
when first impressions are so important, why wait until you are
selling your home to dabble in a bit of door decor?

FRONT AND INTERIOR DOORS

USEFUL CONTACT

THE VICTORIAN SOCIETY
ADDRESS 1 Priory Gardens, Bedford Park, London, W4 1TT
TEL 0181 994 1019
Colour leaflet on restoring/replacing Victorian doors costs £3.

BRITISH GATES AND TIMBER 🚗

ADDRESS Biddenden, near Ashford, Kent, TN27 8DD
TEL 01580 291555   **FAX** 01580 292011
This well-established company (founded 1936), specialise in reproduction
traditional Tudor doors, with antique iron fittings. Orders take around six
weeks. Traditional doors in English oak cost £751.90 plus VAT; in oroko,
£550 plus VAT; and in Brazilian mahogany, £623 plus VAT.
RAIL *Headcorn* • **OPEN** *Mon–Sat 8am–5pm* • **SERVICES** *Catalogues.
Nationwide deliveries*

CLASSIC BUILDERS AND JOINERS

ADDRESS 211 Harrow View, Harrow, Middx, HA1 4SS
TEL 0181 863 6767   **FAX** 0181 863 6903
They make any size or shape of door – see around 100 on display, with a
starting price of around £180. Styles include antique-effects and stained
glass. Plus vast selection of handles and fittings, including all security products.
TUBE *West Harrow* • **OPEN** *Mon Tues Thurs Fri 9am–5.30pm. Wed Sat
9am–1pm* • **SERVICES** *Deliveries and fitting. Can make good after
break-ins. Building work*

COTSWOOD DOOR SPECIALISTS

ADDRESS 5 Hampden Way, Southgate, N14 5DJ
TEL 0181 368 1664   **FAX** 0181 368 9635
This family business – trading for over 30 years – can install hardwood
front, internal and garage doors of any shape or size. Front doors cost
from around £50 to £1500.
OPEN *Mon–Fri 8am–5.30pm. Sat 9am–4pm* • **TUBE** *Southgate* • **SERVICES**
Installation and security • **ALSO AT** *63a Park Road, Kingston Hill, Kingston-
upon-Thames, Surrey KT2 6DE (0181 546 3621)*

DARWIN BESPOKE FURNITURE MAKERS

ADDRESS 38A Darwin Road, W5 4BD
TEL/FAX 0181 560 0424
Joinery company specialising in handmade period reproduction doors
usually in mahogany or oak, adding hand-carved mouldings if desired.
TUBE *South Ealing* • **OPEN** *Mon–Fri 9am–5pm*

DEACON & SANDYS 🚗

ADDRESS Unit 3, Apple Pie Farm, Cranbrook Road, Benenden, Kent, TN17 4EU
TEL 01580 243331   **FAX** 01580 243301

These specialists in architectural woodwork can make oak planked and panelled doors based on original 17th- and 18th-century designs, with moulded frames and hand-carving if required. Orders take around four weeks. Plus wall panelling, and staircase balusters. Doors start at £760 (exterior); £275 (interior). They also make hand-finished refectory tables from £1720.
RAIL *Staplehurst* • **OPEN** *By appointment* • **SERVICES** *Nationwide deliveries/installations*

IN DOORS

ADDRESS Beechingwood Farm, Beechingwood Lane, Platt, Sevenoaks, Kent, TN15 8QN
TEL 01732 887445 **FAX** 01732 887446
A stock of over 1,000 repaired and restored interior, exterior and cupboard doors. Also make doors using old timber in pine or hardwoods for extensions or restorations. Plus reproduction door/window furniture, including their own oak latch sets.
OPEN *Mon–Fri 9am–5pm. Sat 9am–12.30* • **SERVICES** *Clean and restore windows, doors, door frames, wainscotting and floors. Paint stripping*

JUST DOORS

ADDRESS 126 West Green Road, Tottenham, N15 5AA
TEL 0181 800 3118 **FAX** 0181 376 4133
New external or internal doors in stock or to order, in pine, mahogany, and glass.
TUBE *Seven Sisters* • **OPEN** *Mon–Fri 8.30am–5pm. Sat by appointment* • **SERVICES** *Fitting including all locks and bolts etc*

THE LONDON DOOR COMPANY

ADDRESS 153 St John's Hill, SW11 1TQ
TEL 0171 223 7243 **FAX** 0171 223 7296
This was London's first specialist door business. Now they have over 30 period designs in stock, or they can make to order. 'We try to create a door that's sympathetic for the property, but we don't do restoration just for the sake of it: we have modern as well as period models. Houses should develop with the people who live in them, and reflect individual personality.' Decorative glazing in etched or bevelled brilliant-cut or stained glass. Plus all door furniture and top-quality security products.
RAIL *Clapham Junction* • **OPEN** *Mon–Sat 9am–5pm* • **SERVICES** *Doors made to order. Fitting, including security products. Stained glass panels, screens and partitions made to order*

ORIGINAL DOORS

ADDRESS 93 Endwell Road, Brockley Cross, SE4 2NF
TEL 0171 252 8109
Friendly husband-and-wife team sell second-hand ('reclaimed') period doors, shutters and old pine kitchens. 'Buy a door and save a tree.' Plus traditional stripped pine architectural fittings/doors.
TUBE *New Cross* • **OPEN** *10am–6pm Mon–Sat. Sun by appointment* • **SERVICES** *Stripping service for huge range of items, including woodwork and metal*

PECO OF HAMPTON

ADDRESS 72 Station Road, Hampton, Middx, TW12 2BT
TEL 0181 979 8310   **FAX** 0181 941 3319
This obliging family business, trading for nearly 30 years, has over 2,500 period doors in stock, many with stained and etched glass.
RAIL *Hampton* • **OPEN** *Mon–Sat 8.15am–5.15pm* • **SERVICES** *Workshop makes and repairs stained glass. Service for stripping wood*

THE PERIOD HOUSE GROUP ✉

ADDRESS Fold Court, Buttercrambe, York, YO41 1AU
TEL/FAX 01759 373484/01759 373495
Planked and ledged country-style doors made from re-claimed timber with a hand-waxed finish. These have rose-head nails, and you can add their hand-forged iron latches and hinges – they say they are the largest UK supplier of this type of ironware.
SERVICES *Catalogue. Nationwide deliveries within 48 hours*

TODD DOORS

ADDRESS 112–116 Church Road, Northolt, UB5 5AE
TEL 0181 845 2493   **FAX** 0181 845 7579
Over 3,000 interior/exterior hardwood doors in stock, in many sizes, prices to suit all pockets – 'largest showroom in South East,' they say. Fixtures and fittings – hardware for emergency doors, insurance-rated locks. Bevelled, coloured, frosted, etched and sand-blasted glass in double or triple-glazed units – with handmade leadlights to order.
TUBE *Northolt* • **OPEN** *Mon–Wed 8am–5.30pm. Thurs 8am–7pm. Fri 8am–5.30pm. Sat 9.am–5.30pm* • **SERVICES** *Fitting and finishing. Brochures, deliveries*

DOOR FURNITURE AND SPECIALIST IRONMONGERY

Door furniture is a strange term that covers knobs, handles, knockers, letter boxes and the like – important finishing touches to set off your doors, and windows, too.

ALLGOOD ARCHITECTURAL HARDWARE

ADDRESS 297 Euston Road, NW1 3AQ
TEL 0171 387 9951   **FAX** 0171 383 7950
Modern distinctive designs, including FSB's unique range including handles by Jasper Morrison, Philippe Starck, Nicholas Grimshaw and Richard Rogers. This is a showroom for architects and specifiers. The public can buy at the trade counter, although you will have to wait for your order to come down from Birmingham.
TUBE *Warren Street* • **OPEN** *Mon–Fri 9am–12.30pm; 2pm–5pm*

J D BEARDMORE

ADDRESS 17 Pall Mall, SW1Y 5LU
TEL 0171 670 1000 **FAX** 0171 670 1010

Come here for old-fashioned solid brass, presented with old-fashioned service – this is one of London's great old companies, dating back to 1860, but only recently moved to this showroom. They know everything about knobs, knockers, handles, hinges, catches and so on, and have the stock to back it up, from tiny brass handles and knobs to wrought-iron rings for gates. Their brass handles are made in England from original moulds – cheaper handles elsewhere could be imported, with weight, detail and finish all inferior (these may not even be solid brass, but plated onto grey metal). Simple solid brass knobs from £20 to £25. Ironmongery is one branch of British engineering still thriving. Plus wrought iron, porcelain, crystal and contemporary door furniture, and special finishes from antique gold to verdigris. 'From Tudor cottage and Regency palace to thirties semi or nineties loft, we've got something to suit.'

TUBE *Piccadilly Circus* • **OPEN** *Mon–Fri 9am–5.30pm. Sat 9am–1.30pm*
• **SERVICES** *Bespoke work of all kinds. Free mail-order catalogue*

CHARLES HARDEN

ADDRESS 14 Chiltern Street, W1M 1PO
TEL 0171 935 2032

This faithful one-man business has been selling door furniture in Marylebone since 1928. China specialists with a range 'as big as any in the country', with knobs from around £8 upwards. Also knobs and handles in brass and glass, plus fittings for window and bathrooms – and 'cheaper than competitors'.

TUBE *Baker Street* • **OPEN** *Mon–Fri 9.30am–5pm (please telephone first)*
• **SERVICES** *Samples copied*

F W COLLINS & SON

ADDRESS 14 Earlham Street, WC2H 9LN
TEL 0171 836 3964 **FAX** 0171 836 3964

Trading over 150 years: a Mr Collins is still in charge. All kinds of ironmongery is crammed into this delightful little shop, with its old wooden counter, pavement wares, pigeon-holes and little drawers – a delicious touch of Dickens in Covent Garden.

TUBE *Leicester Square* • **OPEN** *Mon–Fri 9am–6pm. Sat 10am–6pm*
• **SERVICES** *Key cutting*

DANICO BRASS

ADDRESS 31–35 Winchester Road, Swiss Cottage, NW3 3NR
TEL 0171 483 4477 **FAX** 0171 722 7992

Annelise and Ashok Daryani run a friendly independent business, with three generations of hardware experience. Showroom has over 10,000 items – all sorts of handles, latches, knobs and catches, in finishes from shiny brass to gleaming chrome and black iron. Modern Jado lever handles from Germany are particularly unusual. Plus an impressive selection of decorative metal grilles.

TUBE *Swiss Cottage* • **OPEN** *Mon–Fri 9.30am–6pm. Late night Thurs 7.45pm*
• **SERVICES** *Items can be made to order in special designs/finishes. Brass frames made to measure for radiator grilles*

FRANCHI INTERNATIONAL
ADDRESS Unit 2–11, Chelsea Harbour Design Centre, Lots Road, SW10 0XE
TEL 0171 351 4554   **FAX** 0171 351 2803
Stunning range of unusual European handles, including an elegant design
by Sir Norman Foster.
TUBE *Earls Court + C3 bus/Sloane Square + 11, 22 bus* • **OPEN** *Mon–Fri
8.30am–6pm. Other times by appointment*

FRANCO-FILE ✉
ADDRESS Box 31, Tiverton, Devon, EX16 4YU
TEL/FAX 01884 253556
Traditional imported French blue-and-white enamelled house numbers
and signs.

FULHAM BRASS AND IRONMONGERY
ADDRESS 905 Fulham Road, SW6 5HV
TEL 0171 736 3246   **FAX** 0171 736 3362
Friendly service from partners established in 1985, and a useful port of call
for lever locks, handles, letter plates, and radiator grilles. Many styles for
door handles – brass, chrome, bronze, or black antique iron. Plus antique
style cabinet fittings, bathroom accessories and curtain fittings. Chubb
security centre.
TUBE *Parson's Green* • **OPEN** *Mon–Fri 9am–5.30pm. Sat 10am–4pm*
• **SERVICES** *Engraving*

GHISLAINE STEWART
ADDRESS 110 Fentiman Road, SW8 1QA
TEL/FAX 0171 820 9440
Seeking something exotic for your door? Here are knobs in rare timbers or
sculptural shapes in resin in a choice of finishes including antique bronze
and nickel.
TUBE *Vauxhall* • **OPEN** *By appointment* • **SERVICES** *Mail-order catalogue,
£2.50. Special designs to order*

GLOVER & SMITH ✉
ADDRESS 9a Winchester Street, Overton, Basingstoke, Hants, RG25 3HR
TEL/FAX 01256 773012
Delightful young designers with a growing reputation for charming hand-
cast solid pewter handles, hooks and drawer pulls shaped into starfishes,
twigs, shells and so on. Most beguiling.
SERVICES *Mail-order catalogue*

THE HANDMADE GLASS COMPANY
ADDRESS Roxby Place, SW6 1RF
TEL 0171 610 3344   **FAX** 0171 610 3355
Superb custom-made glass knobs accented with silver and gold leaf, plus a
range in clear contemporary colours. From £15 to £75 each.
TUBE *West Brompton (closed weekends)/Earls Court* • **OPEN** *Mon–Fri
10am–5pm. Sat 10am–1pm (but please check first)* • **SERVICES** *Mail-order
(p&p costs £5)*

HAUTE DECO

ADDRESS 556 King's Road, SW6 2DZ
TEL 0171 736 7171   **FAX** 0171 736 8484

Giving London something to grasp at is Parisian-born Marie-Veronique Swannell, who provides handles with flair from six French makers: small-scale furnishing fantasies in resin (35 colours) and bronze. Here the humble door knob becomes a miniature sculpture – from organic fluid shapes to dolphins, shells, flowers, and even a crocodile. Cupboard and drawer knobs cost around £15. Use to re-vamp junk furniture, or to customise low-budget kitchen units.

TUBE *Fulham Broadway* • **OPEN** *Mon–Sat 10am–6pm*
• **SERVICES** *Custom-made designs. Nationwide deliveries*

LOCKS AND HANDLES
(ARCHITECTURAL COMPONENTS)

ADDRESS 8 Exhibition Road, SW7 2HF
TEL 0171 584 6800   **FAX** 0171 589 4928

En route to the V & A, stop off for an inspirational browse – all the charm of an old-fashioned hardware store (in private ownership for 40 years) married to exciting new contemporary designs. Good displays and stocks of authentic period brass door and window furniture, plus alternatives in wood, crystal-clear acrylic, wrought iron etc. Bathroom accessories; radiator and ventilator grilles; hooks and curtain tie-backs; and security fittings. All to high decorative standards and with friendly, knowledgeable service.

TUBE *South Kensington* • **OPEN** *Mon–Fri 9am–5pm. Sat 9am–9.30pm*
• **SERVICES** *A veritable bible of a catalogue – £6 refundable against orders over £50. Brass curtain poles cut to length*

NU-LINE

ADDRESS 315 Westbourne Park Grove, W11 1EF
TEL 0171 727 7748   **FAX** 0171 792 9451

Busy builders merchant with excellent local reputation for friendly service, and (in addition to all the usual bathroom fittings, paints and so on) good displays of handles, hinges, knobs and fittings of all kinds, including black wrought iron and brass.

TUBE *Ladbroke Grove/Westbourne Park*
• **OPEN** *Mon–Fri 7.30am–5.30pm. Sat 8am–1pm*

PURVES & PURVES

See UNDER ONE ROOF: FURNISHING SPECIALISTS, page 12.
Good for modern knobs.

ROMANYS ARCHITECTURAL IRONMONGERS

ADDRESS 52–56 Camden High Street, NW1 0LT
TEL 0171 387 2579   **FAX** 0171 383 2377

At this old-established hardware store, find a good selection of door fittings, from traditional brass and black iron to streamlined modern aluminium.

TUBE *Camden Town* • **OPEN** *Mon–Fri 8am–5pm. Sat 9am–5pm*

A TOUCH OF BRASS

ADDRESS 210 Fulham Road, SW10 9PJ
TEL 0171 352 5495/351 2255 **FAX** 0171 352 4682
Established in 1982 by William Benham, this is the company that sells official replicas of the No 10 Downing Street lion door knocker. Good displays and stocks of door and window fittings, plus security products. A huge variety of finishes and products – brass, antique brass, chrome, black iron, nickel, steel, Perspex and bronze.
TUBE *South Kensington* • **OPEN** *Mon–Fri 9am–5pm. Sat 10am–5pm*
• **SERVICES** *Catalogue. Mail-order* • **ALSO AT** *Concession on second floor of Harrods (0171 581 1992)* • **SERVICES** *Mail-order catalogue. Made-to-measure radiator cases*

TURNSTYLE DESIGNS ✉

ADDRESS Village Street, Bishop's Tawton, Barnstaple, Devon, EX32 0DG
TEL 01271 325325 **FAX** 01271 328248
Using a resin-based material which has a hard stone-like finish, this firm fashion a series of fanciful knobs and handles in the shape of shells, frogs, cats, birds, ammonites and so on.
SERVICES *Mail-order catalogue*

WINDOWS

- **General glass merchants** *page 206*
- **Replacement windows** *page 207*
- **Stained, decorative and special glass** *page 208*
- **Shutters, awnings and grilles** *page 211*

GENERAL GLASS MERCHANTS

USEFUL CONTACT

THE GLASS AND GLAZING FEDERATION
ADDRESS 44–48 Borough High Street, SE1 1XB
TEL 0171 403 7177 **FAX** 0171 357 7458
Leaflets on choosing windows and glass (including safety glass), and conservatories. They can recommend a member glass merchant in your area.

CHELSEA GLASS

ADDRESS 650–651 Portslade Road, SW8 3DH
TEL 0171 720 6905 **FAX** 0171 978 2827
'Anything and everything in glass' from an obliging old-established company, who were in the Fulham Road, before rate increases pushed them out. All types of glass cut to size while you wait. Cut and bevel glass for shelves and table tops. Wide range of special mirror glass (antiqued and tinted) and mirrors. They make up display cases, and have even ground chips down from drinking glasses.

RAIL *Wandsworth Road* • **OPEN** *Mon–Fri 8am–5.30pm. Sat 8am–12 noon*
• **SERVICES** *Cut, install. Sand-blasting and acid-etching. Mirror restoration*

PREEDY GLASS
ADDRESS Lamb Works, North Road, N7 9DP
TEL 0171 700 0377   **FAX** 0171 700 7579
Old-established glass merchants who cut and fit all types of glass (including laminated safety glass, and wired glass), and polish off sharp edges for shower screens, table tops and so on. Special services include cutting edge profiles on glass up to 1 in thick, sand-blasting, and acid-etching. Special products include extra-clear glass and mirrors, coloured and antiqued mirror glass, and special ironmongery for glass – for example hinges for glass doors and shower screens.
TUBE *Caledonian Road* • **OPEN** *Mon–Fri 8am–5pm* • **SERVICES** *Cut to size, install. Sand-blasting, acid-etching. Mirror restoration* • **ALSO AT** *Stanley Works, 7B Coronation Road, NW10 (0181 965 1323)*

RANKINS (GLASS) COMPANY
ADDRESS 24–34 Pearson Street, E2 8JD
TEL 0171 729 4200   **FAX** 0171 729 7135
Comprehensive range of sheet glass – in particular fire-resistant, decorative, low-reflective, and conservation glass. Also mirrors, sculptured designs, and unusual shapes for furniture and interior design.
TUBE *Liverpool Street + 149, 242 bus* • **OPEN** *Mon–Fri 8am–1pm; 1.30pm–4.30pm* • **SERVICES** *Cut to size, install. Acid-etching, sand-blasting. Tempering (toughening service) for ordinary glass*

REPLACEMENT WINDOWS

See also architectural joinery companies listed under STAIRCASES, page 212.

JOHN SAMBROOK
TEL 01797 252615
Based in East Sussex, this travelling craftsman is famous for exact copies of Georgian fanlights (an otherwise extinct skill). He can also do rooflights and period metal windows. Phone to discuss requirements.

KARTERS BOX SASH WINDOWS
ADDRESS 96 Vallentin Road, E17 3JH
TEL/FAX 0181 521 7815
Make and refurbish traditional box sash windows. Draught-proofing for new or existing windows
OPEN *Mon–Fri 9am–5pm* • **SERVICES** *Make, install, renovate*

THE LONDON WOOD COMPANY
ADDRESS 28 Beulay Road, SW19 3SB
TEL/FAX 0181 241 3179
Box sash window renovation – rotting sills, draughts, broken cords etc.
OPEN *By appointment* • **SERVICES** *Window renovation*

THE ORIGINAL BOX SASH WINDOW COMPANY
ADDRESS Unit 10, Bridgwater Way, Windsor, Berks, SL4 1RD
TEL 01753 858196 **FAX** 01753 857827
Replacement traditional box sash windows in pine with hardwood sills,
single glass, or double-glazed.
RAIL *Windsor* • **OPEN** *Mon–Fri 9am–5.30pm* • **SERVICES** *Make, install*

REFURB-A-SASH
ADDRESS Queens Joinery, Queens Road, Twickenham, TW1 4LJ
TEL 0181 892 1166 **FAX** 0181 892 0055
The name says it all – can repair/restore existing windows, or hand-make
replacements by traditional joinery methods.
OPEN *By appointment* • **SERVICES** *Make, install, renovate*

STAINED, DECORATIVE AND SPECIAL GLASS

Many salvage merchants (listed under ARCHITECTURAL SALVAGE,
page 214) have bits of stained glass to fix into an existing
window, or – better still – have a window made to fit. This section
also includes clear and patterned glass for old windows.

CAROLINE SWASH
ADDRESS 88 Woodwarde Road, SE22 8UT
TEL 0181 693 6574
Glassmaking runs in the family: Caroline, well-known as a glass artist, is
the third generation, and famous for her beautiful windows and panels.
TUBE *North Dulwich* • **OPEN** *By appointment only*

GODDARD AND GIBBS
ADDRESS 41–49 Kingsland Road, E2 8AD
TEL 0171 739 6563 **FAX** 0171 739 1979
Dates back to 1868. Prestigious commissions have included the Houses
of Parliament and St Paul's Cathedral no less. But private clients are
welcome. Stained Glass Supplies is at same address, with a huge range of
antique/decorative glass, DIY stained-glass materials and lamp accessories.
TUBE *Old Street* • **OPEN** *Mon–Fri 8am–5pm*

JAMES PREECE STAINED GLASS
ADDRESS 18a Rutland Park Gardens, Willesden Green, NW2 4RG
TEL 0181 459 2314
Contemporary and traditional designs for windows, doors, skylights etc.
TUBE *Willesden Green* • **OPEN** *By appointment only*

KATE BADEN FULLER
ADDRESS 34 Elfort Road, N5 1AZ
TEL/FAX 0171 354 3842
One of London's finest modern stained-glass artists. Also holds regular short
stained-glass courses for beginners – ring for details.

LEAD AND LIGHT
ADDRESS 35a Hartland Road, NW1 8DB
TEL 0171 485 0997   **FAX** 0171 284 2660
Large studio/warehouse for stained-glass work and leaded lights.
Also lighting, etched glass, and coloured glass, and supplies for DIY.
TUBE *Chalk Farm/Camden* • **OPEN** *Mon–Fri 9am–5.30pm. Sat
10am–5.30pm* • **SERVICES** *Design service. Coloured glass cut to size*

THE LONDON CROWN GLASS COMPANY
ADDRESS 21 Harpsden Road, Henley-on-Thames, Oxon, RG9 1EE
TEL 01491 413227   **FAX** 01491 413228
Authentic glass for period buildings – 1700–1920 – but not coloured glass
or glass for leaded lights.
OPEN *By appointment* • **SERVICES** *Orders over £70 can be delivered –
single panes must be collected*

MARIA MCCLAFFERTY DESIGN
ADDRESS 11 Hillside Road, SW2 3HL
TEL 0181 671 6782   **FAX** 0181 674 6849
Experienced stained-glass artist who designs and makes stained and/or
etched and engraved panels for doors, windows, screens, skylights and so
on. Reproductions or startlingly original modern designs – these can be
panels to sit inside a window so you can move them from house to house.
RAIL *Streatham Hill/Tulse Hill* • **OPEN** *By appointment only* • **SERVICES**
Installation. Repairs and restorations

NEIL PHILLIPS STAINED GLASS
ADDRESS 99 Portobello Road, W11 2QB
TEL 0171 229 2113   **FAX** 0171 229 1963
This shop is the outpost for large specialist workshops making and restoring
stained glass in Birmingham since 1838. Beautiful stained-glass panels,
including complete windows, are lovingly rescued, ready to find a new
home. Small fragments and hanging panels can cost as little as £20 to
£50, and a panel for a door could be £150 to £200. Larger pieces: from
£400 upwards.
TUBE *Notting Hill Gate* • **OPEN** *Mon–Fri 10am–4pm. Sat 8am–4pm*
• **SERVICES** *Restoration, in-situ within 10 miles of workshop, or for jobs
of a reasonable size*

PHILIP BRADBURY GLASS
ADDRESS 83 Blackstock Road, N4 2JW
TEL 0171 226 2919   **FAX** 0171 359 6303
This workshop of five craftsmen makes to order a range of 16 acid-etched
patterns on new glass, to suit period properties – price for windows is
£12.50 sq ft. They also etch patterns on laminated safety glass for doors
(£16.50 sq ft), make leaded lights to order, and do brilliant-cut work to
match existing panels for restoration.
TUBE *Finsbury Park* • **OPEN** *Mon–Fri 9.30am–5.30pm. Sat 10am–2pm*
• **SERVICES** *Catalogue. Install*

PRISMS STAINED GLASS DESIGN

ADDRESS Unit 31, Kingsgate Workshops, 114 Kingsgate Road, NW6 2JG
TEL 0171 624 3240   **FAX** 0171 328 7878

Beverley Bryon creates modern or traditional designs for stained glass (windows, screens, lighting, skylights, door panels) using painting, sandblasting, fusing and slumping, and silver staining. She does lots of work for private houses. 'I love implementing a client's own ideas, and I have a flexible approach where budgets are concerned.'

TUBE *West Hampstead* • **OPEN** *By appointment* • **SERVICES** *Make, install*

RAY BRADLEY

ADDRESS 3 Orchard Studios, Brook Green, W6 7BU
TEL 0171 602 1840

Well-known artist who makes stained glass for all situations on any scale. He also does decorative work on sheet glass using techniques such as sand-blasting, acid-etching, enamelling, gilding and silvering. He has worked extensively in this country and abroad, and his pieces are in private collections and the V&A museum.

TUBE *Hammersmith* • **OPEN** *By appointment*

THE STAINED GLASS PLACE

ADDRESS 3 Turnham Green Terrace Mews, W4 1QU
TEL 0181 747 8218

Lou Spencer, an experienced artist who has worked in stained glass for 20 years, is friendly and approachable for domestic commissions, making windows, door panels, and screens in modern or traditional designs. 'Sometimes people want me to copy what's there already, or to re-create what was there before. Or they have their own ideas and we start from scratch.' Two long narrow panels for a door might cost from around £300.

TUBE *Turnham Green* • **OPEN** *By appointment* • **SERVICES** *Make, install. Repairs and restorations*

STAINED GLASS SHOP

ADDRESS 62 Fairfield Street, SW18 1DY
TEL 0181 874 8822   **FAX** 0181 870 0056

David Meakin runs a shop/workshop where you can commission traditional designs for windows, door panels or leaded lights, at prices from around £100. He also sells small ready-made panels and materials for DIY.

RAIL *Wandsworth Town* • **OPEN** *Mon–Fri 8am–5pm* • **SERVICES** *Make, install. Repairs and restorations*

STONEY PARSONS STAINED GLASS

ADDRESS 231 Aberdeen House, 22–24 Highbury Grove, N5 2EA
TEL/FAX 0171 226 4241

Imaginative stained-glass artist interprets carefully the ideas of her clients, making front door panels, windows, screens and so on. The beautiful iris panel on display in her workshop has inspired several commissions.

OPEN *By appointment*

TOWNSENDS

See HEATING: FIREPLACES, page 194. North London workshop for stained and etched glass panels, plus restorations, in-situ if necessary.

SHUTTERS, AWNINGS AND GRILLES

AMERICAN SHUTTERS

ADDRESS 72 Station Road, SW13 0LS
TEL 0181 876 5905   **FAX** 0181 878 9548
Exclusive US designs in a choice of wood stains and colours, with adjustable louvres in choice of slat widths. Arched tops to order. Also traditional solid panel designs. All panels are custom-made in America to order. No showroom – ring/fax for brochure.
SERVICES *Measure, make, install* • **WEBSITE** *www.americanshutters.co.uk*

BENBOW'S

ADDRESS Benbow Yard, Townley Street, SE17 1DZ
TEL 0171 701 0208   **FAX** 0171 703 3254
Steven Benbow is the fourth generation of blacksmiths with a working forge on the same premises. He does all iron and steel work, repairing and making security grilles and staircases, and repairing gates and railings.
TUBE *Elephant & Castle* • **OPEN** *Mon–Fri 6.30am–6pm*

CAPRICORN ARCHITECTURAL IRONWORK

See STAIRCASES, page 212. Decorative metal grilles.

GODINGTON FORGE

ADDRESS Godington, Bicester, Oxon, OX6 9AF
TEL 01869 277 423
Richard List is a blacksmith who specialises in security. He will make a fine tracery of metalwork for windows or door grilles, inside or out.
OPEN *Home visits in London by appointment*

THE HOUSE OF SHUTTERS

ADDRESS Studio 2, The Birches Business Centre, Sesley, Chichester, West Sussex, PO20 9EP
TEL 01243 603020/0171 610 4624   **FAX** 01243 603069
Custom-made interior pine shutters in a good range of sizes and finishes. Ring, write or fax for brochure.
SERVICES *Measure, make, install*

PLANTATION SHUTTERS

ADDRESS 131 Putney Bridge Road, SW15 2PA
TEL 0181 871 9333/0181 871 9222   **FAX** 0181 871 0041
The only wooden shutter suppliers with a London showroom. Shutters are made to order in the UK from bass, an American hardwood, finished to almost any stain or colour. Two slat widths: 32 mm and 48 mm.

Orders take around three weeks. Also wooden venetians, metal venetians, Pinoleum and roller blinds from designer fabrics.
TUBE *East Putney* • **OPEN** *Mon–Fri 9am–6pm* • **WEBSITE** *www.plantation.demon.co.uk* • **SERVICES** *Measure, make, install*

J H PORTER & SON
ADDRESS 13 Cranleigh Mews, Cabul Road, SW11 2QL
TEL 0171 978 5576   **FAX** 0171 924 7081
This forge does all kinds of iron and steel work, including making security grilles, furniture, brackets, staircases and so on – 'sometimes people don't even visit. They just fax us measurements and a drawing'.
RAIL *Clapham Junction* • **OPEN** *Mon–Fri 8am–5.30pm*

THE SHUTTER SHOP
ADDRESS Queensbury House, Dilly Lane, Hartley Wintney, Hants, RG27 8EQ
TEL 0171 229 9095/01252 844575   **FAX** 01252 844718
Shutters with movable louvres in a choice of four widths custom-made in the UK from hardwoods, painted or stained in lots of colours. Alternatively, plain solid shutters, or a style with raised panels. Also: fantops, arched tops, and special shapes made from templates. No showroom – ring, write or fax for brochure.
SERVICES *Measure, make, install*

SIX SMITHS
See FURNITURE: GLASS, METAL AND LEATHER, page 167. Consumate creators of grilles to keep the burglars out and the imagination in.

STAIRCASES

'Halfway up the stairs
Isn't up
And isn't down.'
A A Milne (1882–1956), *When We Were Very Young*

BENBOW'S
See WINDOWS: SHUTTERS, AWNINGS AND GRILLES, page 211.
South London forge experienced in metal staircase manufacture.

E J BUSHELL
ADDRESS 453 Sunleigh Road, Wembley, Middx, HA0 4OR
TEL 0181 900 2905   **FAX** 0181 900 1637
These joiners do staircases and windows, and all wood turning for spindles – if it's not standard, they will match an existing one.
TUBE *Alperton* • **OPEN** *Mon–Fri 8am–5pm*

CAPRICORN ARCHITECTURAL IRONWORK
ADDRESS Tasso Forge, Tasso Yard, 56 Tasso Road, W6 8LZ
TEL/FAX 0171 381 4235
The promise from one of London's most famous metalworkers is 'absolutely

anything from a candlestick to a large spiral staircase, made to your design or theirs'. Railings, gates and so on.
TUBE *Barons Court* • **OPEN** *Mon–Fri 9am–6pm*

THE CAST IRON SHOP (R BLEASDALE)

ADDRESS 394 Caledonian Road, Islington, N1 1DW
TEL 0171 609 0934   **FAX** 0171 607 7565
Bleasdales have been making London's metalwork for nearly 30 years. It's worth a special journey to visit their large showroom with factory and more showrooms opposite. Ornate Victorian spiral staircases, straight Victorian staircases, traditional railings, balconies and so on, are made to old patterns using original moulds. Also ornate floor grilles and rose arches.
TUBE *Caledonian Road* • **OPEN** *Mon–Fri 10am–5pm. Sat 10.30am–1pm*

HEARNS (SPECIALISED) JOINERY

ADDRESS 101 Waldegrave Road, Teddington, Middx, TW11 8LW
TEL 0181 977 0032   **FAX** 0181 977 1655
An impressive workshop stretching over half an acre – craftsmen make by hand and to order all kinds of special joinery, including doors, windows, conservatories, kitchens and general furniture. Famous for their ornate staircases which they make and fit to any design. 'We combine computer technology with tried and tested hand skills.'
RAIL *Teddington* • **OPEN** *Mon–Fri 8am–5.30pm* • **SERVICES** *Manufacture, install*

E A HIGGINSON AND CO

ADDRESS Unit 1, Carlisle Road, NW9 0HD
TEL 0181 200 4848   **FAX** 0181 200 8249
This family business of architectural joiners makes a wide variety of staircase styles to order. They also import wooden and steel Italian spiral staircase designs.
TUBE *Burnt Oak* • **OPEN** *Mon–Fri 9am–5pm or by appointment*
• **SERVICES** *Staircase design and manufacture*

MULLEN AND LUMSDEN

ADDRESS 28 Elder Sreet, E1 6BT
TEL 0171 377 8544   **FAX** 0171 377 9342
All architectural joinery, including made-to-measure staircases.
TUBE *Liverpool Street* • **OPEN** *Mon–Fri 8am–6pm*

J H PORTER & SON

See WINDOWS: SHUTTERS, AWNINGS AND GRILLES, page 211.
Battersea forge experienced in metal staircase manufacture.

STAIRWAYS PRODUCTS

ADDRESS 102 Chingford Mount Road, E4 9AA
TEL/FAX 0181 527 6180
Manufacturers of traditional and open-plan wooden stairways and spindles.
TUBE *Walthamstow Central* • **OPEN** *Mon Tues Thurs Fri 10am–4pm. Sat 10am–2pm* • **SERVICES** *Home surveys. Manufacture and install*

WANSDOWN JOINERY WORKS
ADDRESS 327+339 Lillie Road, Fulham Cross, SW6 7NR
TEL 0171 385 0351   **FAX** 0171 381 8997
'We can do anything and everything that can be made out of wood!'
In particular, they make period staircases and fit out panelled rooms.
Plus all architectural joinery.
TUBE Fulham Broadway • **OPEN** Mon–Fri 8am–5.30pm

ARCHITECTURAL SALVAGE

'When we build, let us think we build for ever.'
John Ruskin (1819–1900)

Whatever the nobility of Ruskin's aspirations, sadly buildings come down or are re-fitted all the time, but luckily the scavenging trade – known more grandly as architectural antiques – is ever-growing. Here is a fruitful source for many looks – romantic, gothic, flamboyant, eclectic, historic. You can find complete fireplaces, stained-glass windows, sets of old tiles, pieces of stone carving. Underpinning the fancy bits are the yards and warehouses that supply reclaimed building materials – timber for floors, slates for roofs, bricks for weathered walls and so on. Many outfits combine the two. Measure your spaces carefully, empty your car boot, and sally forth.

USEFUL CONTACT

SALVO
TEL 01890 820333
They can provide a complete register of salvage merchants for your area – £5.75.
WEBSITE www.salvo.co.uk

ALFRED G CAWLEY
ADDRESS Havering Farm, Guildford Road, Fend, Surrey, GU4 7QA
TEL 01483 232398
Mainly a yard for all sizes of timber but they also have some demolished building materials including bricks, tiles and windows. Plus some bathroom fittings and doors. Phone ahead to check stocks.
OPEN Mon–Fri 8am–5pm. Sat 8am–1pm

ARCHITECTURAL SALVAGE CENTRE
ADDRESS 30–32 Stamford Road, N1 4JL
TEL 0171 923 0783   **FAX** 0171 923 9458
Well-organised selections of period fixtures and fittings, including ironwork, sinks, basins, cast-iron baths (from £95) and loos. Old doors from around

£25. Cast-iron radiators from £9 a section. Plus lots of smaller items such as old switches and door knobs. Also garden finds, such as statues and old park benches.

RAIL Dalston Kingsland • **OPEN** Mon–Sat 9am–6pm
• **SERVICES** Shot-blasting and metal polishing

CHURCHILL'S ARCHITECTURAL SALVAGE
ADDRESS 186–188 Old Kent Road, SE1 5TY
TEL 0171 708 4308 **TEL** 0171 708 4100
They have lots of old fireplaces (unrestored from around £75), plus decorative ironwork and bathroom fittings (taps from around £20 a pair). An Edwardian kitchen sink could cost from £25 to £30. Also reclaimed door furniture, including knobs, knockers and so on. Garden furniture (old teak bench, around £200) ornaments, urns, statues. Occasionally, you might find some pine furniture. They promise 'impartial advice.'
TUBE Elephant and Castle • **OPEN** Mon–Sat 10.30am–5.30pm
• **SERVICES** Fireplace restoration

DRUMMONDS ARCHITECTURAL
ADDRESS The Kirkpatrick Buildings, 25 London Road, Hindhead, Surrey, GU26 6AB
TEL 01428 609444 **FAX** 01428 609445
Director Drummond Shaw offers 'anything and everything in architectural salvage...it's irritating when you go somewhere and only get half the materials.' His stock is certainly comprehensive enough to make a special journey worthwhile. There's a heavy goods yard for old weathered materials, such as bricks, tiles, and chimney pots. Also find stone window-sills, and stone floor and wall tiles, plus beams, floorboards, mouldings, and staircases. Cast-iron radiators and guttering. Particularly good for restored bathroom fittings. Architectural antiques include fireplaces, grates, firebacks and guards, plus stained glass and unusual windows. Decorative pieces include chandeliers, lights, light switches, gilt and attractive mirrors, along with columns and pillars. Garden items feature fountains, sundials, birdbaths, busts, urns, gates, and decorative ironwork, along with arches, railings, and paving. They also make repro cast-iron baths.
OPEN Mon–Sat 9.30am–5.30pm. Sun 10am–4pm • **SERVICES** Original vitreous bath re-enamelling. Shot-blasting, stripping, and renovation

FENS RESTORATION
ADDRESS 46 Lots Road, SW10 0QF
TEL 0171 352 9883
Reclaimed doors, ready-stripped, can cost from about £85, depending on their size and decorative appeal. They also have some bathroom fittings – for example, Edwardian brass bath mixer, around £320. The selection of furniture varies all the time, but might include old pine, painted pieces and old French furniture.
TUBE Sloane Square/South Kensington • **OPEN** Mon–Fri 9am–5pm. Sat by appointment only • **SERVICES** Wood and metal stripping. Restoration and repairs to all kinds of furniture – from mending a chair leg to re-polishing a large table, or restoring an antique

FLOYDS BUILDING MATERIALS (FBM)

ADDRESS 349–357 Ilderton Road, SE15 1NW
TEL 0171 639 6991 **FAX** 0171 252 8017
This general builders merchant also sells reclaimed yellow and mixed
London stock bricks and old Welsh slates. Plus DIY materials.
TUBE *New Cross/New Cross Gate* • **OPEN** *Mon–Fri 8am–5.30pm.
Sat 8am–1pm*

GROVE GREEN ANTIQUES

ADDRESS 108 Grove Green Road, Leyton, E11 4EL
TEL/FAX 0181 558 7885
Partly shop and partly yard with 'just about everything – and all original.'
Fireplaces – for example restored cast-iron – from around £250. Internal
panelled doors, fully restored, from around £80. Stained glass – a small
panel around 2 ft sq costs about £35, large pieces up to £350. Also
lanterns and leaded lights. Bathroom fittings (mixer tap, £45), including
Victorian baths and loos. Old sinks from about £25, and cast-iron radiators
from £50 to £350. Garden items and some chimney pots.
TUBE *Leytonstone* • **OPEN** *Mon–Sun 9am–6pm* • **SERVICES** *Metal and
wood stripping. Restore old doors, replacing stained glass panels.
Fireplace restoration*

THE HOUSE HOSPITAL

ADDRESS 9 Ferrier Street, SW18 1SW
TEL 0181 870 8202
Specialise in cast-iron radiators. Also broad range of salvaged goods.
Doors/brass handles. Bathroom fittings: baths, basins, taps. Victorian
gates/railings.
RAIL *Wandsworth Town* • **OPEN** *Mon–Sat 10am–5pm* • **SERVICES**
Sandblasting. Door-stripping

HOUSE OF STEEL

ADDRESS 400 Caledonian Road, N1 1DN
TEL/FAX 0171 607 5889
Judy Cole – Ms Metalwork – has been the presiding genius over this large
warehouse with its showrooms and workshops for 20 years. Original
cast-iron fireplaces, unrestored, from around £100. Or she will make you
a new one – 'though funnily enough they work out more expensive'. Plus
railings, gates, staircases, door knobs etc. Also light fittings, cast-iron and
steel garden and interior furniture and fire accessories – antique, or repro.
What she hasn't got, she'll get or copy.
TUBE *Caledonian Road* • **OPEN** *Mon–Fri 11am–6pm. Sat by appointment
only* • **SERVICES** *All metalwork to order. Restorations (railings, gates and so
on), in situ if necessary. Courtyard parking*

LASSCO (LONDON ARCHITECTURAL SALVAGE AND SUPPLY CO)

ADDRESS St Michael's, Mark Street, off Paul Street, EC2A 4ER
TEL 0171 739 0448 **FAX** 0171 729 6853
This de-consecrated church is unbeatable for atmosphere. As London's old
buildings (sadly) get demolished, this firm acquires the best pieces, with
impeccable pedigrees – from government offices, hotels, mansions, and

even other churches. The result is an awe-inspiring selection of fine architectural antiques, chimneypieces, and garden ornaments, albeit on the pricey side. To supply the growing demand for the more serviceable workaday items for London's home owners, LASSCO has split itself into various specialist sections, see below.

TUBE *Old Street* • **OPEN** *7 days 10am–5pm* • **WEBSITE** *www.lassco.co.uk*
• **SERVICES** *Brochure, price list. Shipping*

LASSCO FLOORING

ADDRESS 41 Maltby Street, Bermondsey, SE1 3PA
TEL 0171 237 4488   **FAX** 0171 237 2564
LASSCO (see above) has been so successful, it's split into specialised units. This warehouse concentrates on wooden floors, including homegrown, foreign and reclaimed hardwood parquet, and Victorian pine boards. Parquet costs from around £15 a square metre up to £150 for the finest types; reclaimed pine boards are around £21.50. Also some old terracotta and flagstones.

TUBE *London Bridge* • **OPEN** *Mon–Sat 10am–5pm* • **WEBSITE**
www.lassco.co.uk • **SERVICES** *Brochure, price list. Recommend fitters*

LASSCO RBK

ADDRESS Britannia Walk, Islington, N1 7LU
TEL 0171 336 8221   **FAX** 0171 336 8224
Yet more LASSCO – RBK stands for radiators, bathrooms and kitchens and you'll find a huge selection of reclaimed cast-iron radiators tested and ready to install. Choose from various finishes, which can up to double the price. For example, a radiator 30 in high and 24 in wide, simply shot-blasted might cost around £150. Primed, ready for painting, it would be £175. Lacquered against rusting, £200. Powder-coated in a huge choice of colours, £225. Burnished, £300. Also teak worktops – for example, a 5 ft length, unrestored, £125. Plus bathtubs and bathroom fittings and Belfast sinks, from £45 to £100.

TUBE *Old Street* • **OPEN** *Mon–Sat 10am–5pm* • **WEBSITE** *www.lassco.co.uk*
• **SERVICES** *Restoration services include re-enamelling, re-polishing, and shot-blasting*

LASSCO TRADE WAREHOUSE

ADDRESS Britannia Walk, Islington, N1 7LU
TEL 0171 490 1000   **FAX** 0171 336 8224
LASSCO has developed a formidable reputation in architectural salvage, and often gets offered items in bulk from large institutions, such as museums, colleges and banks. They don't want to display these in the main church showroom (see above) as the result would be cluttered. So this is where you can find quantities of, for example, mahogany display cabinets (from £600), and four-panelled doors (£50 to £60, unrestored) plus library tables, stained glass, lighting, and panelled rooms.

TUBE *Old Street* • **OPEN** *Mon–Sat 10am–5pm* • **WEBSITE** *www.lassco.co.uk*

LAZDAN

ADDRESS 218 Bow Common Lane, Bow Common, E3
TEL 0181 981 4632/3484   **FAX** 0181 980 5395
Used bricks and slates in large quantities.

TUBE *Mile End* • **OPEN** *Mon–Fri 8am–5pm. Sat 8am–noon*

RECLAIMED BUILDING MATERIAL SUPPLIES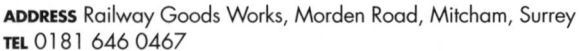

ADDRESS Railway Goods Works, Morden Road, Mitcham, Surrey
TEL 0181 646 0467
Second-hand building materials: 'anything and everything for building a
house.' Doors, tiles, slates, bricks, timber, railings, fences and so on.
TUBE *Morden* • **OPEN** *Mon–Sat 7am–5pm*

TSAR ARCHITECTURAL

ADDRESS 487 Liverpool Road, Islington, N7 8PG
TEL 0171 609 4238   **FAX** 0171 609 1883
Tiles and period fireplaces. Own foundry makes reproduction brass fittings,
garden furniture, statues and urns.
TUBE *Highbury and Islington* • **OPEN** *Mon–Sat 10am–6pm* • **SERVICES**
Restoration service for marble fireplaces. Fireplace installations

WILLIAM FRY & CO (SCRAP METAL MERCHANTS)

ADDRESS Mitre Works, Neasden Goods Depot, Neasden Lane, NW10 2UG
TEL 0181 459 5141   **FAX** 0181 459 2290
TUBE *Neasden* • **OPEN** *Mon–Fri 8am–5pm. Sat 8am–12 noon*
*New and second-hand rolled steel joints (RSJs) for through lounges,
extensions etc* • **SERVICES** *Delivery*

WHITEWAY AND WALDRON

ADDRESS 305 Munster Road, SW6 6BJ
TEL/FAX 0171 381 3195
Ecclesiastical atmosphere and a wonderful source of unusual decorative
architectural fittings, salvaged from more pious times. Stained glass,
church furnishings, statuary and doors.
TUBE *Fulham Broadway* • **OPEN** *Mon–Fri 10am–6pm. Sat 11am–4pm*
• **SERVICES** *Shipping/valuations*

ANTIQUES

> *'What make ye and what strive ye for? Keep ye thought*
> *Of us, or in new excellence divine*
> *Is old forgot ? or do ye count for nought*
> *What Greek did and what Florentine?'*
> Robert Bridges (1844–1930)

You can furnish a whole room with antiques, or just add the odd
pieces for a softening, humanising effect. The sources in London
are endless, and the subject of books in themselves, so this chapter
is just a taster of what's out there. A good starting point is a current
copy of *The Collector*, a small bi-monthly magazine free from
good antiques shops (or send sae to 54 Uxbridge Road, W12 8LP;
0181 740 7020). It lists around 300 specialist dealers by subjects
and areas. When buying from a dealer, a window sticker

indicating membership of a professional association is reassuring. Look for initials LAPADA (The Association of Art and Antique Dealers) and/or BADA (The British Antique Dealers Association). This is evidence of a good reputation and trustworthy business practices. AUCTIONS are listed on page 231. For old beds, see BEDROOMS AND BEDS: TRADITIONAL BEDS, page 139.

USEFUL CONTACT

LAPADA, THE ASSOCIATION OF ART AND ANTIQUES DEALERS
ADDRESS 535 King's Road, SW10 0SZ
TEL 0171 823 3511   **FAX** 0171 823 3522
LAPADA will help you find a specialised dealer in what you are looking for. They also have free care leaflets on antiques, including furniture, silver, porcelain, and prints and pictures.

GENERAL SOURCES

ALFIES ANTIQUE MARKET
ADDRESS 13–25 Church Street, NW8 8DT
TEL 0171 723 6066   **FAX** 0171 724 0999
Largest covered market in the UK – a vast warren of 270 dealers with around 370 stands over four storeys. Many specialise, which makes a trip all the more fruitful. Decorative antiques, antique jewellery, dolls and toys, costume and textiles, silverware, ceramics and glass, pictures and prints, Arts and Crafts, Art Nouveau, Art Deco and 20th-century collectibles, prices from a few pounds to a few thousand. Friendly atmosphere.
TUBE *Marylebone/Baker Street/Edgware Road* • **OPEN** *Tues–Sat 10am–6pm* • **SERVICES** *Pleasant cafe*

ANTIQUARIUS
ADDRESS 131–141 King's Road, SW3
TEL 0171 351 5353   **FAX** 0171 351 5350
Over 120 dealers with a wide range of antiques from all periods – clocks, watches, silver, glass, jewellery, antiquarian books, boxes, paintings, prints and porcelain. They're proud of the recent redecoration and addition of air conditioning.
TUBE *Sloane Square* • **OPEN** *Mon–Sat 10am–6pm* • **SERVICES** *Cafe, bureau de change. Jewellery repairs and antique restorations*

BERMONDSEY MARKET
ADDRESS Bermondsey Square, SE1
This is the most famous antiques street market in South England with around 350 stalls outside, plus another 150 indoors. Old silver, jewellery, pictures, glass, ornaments, medals, furniture and kitchenware.
TUBE *London Bridge* • **OPEN** *Fri 5am–1.30pm*

BOND STREET ANTIQUES CENTRE
ADDRESS 124 New Bond Street, W1 9AE
TEL 0171 351 5353 **FAX** 0171 351 5350
Top traders sell silver, jewellery, watches, porcelain, Oriental antiques
and glass.
TUBE *Bond Street* • **OPEN** *Mon–Fri 10am–5.45pm. Sat 11am–5.30pm*

BOURBON-HANBY ANTIQUES CENTRE
ADDRESS 151 Sydney Street, SW3
TEL 0171 352 2106 **FAX** 0171 565 0003
Complex of small interesting shops with specialist traders – including
antique fabrics, Oriental porcelain, thirties china.
TUBE *Sloane Square/South Kensington + 11, 19, 22 49 bus*
• **OPEN** *Mon–Sat 10am–6pm. Sun 11am–5pm*

CAMDEN PASSAGE ANTIQUE MARKET
ADDRESS Camden Passage, The Angel, Islington, N1
World-famous antique market, with hosts of little stalls packing a villagey
pedestrianised 18th-century street, overflowing into the area all around.
You can find anything if you hunt hard enough, including furniture and
furnishings, old dolls, prints, silver, jewellery and china. The area also has
around 200 antique shops, some grouped together in arcades, but some
are only open on market days.
TUBE *Angel* • **OPEN** *Wed 6.30am–3pm. Sat 8am–4pm* • **SHOPS** *Tues–Sat
10am–5pm (some close early Thurs; some only open market days)*

FURNITURE CAVE
ADDRESS 533 King's Road, SW10 0TZ
TEL 0171 352 4229 **FAX** 0171 352 3654
One of the largest collections of antique furniture in London, with 15
independent dealers. 17th- to 18th-century English and Continental
furniture and furnishings, decorative accessories and collectibles, lighting,
porcelain, architectural salvage, garden ornaments, Oriental furniture,
paintings.
TUBE *Fulham Broadway* • **OPEN** *Mon–Sat 10am–6pm. Sun 11am–4pm*
• **SERVICES** *Small sandwich bar*

GRAYS ANTIQUE MARKET
ADDRESS 1–7 Davies Mews and 58 Davies Street, W1Y 2JP
TEL 0171 629 7034 **FAX** 0171 493 9344
Watch out for the tributary of the River Tyburn running through the
basement of the Mews building! Together these buildings house around
180 dealers – they're strongest for jewellery, but you'll also find old
textiles, prints, ceramics and other collectibles.
TUBE *Bond Street* • **OPEN** *Mon–Fri 10am–6pm* • **SERVICES** *Cafe*

LONDON SILVER VAULTS
ADDRESS 53–64 Chancery Lane, EC2A 1QT
TEL 0171 242 3844
Modern and antique silver, including cutlery, frames, tea and coffee pots,
candlesticks and so on.
TUBE *Chancery Lane* • **OPEN** *Mon–Fri 9am–5.30pm. Sat 9am–1pm*

THE MALL ANTIQUES ARCADE
ADDRESS Camden Passage, 359 Upper Street, N1 0PD
TEL 0171 351 5353   **FAX** 0171 351 5350
Wide range of antiques from 35 dealers, with furniture on the lower
ground floor.
TUBE *Angel* • **OPEN** *Tues Thurs Fri 10am–5pm. Wed 7.30am–5pm.
Sat 9am–6pm* • **SERVICES** *Restaurant*

NORTHCOTE ROAD ANTIQUES MARKET
ADDRESS 155a Northcote Road, SW11 6QB
TEL 0171 228 6850
Charming concentration of small stalls, with many specialist dealers –
kitchenalia, thirties ceramics, art nouveau and so on. There's an annexe
further along the street.
RAIL *Clapham Junction* • **OPEN** *Mon–Sat 10am–6pm. Sun 12 noon–5pm*

PORTOBELLO ROAD
ADDRESS Portobello Road, W10 and W11
Street market. For bargain antiques at the South end, go very early,
although there are stalls for antiques and collectibles all day.
TUBE *Notting Hill Gate/Ladbroke Grove* • **OPEN** *5am–1pm*

ARTS & CRAFTS, ART NOUVEAU, DECO AND RETRO

ART FURNITURE
ADDRESS 158 Camden High Street, NW1 9PA
TEL 0171 267 4324   **FAX** 0171 267 5199
Arts and crafts and art deco furniture.
TUBE *Camden Town* • **OPEN** *7 days 12 noon–5pm*
• **WEBSITE** *www.gen.com/creative-eye/art-f/*

THE ARTS AND CRAFTS FURNITURE COMPANY
ADDRESS 49 Sheen Lane, East Sheen, SW14 8AB
TEL/FAX 0181 876 6544
Three showrooms with arts and crafts furniture and decorative arts.
RAIL *Mortlake* • **OPEN** *Mon–Sat 10am–6pm* • **SERVICES** *Restoration.
Catalogue (please send first-class stamp)*

DECO INSPIRED
ADDRESS 67 Monmouth Street, WC2H 9DG
TEL/FAX 0171 240 5719
Three times a year, Nikki Chaman goes to the States and brings back
the best pieces from the twenties to the seventies, including lamps, furniture
and ornaments. Here she has them so lovingly restored people ask if they're
repro. 'But they're not,' she says with pride. Prices from £20 to £3,000.
TUBE *Leicester Square/Covent Garden* • **OPEN** *Mon–Sat 11am–7pm.
Sun 2pm–6pm*

FLYING DUCK ENTERPRISES
ADDRESS 320/322 Creek Road, SE10 9SW
TEL 0181 858 1964   **FAX** 0181 852 3215
From kitsch to cool, Carolyn Shrosbree and James Lowe are veteran hunters of design finds from the fifties onwards – their business is celebrating its 12th year with three years as a shop. They have china, furniture, lights, curtains, bar stools and bars – and (a new addition) original fifties diner furniture from the States. 'We look for pieces in mint condition but restore sensitively if necessary.'
RAIL *Greenwich* • **OPEN** *Tues–Fri 12 noon–6pm. Sat Sun 10.30am–6pm*
• **SERVICES** *Mail-order catalogue*

METRO RETRO/OUT OF TIME
ADDRESS 21 Canonbury Lane, N1 2AS
TEL 0171 354 5755/0171 288 1086   **FAX** 01245 442047
Out of Time sells forties and fifties kitsch and home accessories, sharing a cramped but fascinating narrow showroom off Upper Street with Metro Retro, who do stylish old fridges and other electrical appliances, furniture, and lighting. Fully restored electric fans, 1920s–1950s, £85. Bakelite telephones, 1930s–1950s, converted to UK telephone system, £90. Original factory and school clocks with quartz movements from £65.
TUBE *Highbury & Islington* • **OPEN** *7 days 10am–6pm*
• **WEBSITE** *www.metroretro.co.uk*

PLANET BAZAAR
ADDRESS 151 Drummond Street, NW1 2PB
TEL/FAX 0171 387 8326
In her spacey gallery, Maureen Silverman assembles the best of fifties to eighties design – furniture, lighting, art, books, ceramics, glass and eccentricities.
TUBE *Warren Street/Euston Square* • **OPEN** *Tues–Sat 11.30am–7pm or by appointment* • **WEBSITE** *www.planetbazaar.co.uk* • **SERVICES** *On-going programme of exhibitions*

RADIO DAYS
ADDRESS 87 Lower Marsh, SE12 7AB
TEL/FAX 0171 928 0800
Vintage radios from £65, with original parts but fully serviced and in working order. Also collectibles and memorabilia from the twenties to the seventies. Cocktail bars from around £95. Cocktail cabinets from £75. Tubular seventies table with smoked glass top and four chairs, £125.
TUBE *Waterloo* • **OPEN** *Mon–Sat 11am–5pm. Other times by appointment – just phone*

RETRO HOME
ADDRESS 20 Pembridge Road, W11 3HL
TEL 0171 221 2055   **FAX** 0171 727 4185
This long narrow show space is packed tight with post-war furniture, pottery, glass, plastics and lighting, from fifties through to kitsch.
TUBE *Notting Hill Gate* • **OPEN** *7 days 10am–8pm* • **SERVICES** *Mail-order*

TOMTOM
ADDRESS 42 New Compton Street, WC2H 8DA
TEL/FAX 0171 240 7909
How cool can you be? TomTom shows the way with classic pieces from the
fifties, sixties and seventies – anything from a £10 pen tidy to a Florence
Knoll conference table at £1,295. Large pieces are ideal for the modern
loft space. Ceramics and glass, and radio and tvs in working order.
TUBE *Tottenham Court Road* • **OPEN** *Tues–Fri 12 noon–7pm. Sat 11am–6pm*

VISTO
ADDRESS 41 Pembridge Road, W11 3HG
TEL 0171 243 4392   **FAX** 0171 243 1374
Hilary Little has turned her small shop into memory lane for those of a certain
age who can remember boomerang coffee tables and all that fifties jazz.
TUBE *Notting Hill Gate* • **OPEN** *Mon–Fri 11am–6pm. Sat 10am–6pm*

SECURITY SPECIALISTS

Buzz, buzz... 'Operation Bumblebee' is stinging the thieves.
This Metropolitan Police initiative which began in North East
London in 1991-2, has halted the steady rise in burglary.
Gradually domestic break-ins are reducing. But the police still need
help, and it is in your own interest to protect your property and
personal safety with vigilance. Contact your local Metropolitan
Police Crime Prevention Officer (CPO) by telephoning your local
police station. A specially-trained officer will give free security
advice, taking into account any individual or local problems.
If locked out after hours, telephone your local police for the
number of a local emergency locksmith.

USEFUL CONTACTS

For security work in your home, use firms who are members of the
following trade associations:

THE MASTER LOCKSMITHS ASSOCIATION (MLA)
TEL 01327 262255   **FREEPHONE** 0800 783 1498
Will supply the name of an inspected member in your area.

NATIONAL APPROVAL COUNCIL FOR SECURITY SYSTEMS (NACOSS)
TEL 01628 637512
Will supply the name of an approved member in your area.
WEBSITE *www.nacoss.org*

BANHAM PATENT LOCKS

ADDRESS 233–235 Kensington High Street, W8 6SF
TEL 0171 622 5151   **FAX** 0171 498 2461

In 1926 W F Banham (motto: 'Another Burglar Foiled') invented the first automatic door bolt. They make and install their own patented locks, and install other leading brands. Supply and install security grilles, safes, entry telephones, and alarms. Own central monitoring service, with a unique 24-hour key-holding service. Locks, alarms, grilles, window bars, folding door gates. 24-hour emergency alarm service. Fire alarms, CCTV and video systems.

TUBE *High Street Kensington* • **OPEN** *Mon–Fri 9am–5.30pm. Sat 9am–5pm*
• **SERVICES** *Supply, install*

BARRS SECURITY

ADDRESS 329 Fulham Palace Road, SW6 6PE
TEL 0171 736 7668   **FAX** 0171 731 4502

In stock are most makes of locks and safes, with a busy workshop at the rear for special orders.

TUBE *Putney Bridge* • **OPEN** *Mon–Thurs 9am–5.30pm. Fri 9am–5pm*
• **SERVICES** *Supply, install. 24-hour emergency service*

BARRY BROS SECURITY DEVICES

ADDRESS 121–123 Praed Street, W2 1RL
TEL 0171 262 9009   **FAX** 0171 262 5005

A showroom over two floors displays all the goods and services this flourishing family firm can offer. Founded by Jack Barry in 1945 – now run by sons John, Frank and Orlando: security with a human face. Own London-wide installation service for all types of locks, alarms, fire-extinguishers, fire-escape equipment, fireproof cabinets, safes, grilles and security doors. Trained staff, own fitters; members of both the MLA and NACOSS.

TUBE *Paddington* • **OPEN** *Mon–Fri 8.30am–6pm. Sat 9am–5pm*
• **SERVICES** *Supply, install and maintain*

A BUCKENAM (LOCKSMITHS)

ADDRESS Rear of 158 Blackstock Road, Highbury, N5 1HA
TEL 0171 226 8734   **FAX** 0171 354 3818

Reliable family firm – trading for over 30 years; speedy, friendly service for all security products including high security locks. Vehicle key specialists

TUBE *Arsenal* • **OPEN** *Mon–Fri 9am–6pm. Wed 9am–7pm*
• **SERVICES** *Advise, supply, fit*

C & M APOSTOLIDES

ADDRESS 257 Wood Street, E17 3NG
TEL 0181 923 5050   **FAX** 0181 923 6060

Michaele 'You don't have to be rich to need a safe' Apostolides is a great-grandson of the original founder – and very English. His company is one of London's best-known specialists in safe installations and removal, with its own workshops. Safe types include under-floor, wall, and bolt-down, with access by key, combination or digital electronics. Prices from around £300.

TUBE *Walthamstow Central* • **OPEN** *By appointment*

CHISWICK SECURITY

ADDRESS 5 Chiswick Terrace, Acton Lane, W4 5LY
TEL 0181 994 1474
Re-assuring family firm: Bob Efford, and his two sons Colin and Simon.
24-hour locksmiths and carpenters, with MLA and NACOSS membership.
They will arrive within half an hour (sometimes sooner) for lock-outs within the
London area. Around 50 per cent of locks can be opened without damage,
they say. Average call-out fee is £50 plus VAT and materials. Night-time calls
are routed through a director's home, who then alerts the duty locksmith.
TUBE *Chiswick Park* • **OPEN** *Mon–Fri 9am–5.30pm. Sat 9am–5pm*

CSG

ADDRESS 13 Crucifix Lane, SE1 3JW
TEL 0171 378 8118   **FAX** 0171 378 8453
A good source for all security products.
TUBE *London Bridge* • **OPEN** *Mon–Fri 9am–5pm*
• **SERVICES** *Supply/install all locks*

DENNIS LOCK AND KEY SERVICES

ADDRESS 139 Wood Street, Walthamstow, E17 3LX
TEL 0181 520 7450
FAX 0181 521 8376
A full range of all security products.
TUBE *Walthamstow Central Tube* • **OPEN** *Mon–Fri 9am–5.30pm
Sat 9am–1.30pm* • **SERVICES** *Supply, install. After-hours emergency
service – 0181 521 2444*

FGW LOCKSMITHS LTD

ADDRESS 129 Whitecross Street, EC1 8JL
TEL 0171 253 9454/9721
You can trust a family firm that's been trading for over 100 years. They sell
all kinds of locks, tools, alarms, security bars and so on, and take care to
train their staff.
TUBE *Barbican* • **OPEN** *Mon–Fri 7am–3.30pm* • **SERVICES** *Supply, install*

FINCH DIY STORES

ADDRESS 329–333 Regent's Park Road, Finchley, NW3 IDP
TEL 0181 346 4417   **FAX** 0181 343 3115
Trading for over 25 years, this friendly, knowledgeable family firm sells all
kinds of locks for doors, windows, patio doors etc. Plus various security
devices, including security bars for windows, and property-marking kits.
They are safe engineers and full security specialists.
TUBE *Finchley Central* • **OPEN** *Mon–Sat 8.15am–6pm.
Sun 9.30am–1.30pm* • **SERVICES** *Lock-fitting, key cutting*

MARKET LOCK AND SAFE

ADDRESS 3 Manchester Road, E14 3BD
TEL 0171 515 2121/987 5757   **FAX** 0171 537 4938
This small, friendly family locksmith offers a wide range of security products
and services.
DLR *Island Gardens* • **OPEN** *Mon–Fri 8.30am–5.30pm. Sat 9am–1pm*
• **SERVICES** *Key cutting, supply/install, repairs*

R AND R SECURITY SERVICES
ADDRESS 169 South Ealing Road, W5 4QP
TEL 0181 847 3129/847 4404 **FAX** 0181 560 3413
Established for nearly ten years, they can supply and fit all kinds of
locks, alarms, safes and grilles. Key specialists and experts in burglary
prevention and fire protection.
TUBE *South Ealing* • **OPEN** *Mon–Fri 9am–5pm. Sat 9am–1pm*
• **SERVICES** *Supply and fit*

J REEDER LOCK AND SAFE CO LTD
ADDRESS 587 Barking Road, Plaistow, E13 9E2
TEL 0181 472 3431/0171 476 5450 **FAX** 0181 503 4145
These specialist locksmiths and safe engineers can supply and fit all kinds
of locks, providing expert advice on all security problems.
TUBE *Plaistow/Upton Park* • **OPEN** *Mon–Fri 8.30am–5.30pm*
• **SERVICES** *Supply, install*

SAXON SECURITY LOCKS
ADDRESS 208 Mitcham Road, Amen Corner, SW17 9NN
TEL 0181 767 6281 **FAX** 0181 767 7380
Expert advice combined with speedy fitting. They can make to measure
various kinds of sliding gates and security grilles; safe experts. They
operate a registered key system.
TUBE *Tooting Broadway* • **OPEN** *Mon–Fri 8.30am–5.30pm.*
Sat 10am–4pm • **SERVICES** *Supply and fit*

TRAFALGAR LOCK AND KEY CO
ADDRESS 36 Kennington Road, SE1 7BL
TEL 0171 928 0639 **FAX** 0171 620 0484
This firm can handle all aspects of security, with advice and supply of
various types of locks and safes.
TUBE *Lambeth North* • **OPEN** *Mon–Fri 9am–5.30pm (both branches)*
• **SERVICES** *Access control* • **ALSO AT** *110 Trafalgar Road, Greenwich SE10
(0181 853 3614)*

WILLET A/C/T SECURITY INSTALLATIONS
ADDRESS 4 Loampit Hill, Lewisham, SE13 7SW
TEL 0181 692 1080 **FAX** 0181 692 2428
Supply and install all types of security equipment.
RAIL *Lewisham* • **OPEN** *Mon–Fri 8.30am–5.30pm. Sat 10am–4pm*
• **SERVICES** *Supply/install. Emergency locksmith service*

MARKETS

The best place to collect unique affordable accessories for all
sorts of looks, from kitsch to country, is at a market, and London
is known as the best market town in Europe. London's market
traders are usually very honest and take a pride in sticking to a
regular pitch. Your legal rights are the same as when you buy
from a shop, but in practice will be difficult to enforce – so always
examine purchases carefully. Watch out for pickpockets and

thieves – don't carry money in backpacks, open handbags or in trouser back pockets. Take an umbrella and some extra bags to get your treasures home. Start as early as you can, and leave time to enjoy the general atmosphere. Some so-called antique 'markets' are really a warren of little shops trading on a more or less daily basis under one roof. These are listed in the chapter on ANTIQUES, page 218.

BERMONDSEY MARKET

ADDRESS Bermondsey Square, SE1
This is the most famous antiques market in South England with around 350 stalls outside, plus another 150 indoors. Dealers and serious buyers hunt for old silver, jewellery, pictures, glass, ornaments, medals, furniture and kitchenware. Tourists and locals just goggle.
TUBE *London Bridge* • **OPEN** *Fri 5am–1.30pm*

BERWICK STREET MARKET

ADDRESS Berwick Street (leading into Rupert Street), W1
Mainly fruit and veg. Some cut-price clothing and household goods.
TUBE *Leicester Square* • **OPEN** *Mon–Sat 8am–5pm*

BETHNAL GREEN MARKET

ADDRESS Bethnal Green Road, E1
Food, toys and household goods.
TUBE *Bethnal Green* • **OPEN** *Mon–Sat 8am–6pm. Thurs 8am–1pm*

BRICK LANE

ADDRESS Shoreditch, E1 and E2
One of the more popular London markets. Serious collectors have been, shopped and gone before 9am. Antiques, crockery, electrical equipment, furniture, carpets.
TUBE *Liverpool Street/Aldgate East/Old Street* • **OPEN** *Sun 8am–1pm*

BRIXTON MARKET

ADDRESS Electric Avenue, Pope's Road, Brixton Station Road, SW9
Household, haberdashery and bric-a-brac. Despite the area's bad reputation, this is a friendly bustling place, near the tube, with lots of ethnic treasures.
TUBE *Brixton* • **OPEN** *Mon–Sat 8am–6pm. Wed 8am–1pm*

CAMDEN LOCK

ADDRESS Commercial Place, Camden High Street, NW1
Seething, pulsating mass of tourists and locals: not for the faint-hearted or squeamish! Atmosphere veers schizophrenically between hip and hippy. Overflows into adjacent areas: Electric Ballroom, Canal Market, Chalk Farm market. Particularly strong on handmade crafts: many craftspeople work to commission in the adjacent workshops. The Stables (off Chalk Farm Road, opposite junction with Hartland Road) is a focus for retro furnishing classics at the weekend (8am–6pm).
TUBE *Camden* • **OPEN** *Thurs–Sun 9am–5.30pm, but best – and most crowded – at weekends. Covered market open 7 days 10am–6pm*

CAMDEN PASSAGE
ADDRESS Camden Passage, Islington, N1
Antiques, Art Nouveau, Art Deco, clocks, maps and prints, antique toys –
a friendly mass of traders, many with small shops/arcades only open on
market days.
TUBE *Angel* • **OPEN** *Wed 6.30am–3pm. Sat 8am–4pm*

CHURCH STREET
ADDRESS Church Street, W2
Household goods, junk, antiques and bric-a-brac.
TUBE *Edgware Road* • **OPEN** *Tues–Sat 8am–5pm*

COLUMBIA ROAD MARKET
ADDRESS Columbia Road, E2
Plant and flower bargains – greenfingers in the know go for bargains
which change according to the season – bedding plants in June,
Christmas trees in December. Plus specialist shops and studios.
TUBE *Shoreditch* • **OPEN** *Sun 8am–1pm*

COVENT GARDEN CRAFT MARKET
ADDRESS The Apple Market, Covent Garden, WC2
Pretty (and sometimes pretty pricey) stalls have replaced the old fruit-and-
veg market which had been there since the early 1600s. They're laden
with handicrafts, often unusual. Traders vary from day to day, but have
regular pitches. You'll be buying from the makers in many cases. Free street
entertainment adds to the atmosphere – music, jugglers miming. A fun
day out, but crowded with tourists in summer.
TUBE *Covent Garden – but gets very crowded so use Leicester Square in
the height of the season* • **OPEN** *Mon 6am–4pm (antiques). Tues–Sun
9am–6pm (crafts)*

DEPTFORD MARKET
ADDRESS High Street, Douglas Way, Deptford, SE8
General household, bric-a-brac, second-hand, wickerwork, lampshades.
TUBE *New Cross* • **OPEN** *Wed Fri Sat 8.30am–5pm*

EARLS COURT MARKET
ADDRESS Lillie Road, SW6
Bed linen, electrical goods, general household goods.
TUBE *Earls Court* • **OPEN** *Sun 8am–1pm*

GREENWICH MARKET
ADDRESS Church Street, Greenwich High Road, SE10
Books, antiques, bric-a-brac. Particularly good for fine craftwork and small
pieces of handmade furniture. Most atmospheric way to travel is by boat
from Westminster or Charing Cross piers.
RAIL *Greenwich* • **OPEN** *Sat Sun 9am–5pm*

HACKNEY WICK CAR BOOT MARKET
ADDRESS Hackney Wick Greyhound Stadium, Waterden Road, E15
You never know what you might find!
RAIL *Hackney Wick* • **OPEN** *Sun 6am–2pm*

MARKETS

HAMPSTEAD COMMUNITY MARKET
ADDRESS Hampstead High Street, NW3
Pictures, antiques, crafts, junk. Plus wonderful homemade cakes.
TUBE *Hampstead* • **OPEN** *Mon–Sat 9.30am–6pm*

INVERNESS STREET MARKET
ADDRESS off Camden High Street, NW1
Bric-a-brac, junk. Browse for old tools, lighting and old kitchenware.
TUBE *Camden* • **OPEN** *Sat Sun 9am–5pm*

JUBILEE MARKET
ADDRESS Covent Garden, WC2
Emphasis on clothing and tourist goods. Special days: Mon: bric-a-brac
and antiques. Sat and Sun: crafts and ceramics.
TUBE *Covent Garden* • **OPEN** *7 days 9am–6pm*

KINGSLAND WASTE MARKET
ADDRESS Kingsland Road, E8
Large market selling a mixture of goods. DIY tools, house paints, electrical
goods, second-hand furniture.
RAIL *Dalston Junction* • **OPEN** *Mon–Sat 9am–5pm*

LAMBETH WALK MARKET
ADDRESS Lambeth Walk, SE11
Household goods.
TUBE *Vauxhall/Lambeth North* • **OPEN** *Mon–Sat 8am–6pm. Thurs 8am–1pm*

LEATHER LANE MARKET
ADDRESS Leather Lane, EC1
Office workers throng this general lunchtime market: good for plants.
TUBE *Chancery Lane* • **OPEN** *Mon–Fri 12 noon–2.30pm*

LOWER MARSH
ADDRESS Lambeth, SE1
General household goods.
TUBE *Waterloo* • **OPEN** *Mon–Sat 10.45am–3pm*

NORTH END ROAD MARKET
ADDRESS North End Road, SW6
Hardware, electrical goods, kitchen/bathroom ware, bed linen.
TUBE *Fulham Broadway* • **OPEN** *Mon–Sat 9am–5pm. Thurs 9am–1pm*

NORTHCOTE ROAD MARKET
ADDRESS Northcote Road, SW11
General household goods.
RAIL *Clapham Common* • **OPEN** *Mon–Sat 7am–6.15pm*

PETTICOAT LANE MARKET
ADDRESS Middlesex Street, E1 (it spreads into the surrounding streets)
Confusingly, you won't find Petticoat Lane on any map as it's actually in

Middlesex Street. This market is beloved for cheap clothing. Also china, household goods and junk. Go early for the best buys, listen to the traders' practised patter – and watch out for tourists.
TUBE *Liverpool Street* • **OPEN** *Sun 9am–2pm*

PORTOBELLO ROAD
ADDRESS Portobello Road, W10 and W11
Where once there was just a track to an old Porto Bello Farm, every Saturday there's a famous crowded street market – perhaps the longest in the world plus an interesting mix of shops. For bargain antiques at the south end, go very early (before 8am if possible), although there are stalls for antiques and collectibles all day. The centre of the street is dominated by clothing, including cut-price fashion, and fruit and veg, which give way to an intriguing mix of ethnic and modern arts and crafts spreading out under the huge Westway arch. This part is liveliest in the afternoon, with impromptu performances of music and mime.
TUBE *Notting Hill Gate/Ladbroke Grove* • **OPEN** *8am–5pm (earlier for antiques)*

PUTNEY FLEA MARKET
ADDRESS Putney Hill, SW15
Bric-a-brac, junk.
TUBE *East Putney* • **OPEN** *Fri Sat 9am–5pm*

ROMAN ROAD MARKET
ADDRESS Roman Road, E3
Cut-price clothing. Designer seconds and samples. Household goods, linen and plants.
TUBE *Mile End* • **OPEN** *Thurs 8.30am–5pm. Sat 9am–5pm*

SHEPHERD'S BUSH MARKET
ADDRESS Uxbridge and Goldhawk Roads, W12
Crockery, bric-a-brac, kitchen utensils, carpets, rugs, vinyl flooring, bedding, furnishing fabrics, electrical goods and haberdashery.
TUBE *Goldhawk Road* • **OPEN** *Mon–Sat 9am–4.30pm. Thurs 9am–1pm*

SPITALFIELDS MARKET
ADDRESS off Commercial Street, E1
Spitalfields Market is housed in a huge Victorian glass-roofed fruit-and-veg complex which comes alive every Sunday. There are craft stalls and an organic food market for country-fresh vegetables, fruit, bread, cakes and meat. Recently, half was about to be 'developed', but the scheme fell though at the last minute. Sadly, many of the specialist shops around the market's edge had already been given notice to quit. Now, businesses are creeping back again, and they all stay open on Sunday, when you'll also find an incredible choice of places to eat, making this a fun day out – even if it rains, because the whole complex is under cover.
TUBE *Liverpool Street/Moorgate* • **OPEN** *Sun 10am–3pm. Some weekday activity*

WALTHAMSTOW MARKET
ADDRESS High Street, Walthamstow, E17
Kitchenware, good quality crystal.
TUBE *Walthamstow Central* • **OPEN** *Thurs–Sat 8am–5pm*

WELL STREET MARKET
ADDRESS Well Street, Hackney, E9
General household goods.
TUBE *Hackney Central* • **OPEN** *Mon–Sat 8am–5pm*

WEMBLEY MARKET
ADDRESS Wembley Stadium Car Park, Middx
A vast market – good for clothes, with household goods, too: china, linens, gadgets, and gimmicks. You can even find large pieces of furniture like sofas and chairs.
TUBE *Wembley Park* • **OPEN** *Sun 8am–1pm*

WOOLWICH MARKET
ADDRESS Beresford Square, Woolwich, SE18
General items and household goods.
RAIL *Woolwich* • **OPEN** *Tues–Sat 9am–5pm. Thurs–Sat 9am–3pm*

AUCTIONS

'Groucho: We're going to have an auction
Chico: I came over here on the Atlantic auction.'
Marx Brothers film, *The Coconuts*. Script by George S Kaufman and M Ryskind

Details were correct at the time of going to press but please phone to check specifics.

There's a mystique that surrounds buying at auction but it's a good way of kitting out a home – particularly for large pieces of furniture. Viewing is essential – allow plenty of time for thorough inspections. A catalogue is also a must – it will only be expensive for prestige art auctions. Check catalogue descriptions and 'lot' (identification) numbers against goods. Take a tape measure with you to check dimensions, plus a rough plan of the rooms you want to furnish.

Many catalogues are available by mail order or by subscription. Beware of the letters AF beside the description of a lot: they stand for 'as found' and may indicate trouble. Estimates are just that – anything can happen on the day. Fix an upper price limit in your mind and stick to it.

Bid by raising your catalogue, or calling out. Don't be intimidated by tales of 'dealers rings' and so forth. Remember, the auctioneer is interested in you as a customer, particularly at a time when so many dealers can no longer afford to buy. Indeed, it may well be their bankrupt stock that is under auction.

Bids progress in even increments according to value, but may creep up by as little as £1 when the end is nigh. Don't worry about special signs: blow your nose if you want to. Buyers are usually charged a premium (auctioneer's commission) of around 10 per cent of their accepted bid. VAT is charged on this. Find out the latest you can collect: after that you may be charged storage. Auctioneers won't accept cheques for large amounts without special arrangements, and smaller houses may not take credit cards.

London's 'big four' are world famous, with prestigious auctions and international bids by phone or electronically. If you're in their league, here are their details.

BONHAMS
ADDRESS Montpelier Street, Knightsbridge, SW7 1HH
TEL 0171 393 3900   **FAX** 0171 393 3905
TUBE *Knightsbridge* • **WEBSITE** *www.bonhams.com*

CHRISTIES
ADDRESS 8 King Street, SW1Y 6QT
TEL 0171 839 9060   **FAX** 0171 839 1611
TUBE *Green Park* • **WEBSITE** *www.christies.com*
• **ALSO AT** *85 Old Brompton Road, South Kensington, SW7 3LQ*

PHILLIPS
ADDRESS 101 New Bond Street, W1Y 0AS
TEL 0171 629 6602   **FAX** 0171 629 8876
TUBE *Bond Street* • **WEBSITE** *www.phillips-auctions.com*
• **ALSO AT** *10 Salem Road, Bayswater, W2 4DL (0171 229 9090)*

SOTHEBY'S
ADDRESS 34–35 New Bond Street, W1A 2AA
TEL 0171 493 8080   **FAX** 0171 293 5989
TUBE *Bond Street/Oxford Circus* • **WEBSITE** *www.sothebys.com*

However, it's the thriving local houses that provide the bargains.

ACADEMY AUCTIONEERS
ADDRESS Northcote House, Northcote Avenue, W5 3UR
TEL 0181 579 7466   **FAX** 0181 579 0511
Jewellery, clocks, ceramics, oriental crafts, furniture, carpets etc.
TUBE *Ealing Broadway* • **VIEWINGS** Mon 2–8pm. Tues 9.30am–4.30pm. Wed 9.30am – sale • **SALES** Wed noon (smaller items). Thurs 4pm (larger items)

BAINBRIDGE'S
ADDRESS Station Parade, Ickenham Road, West Ruislip, Middx
TEL 0181 579 2966   **FAX** 01895 623 621
Clothes, silver, bric-a-brac, house clearances, antiques and jewellery.

TUBE *West Ruislip* • **VIEWINGS** *Wed 1pm–7pm. Thurs 9.30am–sale*
• **SALES** *Thurs 11am every 4 weeks*

BLACK HORSE AGENCIES AMBROSE

ADDRESS 149 High Road, Loughton, Essex, 1G10 4LZ
TEL 0181 502 3951 **FAX** 0181 532 0833
Ceramics, glass, oriental arts, postcards, cigarette cards, clocks,
barometers, paintings – oil and watercolour – teddy bears, furniture etc.
TUBE *Loughton* • **VIEWINGS** *Sat 9am–4pm. Mon 9am–6pm. Tues 9am–7pm*
• **SALES** *Specialist sales: Thurs 11am. Antique furniture sale: Fri 11am.
Both monthly*

BONHAMS LOTS ROAD

ADDRESS 65–69 Lots Road, SW10 0RN
TEL 0171 393 3900 **FAX** 0171 393 3905
English and continental furniture and furnishings. Also sales for ceramics/
glass, silver/jewellery.
TUBE *Fulham Broadwal/Sloane Square + 22 Bus* • **VIEWING** *Sat Sun
10am–4.30pm. Mon 10am–7pm. Tues 10am–6pm* • **SALE** *Tues 6pm
every 2 weeks* • **WEBSITE** *www.bonhams.com*

CHANCELLORS AUCTIONS AT KINGSTON

ADDRESS 74 London Road, Kingston upon Thames, Surrey, KT2 6PX
TEL 0181 541 4139 **FAX** 0181 547 0210
General weekly sales, monthly antique/fine art sales. General household
clearances three times a month.
RAIL *Kingston* • **VIEWINGS** *Wed 2–8pm. Thurs 9–10.30am*
• **SALES** *General weekly sale Thurs 10.30am. Monthly antique/fine art sales
(ring for details)* • **WEBSITE** *www.chancellors.co.uk*

CRITERION SALEROOMS

ADDRESS 53 Essex Road, Islington, N1 2BN
TEL 0171 359 5707 **FAX** 0171 354 9843
Antique furniture, general antiques, decorative items.
TUBE *Angel* • **VIEWING** *Fri 4–8pm. Sat and Sun 10am–6pm. Mon 10am–sale*
• **SALES** *Every Mon 6pm* • **WEBSITE** *www.criterion-auctioneers.co.uk*

FORREST AND CO

ADDRESS 17–31 Gibbins Road, Stratford, E15 2HV
TEL 0181 534 2931 **FAX** 0181 503 0251
'General goods' plus occasional sales of antiques.
RAIL *Stratford* • **VIEWINGS** *Wed (fortnightly) 10am–5pm*
• **SALES** *Thurs (fortnightly) 11am*

FRANK G BOWEN

ADDRESS Malcom Road, E1
TEL 0171 790 7272 **FAX** 0171 790 7373
Liquidated stocks of office equipment from official receivers.
TUBE *Bethnal Green* • **VIEWING** *Day before sale 9am–5pm*
• **SALES** *Thurs every 2–4 weeks*

GENERAL AUCTIONS
ADDRESS 63–65 Garrett Lane, SW18 4AA
TEL 0181 874 2955 **FAX** 0181 877 3583
Sales of bankrupt and liquidated stock. Also seized goods from
Customs and Excise.
RAIL *Wandsworth Town* • **VIEWINGS** *Sat 10am–3pm*
• **SALES** *Mon 11am–noon. Miscellaneous sale approx 12 noon–5pm*
• **WEBSITE** *www.auction.u-net.com*

R F GREASBY
ADDRESS 211 Longley Road, SW17 9LG
TEL 0181 672 2972 **FAX** 0181 767 8616
Sales include goods from lost property for London Transport, confiscated
goods from Customs and Excise, bailiffs and county courts.
TUBE *Tooting Broadway* • **VIEWINGS** *Mon (fortnightly) 4–8.30pm*
• **SALES** *Tues (fortnightly) 10am*

HORNSEY AUCTIONS
ADDRESS 54–56 High Street, Hornsey, N8 7NX
TEL 0181 341 1156 **TEL** 0181 340 5334
General sales, antiques, porcelain, house clearance, 'Anything of value!'
TUBE *Turnpike Lane + 144 bus* • **VIEWINGS** *Tues 5–8pm. All day Wed*
• **SALES** *Wed 6.30pm (weekly)*

LOTS ROAD CHELSEA AUCTION GALLERIES
ADDRESS 71–73 Lots Road, SW10 0RN
TEL 0171 351 7771 **FAX** 0171 376 8349
Modern/repro furniture, general antiques, garden furniture, statuary,
ethnic furniture, tribal art.
TUBE *Fulham Broadway* • **VIEWINGS** *All day Monday. Thurs 5–7pm.
Fri 10am–4pm. Sat Sun 10am–4pm* • **SALES** *Modern sale Mon 1pm.
Antiques sale Mon 6pm* • **SERVICES** *Organic vegetarian cafe, Link Live
(0336 411263)*

LLOYDS INTERNATIONAL
ADDRESS 118 Putney Bridge Road, SW15 2NQ
TEL 0181 788 7777 **FAX** 0181 874 5390
TUBE *East Putney* • **VIEWINGS** *Customs/lost property: Wed (fortnightly)
10am–6pm. Furniture: Fri (fortnightly) 9.30am–7.30pm* • **SALES** *Customs/
lost property: Wed (fortnightly) from 6.30pm. Furniture: Sat (fortnightly)
11am–3pm* • **WEBSITE** *visitweb.com.lloyds-international*

RICHMOND & SURREY AUCTIONS
ADDRESS Old Railway Parcel Depot, Richmond Station, Kew Road,
Richmond, Surrey, TW10 2NA
TEL 0181 948 6677 **FAX** 0181 948 2021
Cosy atmosphere inside Richmond station, with around 400 mixed lots of
furniture (modern and antique), glass, ceramics, and statuary.
VIEWINGS *Wed 4pm–8pm. Thurs 10am–6pm* • **SALES** *Thurs 6pm*

RIVERSIDE AUCTIONS

ADDRESS 400 Caledonian Road, N1 1DN
TEL 0171 700 6022 **FAX** 0171 700 6696
Speciality here is used catering equipment – your chance to acquire
a trendy range cooker or stainless steel workbench for the proverbial
song. For example, cookers from around £300; trollies for around £90;
workbenches, from around £20 to £25 a foot – 'cheaper than a wood
table'.
VIEWING Mon–Fri 2pm–5.30pm • **SALES** Fortnightly Mon 11am

ROSANS AND COMPANY

ADDRESS Croydon Auction Rooms, 144–150 London Road,
Croydon, Surrey, CR0 2TD
TEL 0181 688 1123 **FAX** 0181 760 0582
Household clearance, bankrupt stock and some vehicles.
VIEWINGS Fri 9.30am–4.30pm • **SALES** Sat 10am (fortnightly)
• **SERVICES** Catalogue

ROSEBERY'S

ADDRESS 74–76 Knights Hill, SE27 0JD
TEL 0181 761 2522 **FAX** 0181 761 2524
Antiques/general sales. Periodically have speciality sales, ie toys,
decorative arts, musical instruments. Phone for details.
RAIL West Norwood • **VIEWINGS** Sun (before sale, fortnightly)
2.30–5.30pm. Mon 10am–7.30pm. Tues of sale from 9.30am
• **SALES** Tues 12 noon (fortnightly)

SOUTHGATE AUCTION ROOMS

ADDRESS 55 High Street, N14 6LD
TEL 0181 886 7888 **FAX** 0181 882 4421
General household goods.
TUBE Southgate • **VIEWINGS** Sat 9am–1pm. Mon 9am–5pm
• **SALES** Mon 5pm

INDEX